THE SPORTS SPEED SYSTEM

HOW TO BUILD THE ULTIMATE TEAM SPORT SPRINTER

Written By

Sam Portland

The Sports Speed System
How To Build The Ultimate Team Sport Sprinter

Sam Portland

Copyright © 2022
Written by Sam Portland
ISBN: 978-1-3999-9384-5

All rights reserved. No part of this book may be reproduced in any form without permission in writing from the publisher, except for brief quotations embodied in critical articles or reviews.

Dedication

*To the athletes, the coaches and the sports I love to play.
I couldn't have done this without you.*

"Does history record any case in which the majority was right"

Robert Heinlein

PREFACE

Dear reader,

Sports speed: How to build the ultimate team sports sprinter is written primarily for the strength and conditioning coach with a keen aptitude for team Sports. However this book is also incredibly useful for any tactical coach or physiotherapist with the aim of developing speed that translates to the competition arena. This book will also serve as a tremendous guide for medical practitioners who need practical guidance for returning players from injury.

I've been a coach for many years, but alongside that as a coach I've always held tightly to my identity as an athlete. This is because my athletic career is what led me into coaching. I've always prided myself on being able to truly understand the nature of training and performance by experimenting on myself and observing how it affected my own play.

I am a true believer that speed is something that needs to be felt in order to be trained and coached. I believe that speed is something that stays with us, inside our body for a long time.

What is so different about the Sports Speed System?

The sports speed system is the coming together of many different training methods, principles, and approaches. These have been implemented, and deliberately placed with one goal in mind: speed. Through its holistic design we go beyond asking how do we improve speed, we are asking the question of how do we improve speed on the field of play? To do this effectively, it requires a well thought out coaching process that knows when not to further develop biomotor abilities such as strength and power but to do the complete opposite and understand the times of when we have to learn to utilise what we already have. This is where the seamless approach of the four main pillars of the sports speed system truly thrives. With the constant question of "Does this training support the overall goal", we know exactly when to remove certain types of training to prioritise more important ones. The System works backwards from the overall goal of winning matches and games and develops the things that we need to in order to excel in these disciplines. This is not just another training program, it is a system that creates results.

Why did I decide to publish this book?

Throughout the course of my coaching career I have always taken a lot of pride in my ideas around how training should be applied to the team sport athlete. This came from just having coffee with coaches and general conversation but also through the inherent education that I would give to my athletes in order for them to understand why they are doing the training that they are.

Alongside this I do truly feel that the origins of the strength and conditioning profession and the primary guiding principles have been somewhat forgotten and one of the biggest challenges that I have faced with this book is to bring those principles back to life. The origins of performance training were founded in the Olympic disciplines and therefore cannot be literally applied to the development of the team sport athlete. However, if carefully blended with a holistic approach, and a deep understanding of their application is present, we are able to create exciting athletes who can fully express themselves in the field of play. In many conversations with coaches I always reference the emergence of the mixed martial arts discipline. At its inception you had many different disciplines such as wrestlers and kickboxers trying to win a fight, very shortly after it was realised that we had to create Mixed Martial artists. I personally feel that at this current level of applied training within team sports we are similar to the birth of mixed martial arts, trying to create athletes who run like sprinters, lift weights like powerlifters and run like middle distance runners all in the attempt to optimise for performance. This is why I have written this book, so we can start to create team sport sprinters in an attempt to unify all the individual qualities to support the overall goal of winning games and excelling in the tactical realms of field sports.

Final Remarks

Just like anything worth having, speed takes time to develop. However with the sports speed system you are able to maximise the early transfer, and create continual improvements and adaptations over time. The resources and programs provided will give you a strong foothold in how you can utilise and implement this system within your training approach. section one of general speed is where most people stop their speed training, it is your job and your responsibility to make sure that you go the actual miles to create and make the difference.

Yours Sincerely,

Sam Portland

THANKS AND ACKNOWLEDGMENTS

The people involved in this book have been vital to the organisation of my mind and help me piece it all together in a logical order and maintain some what of a normal life in the process.

Firstly I would like to thank Jonty Simson who assisted me on editing the book and ensuring I keep the original meaning of my work. A man who I value tremendously and a great coaching mind. Secondly, I would like to thank all the athletes who I have and will conditnue to help with my coaching. Without you this doesn't exist. I would like to thank the coaches who have trusted me to share my ideas with them to guide their coaching and push me to develop my work. I hope this book inspired you further and we continue to grow together.

I would like to thank Emma Nightingale, my partner and the lady who always reminds me of who I am, loves me and motivates me to follow this path by my side.

Lastly I would like to thank my parents Lisa and Keith who have taught me the power to believe in myself and encouraged me to go after my passion staying true to who I am.

CONTENTS

Preface v

Thanks and Acknowledgments vii

Contents ix

Introduction xv

The Sports Speed System 1

    What is the Sports Speed System 1

    Evolution and Inspiration of the Sports Speed System 2

    How to use this book..3

The Frameworks of the Sports Speed System 6

    Framework 1: Speed Age 6

        Speed Age and Program Considerations...8

    Framework 2: Learn Load and Execute 11

    Framework 3: Drill Stacking 12

    Framework 4: Stable to Unstable 15

    Framework 5: Step By Step 16

    Framework 6: Curve Loading 19

    Framework 7: Non Linear Sprinting 22

General Speed 25

    Transfer of Training 25

    Applied Physics of Sprinting..28

        Newton's Laws applied to sprinting 30

        Momentum and Impulse 31

        Stiffness and Springiness 32

        Circular Motion and Centrifugal Force 32

    Physiology of Sprinting 34

        Energy System Foundations...34

        Training as an energy system development tool.....................................36

        Muscle Mechanics and Speed 37

        Elastic vs. Muscle-Driven Sprinters..39

        Elastic-Driven Sprinters..39

        Reflexes and Speed Training 41

The Fascial System and Speed Training 43
The Muscular and Nervous System Responses in Training 45

Coaching Speed Coaching Speed In Team Sports 47
The Challenge of Coaching Speed in Team Sports 47
Sprint Times of Varying Sports 48
Maximum Speeds of Various Sports 49
Fundamental Skill Acquisition and Coaching 49
The Importance of Deliberate Practice in the Development of General Speed 51
Displacement and Sprinting 52
Error Detection In Speed Training 57
Technical Models in Sprinting Movements 62
Understanding the Gait Cycle 62
      Effective Acceleration 65
Rotation and Compensation Combined with Axis and Planes of motion 70
Training and Development of Deceleration Abilities in Team Sport Athletes ... 76
Team Sport Athlete Archetypes: Understanding Physical Biases 80
Anthropometrics and Team Sport Sprinting 81
Mastering the Process of Sports Speed 85

Exercise Classification for Speed 87
Bondarchuk's Exercise Classification 89
Dynamic Correspondence 91
Transfer of Training 93
Conjugated Training Effects (CTE) 93
Body Links 95
Exploring Part, Whole, and Mixed Methods of Motor Learning with respect
    to Exercise Classification 96
The Law of Accommodation 98
SAID Principle 99
Exercise Classification for Team Sports Speed Training: Bridging the Practical Gaps ... 100
Layering the Force-Velocity Curve to Build Sprint Training Programs 102
Utilising Exercise Classification and Strength Types in Speed Training Programs ... 105
Organising Speed Training: Defining Progression within Exercise Qualification ... 106
The Thought Process of Speed Training: From Problem Solving to Execution ... 108

A Systematic Approach to Exercise Classification of Speed 113
Weight Training for Speed 113
The Role of Strength Training and Transfer 113
Consideration of Size Principle and Intent When Programming Weight for
    Speed Development 116
Complimentary Weight Room Programming for Speed 117
Strength in the Context of Sprinting 122
Ballistic Training for Speed: Programming and Progressions 124

Maximising Speed with Jump and Plyometric Training	131
Programming for Speed	134
Fundamental Principles of Constructing Training Programs, Periodisation, and Training Organisation	135
Training Cycle Layout: Macrocycle, Mesocycles, and Microcycles	138
Tools and Modalities for Speed Development	141
Volume Considerations for Speed Training Programs	144
Intensity Considerations in Speed Training Programs	145
Modifying Track and Field Models for Team Sports	148
Speed Zones	149
The Motor Learning Response and Exercise Exposure	152
Planning for Speed Training Programs	166
Multi-Year Periodisation Considerations for Team Sport Athletes using the Sports Speed System	168
Principles of Multi-Year Periodization	169
Speed Gate Golf	172
The Psychology of Speed Gate Golf: Unlocking Peak Performance	173
Gamification of Speed Gate Golf: Igniting Competence and Motivation	177
Cognitive Behavioral Techniques and Speed Gate Golf: A Path to Performance Enhancement	178
Unleashing Positive Feedback Loops in Speed Gate Golf for Optimal Performance	180
Enhancing Motor Learning in Speed Gate Golf	182
Enhancing Motivation through Athlete Groupings in Speed Gate Golf	184
Implementing Speed Gate Golf	186

Using Data In Team Sport Sprinting **188**

Big Picture Thinking: Leveraging Data in Team Sports for Optimal Performance	188
Decision Making and Athlete Performance: Leveraging Data to Drive Success	190
Speed Gates: Enhancing Performance Through Data Analysis	192
Using Force Platforms to Enhance Your Speed Training Program	193
Categorisation and Decision-Making: Maximising the Potential of Force Platforms	195
Combining Metrics for Powerful Data	197
Utilising GPS Data to optimise Speed Programs	199
Enhancing Your Speed Program with Slow Motion Video Analysis	200

Rehabilitation and the Sports Speed System **201**

Understanding Team Sport Sprinting	205
When to transition to Specific Speed	206
Specific Speed and Motor Learning	208
The Direction of Training	208
The Data Behind Team Sport Sprinting	208
Vision, Timing and Distance	213

How to Build Specific Speed	215
Increasing Specialisation	218
Speed and Game Skills	219
Understanding Space	220
High Frequency Actions in Team Sports to Create Special Speed	221
Situations in Field and Team Sports	223
The Sport Involvement Continuum	223
Skill Acquisition and Speed in Team Sports	225
The Three Stages of Motor Learning	225
Implicit and Explicit Learning for Special Speed Development	227
The Ecological Approach to Skill Acquisition in Team Sports	229
Perception-Action Cycle: Enhancing Decision-Making	231
The Importance of Play in Learning Skills for Sports Speed	233
Skill - Drill - Practice - Perform	235
Special Speed Preparation Progression	237
Coaching Styles and Special Speed	237
Scheduling Speed Training in Team Sports	240
Determining Successful Transfer of Speed	245
Implementing Tactical Speed in Practice	247
Bringing it All Together: Matches	248
The Sports Speed System: Coaches Roadmap	252
The Exercises of The Sports Speed System	253
Warm Up Drills	254
A Series	254
B Series	264
The Use of Single Leg Drills and Variations	271
Acceleration Progressions - please refer to the drill stacking model for further understanding.	272
Ankle Series	273
Knee Series	283
Hip Series	292
Hip Flexion Series	301
Lumbar Pelvic considerations	303
Using Wall Drills to Develop the Acceleration Pattern	306
Mastering the Unilateral Positions	307
Building Unilateral to Exchange	309
Finding the Second Exchange	310
Developing Wall Rhythm	311
Introducing External Load	311

      Introducing Pattern Movements in the Sports Speed System...311
      Specific and Specialised Exercises for Developing Acceleration....................................315
      Maximum Velocity Exercises within the Sports Speed System 342
  Step Loading Table for 0-15 Step Acceleration 347
  Speed Gate Setup Considerations 348
  Technique Analysis Videos - Scan QR CODES 348
      Sports Speed Training Cycles 349

Google Sheet Calculators - Scan QR Code to Acces these..364
  Force Velocity Profile...364
  Dynamic Strength Index 364
  Effect Size Calculator...364

Jump training Progressions 364
  Jump methods and exercise progressions..365
      1.   Landing + Non countermovement Jumps..365
      Drop Landings...365
      Non-Countermovement Jump + Land...366
      Countermovement and Land..367
      2.   Extensive..368
      Pogo Series 368
      Extensive Series 369
      Advanced Extensive 370
      3. Intensive...370
      Long Coupling...370
      Short Coupling..371
      Altitude Landings..371
      Introduction to Weighted Jumps 372
      Weighted Non-Countermovement Jumps 372
      Weighted Eccentric Focus Jumps...373
      Weighted Extensive Jumps 373
      Weighted Medicine Ball Pogo Series 373
      Weighted Extensive Jumps 374
      Extensive Overspeed Jumps 374
      Weighted Intensive 375
      Long Coupling...375
      Short Coupling..375
      Drop Jumps 375
      Depth Jumps 376
      Programming considerations: 377
  Ballistic Exercise Progressions 378
      Classifying a strength or ballistic exercise 378
      Categorising Ballistic Modalities..379

- Ballistic Exercises Based on Classification for Speed 380
- Gym based Exercises 380
- Weighted jumps 381
- Medicine Ball Throws 381
- Resisted specific movement 382
- Measuring & Tracking 383

Example Programs & Sessions 383

Biomechanical Factors of Speed in Sprinting 383
- 1. Hip Joint 385
- 2. Knee Joint 385
- 3. Ankle Joint 385
- Practical Examples and Coaching Considerations 386

Brodmann Areas Of The Brain 386

INTRODUCTION

Writing a book was the last thing I thought I would do. But I've done a lot of things I didn't think I'd do. So here it is.

This is my Sports Speed System. How I develop speed with my athletes. I've written it out as best I can to give you the playbook. The how and not the what or the why. The way I think and how I see speed.

My journey into speed came from having to learn how to teach what I took for granted. As a young promising rugby player who scored more tries from inside my own half than the opposition. Speed was never a question. I was born with it.

Following injury, and losing my chance at professional rugby, I turned my attention to coaching. But when I had to teach speed, I was stuck. I threw myself into books from Tom Tellez, Michael Yessis, and the great Yuri Verkhoshansky. As I obsessed over this. I didn't yet know what solving this problem would lead me to become, back then there was only one thing on my mind. How can I make the athletes that I work with fast? Really Fast. And not just fast on the track. Fast on the field of play. Where it matters. The only place it truly matters.

As you read this book I want you to keep an open mind. Scribble all over it and most importantly go and apply it. Don't let it just collect dust on the bookshelf. Make it the secret weapon in your coaching toolbox.

THE SPORTS SPEED SYSTEM

WHAT IS THE SPORTS SPEED SYSTEM

Speed is the essence of athletic success, and the Sports Speed System stands as a groundbreaking approach designed to make athletes faster on the field. This system revolves around four core elements, progressively enhancing different facets of an athlete's speed.

Most field sports or team sports rely on speed as a distinguishing factor that defines performance on the field. From a physical preparation standpoint it is at the top of the hierarchy as a performance variable. The image below summarises how I view the role of speed and its contribution to field sports. Using this as an overarching framework we are able to create Sports Speed.

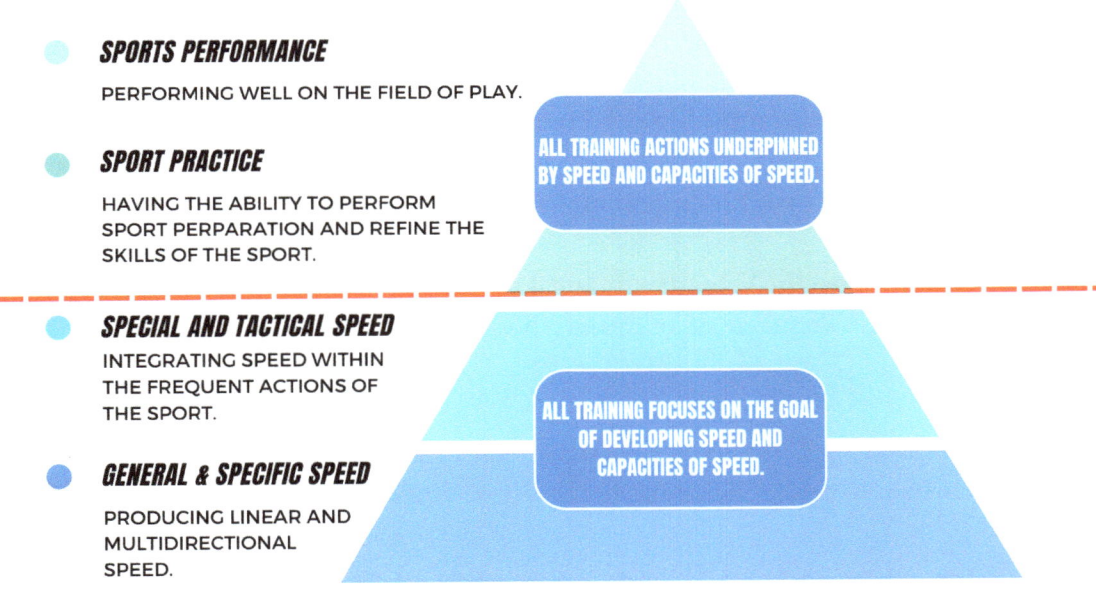

There is a key difference when separating preparation for the demand of the sport and then preparing to play the sport itself. The way I consider this within the sports speed system is that everything under the red line must contribute to the development of speed and capacities of speed. Whereas, as soon as training crosses the threshold into sport practice all actions are underpinned by the work we have previously conducted in preparation training. This is where we need to learn to see if the adaptations being created are working and how/if we need to tweak the approach to develop athletes further.

As a physical preparation specialist this pyramid below will be your guide to help you develop training programs and preparation cycles to enhance and optimise your athletes performance.

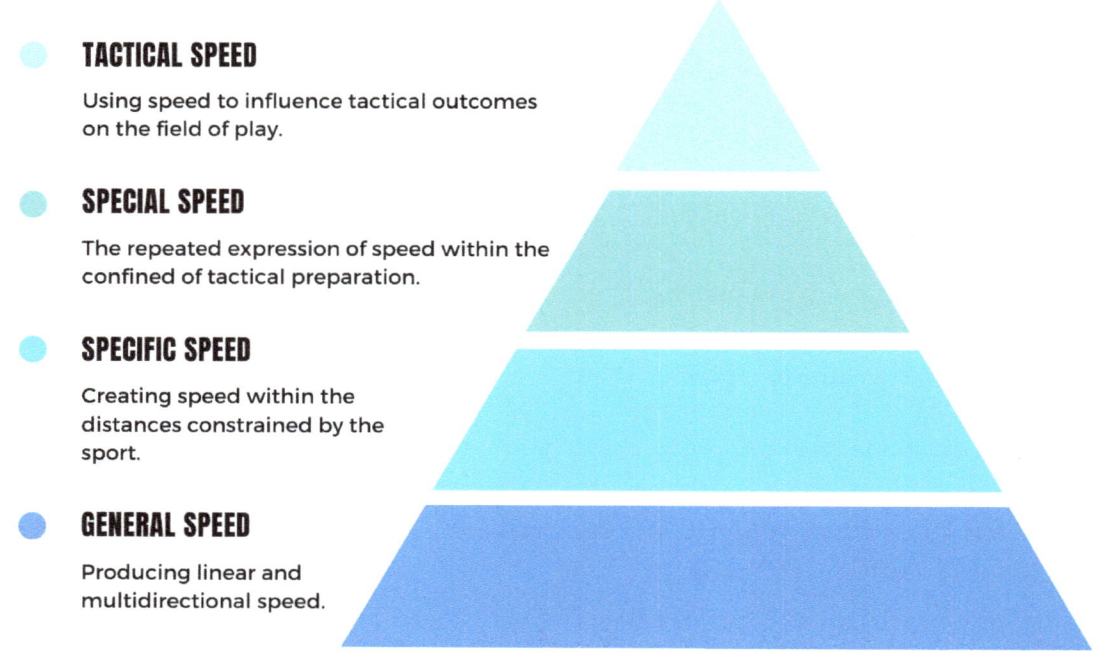

1. General Speed: Running in a Straight Line or Pre-planned Change of Direction- The foundation of the system, general speed, focuses on running in a straight line then introducing pre-planned change of Direction. This fundamental skill forms the basis for more complex speed elements.

2. Specific Speed: Distance-Specific Velocity - Tailored to field distances, specific speed hones in on running fast in relation to the specific demands of the game. It's about translating general speed into field-specific scenarios.

3. Specialised Speed: Mastering Changes of Direction - Specialised speed addresses the nuances of the game, incorporating elements like changes of direction, decelerations, and evasion patterns. It's about being agile and reactive on the field.

4. Tactical Speed: Integrating with Game Dynamics - The pinnacle of the system, tactical speed combines all elements with the use of a ball or implement, strategically increasing the likelihood of scoring or winning. It's not just about individual speed but how it contributes to the team's success.

EVOLUTION AND INSPIRATION OF THE SPORTS SPEED SYSTEM

Holistic Approach of the Sports Speed System

The genesis of the Sports Speed System is rooted in a coaching journey that has guided athletes from park enthusiasts to professional rugby players and beyond. This system, born from this diverse coaching experience, offers a logical, progressive, and measurable approach. It grants coaches the freedom to design sessions while maintaining a sharp focus on technical output and physical improvements.

Specific Training Methodologies Unique to the Sports Speed System

The system's unique training methodologies set it apart. "Speed Gate Golf" introduces a stress inoculation process, utilising submaximal acceleration and running to enhance strength, power, and speed. The emphasis on long accelerations and submaximal acceleration allows athletes to train at levels conducive to sustained improvement.

The Sports Speed System challenges conventional methodologies by spotlighting the potency of submaximal sprinting. It refutes the misconception that maximum effort is the sole path to speed improvement. Submaximal sprinting, a hallmark of this system, is a powerful tool for developing general, specific, specialised, and tactical speed in team sport athletes.

At its core, the system takes a holistic approach by prioritising the primary goal of running quickly in a straight line. Once this foundational skill is achieved, it opens avenues for integrated decision-making with technical and tactical coaches, leading to enhanced game performance.

Psychology plays a crucial role in the Sports Speed System, particularly evident in the "Speed Gate Golf" strategy. Athletes not only enhance their physical abilities but also gain a deep understanding of their speed and how their body. This integration fosters relaxation, positively impacting mindset, and enables athletes to train their bodies like true team sports sprinters. What sets the Sports Speed System apart is its origin within the team sport environment. Tested extensively with team sport athletes, the system goes beyond merely enhancing straight-line speed. It addresses the critical ability to repeatedly reduce speed on the field, a skill often overlooked in traditional speed training.

A standout feature is the "drill stacking methodology," a highly impactful strategy allowing the reverse engineering of sprinting movements down to local muscles. Athletes and coaches benefit from how this methodology builds a narrative across sessions and training programs, creating a comprehensive and effective approach to speed training.

In conclusion, the Sports Speed System stands as a testament to innovation in the realm of athletic performance. Its holistic approach, unique methodologies, and emphasis on real-world application make it a game-changer for athletes and coaches seeking to unlock their full speed potential.

HOW TO USE THIS BOOK

I challenged myself when writing this book to create a book that evolves with you. There are many layers within the creation of the sports speed system. But that does not mean that you cannot start using it right away. As you and your athletes progress I want you to keep referring back to this book as a guide. Like many books I have read I will never exhaust them as I learn something new everytime I pick it up. This chapter serves as your compass, guiding you through the pages that promise to be a constant reference in your pursuit of speed excellence.

Getting Acquainted with the Frameworks

Before diving into the specifics, read through the main classifications that underpin the system. The Sports Speed System is built on four pillars: General Speed, Specific Speed, Specialised Speed, and Tactical Speed.

There are also 7 major frameworks that have been crafted to help you coach and plan effectively. These elements form the bedrock of your journey to becoming faster on the field.

Action Steps:
- Familiarise yourself with the four pillars, understanding their unique contributions to your overall speed development.
- Read through the frameworks of the system and think about how you can apply them in your coaching process.
- Reflect on your current strengths and weaknesses in each pillar, setting the stage for targeted improvements.
- Recognise the freedom this system provides coaches, allowing for tailored sessions while maintaining a focus on technical and physical advancements.

Unique Training Methodologies

This guide introduces you to unique training methodologies that set the Sports Speed System apart. "Speed Gate Golf" and the emphasis on submaximal acceleration are key components. Learn how these methodologies enhance strength, power, and speed, providing a novel approach to your training routine.

Action Steps:
- Explore the intricacies of "Speed Gate Golf" and understand its role as a stress inoculation process.
- Embrace the advantages of submaximal acceleration in building a robust foundation for continuous improvement.

Bridging the Gap: Holistic Approach

One of the defining features of the Sports Speed System is its holistic approach. At its core is the goal of running fast in a straight line to then translate to the field. Explore how achieving this foundational skill opens avenues for integrated decisions with technical and tactical coaches, ultimately enhancing your game performance.

Action Steps:
- Acknowledge the primary goal of running fast in a straight line and recognise its far-reaching impact.
- Contemplate how a holistic approach aligns with your personal speed goals and the dynamics of your chosen sport.

Psychological Integration

Speed isn't just about physical prowess; it's a mental game too. Discover the psychology of sprinting embedded in the Sports Speed System. A closer look at "Speed Gate Golf" reveals how understanding your velocity and nervous system responses fosters relaxation, positively impacting your mindset.

Action Steps:
- Engage with the psychological elements of sprinting, recognizing their integral role in your overall speed development.

- Consider how the integration of psychology aligns with your training philosophy and personal growth objectives.

What Sets the Sports Speed System Apart

Uncover the primary factor that distinguishes the Sports Speed System — its origin within the team sport environment. Tested extensively with team sport athletes, this system goes beyond straight-line speed, addressing the crucial ability to repeatedly reduce speed on the field.

Action Steps:
- Reflect on how your sport-specific demands align with the Sports Speed System's focus on reducing speed on the field.
- Consider the advantages this system brings to team sport athletes, elevating your understanding of its practical applications.

Impactful Innovations and Features

Delve into the impactful innovations within the Sports Speed System, including the 'drill stacking methodology.' Understand how this strategy allows the reverse engineering of sprinting movements, creating a narrative across sessions and training programs.

Action Steps:
- Grasp the essence of the 'drill stacking methodology' and its role in building a comprehensive narrative.
- Explore how these innovations resonate with your preferred training style and align with your performance goals.

Practical Training

Before you just jump into the Sports Speed System, construct a loose plan or use the one provided in this book to help you experience the system.

Action Steps:
- Develop a weekly training program that lets you explore the different training elements in the system.

Congratulations on starting your journey with "The Sports Speed System." This section will help you lay the foundation for an immersive and transformative experience. As you navigate through the subsequent chapters, remember that this guide is not just a book; it's a companion in your ongoing quest for speed mastery.

THE FRAMEWORKS OF THE SPORTS SPEED SYSTEM

In this chapter we will be laying the foundation for the rest of the book. Each chapter stacks upon what came before, compounding to deepen your understanding of the system. This starts with the frameworks; they are the heartbeat of the system, and bring this powerful speed training solution to life.

Framework 1: Speed Age

Speed age is a framework that is used to identify an athlete's current level of specialisation. It takes into consideration the amount of time spent performing deliberate, structured and progressive speed training. Speed age is a concept that combines and applies two separate ideas from other fields, creating something that feeds into every level of the sports speed system. I will now explain these for reference.

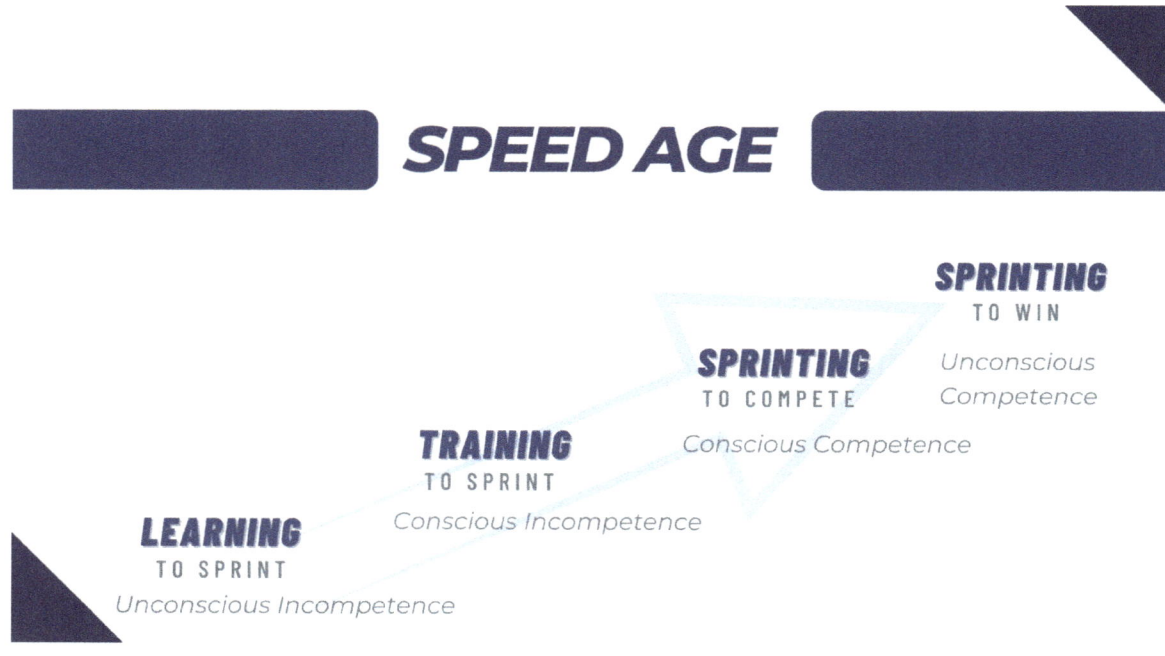

Training Age - Tudor Bompa

Tudor Bompa is known as "the father of periodisation" and has made significant contributions to the understanding and application of training methodology in sports.

The concept of training age refers to the cumulative amount of time an individual has been engaged in systematic training or physical activity. This is such a crucial factor when considering the application of speed training for field sport athletes as a majority of them have not had the necessary exposures to deem them "qualified" with a higher speed age. When we use the term "qualified" or "qualification" with respect to training, we are referring to the athletes ability to perform the task correctly and have the physical competency to tolerate the stress that the exercises can place on the individual.

Training age takes into account the physiological adaptations, skill acquisition, and performance improvements that occur over time as a result of consistent training. It goes beyond simply measuring the chronological age of an individual and recognizes that two individuals of the same age may have vastly different levels of training experience and adaptations.

A person with a higher training age is likely to have developed a higher level of speed, strength, endurance, and sport-specific skills compared to someone with a lower training age. This is because the body adapts to the demands placed upon it during training, leading to improved physical capabilities and performance.

Understanding an individual's training age is crucial for developing appropriate training programs. Beginners with a low training age require a focus on building a foundation of strength, developing proper movement patterns, and gradually increasing training volume and intensity to avoid injury and allow for adaptation. On the other hand, individuals with a higher training age may require more advanced training techniques, higher training volumes, and increased complexity to continue progressing. This is a key element of speed age. What is often found in athletes is a high training age but a low speed age. This is due to the lack of attention placed on speed.

By considering an individual's training age, coaches, trainers, and athletes can tailor training programs to meet their specific needs, ensuring optimal progression, minimising the risk of overtraining, and maximising performance gains. It is important to note that training age is just one of many factors to consider in program design, and other individual differences should always be taken into account.

In summary, training age represents the accumulated experience and adaptations an individual has gained through consistent training. It guides the development of appropriate training programs and helps to optimise training progression based on an individual's level of fitness and skill.

Stages of Competence
The four stages of competency, often referred to as the "conscious competence" learning model, describe the process of acquiring and developing skills or knowledge. This model was popularised by Noel Burch. This model is a must have tool for coaches as it guides perspective and facilitates the learner and effective learning environments.

1. **Unconscious Incompetence:** In this initial stage, individuals lack awareness or knowledge of a particular skill or knowledge area. They are unaware of their incompetence and may not recognize the need to develop the skill. They may make mistakes or have poor performance without realising it. An example of this is an athlete mistaking moving fast for running fast. This is where you will see an athlete in an attempt to accelerate quickly, move their arms and legs aggressively and frantically but not actually create a significant change in speed as they have not moved their centre of mass well.

2. **Conscious Incompetence:** At this stage, individuals become aware of their incompetence. They recognize that they lack the necessary skills or knowledge and understand that there is room for improvement. They may seek guidance, training, or resources to address their deficiencies and actively work towards acquiring the desired competency. An example of this is when an athlete is able to recognise their technical mistakes during training.

3. **Conscious Competence:** In this stage, individuals have acquired the necessary skills or knowledge, but applying them requires conscious effort and concentration. They can perform the task or demonstrate the skill successfully, but it may still require active thinking, planning, or focusing on the steps involved. Practice and repetition are typically needed to reinforce competence and increase proficiency. At this stage you will have an athlete who can move well and produce good speed performances in training, but struggle to utilise this speed in the field of play. There is a lot of thought in the action of movement.

4. **Unconscious Competence:** At the final stage, individuals have developed a high level of competency, and the skill or knowledge becomes almost automatic. They can perform the task effortlessly and without conscious effort. The skills have been internalised, and individuals can execute them effectively and efficiently, often without even realising the complex processes involved. An athlete achieving this stage is great for a coach to see. The athlete is able to perform the task demands of the sport, passing, hitting etc while maintaining high levels of speed throughout. The tasks of the game do not hinder the performance of speed and vice versa.

It's important to note that progression through these stages may vary for each individual and depend on factors such as the complexity of the skill, prior experience, and the amount of practice or training undertaken. It is also to acknowledge that athletes can revisit each stage of competency with every level of improvement they make. As new speeds are attained, athletes have to refine their skill sets to master the higher intensity of the new level of speed.

Understanding these stages can help individuals and educators recognize where they or others are in the learning process. It encourages a growth mindset and emphasises the importance of practice, feedback, and continuous learning to progress from unconscious incompetence to unconscious competence. An athlete with a higher speed age has more of the skills of sprinting at the unconscious competence stage, and has been through many cycles of the process. The athlete with the younger speed age may only have made one refinement to how they sprint the whole time they've been sprinting, because when they were 13 their coach told them to "run more upright". Each revolution through the stages will be a bigger and easier leap forwards for this athlete compared to the athlete with the high speed age who might take 2 years to really integrate a change in their preactivation sequencing into their mechanics at top speed.

Team sport athletes fall into the trap of having a high "training age" but a low "speed age". This is due to the lack of specific training exposures and the structured deliberate learning that is required to master sprinting in sports.

Speed Age and Program Considerations

Speed development is a multifaceted process that requires careful consideration of an athlete's speed age and program design. Understanding the different stages of speed development and tailoring interventions accordingly can maximise training effectiveness. In this chapter, we will explore the stages of learning to sprint, training to sprint, sprinting to compete, and sprinting to win, and delve into the key factors to consider at each stage.

1. Learning to Sprint

The initial stage of learning to sprint is characterised by unconscious incompetence. Athletes in this stage may lack awareness of their current skill level and possess a low speed training age in relation to their biological age. Additionally, their physical capacity is limited, indicating the need for specific training. As a coach or trainer, it is crucial to conduct a thorough needs analysis using the sports speed frameworks to improve the athletes physiology, determining the appropriate educational level (how much the athlete knows about the basics of speed), loading strategies based on physical capacity (what level of intensity you can use to create adaptation), and coaching techniques to facilitate progress. Many individuals find themselves in this stage, eager to advance their skills and reach the next level. At this stage we create adaptation through developing basic mechanics and physiological a

2. Training to Sprint

Transitioning to the training to sprint stage, athletes enter a phase of conscious incompetence. Here, their speed training age becomes moderate, and they have developed a certain level of physical capacity. Technical loading plays a significant role at this stage, as athletes need to refine their skills and improve specific aspects of their performance. We create technical loading by placing emphasis on mastering the technical abilities of the athlete. This stresses the cognitive capacities of the athlete. We use exercise to stress the learned ability of the athlete. If the skill of movement breaks down too quickly then we know there is more performance gain to be made easily just by improving the skill. Professionals in various sports often find themselves in this stage, seeking to optimise their abilities and bridge the gap to higher levels of competition.

Time dependency is a crucial consideration throughout the speed development process. As athletes progress, they gain a better understanding of the basics and acquire knowledge of the fundamental specific speed movement skills and relevant drills *(see appendix)*. As we will unpack in framework 2: Learn Load Execute creating associative experiences from slow controlled movements to fast aggressive movements to enhance the athletes learning and performance. To support this we will use specific types of strength training and monitoring of important data to address any deficiencies in length, frequency, or contact quality. Technical loading, which involves coaching and teaching, is instrumental in helping athletes piece together the necessary skills and optimise their performance.

3. Sprinting to Compete

Moving forward to the sprinting to compete stage, the objective is to convert physical capacities into competitive execution. Coaches must discern when to eliminate unnecessary elements and prioritise essential components for optimal performance. For example coaches can become over reliant on running drills too often and add more drills as opposed to changing or decreasing the amount of drills covered to conserve energy for more specific training. It is a developmental phase where athletes must demonstrate their abilities and execute with precision.

4. Sprinting to Win

Finally, in the sprinting to win stage, athletes have a clear understanding of their requirements and possess advanced coaching skills. They collaborate with coaches to enhance their learning experience and operate as high-level sprinters, achieving speeds of ten metres per second or higher. This stage focuses on the development of leading indicator metrics, such as efficiency metrics, to evaluate progress. Fine-tuning the residency program and physical loading capabilities become paramount, with technical execution serving as the ultimate goal.

When designing a program for speed, it is crucial to consider the law of accommodation. Athletes must progress and ascend through the different stages to prevent stagnation and inhibit their development. By utilising a simple framework and understanding the specific needs of each stage, coaches and trainers can effectively develop the necessary skills and propel athletes towards their speed goals. This table below provides a snapshot of how training progresses through the speed ages.

Speed Age	Entry KPI	Exit KPI	Means of Training
Learn to Sprint	0-2 years of Sports Speed Training	Rate of Progress stagnates	Heavy resisted sleds, highly stable training. Technical Sprinting
Train to Sprint	2-4 years of Sports Speed Training		Light resistance, moderate stability training.
Sprint to Compete	4-6 Years of Sports Speed Training	No exit criteria - this is 90+% of potential is exhausted and performance optimisation is the priority.	Max Speed, Overspeed Sprinting variations
Sprint to Win			

In conclusion, speed age and program considerations play a vital role in optimising speed development. By recognising the stages of learning to sprint, training to sprint, sprinting to compete, and sprinting to win, coaches can tailor interventions to address the unique needs of athletes at each stage. A well-designed program, coupled with strategic progression, can unlock an athlete's full potential and facilitate continuous growth in speed and performance.

Framework 2: Learn Load and Execute

The second framework is called **learn-load-execute**. It is a theory derived from skill acquisition research and is based on the work of Fitts and Posner. The Fitts and Posner model is a 3 stage process of skill acquisition.

1. Cognitive Stage *(Learn)*: The cognitive stage is the initial phase of motor learning. During this stage, learners are unfamiliar with the skill and need to understand its basic components. They rely on conscious thought, attention, and observation to grasp the task's requirements and develop a mental representation of the skill. Movements are often inconsistent, and errors are common. Feedback and guidance from instructors or more experienced individuals are crucial in this stage to establish a foundation for skill acquisition.

2. Associative Stage *(Load)*: In the associative stage, learners have acquired the basic fundamentals of the skill and start refining their movements. They focus on reducing errors, improving coordination, and becoming more consistent. They gradually shift from relying on conscious thought to more automatic and intuitive movements. Practice plays a vital role during this stage, as learners refine their technique, adjust timing and coordination, and gain a deeper understanding of the skill's nuances. Feedback and self-correction become increasingly important in fine-tuning movements. I know that the term "load" might lead you to believe that we are to place external load on the athletes through bands etc but we can do this in other ways. When considering associative learning response we can place a cognitive load on the athlete to stress the mental capacity of the skill learned in the previous step of the framework. Or alternatively we can use resistance to act as a constraint or too to develop physical qualities. As a coach it is your job to determine which is needed more.

3. Autonomous Stage *(Execute)*: The autonomous stage represents the final phase of motor learning, characterised by skilled and automatic performance. Learners in this stage can perform the skill proficiently with minimal conscious effort. Movements are fluid, precise, and efficient. Learners can focus on strategy, decision-making, and higher-level aspects of the task rather than on the basic mechanics. Feedback is still valuable but typically comes from self-reflection or occasional external sources to maintain and refine performance.

It's important to note that the progression through these stages is not always linear, and individuals may move back and forth between stages depending on factors such as complexity, practice intensity, and individual differences. The model provides a framework for understanding the learning process and highlights the evolution from cognitive engagement to more automatic and skilled performance.

But how do we apply this framework to coaching speed? Understanding the stages of motor learning helps coaches and athletes tailor instruction, provide appropriate feedback, and design training sessions that facilitate skill development and progression.

One of the often overlooked variables in this framework is that it is cyclical in nature. This means that you can work through each step multiple times through a session, choosing a learn drill then a complimentary loading drill, assessing if there is any immediate change (good or bad) and then working back to learn or execute. This means that athletes will cycle through this framework many times to master skills and physical qualities. From the work of Fitts and Posner, we must acknowledge that skill acquisition is not linear. Therefore we need to repeat these phases and can repeat these phases multiple times in a session if we need to. A typical starting cycle would be to help an athlete overcome poor initial projection. Taken from the "Cheat Sheet '' later in the book, this is how I would typically cycle an athlete through Learn Load Execute to increase the athlete's ability to perform this skill. At the rear of the book you will find a full walk through of how to use the system most effectively.

STEP 1		LEARN	LOAD	EXECUTE
1	Poor Initial rate of projection	Stable Bilateral Wall Projection	Banded Load and Smash - Bilateral - Unilateral	1 Step Push

Putting this framework into practice requires the use of the next framework. Drill stacking. By understanding the three stages and focusing on creating effective speed exposures that have a developmental thread within them, we can help our athletes perform at their best. This framework will be used at the beginning of almost every session after the warm up. This ultimately creates an acceleration in learning and enhances the transfer of speed faster. Remember, practice does not make perfect. Only perfect practice makes perfect.

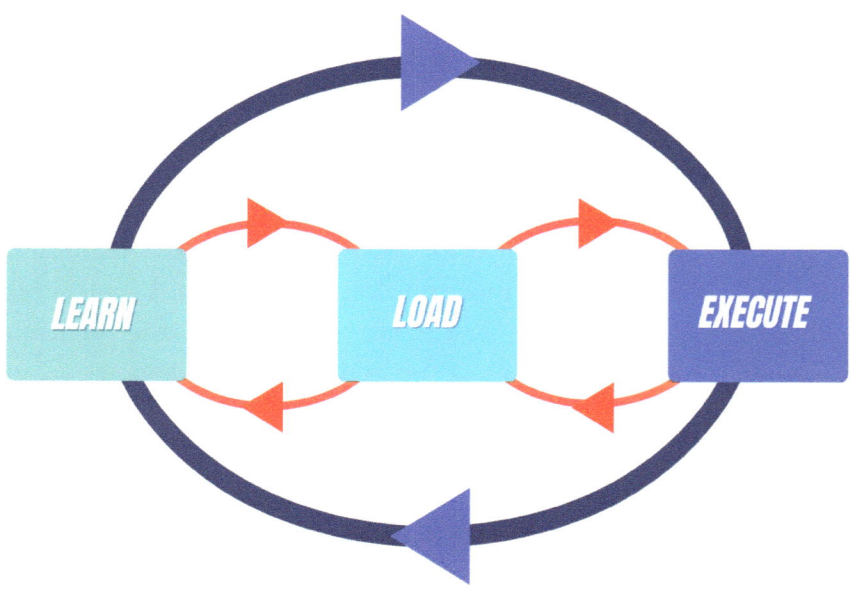

Before we move into drill stacking I would like to point out how the frameworks compliment one another. I will continue to do so as we stack the frameworks.

- *Speed age allows us to identify where the athlete is ready to start their journey.*
- *Learn Load Execute gives us the coaching frameworks to build effective coaching sessions.*

Framework 3: Drill Stacking

Drill stacking is a motor learning theory-based approach that helps coaches organise and structure their training programs for athletes. It integrates the principles of exercise classification and dynamic correspondence.

This helps ensure athletes are guided through a progressive stream of training. This framework is the first place all coaches should start when planning sessions as it fits directly into the Learn Load Execute framework.

The primary goal of drill stacking is to increase exposure to complexity and task specificity in a subtle way. It involves gradually exposing athletes to more challenging exercises and drills that have been trained in part previously. Performed with repetition the athletes are able to push themselves to get better but making slight changes in the movements and the way in which they are performed. The approach is easily applicable to large numbers of athletes.

Drill stacking is based upon the law of accommodation; if an athlete is exposed to a certain level of stimulus for a prolonged period of time that stimulus will stop being an effective tool for training adaptation..Drill stacking uses this to achieve an improved equilibrium in physical and technical capacity which allows the athletes to benefit from increasing levels of intensity, complexity, and specificity in training. . For example, specific strength at the ankle is required for lots of sporting actions, and through drill stacking, we seamlessly improve the capacity of the joint whilst teaching it to perform more complex tasks

DRILL STACKING

DRILL STACKING
- **Skill**
  - Acceleration (Steps 1-3)
  - Acceleration (Steps 4-7)
  - Max Velocity
  - Transitional Non-Linear Sprinting
- **Pattern**
  - Project
  - Project - Exchange
  - Project - Exchange - Contact
  - Project - Exchange - Contact - Project
- **Movement**
  - Triple Flexion
  - Triple Extension
  - Swing
  - Retraction
- **Segment**
  - Ankle Stiffness
  - Knee Extension
  - Hip Extension
  - Lumbar Pelvic Rotation

Drill stacking involves breaking down the movement into segments, understanding the pattern of the movement, and then applying the necessary drills to improve the movement. For example, ankle stiffness, knee extension, hip extension, and lumbar pelvic rotation are the key lower limb segmental movements that most coaches need to focus on. The movements involved in drill stacking for sprinting include triple extension, triple flexion, swing, and retraction. After you start to isolate and improve the segments and movements, you are able to implement these into the pattern you are trying to influence.

To implement drill stacking, coaches need to create a stack of exercises that progress in specificity and complexity. Coaches start with basic exercises and then replace them with more complex ones as athletes improve. The progression is non-linear, and coaches need to focus on the deficits they want to change and the adaptations they want to create.

Drill stacking creates leading indicators for coaches and athletes to use. A leading indicator is a piece of data that allows us as coaches to anticipate the challenges which will occur during the next phase of training. For example if an athlete is poor in a specific body segment , this indicates that the athlete will most likely struggle with more complex movements which that segment drives. As athletes progress, coaches can rotate drills and replace them with more complex ones, creating a path of progression that elevates athletes. Drill stacking is agile in approach, allowing coaches to create hyper-specificity in a certain element and apply it to different circumstances.

Drill stacking really came to life with me one day when I was coaching a professional rugby athlete who was so strong in the gym but just couldn't use this strength. He was a bigger player and really relied on his size to get him out of trouble. He pulled me aside one day and asked me if I could help him out before training. Feeling like he needed to get the extra edge in his game he knew speed was his achilles heel. Being such a brutish athlete he was heavy and cumbersome in nature. So I knew I had to break down speed to a joint by joint approach. "We are going to train for speed like you train for bigger biceps," I told him. I knew full well that if I started pushing him with accelerations and such he would get hurt, I also didn't want to tire him out for training so we took our time. We focused on being loose and fluid and then started with the ankle. Loading him up segment by segment, movement by movement. "It's like my body is working again" he told me after a training session and it was true. Drill stacking became a staple in his pre training and pre match routine. Sprinkling across the week in small amounts made huge differences in a matter of weeks. That's when I knew I was onto something big. That's when I knew I had to get it in every speed program there is.

Choosing the right exercises when implementing the drill stacking framework is really important. To do so I advise you start with the specific segment you want to influence based on the specific outcome you want to create. I advice hip extension as a very good starting point for most athletes. Select appropriate exercises that encourages the development of the segment and then progress from there increasing the way that hip extension is expressed. In later chapters of the book we will dive into special strength and body links that will help you create a greater understanding of the application of drill stacking. You will find examples of this in the appendix to guide you further.

In summary, drill stacking is a highly applicable and easy-to-use motor learning theory-based approach that helps coaches organise their training programs for athletes. By breaking down movements into segments and understanding the necessary movement skills and capacities, coaches can create a stack of exercises that progressively increase in specificity and complexity, heightening performance..

- *Speed age allows us to identify where the athlete is ready to start their journey.*
- *Learn Load Execute gives us the coaching frameworks to build effective coaching sessions with.*
- *Drill stacking breaks down the movements to highlight what to train in according to where we see there are specific skill or strength deficits. It is advised to always start with segment and work upward from there.*

Framework 4: Stable to Unstable

The stable to unstable framework creates a systematic approach to decreasing stability whilst increasing velocity. Stability is a variable that is often overlooked in training speed. In the context of speed training, stability can be defined as to how much external resistance or support an athlete is given to control the body and how much time is spent on the ground. Support can be a literal immovable object (e.g. a wall) or an object that moves which also balances the torso (push sled). As an athlete moves progressively faster the less stability they have, as there is less time to make corrections to position and trajectory. Therefore creating a training framework which systematically increases the amount of instability an athlete has to overcome is an incredibly powerful training tool. As a coach you are able to manipulate this continuum, to seamlessly transfer the learned skills and physical adaptations made under more stable conditions to higher velocities. The framework is exemplified in a child learning to ride a bike. The stabilisers allow the child to push hard, move fast and steer without falling off. Then with the new level of specific balance and strength, the stabilisers can be removed limiting the risk of injury.

Utilising the previous frameworks (Learn Load Execute and Drill Stacking) as coaches we are able to create simple and effective training solutions. This involves reverse engineering specific movements to create specific exercises and systematically unloading stability to support learning. It allows the athlete to formally associate the single exercises with the desired outcome, painting the picture of speed development and constantly reinforcing the overall aim of the session and training. You will find specific examples of these exercises in the "Exercises of the Sports Speed System Chapter". There is a push-pull process within the system, which means we can pick exercises to push the training forwards and test how the athlete performs with less stability and we can then pull back if we need to in order to refine the athlete more. This feedback and control stops the athlete from returning to old habits as a means of survival. It is important to re-emphasize, as discussed with speed age, that everytime a new level of performance is attained the athlete must learn to use their motor skills at this new, higher intensity. Training the new, higher output under more stable conditions allows us to ensure that the new improvement is ingrained into the athlete.

The more stable movements train and improve an athlete's specific strength. This prepares the athlete to encounter a lack of stability, such as rapidly placing one foot in front of the other in space. They are then able to use that strength to acquire a new level of motor control. This improves how the athlete not only applies force but the efficiency with which this force is applied.

It is important to monitor the athlete's physical and psychological reactions to the added instability and ensure that we do not push them too far too soon. The key to success with this framework is to balance the push and pull, to meet the needs of the athlete in front of you.

For your reference here are some examples of the exercises and where they fit on the continuum below. These exercises are explained on a deeper level in the "Exercises of the Sports Speed System Chapter".

Stable		Stable - Unstable		Unstable - Stable			Unstable	
Segmented	Connected Movement	Segmented	Connected Movement	Hand Supported	Hand Supported Hip Resisted	Hip Resisted	Sprinting	Overspeed Sprinting
Ankle / Knee / Hip Emphasis	Full Range Joint or Multi Joint Action	Single Leg Ankle Flexion Extension	Single Exchange Pattern	Prowler March	Prowler March with Hip Resistance	Resisted Sled March	Long Acceleration	Assisted Max Speed
Overcoming Isometrics	Unilateral Load and Smash	Single Leg Hip Flexion Extension	Kneeling Wall Shoot	One Step Push	Prowler Prance with Hip Resistance	Resisted Sled Prance	Fly Sprints	Assisted Drills

- *Speed age allows us to identify where the athlete is ready to start their journey.*
- *Learn Load Execute gives us the coaching frameworks to build effective coaching sessions with.*
- *Drill stacking breaks down the movements to highlight what to train.*
- *Stable to unstable shows how to gradually improve the motor control of these movements.*

Framework 5: Step By Step

Know what you need to see

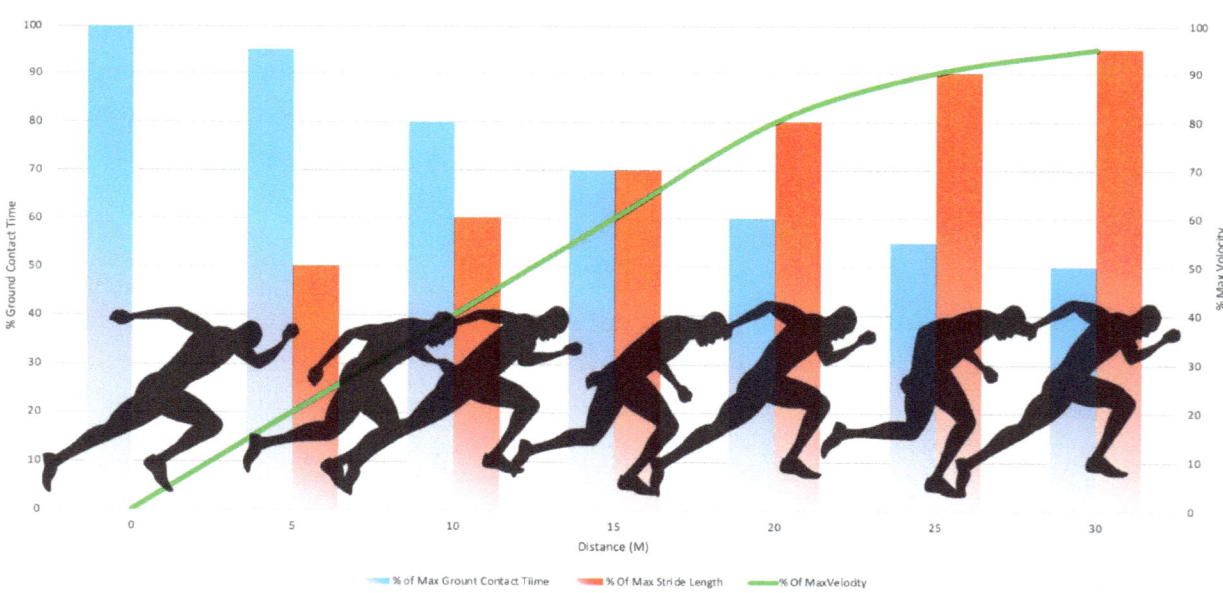

Framework five is a step-by-step approach that breaks down the phases from acceleration to maximum velocity. This framework emphasises the relationships between ground contact, stride length, and stride rate. This framework takes the literal approach of building speed from step 0 and upwards to ensure optimisation of speed. Note we do not just work 1 step at a time we compound steps as we go. An exercise often used is a 1 step push (See appendix) and use a run off distance. The emphasis is on step 1 and then using the other steps to work on technique. We will then introduce a 2 step push and so on to fine tune technique and

WWW.SAMPORTLAND.COM

effective force application. In team sports we have limited time to express speed and this framework ensures we maximise every step. Using drill stacking from the top down. We look at breaking acceleration into steps 1-3 and steps 4-7, emphasising the specific qualities desired during these phases and combining the steps together. We use step screenings to identify the change in technique and physical output per step. In sprinting activity the body position of the athlete changes every step and this needs to be coached and monitored.

To further the understanding of the step by step approach we need to consider the relationship between time spent on the ground and time spent in the air. For example, If the athlete spends too long on the ground this will decrease the stride frequency and therefore shortening the stride length. This is due to the fact that if you spend longer on the ground and your centre of mass is constantly moving forward or even increasing speed you will be forced to shorten your stride to prevent the risk of falling over. This will result in a net decrease in speed.

The step by step process involves analysing the technical and physical aspects of each step to create effective horizontal and vertical displacements. The goal is to generate vast amounts of momentum by ensuring that velocity is changing every step and that athletes are finding the next progression through key technical positions.

It is important to understand how the point of ground contact influences momentum, acceleration, and net velocity. Whether the point of contact is ahead, or behind the centre of mass determines whether we create a braking force or a propulsive force.

The concepts of braking and propulsive forces play a pivotal role in optimising an athlete's performance.

Braking forces reduce an athlete's forward momentum. They occur when the net reaction force from the ground opposes the direction of travel, typically when ground contact occurs too far ahead of the centre of mass. While it might seem counterintuitive to discuss deceleration in a sport focused on speed, controlled braking is essential during various phases of sprinting. As an athlete transitions from acceleration to maintaining maximum speed, controlled breaking allows for smoother transitions within the phases of the gait cycle and conserves energy. It also enables the athlete to efficiently reposition their limbs for the next stride. Braking force is essential to the development of speed and how speed builds through our steps.

Propulsive force is any reaction force the athlete creates against the ground that is a net forwards direction. This force is particularly crucial during the acceleration phase, where athletes need to overcome inertia and rapidly increase their velocity. Maximising propulsive force ensures that the athlete can reach their desired velocity quickly. Which is why the point of contact is so important when considering the step by step framework. Which is a guide to help you as a coach build your athletes speed in a literal step by step fashion to ensure you are maximising every ground contact to its fullest.

The displacement of the centre of mass refers to the movement of an athlete's overall body weight during sprinting. We can establish this by looking at the distance that the hip travels after the point of vertical alignment (full support) has been established (see image below). This action and distance covered enables the process of effective acceleration. Throughout an acceleration effort maintaining an optimal displacement is essential for efficient mechanics and energy conservation. This is because the athlete is able to exchange their legs underneath their hips effectively. The displacement (forward and gradually up) creates time for this action to take place. Less initial displacement will decrease the time available to exchange legs and shorten the athletes stride decreasing speed. These concepts are discussed in greater detail within the chapter Applied Physics of Sprinting.

The step-by-step framework helps identify deficits in technical and physical relationships, and it involves understanding exercise classification, horizontal versus vertical displacement, and effective displacement. When examining a specific step in a run we can identify the desired technical model. Whilst subtle differences occur this detail is vital. As we will discuss in the physics chapter of this book we have to create propulsion and orientate the athletes centre of mass in the direction that we want to go. When we develop early acceleration with athletes, using this framework often an athlete will start to stumble forward as they begin to produce more force. This will raise an alarm to use framework 1 to refine posture and work on an athlete's ability to exchange legs faster in the air. When we find an "error" it is an opportunity to implement a quick intervention to support our skill outcome.

By focusing on steps one through seven, coaches can create rapid acceleration , reach maximum velocity faster, and optimise the points of contact.

This process can be made very easy to apply when we look at the common issues that a majority of team sport athletes face. For example not being able to create significant horizontal displacement in initial steps of acceleration. We also tend to see athletes who will overstride during their initial acceleration. Overstriding in the context of sprinting is when the foot makes contact with the ground ahead of the centre of mass. This causes the athlete to create too much braking force early in the contact, limiting their ability to accelerate efficiently. Taking the step by step approach the development of acceleration and top speed helps to eliminate many of the issues athletes face. Overall, Framework five provides a comprehensive approach to building acceleration power and maximising velocity by analysing each step of the process.

- *Speed age allows us to identify where the athlete is ready to start their journey.*
- *Learn Load Execute gives us the coaching frameworks to build effective coaching sessions.*
- *Drill stacking breaks down the movements to highlight what to train*
- *Stable to unstable show how to gradually improve the motor control of these movements*
- *Step by step allows you to build speed step by step*

Framework 6: Curve Loading

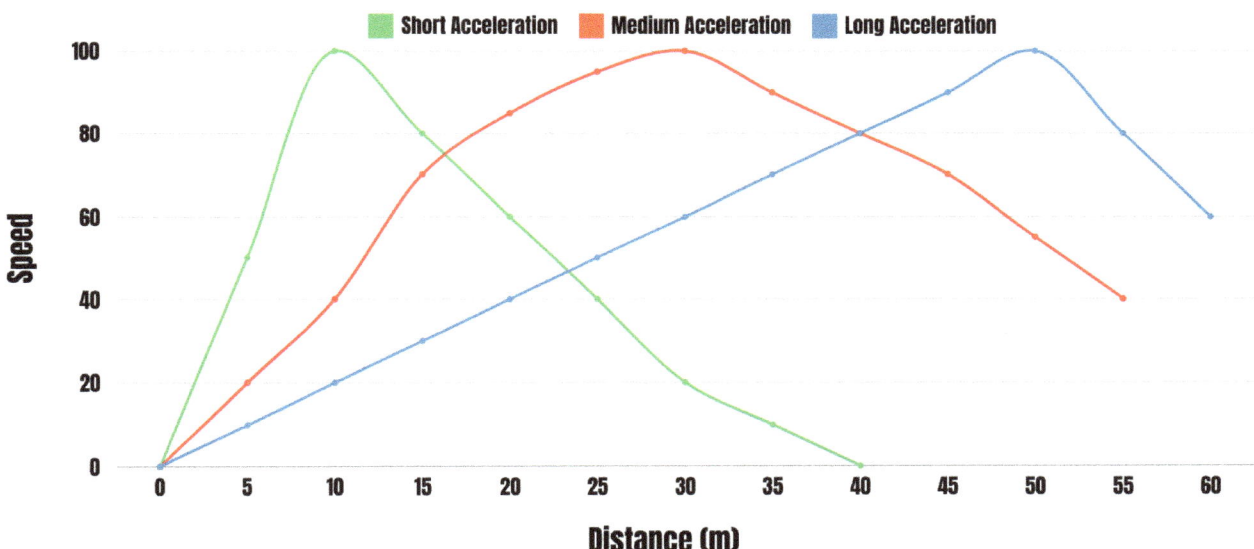

Curve Loading is a key tool for enhancing speed by changing the way you accelerate. This framework explains the role of submaximal speed training. Submaximal training has been widely used in conventional weight room activity for decades with great effect. But within the context of speed training we fail to recognise how to implement this training tool.

This framework focuses on how a given running velocity can create intensity and what the cost of that intensity is. Here are three examples of intensity curves within curve loading. These are based on different magnitudes of acceleration. We can shape the intensity of our sessions based on this very metric. The graph above illustrates how we can find the same resultant velocity whilst accelerating at different rates.

The blue long acceleration (0-50m) curve allows athletes to build up to their maximum speed over a longer distance. This helps coaches understand the athlete's most comfortable rate of acceleration to achieve their ultimate goal of maximum velocity. This is achieved by not limiting the distance that max speed is created and gives the athlete time to build up. Using a simple GPS tracker this can be determined by looking at the distance at which max speed occurred (Not available on all GPS manufacturers). Another byproduct of this method is the accumulation of step load.

Step load is the fatigue cost per step at a given velocity or rate of acceleration. This metric helps us understand how the athletes are being exposed to intensity and volume. This mimics the same way you would look at the fatigue cost of different barbell training. The higher the percentage of maximal speed the greater the fatigue is on the neuromuscular system and the more volume of steps covered will create stress on the energy system and muscular system. When considering the difference between maximal speed training and short acceleration training we make the careful assumption that during maximal speed training there is a great cost to the central nervous system and the neuromuscular system as opposed to short acceleration. During short acceleration we can assume that due to the higher muscular nature of the activity that there is a greater cost at the muscular level. With regards to the energy system considerations to this, how the workouts are structured will determine how stress is placed on the metabolic system. In my experience many team sport athletes lack the ability to handle high volumes of acceleration or maximal speed with a greater density. One assumption made is that a player can run X accelerations in a game therefore they should be able to complete that in training completely disregarding the density at which they are executed. This needs to be taken into consideration when structuring step loads in workouts.

When using longer curves we can mitigate some of the fatigue of sprinting. This is because we are able to increase the window of time an athlete needs to achieve a certain speed. This is primarily aimed at the development of maximal speed. During a longer acceleration we can reduce the mechanical work created by acceleration and gradually expose the athletes to higher speeds with less effort at the beginning of the sprint, as we have removed the initial horizontal displacement.

Lesser Horizontal Displacement   **Greater Horizontal Displacement**

The short acceleration (0-20m) curve creates more intense loading because the rapid acceleration involves bigger forces. It results in an initial peak in velocity but a quick drop off (rate of decay) making it very taxing on the athlete's system, due to the maximal intent and effort that this type of speed requires.

The Medium acceleration curve can be a little bit of a no man's land at times if used in isolation, but the Medium curve is so important to a developing team sport sprinter. It bridges the gap from having a great "burst" of speed to having the ability to continue to accelerate for longer. Some athletes are more anthropometrically predisposed to favour acceleration or top speed due to the nature of their lever lengths. However this is an essential way to accelerate in team sports as field sports require short bursts, long fast covering runs but also 20-30m timed penetrating runs.

Coaches can use the Curve Loading framework to shape the intensity of the training session based on the athlete's qualification and desired adaptations.

Understanding the rate of decay is vital for the coach. This is the rate at which an athlete starts to decelerate after reaching top speed or circa maximal speed. This is a net result of the initial effort put into the time it takes to achieve top speed due to the energy which is required. During short acceleration efforts once peak speed is achieved an athlete will drastically start to decrease speed as opposed to a medium or longer acceleration which decreases at slower rates. This is due to the conservation of energy that these less taxing accelerations require. This should be incorporated within your periodisation to create less taxing speed exposures.

Variable	Short	Medium	Long
Distance	0-20m	20-50m	50-80m
Rate of Decay	High	Medium	Low
Physical Requirement	High Muscular	Muscular / Elastic	High Elastic
Injury Risk	High	Medium	Low
RPE	High	Medium	Low

The way in which speed is created from a muscular skeletal system is not the same for all distances. During shorter acceleration there is a greater demand on the muscular structures of athletes to create the forces required to produce speed very quickly. This is because there is no stored energy within the athletes tendons. This is contrasted within the medium and longer acceleration curves as the athlete with a slower initial acceleration is able to capitalise on the elastic nature of the tendon response. This means that with the longer build ups the muscular skeletal system can shift towards a more elastic dominance in the creation of speed.

Purely from the way in which an athlete attempts to create speed significantly correlates to the risk of injury. In the shorter conditions the athlete is required to put maximal effort into every step thus creating a huge window of opportunity for any form of speed related injury. For example, short accelerations pose a higher risk to pelvic integrity, and spending too much time there can lead to lower limb soft tissue injuries.

When given more time to find speeds athletes can relax and focus on technique and not try to force their speed and let the body create it for them.

Coaches can use the Curve Loading framework to apply density models and create competitions, leading to enhanced performance. Density models are a useful tool that allow coaches to achieve certain speeds with less effort. A density model with regards sprinting is where we open up the distance required to reach a certain percentage of speed. The image below illustrates the different ways you achieve the same percentage of speed. In each of these instances we can manipulate the way our athletes achieve their speed. Applying the density model correctly will be to start with the longer windows of acceleration in early phases of training and work backwards to more sport specific distances. For example a using a long acceleration to achieve 80% of max speed instead of a 30 metre medium acceleration to save the mechanical load on the athlete. Typically team sport athletes struggle with high volumes of mechanical work in speed training due to a lack of speed age, this due to the lack of specific physical preparation required to tolerate this type of work.

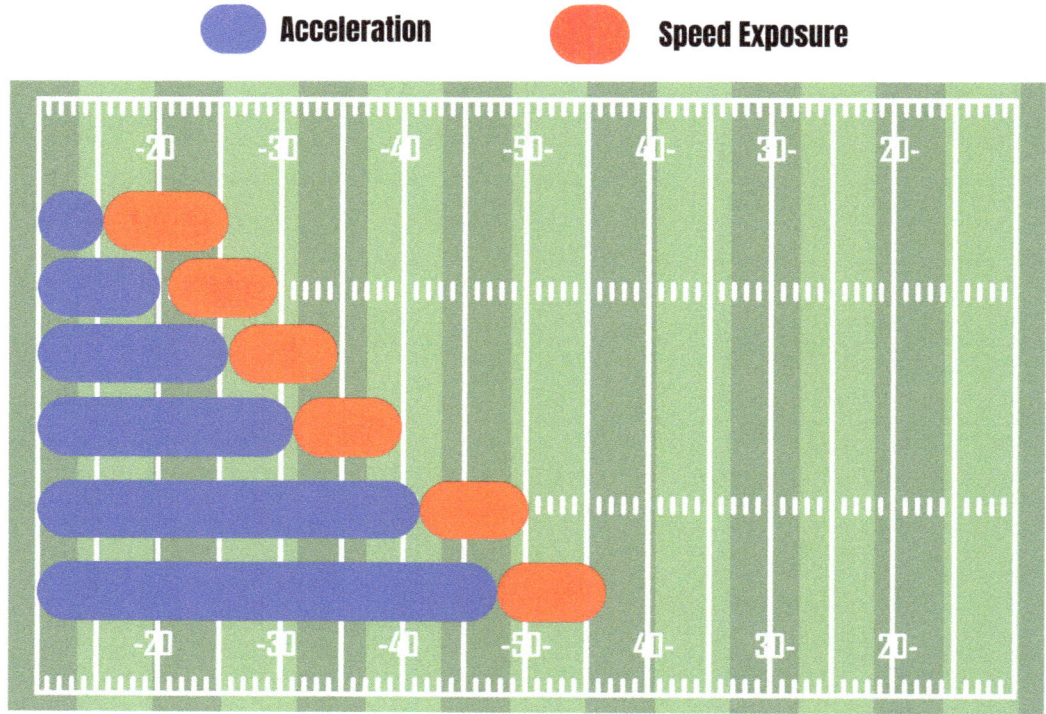

- *Speed age allows us to identify where the athlete is ready to start their journey.*
- *Learn Load Execute gives us the coaching frameworks to build effective coaching sessions.*
- *Drill stacking breaks down the movements to highlight what to train*
- *Stable to unstable show how to gradually improve the motor control of these movements*
- *Step by step allows you to build speed step by step*
- *Curve loading shows you how to shape intensity by varying rate of acceleration.*

Framework 7: Non Linear Sprinting

Non Linear Sprinting is a framework that focuses on teaching how to apply sprinting rules in a non-linear fashion. This framework emphasises the importance of identifying key movement patterns within team sports and understanding the fundamentals of limb organisation that remain constant regardless of direction. The framework also aims to demonstrate the key rules of motion that contribute to non-linear sprinting and create a drill stacking model towards real exposure.

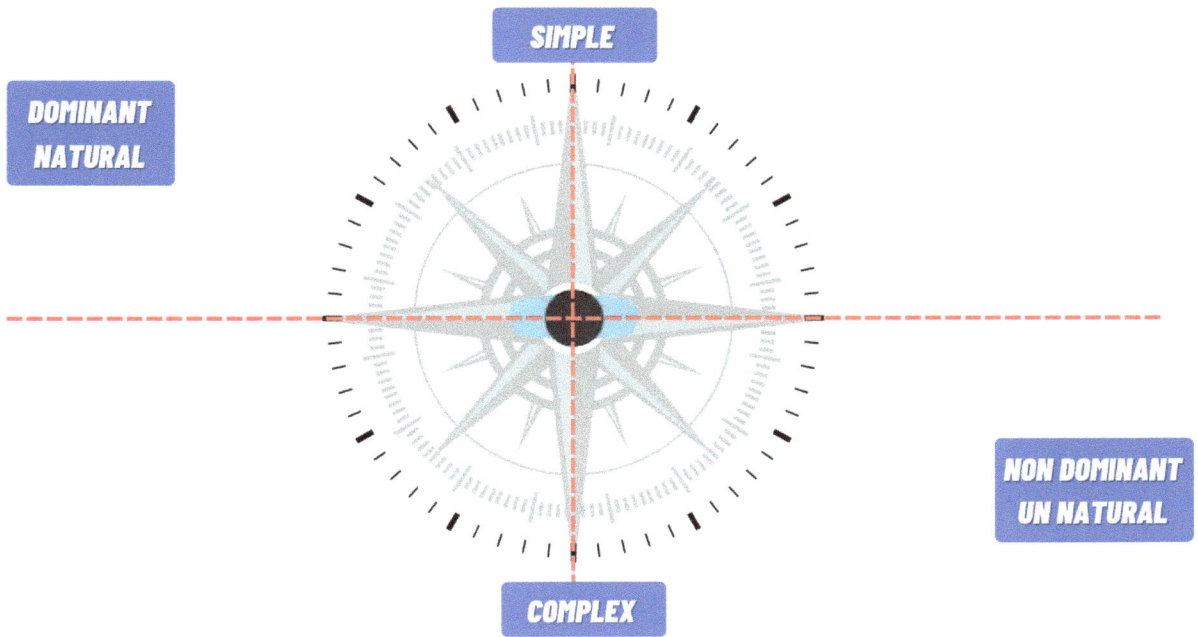

The compass above illustrates the foundational premise on non-linear sprinting. In the application of coaching non-linear movement it is incredibly important to consider dominant and non dominant sides. As coaches we need to speed up the understanding and development of motor learning and motor control so it can be utilised in the context of the game. It is also important to recognise what constitutes simple and complex in this context. In this case it is identified that simple non linear sprinting encompasses anything that involves the net displacement of the athlete being forward. Complete is the direct opposite of this. Therefore it is advised to focus on coaching simple dominant actions first and then progress through the quadrant as illustrated below.

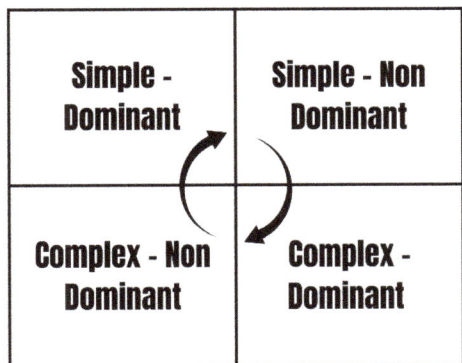

The key to non-linear sprinting is finding the same leg exchange position that one would use for acceleration. They are merely performed at different angles. I have demonstrated this in the image below, where the athlete GB sevens player is demonstrating the same kinematic position in a linear acceleration and a lateral acceleration. When the non linear sprinting framework is applied and coaches effectively we are able to close the game between linear and non linear movement very quickly by forming the associations between movements. Developing these skills is crucial for team sports such as rugby, American football, and soccer, where players need to peel off, drift out, hitch up, or run a comeback route.

INITIAL PUSH OFF

FULL SUPPORT

It is important to assess the level of technical efficiency of athletes during the first few steps of non-linear movements. For every non-linear sprinting pattern, there is a linear sprinting pattern that follows, so it is crucial to be as efficient as possible in our non linear movements to maximise the linear speed actions that follow.

The Non Linear Sprinting framework is an important aspect of coach education and can be applied through drill stacking and subtle progression within learning to achieve the desired results. Coaches should focus on applying this framework in their coaching and understanding of non-linear movements.

- *Speed age allows us to identify where the athlete is ready to start their journey.*
- *Learn Load Execute gives us the coaching frameworks to build effective coaching sessions.*
- *Drill stacking breaks down the movements to highlight what to train*
- *Stable to unstable show how to gradually improve the motor control of these movements*
- *Step by step allows you to build speed step by step*
- *Curve loading shows you how to shape intensity by varying rate of acceleration.*
- *Non linear sprinting allows you to do what you do forward at differing angles.*

GENERAL SPEED

The pillar general speed raises awareness of the true nature of straight line running or pre-planned change of direction. These two qualities whilst specific when considering the traditional classifications of training, are ultimately general qualities when we are training athletes to perform within team sports.

When we consider how we develop an athlete's physical abilities we must consider this in the wider picture of sport preparation. Below I have allocated the ratios of where you need to be spending your time and dedicating your efforts in training for maximum return on training investment.

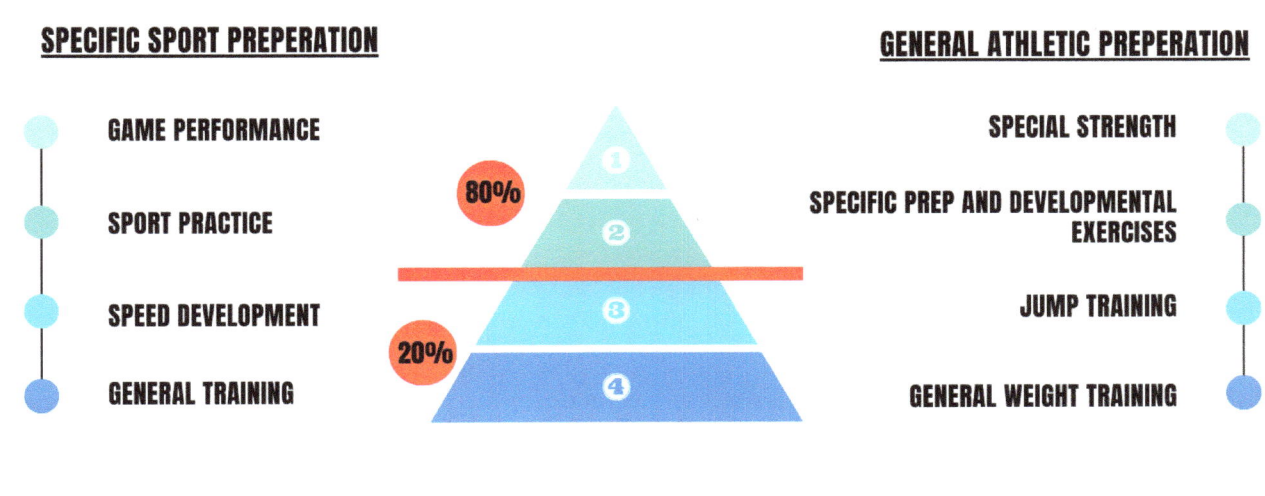

TRANSFER OF TRAINING

The transfer of training forms the backbone of athletic preparation, encompassing the translation of general physical capacities into sport-specific proficiency. Rooted in the methodology of Anatoliy Bondarchuk, this approach entails a strategic progression through three essential phases. These are covered in greater detail later in the book.

Assessing the efficacy of transfer involves the monitoring of athlete responses and performance indicators.

See the picture below to grasp the fundamentals of the transfer of training. It is important to determine the effectiveness of the training to do otherwise we are just wasting time. An example of this is how a resisted sled march will affect an athlete's ability to accelerate faster for a given distance. The trained exercise is the sled march and the untrained exercise is the timed acceleration. Whilst a simple visual calculation, to obtain the results of your training we need to determine effect size.

$$\text{TRANSFER} = \frac{\text{RESULTS GAIN IN NON TRAINED EXERCISE}}{\text{RESULTS GAIN IN TRAINED EXERCISE}}$$

Effect size is a critical statistical measure in sports science, offering a standardised way to quantify the magnitude of changes or differences between two conditions. In the context of speed training, understanding the effect size can help coaches and athletes assess the efficacy of specific training interventions, such as timed resisted sprints, on performance outcomes like unresisted sprint times.

Understanding Effect Size

Effect size provides a clear and interpretable metric that reflects the practical significance of a training intervention. Unlike p-values, which only indicate whether an effect exists, effect size measures the magnitude of the effect, making it a more meaningful indicator for evaluating training outcomes. Commonly used measures of effect size include Cohen's d, Hedge's g, and partial eta squared, with Cohen's d being the most frequently applied in sports science studies.

Calculating Effect Size

Please refer to the appendix resources as I have created a google sheet that houses these calculations for you. To calculate the effect size of timed resisted sprints on unresisted sprint times, follow these steps:

1. Gather Data: Collect pre- and post-intervention sprint times for a group of athletes. Ensure you have a control group that did not undergo the resisted sprint training for a more robust comparison.

2. Calculate the Mean and Standard Deviation: Determine the mean and standard deviation of sprint times for both the pre-intervention and post-intervention conditions in both groups.

3. Compute Cohen's d:
— Calculate the mean difference between the pre- and post-intervention sprint times for the experimental group (those who did the resisted sprints).
— Calculate the mean difference for the control group.
— Subtract the control group's mean difference from the experimental group's mean difference to find the net effect.
— Divide this net effect by the pooled standard deviation (which accounts for variability in both pre- and post-intervention conditions).

The formula for Cohen's d is:

$$d = M1 - M2 / SD\ Pooled$$

where *M*1 and *M*2 are the mean sprint times of the experimental and control groups, respectively, and *SD Pooled* is the pooled standard deviation.

Example Calculation

Suppose you have the following sprint times (in seconds) for a group of athletes:

- Experimental Group (Resisted Sprints):
- Pre-intervention: Mean = 12.5, SD = 0.3
- Post-intervention: Mean = 12.0, SD = 0.2

- Control Group:
- Pre-intervention: Mean = 12.4, SD = 0.3
- Post-intervention: Mean = 12.3, SD = 0.3

First, calculate the mean differences:
- Experimental group: 12.5 - 12.0 = 0.5
- Control group: 12.4 - 12.3 = 0.1

Net effect: 0.5 - 0.1 = 0.4

Next, calculate the pooled standard deviation:

$$SDpooled = \sqrt{\square(SDpre^2 + SDpost^2) \div 2} = \sqrt{\square(0.3^2\square^\square + 0.2^2) \div 2} = 2(0.09 + 0.04) = 0.065 = 0.255$$

Finally, compute Cohen's d:

$$d = 0.4/0.255 \approx 1.57$$

An effect size of 1.57 is considered large, indicating that the timed resisted sprints had a substantial impact on improving unresisted sprint times. Below is a table that demonstrates the magnitude of effect size to determine how effective your interventions have been.

Effect Size (Cohen's d)	Magnitude	Description
0.0 - 0.1	Trivial	No noticeable effect
0.2 - 0.4	Small	Small effect, but might be meaningful
0.5 - 0.7	Medium	Moderate, noticeable effect
0.8 - 1.2	Large	Large, significant effect
1.3 - 1.9	Very Large	Very large effect
2.0 and above	Huge	Huge, extremely significant effect

Understanding the effect size is a key part to the coaching process. This allows coaches to make informed decisions about incorporating more specific training into training regimens. A large effect size suggests significant improvements in unresisted sprint performance, justifying the inclusion of such training methods. Additionally, regular assessment and reorganisation of training programs based on effect size calculations ensure that athletes continue to receive the most effective interventions for their development.

APPLIED PHYSICS OF SPRINTING

Examining the laws of physics can help us to understand sprinting technique, the training aims within sprinting, and what qualities athletes need to achieve their best performances. In this chapter we attempt to provide a logical basis for some of the axioms of sprint training, and give practical interpretations which will give coaches the ability to understand what they see on the field in a framework of Classical mechanics.

Contents
- Definitions
- Newton's Laws
- Momentum and Impulse
- Stiffness and Springiness
- Circular Motion and Centrifugal Force

Definitions

Before we begin, we will define the physical quantities which will be used throughout, and look at where these quantities occur in sports and in sprinting. It may be useful to refer back to this table throughout the chapter. These quantities are either scalars or vectors. Scalars have a magnitude (size) whereas vectors have a magnitude and also a direction. For example temperature is a scalar quantity, whereas velocity is a vector because it has a size and also a direction. It is often useful for us to consider the horizontal and vertical components of a vector quantity separately, or to look at two different horizontal components (e.g an E-W component and a N-S component).

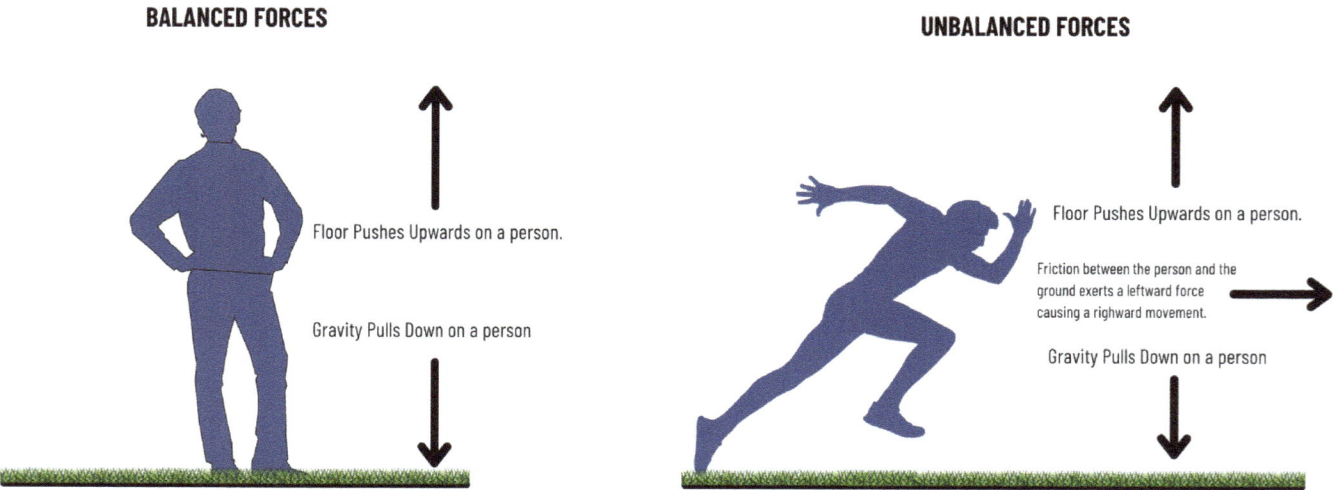

Quantity	Definition	Symbol(s)	Unit(s)
Position	The location of an object in space	–	–
Distance	The amount of space between two positions, **Examples include stride length, the length of a track, the length of a limb**	L	m
Speed	The rate at which an object moves along a path **Examples include how fast a ball moves along its trajectory through the air**	s	m/s
Velocity	The rate at which the position of an object is changing, or very simply how fast it is going. The units metres/second tell us how many metres the object moves every second. Velocity is a vector quantity so it specifies that the movement is in a certain direction. If an athlete runs at a constant speed but changes direction then their velocity has changed too. **Examples include how fast an athlete is running, how fast a ball moves through the air**	v	m/s
Angular Velocity	The rate at which an object is rotating either about its own axis (spin angular velocity), or about an external point (orbital angular velocity) **Examples include how quickly a ball is rotating (spin), how quickly a joint angle is changing (orbital)**	ω	rad/s, revolutions/s
Acceleration	The rate at which the velocity of an object is changing. If an athlete is moving at a constant speed but changing direction, then their velocity is changing, so they are accelerating. The units are metres per second per second. This is describing how many metres per second the velocity changes by each second, and is abbreviated to m/s^2. **Examples include how a ball changes its velocity when struck, how an athletes velocity increases as they break away from a defender**	a	m/s^2
Displacement	The distance an object is away from its starting point. When an athlete jumps up in the air and lands again, they may have travelled a distance of 0.6m, but their displacement is zero. Displacement is a vector quantity and it is frequently broken into horizontal and vertical components	s,x,y	m
Frequency	How often something happens, usually per second. **Examples include stride frequency (how many strides an athlete takes each second), how many times a bike wheel rotates each second**	f	Hz, 1/s
Force	A push or pull on an object. It can act on the whole body of an object like gravity, or act on the surface of an object like friction. Forces cause accelerations to occur. **Examples include gravity, air resistance, friction, pushing out of blocks, pushing off the ground**	F	N, kgm/s^2
Mass	An intrinsic property of an object which determines how much force is needed to accelerate an object	m	kg
Momentum	The product of an object's mass and velocity. It is a vector quantity, so momentum has a certain direction. Momentum is also a conserved quantity, so it does not change unless acted on by an an external force	p	kgm/s, Ns

Quantity	Definition	Symbol(s)	Unit(s)
Impulse	Impulse is the change in momentum an object experiences when acted on by an external force. The change in momentum is the product of the force acting on the object and the time the force is applied for (Δt) Δp = FΔt **Examples include the change in vertical momentum when an athlete contacts the ground and rebounds upwards**	Δp	kgm/s, Ns
Spring Constant/ Stiffness	The amount of force needed to extend or compress a spring by some distance. It is sometimes helpful to think of the body or the leg as a spring. Stiffness is often defined as the resistance of an object or a body to a change in length (McMahon & Cheng, 1990)	k	N/m

Newton's Laws applied to sprinting

Newton's Laws describe how the forces acting on an object affect its motion. We look briefly at some of the implications of each law

1. Law of Inertia. A body remains at rest, or in motion at a constant velocity, unless acted upon by an external force. Athletes must create a force to begin movement or to change their velocity when moving. When a body is at rest all the forces acting on it are balanced, so there is no resultant force, and that body does not accelerate. When an athlete begins to accelerate, they typically go from a stable state with balanced vertical forces and no significant horizontal forces to a state where vertical forces are still balanced, but with the largest possible imbalance in horizontal forces. **Various researchers have found that acceleration performance does not depend on how large the total ground reaction forces produced are, but how large the horizontal component of those forces is**. This emphasises how important acceleration mechanics are, to create forces in the most favourable direction, and good coaching of acceleration revolves around using drills which enhance this skill. Once the athlete reaches top speed, they are no longer accelerating, because all of the force they are generating to push themselves forward is balanced by resistive forces acting against them. To decelerate from top speed back down to stationary requires as much work to be done as it took to achieve top speed in the first place. This is why sprinters decelerate gently after they cross the line, so that slowing down can be assisted by friction and air resistance, rather than having to create large forces themselves. In team sports this is not always an option, so work needs to be done on learning the most efficient ways to decelerate as well as to accelerate.
2. Law of Acceleration. An object accelerates in proportion to the force acting on it, and inversely proportional to its own mass.

$$(1) \ F = ma$$
Force = Mass x Acceleration
$$(2) \ a = F/m$$
Acceleration = Force / Mass

If an athlete creates a force that is twice as large, they will accelerate twice as fast. If one athlete is twice as heavy as another, they will have to create twice as much force to accelerate at the same rate. This is why many coaches are interested in the weights athletes can lift relative to their own bodyweight. Combining this with the square-cube law (When an object increases in size by some multiplier, its new surface area is proportional to the multiplier squared and its new volume is proportional to the multiplier cubed) allows us to understand why acceleration is more difficult for larger, heavier athletes. The force a muscle is capable of producing is proportional to its cross sectional area, but the mass the larger athlete has to move is proportional to their volume, and the law tells us that volume will grow faster than cross sectional area. As such, smaller athletes tend to have greater accelerative abilities, particularly over short distances. This is not only seen through linear acceleration, but also through cuts, steps, and other rapid changes of direction. Playing positions that require these skills tend to be dominated by athletes with lighter builds for this reason, and heavier athletes who do well in these positions often adopt strategies centred more on strength or linear speed than sharp changes of direction. Big athletes who can do both are in very rare air.

3. Law of Action and Reaction. Often stated as "for every action there is an equal and opposite reaction". When one body exerts a force on another, the second body will exert a force of equal magnitude on the first body, acting in the exact opposite direction. As we stand on the ground, we exert a force equal to our weight on it, and the ground pushes back against us, at the same point as we apply force on it. This is called a ground reaction force, and manipulating ground reaction forces is vital to sprinting. The harder we push against the ground, the harder it pushes back against us. If we push hard against the ground vertically, it propels us up into the air, and if we push hard against the ground horizontally, it pushes us horizontally in the opposite direction. At all times in sprinting, we are seeking to maximise ground reaction forces, but we need to make sure that the direction of those ground reaction forces is appropriate for the stage of sprint we are in. During acceleration, we need to make the horizontal component of the ground reaction force as big as possible, whereas at top speed, we try and maximise the vertical component of the ground reaction forces, so that we can get off the ground as quickly as possible.

Momentum and Impulse

As noted above, an object's momentum is the product of its mass and its velocity. An object with a mass of 100kg, moving horizontally at 9m/s has a horizontal momentum of 900kgm/s. Momentum can best be understood by measuring it in Newton seconds. These are an equivalent unit to kgm/s, but more intuitive to think about. If our object has a momentum of 900 Ns, we can bring it to a halt by applying a force of 900 N for 1 second. We could also do this by applying a force of 300 N for 3 seconds, or a force of 100 N for 9 seconds. This brings us to impulse. An impulse is a change in momentum equal to a force multiplied by the time it is applied for. During sprinting, the impulse of each step is the ground contact time multiplied by the average force applied during the step. With each step, the athlete must apply enough vertical impulse to overcome their downwards momentum, get back up into the air and cycle the limbs for the next stride before they return to the ground. Through comparisons with other gait patterns, Weyand et al (2010) found that **Top speed is not about applying the largest possible forces to the ground, but applying creating the required vertical impulses as quickly as possible**. This brings us to the idea that preparation for sprinting should involve getting "strong enough" and learning to produce force as quickly as possible. Many biomechanics researchers have found that ground contact times correlate inversely with top sprint speed (the faster you get off the ground, the faster you run).

Stiffness and Springiness

Elite sprinters contact the ground for less than 0.1 seconds/stride. To reverse their downwards momentum in this time, a huge amount of force is generated in the muscles of the hips and legs and transmitted into the ground. The leg needs to be able to be very stiff to transmit these forces effectively, and the ankle is a joint which often needs particular attention in order to gain the stiffness needed to transmit forces and get off the ground again quickly. Ideally the ankle will remain almost entirely stiff on ground contact, but even elite sprinters enter into some ankle flexion, although through effective harnessing of the stretch reflex, they are able to store and reuse some of the energy lost here. Hooke's law describes what happens when elastic objects (i.e the muscles and connective tissue of an athlete's leg) change length.

$$(3)\ F = kx,$$
Force = Stiffness x Extension

Equation 3 shows that a stiffer limb will change length less than a less stiff limb. In the context of sprinting, this means that on ground contact, an athlete who can generate more stiffness in the ankle and leg will collapse less on contact, and be able to apply force more efficiently to the ground. Elite sprinters are able to generate enough stiffness that their legs change vertical length by less than 2 cm on ground contact, despite handling forces which are large multiples of their body weights in this time. Through progressive exposure, it is possible to build the skills and tissues capacities in athletes which will allow them to handle these forces.

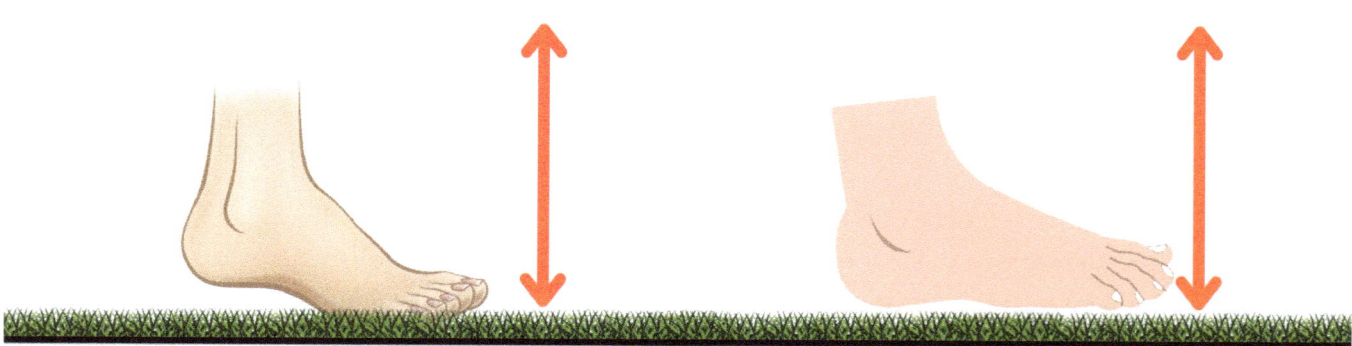

Circular Motion and Centrifugal Force

Team sports contain a great deal of non-linear sprinting and acceleration. Looking at circular motion is a really useful way to understand the forces involved in all forms of curved and non-linear running. It is rare that sports actually require athletes to run in a complete circle (although a great many sports see this as an integral part of the warm up), but running in an arc or a section of a curve is a very common feature of a myriad sporting actions. Running at a constant speed but changing direction requires an athlete to constantly accelerate (recall that acceleration means changing velocity, and your velocity includes your direction as well as your speed).

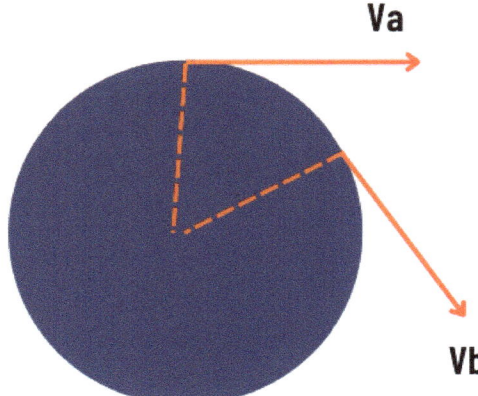

If an athlete runs ¼ of the way around the circle at 7m/s, their N-S velocity has gone from 7m/s down to 0 m/s and their E-W velocity has gone from 0m/s to 7m/s. They have simultaneously decelerated in one direction and accelerated in another, perpendicular direction. This shows us a key feature of circular motion: circular motion can only be maintained when resultant force is being directed at the centre of the circle. For example, imagine swinging a rope with a heavy object tied to the end around yourself in a circle. The only horizontal force that the object experiences is the tension in the rope, due to you pulling it back towards the centre, and this is what keeps it moving in a circle. Likewise, for an athlete to continue running in an arc, they must be creating force towards the centre of the circle. This is called a centripetal acceleration.

$$(4)\ F = mv^2/r$$
Centripetal Force = Mass x velocity^2/radius

We can use the formula for centripetal force to understand how much force an athlete requires to keep running on an arc. If they do not produce this much force, they will either drift away from the centre of the circle, or have to slow down to maintain their course. The amount of force the athlete must produce is proportional to their mass; a heavier athlete must produce proportionally more force than a lighter athlete. The amount of force required to stay on the curve also depends on the velocity squared. This shows us that a small increase in velocity will require an athlete to produce significantly more force (for example a 10% increase in velocity requires a 21% increase in force required to stay on the curve). Finally, the force required is inversely proportional to the radius of the curve. This means that to run a circle or curve with a smaller radius requires much more lateral force to be created. For example, running at the same speed around a circle with a 10m radius only requires half as much lateral force as running at the same speed around a circle with a 5m radius. You can illustrate this to yourself in any sports facility with lots of different markings on the floor. Feel the difference between running the curve of an athletics track, or the centre circle of a football pitch, or the netball D. If you try to accelerate and pick up speed, you will experience the sensation of being thrown outwards by some unseen force. This is centrifugal force, a topic which frequently causes confusion. To an outside observer, there is no such force, but it feels very real, a similar sensation to being in a car as it drives around a bend. Your inertia wants you to keep going in a straight line (see Newton's first law) This arises because your reference frame itself is rotating as you move around the circle, but in every instant your inertia wants you to keep going in a straight line, so you feel its outward tug, and as soon as you choose to break off the circle and run in a straight line, this sensation disappears, as you are no longer fighting your inertia.

When athletes lose speed whilst running a curve they are ultimately failing to create enough force towards the inside of the curve, either through lack of technical ability, or simply through not having the capacity to produce that much force.

PHYSIOLOGY OF SPRINTING

Energy System Foundations

In this chapter we are going to be discussing how to apply physiology to the world of sprinting in team sports. The human body utilises various energy systems to provide the necessary energy for physical activity, including sprinting and sports such as rugby, football (soccer), and American football. All of the energy systems use different mechanisms to generate a molecule called ATP (adenosine triphosphate), which is broken down to power muscle contractions, and other vital cellular processes. The ATP molecule is made of an adenine molecule, a ribose molecule, and a chain of three phosphate molecules. Energy is stored in the phosphate bonds, and breaking a bond to release a phosphate molecule releases this stored energy. Here's a summary of the three primary energy systems and their relevance to these sports:

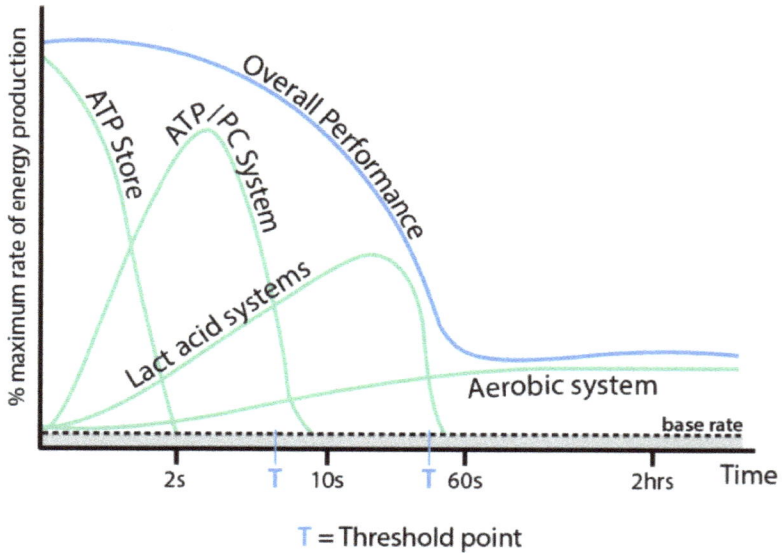

1. **ATP-PCr System (Phosphagen System):** The ATP-PCr system is the energy system used during short, explosive activities like sprints and quick bursts of power. It relies on the stored ATP and phosphocreatine (PCr) to rapidly generate energy. The ATP stores last for a few seconds and then the PC System can enable the system to work for up to 10-15 seconds in total by using PC to reform ATP. Once the system becomes fatigued, it can only be recharged by aerobic metabolism. During sprinting, athletes heavily rely on this system to rapidly produce energy during the explosive acceleration phase and the maximum effort required during the race. In sports like rugby and football, this system is engaged during intense bursts of speed, quick changes in direction, and explosive movements such as tackling or shooting.

2. **Anaerobic Glycolytic System (Lactic System):** The anaerobic glycolytic system provides energy during high-intensity activities lasting from several seconds up to a few minutes. It utilises glucose to generate ATP

without the need for oxygen. Glucose, from the bloodstream, or from stored glycogen, is broken down to produce pyruvate. When the system is working hard, there is only enough oxygen available to use a small amount of pyruvate for efficient aerobic metabolism, so the remaining pyruvate converts to lactate. This regenerates a molecule called NAD+, which is used up in the initial breakdown of glycogen, and regenerating NAD+ by forming lactate allows the breakdown of glycogen to continue, so more ATP can be released. During sprinting, the anaerobic glycolytic system kicks in after the initial burst of ATP-PCr system activity. In sports like rugby and football, this system is heavily utilised during intense periods of play, including short sprints, repetitive high-intensity efforts, and movements requiring power and strength. Using the lactic system intensely also generates fatigue inducing byproducts which can only be cleared by the aerobic system, so it is not possible to maintain large energy outputs with the lactic system for periods longer than a few minutes.

3. **Aerobic System:** The aerobic system supplies energy for longer-duration activities that require sustained effort. It utilises oxygen to break down carbohydrates, fats, and, occasionally, proteins to produce ATP. The aerobic system provides a steady and prolonged energy source, making it essential for endurance events and maintaining performance over extended periods, although it cannot generate ATP as quickly as the other energy systems. In sports like rugby and football, the aerobic system plays a significant role during continuous running, extended periods of play, and maintaining endurance throughout the game. The role of the aerobic energy system is also often overlooked for its role in recovery during and between high intensity bouts of activity. The aerobic system is vital for removing the fatigue inducing byproducts of the other energy systems, and preparing them for high intensity use again. A better developed aerobic system will help athletes to use their anaerobic systems more powerfully and for a greater proportion of the duration of a match.

In team sports, all three energy systems are involved to varying degrees depending on the specific demands of the activity. The relative contributions of each system depend on the duration, intensity, and energy requirements of the task at hand. Training programs for these sports typically involve a combination of conditioning that targets all energy systems to optimise performance and improve overall fitness.

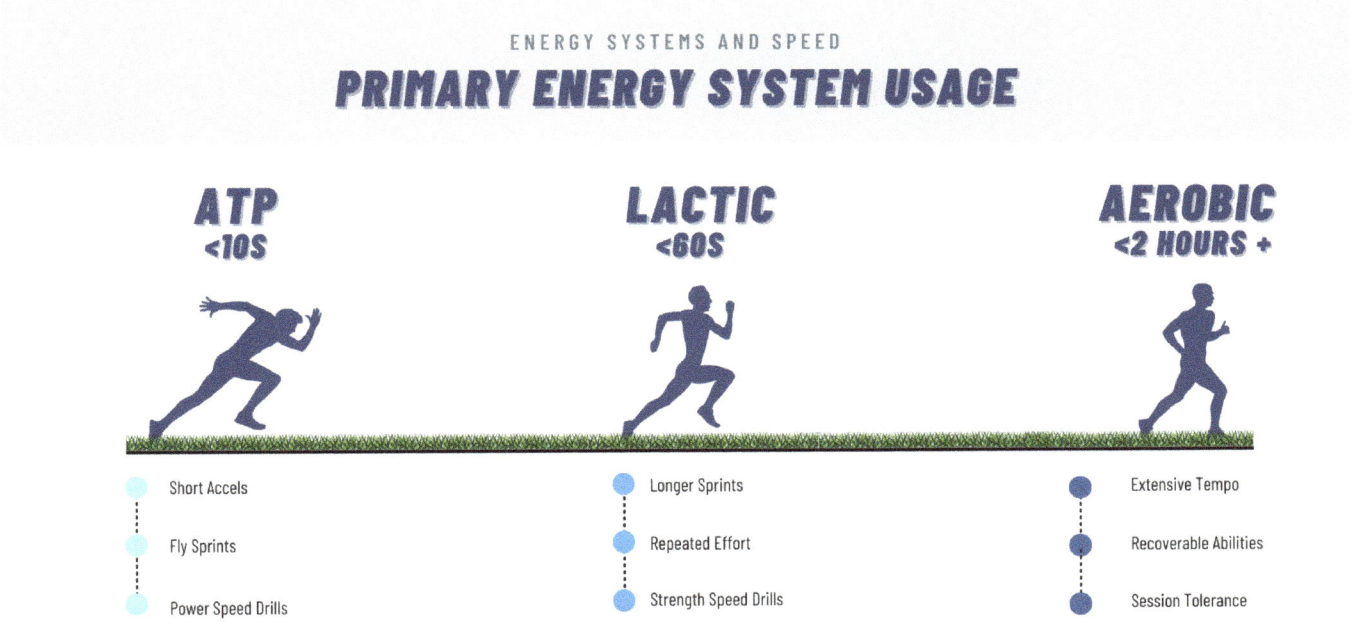

Training as an energy system development tool

It is a great oversight in training when we fail to recognise that all training is an energy system tool. Different modalities enhance an individual's capacity to perform or tolerate work.

We categorise energy system development in three simple ways.

1. **General Conditioning** - Improve foundational capacity to recover from training and train with no consideration to the sport tasks or demands.
2. **Specific Conditioning** - Training that utilises specific exercises and special exercises to improve the task specific outputs of the sport.
3. **Special Conditioning** - Improving the working capacity and repeatability of specific tasks.

In the context of running and sprinting we are able, using this criterion, to produce a progressive stream of exercises to allow suitable conditioning stimulus to develop athletes physiology. Once we appreciate the specific categories of work we are trying to use we can then select the most appropriate tool. Please use the table provided to inform your programming decisions. This is further discussed in the chapter Exercise Classification for Speed.

Descriptor	Reps	Typical work Duration	Work-Rest	% of intensity (Of Max Speed)	% HR Max
Aerobic capacity	1	30-45 Min	NA	20-30%	75%
Aerobic power	3 to 8	1-6 Min	1 to 0.5	30-50%	75-90%
Extensive Tempo	8 to 24	15-40 Sec	1 to 3 - 1 to 4	60-75%	70-85%
Intensive Tempo	8 to 24	4-15 Sec	1 to 6	>75%	85% - 90%
Lactic Intervals	4 to 8	30 Sec	1 to 3 - 1 to 4	100%	NA - Max intent
Repeat Speed	12 to 18	6 Sec	1 to 3 - 1 to 4	100%	NA - Max intent
Speed	6 to 12	3-10 Sec	1 to 10+	100%	NA - Max intent

- **Reps** - A single bout of work. For example; One 30 minute repetition of continuous running.
- **Typical Work Duration** - The amount of time to complete one rep.
- **Work to Rest Ratio** - The relationship between how long an athlete is working compared to the rest duration. For example, a 2:1 work to rest ratio would be 60 seconds work and 30 seconds rest.
- **% of Intensity (Max Speed)** - How fast the athlete should be running in relation to their maximum speed.
- **% HR Max** - The level of desired heart rate for the activity to elicit the physiological adaptations required.
- **Aerobic Capacity** - The overall ability of the cardiovascular, respiratory, and muscular systems to deliver and utilise oxygen and energy substrates.
- **Aerobic Power** - The greatest power output the body can sustain aerobically.

- **Extensive Tempo** - A training method to develop submaximal running to target the development of aerobic capacity.
- **Intensive Tempo** - A training method focused on improving anaerobic capacity, lactate threshold, and speed endurance.
- **Lactic Intervals** - A training method for increasing exercise intensity so you train at or just above your Lactate threshold heart rate. Lactate threshold is intensity at which the blood concentration of lactate and/or lactic acid begins to increase rapidly. It is often expressed as 85% of maximum heart rate or 75% of maximum oxygen intake.
- **Repeat Speed** - A training method for exposing an athlete to greater density of higher velocity running.
- **Speed** - A training methodology exposing an athlete to the soul purpose of developing absolute speed.

When it comes to improving your athletes' speed, it's essential to consider their readiness, qualification, and base aerobic abilities.

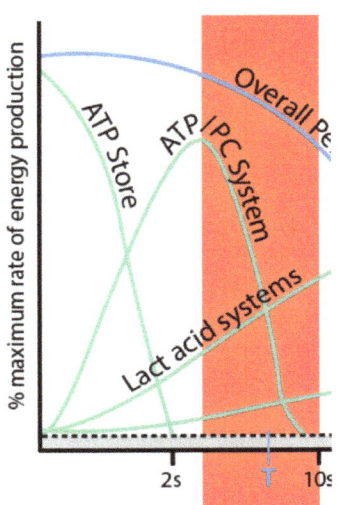

The design of workouts within speed and energy system training is crucial, as certain workouts can create high energy demands, and thus lactic intervals without intending to do so. For example, an athlete in the learning to sprint phases of training does not have the specific development to tolerate high volumes of higher speed running. Therefore, coaches must pay attention to their athletes' recovery abilities and stress their lactic capacity in various scenarios to prepare them for the field. When considering the preparation of athletes from an energy system perspective for team sports, the sport, positional requirement and athlete style will determine the required training methodology.

Keep in mind that energy systems and speed guidelines are rough, and you should determine where your athlete stands. You might not need to perform repeat speed in some situations; instead, focusing on the extensive to intensive sides of tempo at 70-80% Maximal Sprint Speed could be enough to move the needle with a team sport athlete. Deciding what methodology to use can be based on speed age; for example an athlete with a lower speed age will not require the intensity that repeat speed will create to elicit adaptation. Lesser intensity versions such as extensive tempo will be sufficient enough. I have found this to be the case with many team sport athletes. These decisions can also be made based on the specific phase of the preparation cycle with athletes that have greater speed ages. Using a simple progressive overload method of extensive to intensive and then peak with repeat speed training.

Muscle Mechanics and Speed

Muscle mechanics refers to the study of how muscles generate and transmit force to produce movement. It encompasses the understanding of muscle structure, function, and the mechanical principles governing muscle contraction. This section is designed to give you a deeper understanding of muscle physiology and how it relates to speed. In the context of sprinting, an understanding of muscle mechanics is highly relevant as it helps explain the biomechanical factors that contribute to sprint performance. Here's a short summary:

1. **Muscle Contraction:** Sprinting involves powerful and rapid muscle contractions to generate force and propel the body forward. Muscle mechanics examines how muscles contract and generate force through the cross-bridge cycle. In sprinting, muscles primarily rely on fast-twitch muscle fibres that possess a higher capacity for force production and fast contraction speeds.

2. **Force Production:** Muscle mechanics explores how muscles produce force through the interaction between actin and myosin filaments referred toas the sliding filament theory. The force generated by muscle contraction is transmitted through the tendons, which attach muscles to bones. In sprinting, muscles like the quadriceps, hamstrings, and calves generate force to drive forward propulsion and leg movements, such as knee extension and ankle plantar flexion.

3. **Muscle fibre Recruitment:** Sprinting requires the recruitment of a large number of muscle fibres to generate high levels of force. Muscle mechanics helps understand how muscle fibres are recruited and how different types of muscle fibres contribute to sprint performance. Fast-twitch muscle fibres are particularly important for explosive movements and generating the rapid force required for sprinting. There are numerous neuromuscular factors which can be trained to improve the way in which fibres are recruited, allowing the body to produce more powerful efforts. Training can improve the number of fibres recruited, the frequency with which each motor unit fires, and the synchronisation of motor units

4. **Biomechanical Factors:** Muscle mechanics also relates to various biomechanical factors that influence sprinting performance. These factors include muscle length-tension relationships, muscle moment arms, joint angles, and muscle activation patterns. Understanding these factors helps athletes optimise their sprinting technique, such as maximising stride length, generating efficient ground reaction forces, and minimising energy losses during each stride. See Appendix for deeper explanations of these.

5. **Injury Prevention:** Knowledge of muscle mechanics is crucial for preventing injuries during sprinting. Understanding muscle forces, muscle-tendon interactions, and the biomechanics of sprinting can guide athletes in developing proper warm-up routines, conditioning exercises, and training programs that minimise the risk of muscle strains, tears, or other muscle-related injuries.

Muscle mechanics provides valuable insights into the functioning of muscles, their ability to generate force, and their contribution to sprinting performance. This is where the idea of Muscle vs Elastic driven sprinters began. There are two types of sprinters: force-dominant and elastic-dominant, and those with short limbs tend to be more muscular-driven, while those with longer limbs are more tendinous-driven. This makes complete sense based on the muscle architecture these athletes typically possess. However, I urge you not to obsess too much about these details. Instead, understanding the muscle mechanics of your athletes, using drills and exercises that highlight their strengths naturally will suffice. Certain athletes will favour certain things. This is showing you where their natural anthropometric tendencies are.

Elastic Behavioural Properties

- Parallel Elastic Component - Passive Elasticity from muscle membranes.
- Series Elastic Component - Passive Elasticity Derived from tendons when a tensed muscle is stretched.

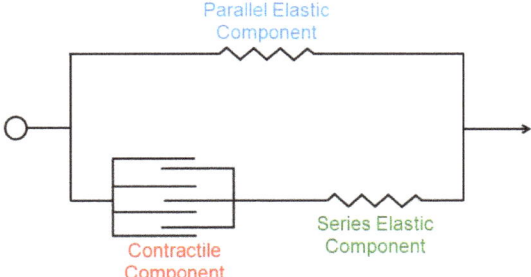

One of the biggest learning opportunities from the understanding of muscle mechanics is found in how we move from muscular to elastic driven activities. Applying the step by step framework, our initial steps are driven by muscular activity, which is building stored energy in our tendons. This begins the process of storing and releasing energy for every step as we accelerate into maximum speed positions where we can continue to create speed using elastic driven activity. Now we will take a look at the differences between elastic and muscle driven sprinters.

Elastic vs. Muscle-Driven Sprinters

Sprinting performance can vary significantly between athletes, often influenced by their predominant reliance on either elastic or muscle-driven mechanisms. Understanding these distinctions can help coaches and athletes tailor training programs to maximise performance. Failing to recognise this can lead you to creating negative transfer with your athletes despite your best efforts. For example training an elastic driven athlete with too much strength work will decrease their elastic properties and subsequently decrease their speed.

Elastic-Driven Sprinters

Elastic-driven sprinters rely heavily on the elastic properties of their tendons and connective tissues to store and release energy during the sprinting cycle. This mechanism is akin to a spring, where energy is absorbed during the ground contact phase and then released during the push-off phase.

Characteristics

1. **High Tendon Stiffness:** Elastic-driven sprinters often possess stiffer tendons, which can store more elastic energy.
2. **Short Ground Contact Time:** They tend to have shorter ground contact times, allowing for rapid energy transfer.
3. **Efficient Use of Stored Energy:** These sprinters efficiently utilise the stored elastic energy, reducing the need for active muscle contraction.

Usain Bolt is the most famous example of an elastic driven sprinter. Widely regarded as one of the greatest sprinters of all time, Bolt is known for his long, powerful strides and efficient use of elastic energy. His ability to maintain top speed with relatively less visible muscle strain exemplifies the characteristics of an elastic-driven sprinter.

Muscle-Driven Sprinters

Muscle-driven sprinters, on the other hand, rely more on active muscle contraction to generate force. These athletes tend to have greater muscle mass and emphasise the role of muscular power in their sprinting performance.

Characteristics

1. **Greater Muscle Mass:** Muscle-driven sprinters often exhibit significant muscle hypertrophy, particularly in the lower body.
2. **Longer Ground Contact Time:** They may have slightly longer ground contact times to maximise the force generated by muscle contractions.
3. **High Force Output:** These sprinters focus on producing high force outputs through active muscle engagement.

Maurice Greene is a great example of a muscle driven sprinter. A dominant force in sprinting during the late 1990s and early 2000s, Greene was known for his powerful build and explosive starts. His sprinting style, characterised by high muscle activation and force production, aligns with the traits of a muscle-driven sprinter.

Implications for Training

Understanding whether an athlete is more elastic or muscle-driven can significantly influence their training regimen. Each type requires a different approach to optimise performance. Here are a couple of key differences in training elastic or muscle driven sprinters. Please keep in mind when reading this that these areas are what differentiate the two sprinter types and not how to explicitly train them. An elastic driven sprinter will need some of what a muscle driven sprinter favours in training but not as much.

Training for Elastic-Driven Sprinters

1. **Plyometrics:** Exercises that enhance the stretch-shortening cycle, such as bounding and hopping are crucial for developing elastic properties.
2. **Shorter Sprint efforts:** Focus on sprint variations with minimal ground contact time to enhance the rapid energy transfer from tendons. For example fly sprints and light resisted accelerations.
3. **Flexibility and Mobility:** Maintaining optimal flexibility and joint mobility ensures efficient use of elastic energy.

Training for Muscle-Driven Sprinters

1. **Strength Training:** Emphasise lower body strength training, including squats, deadlifts, and lunges, to build muscle mass and power.

2. **Longer Sprint efforts:** Incorporate longer sprint effort to improve muscular endurance and force production over extended periods.
3. **Explosive Drills:** Use exercises like power cleans, snatches, and medicine ball throws to develop explosive muscle power.

Practical Application

Coaches should assess their athletes to determine their dominant sprinting mechanism. This can involve biomechanical analysis, force plate testing, and evaluating performance metrics. Once identified, training programs can be tailored to enhance the athlete's natural strengths while addressing any weaknesses.

Reflexes and Speed Training

Reflexes play a vital role in the human body's ability to respond quickly and efficiently to external stimuli. In the context of sprint training, understanding the various reflexes at work can provide valuable insights into optimising performance. This section will explore the stretch reflex, Golgi tendon organ reflex, cross extensor reflex, and stumble reflex, breaking down their mechanisms and relevance to sprint training.

The Stretch Reflex

The stretch reflex, also known as the myotatic reflex, is a protective mechanism that helps maintain muscle length and stability. It occurs in response to a rapid stretch of a muscle, activating a reflex arc involving sensory neurons, interneurons, and motor neurons. The key components of the stretch reflex are:

1. **Muscle Spindle:** The muscle spindle is a sensory organ located within the muscle that detects changes in muscle length. When a muscle is stretched rapidly, the muscle spindle is activated.
2. **Sensory Neurons:** Sensory neurons, known as afferent neurons, carry signals from the muscle spindle to the spinal cord.
3. **Spinal Cord:** The sensory neurons synapse with interneurons in the spinal cord, which transmit signals to motor neurons.
4. **Motor Neurons:** Motor neurons, also called efferent neurons, carry signals from the spinal cord to the muscle, causing it to contract.

The stretch reflex serves a crucial role in sprinting as it helps create rapid muscle contraction. During a sprint, the stretch reflex contributes to the quick and forceful extension of leg muscles on ground contact, shortening ground contact times and enhancing propulsion.

The Golgi Tendon Organ Reflex

The Golgi tendon organ (GTO) reflex functions as a protective mechanism to prevent muscle damage due to excessive tension . It is located at the junction of muscles and tendons, and its main components are:

1. **Golgi Tendon Organ:** The GTO is a sensory receptor that detects changes in muscle tension. When tension within a muscle exceeds a certain threshold, the GTO is stimulated.

2. **Sensory Neurons:** Sensory neurons transmit signals from the GTO to the spinal cord.
3. **Interneurons:** Interneurons within the spinal cord receive signals from the sensory neurons and transmit inhibitory signals to motor neurons.
4. **Motor Neurons:** The inhibitory signals from the interneurons reduce the activity of motor neurons, leading to a decrease in muscle tension.

In sprint training, the GTO reflex helps protect muscles from excessive force and potential injury. It ensures that muscle tension remains within safe limits during explosive movements, allowing sprinters to exert maximum effort without risking muscle damage. Whilst GTOs provide a protective mechanism, their protective function creates a barrier when an athlete is seeking higher outputs of training. Therefore certain methodologies of training are employed to disrupt the role of GTOs. A foundational example of this will be the drop and depth jump variations popularised by Yuri Verkhoshanky. These exercises require athletes to jump off of boxes from great heights to overload the GTOs manipulating the stretch shortening cycle to allow for a greater training stimulus.

The Cross Extensor Reflex

The cross extensor reflex is a reflexive response that provides balance and stability during locomotion. It occurs in conjunction with the withdrawal reflex and involves coordinated movements of the limbs. The key elements of the cross extensor reflex are:

1. **Sensory Neurons:** Sensory neurons detect a noxious stimulus, such as stepping on a sharp object, and transmit signals to the spinal cord.
2. **Interneurons:** Interneurons within the spinal cord receive signals from the sensory neurons and coordinate the reflexive response.
3. **Motor Neurons:** Motor neurons are activated by the interneurons and cause the withdrawal of the injured limb while simultaneously extending and stabilising the opposite limb.

In sprinting, the cross extensor reflex helps maintain balance and stability during rapid and dynamic movements. It ensures that the body maintains equilibrium while generating powerful propulsion forces with each stride by enabling a rapid exchange of limbs.

The Stumble Reflex

The stumble reflex is a rapid automatic response to prevent falling when encountering an obstacle or imbalance. It involves a combination of reflexes, including the stretch reflex,

Golgi tendon organ reflex, and cross extensor reflex. The stumble reflex encompasses the following actions:

1. **Sensory Detection:** Sensory receptors throughout the body detect changes in balance, limb position, and ground contact.

2. **Reflexive Responses:** A coordinated response is triggered, involving muscle contractions, adjustments in body posture, and activation of appropriate reflexes.
3. **Balance Restoration:** The reflexive responses help restore balance, prevent falls, and maintain forward momentum.

In sprint training, the stumble reflex plays a critical role in maintaining stability and preventing falls when encountering unexpected obstacles or uneven surfaces. It allows sprinters to adapt rapidly to their current body position and maintain their speed and stride mechanics in challenging situations. Over time the goal of the coach is to ensure the athlete for a given speed is comfortable with these positions. This allows the athlete to consolidate their learning and performance outcome.

Reflexes are an integral part of sprint training, facilitating rapid and efficient responses to external stimuli. Understanding the stretch reflex, Golgi tendon organ reflex, and stumble reflex provides valuable insights into the mechanisms behind sprint performance and injury prevention. Using this knowledge we are able to understand from a neurological level how rapid movements are created and influence our exercise selection with this. If as coaches we are able to understand the role of these reflexes in sprinting we can then manipulate them and utilise them within the way we structure our training. By incorporating this knowledge into training programs, coaches and athletes can optimise reflexive responses, enhance sprinting technique, and maximise performance on the track.

The Fascial System and Speed Training

For a long time it was accepted that the "musculoskeletal skeletal" system was solely responsible for movement and mechanical leverage. There was a basic understanding that muscles are connected by tendons to bone to create joints and that is how movement is created. This was until the true understanding of the fascial system was recognised and its contribution to movement. The fascial system is a connecting and protective sheath, a complex network of connective tissues that permeates the entire body. It plays a crucial role in movement, speed, and power in sports such as rugby, football, and American football. The fascial system contributes to movement as it is the structure that encases everything within our body. Therefore when considering the posterior chain for example, this only exists because our body's fascia is able to create the link between all of the components of the posterior chain. If the fascia did not exist we wouldn't be able to produce force and create fluid movement in the manner that we can.

This chapter explores the concept of fascial lines and how they contribute to the creation and facilitation of athletic performance. We will examine the role of slings in optimising movement, enhancing speed, and generating power, along with examples of exercises specific to these sports.

Understanding Fascial Lines

Fascial lines are interconnected pathways of tension and force transmission within the fascial system. They form a dynamic web that links different parts of the body, allowing for efficient energy transfer and movement coordination.

Fascial Lines and Movement

Fascial lines play a crucial role in facilitating coordinated and efficient movement in rugby, football, and American football. They provide a platform for force transmission, allowing athletes to generate power and move with fluidity. For example, the line connecting the foot's plantar fascia to the calf muscles is essential for explosive movements like sprinting and cutting due to the force transference needed from a ground contact to create movement. Exercises like "Calf Raises with Foot Roll" can strengthen this line, improving movement mechanics and agility on the field.

Fascial Slings and Speed

Speed is a critical factor in sports, and the fascial system's role in optimising speed is undeniable. Fascial lines store and transmit for elastic energy, enhancing the efficiency of movement. For instance, the line connecting the glutes to the opposite shoulder helps facilitate rapid acceleration. This is due to the contralateral relationship of how locomotion is created. As we extend the hip one side we extend the opposite shoulder to ensure we maximise power and also ensure that we orientate our force in the correct direction. If we did not do this we would move slower and become incredibly unbalanced. Exercises like "Lateral Band Walks" engage this line, strengthening the hip abductors and improving lateral speed and change of direction. This line becomes engaged due to the shoulder creating stability or an anchor for the hip to move effectively. This happens due to the contralateral relationships of opposing shoulders and hips. The resistance applied via the band helps the activation of the muscles in the correct kinetic sequence. This is because the resistance from the band requires effort to move it which then signals the body to activate the most appropriate muscles in their corresponding order to achieve the desired limb action and movement.

Posterior Facial Line During Acceleration.

Training and Optimising the Fascial System

To fully leverage the potential of the fascial system in sports, targeted training is key. By incorporating specific exercises and techniques, athletes can enhance fascial strength, elasticity, and coordination along the relevant lines. Here are some examples of exercises that develop the Fascial system. The reason why they specifically task the fascial system is due to the way they place stress on the body. These exercises are all movement specific actions as opposed to joint specific actions. To learn more about exercise classification please refer to the later chapter in the book.

1. Dynamic Fascia Stretches: Dynamic stretching routines that incorporate movements targeting fascial lines, such as "Walking Lunges with Overhead Reach" or "Walking Quad Pulls," help prepare the body for dynamic movements, enhance range of motion, and improve overall connective tissue flexibility. These movements lengthen the body to its fullest creating an abundance of tension on the body through the fascial systems. This example of an overhead lunge demonstrates the extent to the length of stretch this movement is creating.

2. Sprint Training Variations: Different sprint training exercises such as bouncy runs, long accelerations, wall drills and resisted variations are great. The high velocity nature of these movements create a huge demand on the fascial system to create stability and elasticity. Through this we are directly manipulating it in the most specific way to transfer to speed.

3. Jump and Plyometric Training: Plyometric exercises like "Depth Jumps" or "Bounding" engage the fascial system by rapidly loading and unloading energy. These exercises improve reactive power and explosiveness, benefiting sports that require quick bursts of speed and power. Be sure to use these as an extensive to intensive tool. Extensive refers to jumping intensities that are submaximal in nature and great general conditioning. Intensive jumping refers to activities that are for maximal effort.

4. Specialised Exercises: Incorporating resistance bands or weighted implements into exercises like "Resistance Sled Pushes" or "Kneeling Wall Shoots" activates the fascial system, challenging athletes to develop strength and power throughout the movement patterns that have the greatest transfer to speed. This is because of what this exercise demands of the body. From a static position it has to create immense amounts of tension and propulsive movement. This can only be achieved by the fascial system creating a stable body which will allow the athlete to create movement.

The Muscular and Nervous System Responses in Training

Before delving into the intricate interplay of the muscular and nervous systems in speed training, it's imperative to understand the theoretical underpinning guiding our journey—General Adaptation Syndrome (GAS). Proposed by Hans Selye, this theory elucidates how the body responds to stressors, providing a framework for comprehending the phases of adaptation.

The Stages of General Adaptation Syndrome

Alarm Phase: In the initial encounter with a stressor, the body enters the alarm phase. This phase is characterised by heightened neural and hormonal responses as the body perceives a threat. In the context of speed training, the alarm phase unfolds during the workout itself, triggering acute stress responses in both the muscular and nervous systems.

Resistance Phase: As the stressor persists, the body transitions into the resistance phase. Adaptations occur to enhance the body's ability to cope with the stress. In speed training, this equates to anatomical adaptations such as muscular hypertrophy and improved connective tissue integrity,, increased neural efficiency, and improved coordination—manifestations of the systems preparing for recurrent stress.

Exhaustion Phase: Prolonged or excessive stress leads to the exhaustion phase, where adaptive resources become depleted. Without adequate recovery, this phase poses the risk of fatigue, overtraining, and diminished performance. Recognizing the signs of exhaustion is crucial in crafting effective recovery strategies, safeguarding against burnout.

The Nervous System Response to Training

The nervous system coordinates the intricate dance of muscles. Speed training creates neural adaptations, enhancing the synchronisation and efficiency of motor unit recruitment. High-speed movements refine neural pathways, optimising the interplay between the brain and muscles for swift, precise actions.

Neural recovery involves restoring ion balance, reducing neural fatigue, and fine-tuning coordination. Sleep assumes a pivotal role, allowing the nervous system to recalibrate. Practices like mindfulness contribute to a responsive nervous system, vital for peak speed performance.

The nervous system, being intricately involved in coordination and skill acquisition, demands a more extended recovery period. Post-training recovery for the nervous system may extend to 72 hours or more. Recognising this discrepancy in recovery windows is vital for designing training programs that optimise both systems without inducing undue fatigue.

The adaptability of the nervous system is harnessed through drills emphasising speed, agility, and reaction time, utilising submaximal exercises such long accelerations and technical drills we can create more impactful training exposures more often with less fatigue. Periods of intense effort followed by adequate rest capitalise on neural plasticity, refining the neuromuscular connections essential for rapid acceleration and deceleration. Consistent neural stimulation, coupled with strategic recovery, forms the backbone of effective speed training.

The Muscular System Response to Training

The muscular system, comprising our muscles, tendons, and connective tissues, translates intent into motion. In response to speed training, there is a significant signal to the brain to form the amount of tension created by speed to repair the tissues involved.

Muscular system recovery involves replenishing energy stores, repairing damaged fibres, and removing metabolic byproducts. Adequate rest, nutrition, and targeted interventions like massage or foam rolling play pivotal roles. Protein synthesis, the key driver of muscle repair, is enhanced during recovery, mending and fortifying the fibres for future demands.

Muscles possess a relatively short recovery window compared to the nervous system. The muscles typically recover within 24 to 48 hours of sprint training. With this crucial information we are able to devise recovery strategies and efficient organisation of training to maximise performance. This also helps prevent unnecessary overload that might result in overuse injuries.

In speed training, the muscular system's readiness is paramount. Balancing intensity and recovery becomes crucial to prevent overtraining, ensuring optimal muscular readiness for subsequent sessions. Speed training exercises need the neuromuscular system to be as fresh as possible because of the precise timing and coordination involved, as well as enhancing motor unit recruitment and firing rate.,.

Finding Harmony in Training

Speed training represents a delicate harmony between muscular and neural adaptations. As muscles gain strength and resilience, the nervous system refines its orchestration, fostering a seamless integration of power and precision. The synergy between these systems defines the true essence of speed mastery.

Balancing the recovery needs of the muscular and nervous systems is an art. Periodisation, incorporating varied intensities and recovery modalities, prevents monotony and guards against overtraining. Strategic deloading phases allow both systems to rejuvenate, ensuring sustained progress without the risk of burnout.

The interplay between muscular and neural adaptations forms the cornerstone of maximising speed gains. A holistic approach considers not only the intensity of training but also the quality of recovery. Periodic assessments, adjustments to training stimuli, and mindfulness in recovery practices elevate the potential for breakthroughs in speed performance.

As you progress in your speed coaching or training journey, recognise that the symphony of adaptations within your muscular and nervous systems is ongoing. Embrace the nuances of response and recovery, viewing them not as hurdles but as integral notes in the composition of your speed journey. With each session, each recovery practice, you contribute to a lifelong pursuit of unparalleled speed excellence.

COACHING SPEED COACHING SPEED IN TEAM SPORTS

"The Challenge is to improve the technical efficiency of team sports athletes whilst raising the ceiling of maximal outputs and teach them to use it in the field of play, with minimal time."

The Challenge of Coaching Speed in Team Sports

One of the most significant aspects of coaching is knowing how to apply real coaching paradigms, how to identify errors, correct them, and ensure developmental momentum with your athletes. Coaching requires recognizing when to step back and let things happen, but also when to step forward to make interventions with your athletes.

I was fortunate enough to get exposed to many reps quickly, but I also went down the rabbit hole of trying to find the perfect technical model, trying to prove how smart I was to myself, and then trying to make my athletes look like that model. However, this approach does not work in team sports, where you need to allow things to happen and enjoy the process.

Our challenge is to improve the technical efficiency of team sport athletes while raising the ceiling of maximal output and teaching them to use it in the field of play with minimal time. It sounds like a lot because it is. Therefore, we need to break down and manage our expectations, set goals, and criteria for what we need to do.

Below I have provided you with some tables of normative data that I have compiled with regards to sprint times and sprint velocities. However, once you have achieved these levels, the focus switches to contextual sprinting which is the simulation and replication of sporting actions to utilise the athletes speed to full effect. Something we will explore later within this book.

Sprint Times of Varying Sports

When coaching speed it is important to have a reference of "how fast" an athlete is for their sport. The tables presented are values I have collected from experience and research. However I want to urge you to place value in the journey your athlete is on. Track and monitor the progress they make individually first and then compare to the data later. It is important to note when measuring times with lasers I advocate a 2 point start with a 50cm run in distance before the beam. There is an image of this in the appendix.

Sport	Position	10m Time (s)	20m Time (s)	30m Time (s)	40m Time (s)
Soccer	Professional Player	1.5 - 1.7	2.8 - 3.3	3.4 - 4.5	4.5 - 5.5
American Football	Wide Receiver	1.6 - 1.8	3.0 - 3.5	3.5 - 4.5	4.5 - 5.0
American Football	Lineman	1.9 - 2.2	3.6 - 4.0	4.1 - 5.5	5.5 - 6.5
Rugby	Froward	1.7 - 1.9	3.2 - 3.6	5.0 - 5.5	5.5 - 6.5
Rugby	Back	1.5 - 1.7	2.8 - 3.3	3.4 - 4.5	4.5 - 5.5
Field Hockey	Elite Player	1.8 - 2.0	3.3 - 3.7	5.0 - 5.5	5.5 - 6.5
Lacrosse	Various Positions	1.6 - 1.8	3.0 - 3.5	3.5 - 4.5	4.5 - 5.0
Gaelic Football	Various Positions	1.6 - 1.8	3.0 - 3.5	3.5 - 4.5	4.5 - 5.0
Elite Male Sprinter	100m Specialist	< 1.7	< 2.9	< 4.0	< 4.4
Elite Female Sprinter	100m Specialist	< 1.8	< 3.0	< 4.1	< 4.5

Maximum Speeds of Various Sports

These speeds have been measured using instantaneous velocity from GPS tracking systems.

Sport	Position/Role	Top Speed (mph)	Top Speed (km/h)	Top Speed (m/s)
Soccer	Professional Player	20 - 25 mph	32 - 40 km/h	8.9 - 11.2 m/s
American Football	Running Back, Wide Receiver, Cornerback (In Pads)	20 - 22 mph	32 - 35 km/h	9.0 - 9.8 m/s
Rugby	Backs	20 - 24 mph	32 - 38 km/h	9.0 - 10.8 m/s
Rugby	Forwards	15 - 20 mph	24 - 32 km/h	6.7 - 9.0 m/s
Field Hockey	Elite Player	18 - 20 mph	29 - 32 km/h	8.0 - 9.0 m/s
Lacrosse	Various Positions	15 - 20 mph	24 - 32 km/h	6.7 - 9.0 m/s
Ultimate Frisbee	Various Positions	18 - 20 mph	29 - 32 km/h	8.0 - 9.0 m/s
Gaelic Football	Various Positions	18 - 22 mph	29 - 35 km/h	8.0 - 9.8 m/s
Elite Sprinters (Male)	Track and Field	27 - 28 mph	43 - 45 km/h	12.1 - 12.7 m/s
Elite Sprinters (Female)	Track and Field	24 - 25 mph	38 - 40 km/h	10.7 - 11.1 m/s

Fundamental Skill Acquisition and Coaching

As always it is important to revisit the foundational research and principles when investigating a new area of speed coaching. Nikolai Bernstein's groundbreaking research on skill acquisition and motor control has broader implications for sprinting and field sports. His work on coordination and biomechanics has yielded principles and concepts that can be applied to various athletic movements, including sprinting and field sports like soccer, rugby, and American football.

Bernstein's concept of "redundancy" in motor systems applies to sprinting in field sports, where athletes have multiple potential movement solutions to achieve their desired goals. For instance, during a sprint, athletes have various strategies to optimise their running technique, such as adjusting stride length, arm swing, and body posture. By exploring the available movement options and selecting the most efficient and effective ones through the process of trial and error supported by concurrent coaching, athletes can enhance their sprinting performance. This allows us to steer our thinking away from "perfect" to "effective", which will encourage our athletes to have mental freedom when playing their sport.

Similarly, in field sports, athletes constantly adapt their movements to meet the demands of the game. Whether it's changing direction, evading opponents, or executing complex manoeuvres, athletes exhibit a remarkable ability to exploit their motor systems. They utilise a wide range of movement solutions, and adapt to changing situations to achieve their desired outcomes.

Bernstein's emphasis on proper sequencing of body movements is particularly relevant to sprinting and field sports. Efficient movement patterns involve the coordinated activation and synchronisation of multiple muscle groups and body segments. For example, during sprinting, the legs, arms, and torso work in harmony to generate propulsive force and maintain balance. Athletes who master the sequencing of these movements can achieve greater speed, agility, and fluidity in their performance. When developing speed we must consider what elements are actually consciously trainable against elements that are not. Considering the reflexive nature of speed we must acknowledge that there is a large proportion of speed that is a result of involuntary action. As coaches we must accommodate this through the encouragement of relaxation. The voluntary areas are ones we can directly influence, such as training the athlete to know and understand the key technical positions they need to find in movements and loading them accordingly. This process is essential as in all skill development as if the motor skill is not effectively learned then there is a greater cost to the athlete physically.

Furthermore, Bernstein's concept of dynamic stability holds significance in sprinting and field sports. In dynamic stability, both the base of support and the centre of mass are in motion and effective balance is required. Athletes must develop stability through practice and experience, in order to execute explosive movements with precision and control. Sprinting requires stability to be maintained while generating high levels of force during each stride, while during field sport actions, athletes must navigate dynamic and unpredictable environments while maintaining balance and control.

Building on the work of Bernstein, Yuri Verkhoshanky a renowned sport scientist and researcher identified and explored the idea of "Key movements" of sporting actions. This is integrated into the drill stacking framework. They are portions of a whole movement. For example in acceleration a key movement is hip extension which is only a small part of the bigger movement skill. We are looking to identify and target these 'key movements' possess two distinctive characteristics: firstly, they contribute to the overall improvement of complex movements. They play a vital role in motor learning, meaning that if an individual aims to enhance their sports technique, it becomes essential to focus on improving proficiency in executing these 'key movements' accurately. For example, this hand off action in rugby. The key movements can be identified as hip flexion on the inside leg, arm abduction and elbow flexion on the fending arm combined with hip extension on the outside leg. Creating a successful handoff requires enough force to repel the opponent. That is created by the hip extension combines with the outstretched arm. These movements can be trained deliberately to improve the athletes ability to execute these movements at high speed. This can be integrated into training by implementing whole part whole coaching. Whole part whole coaching involves teaching the entire skill, then breaking it down into smaller parts for focused practice, and finally integrating the parts back into the whole skill for improved performance. Secondly, 'key movements' are integral in increasing the magnitude of force and power exerted, while simultaneously reducing the time required for execution. This is because these movements are identified as those in which the athlete is producing specific force relative to the outcome of the task. This holds particular relevance in sprinting and other sporting movements as mentioned in the previous example.

The combination of these two principles and frameworks allow coaches to engage in deliberate practice to help athletes improve. These concepts are integrated into the areas of exercises classification later discussed in this book.

The Importance of Deliberate Practice in the Development of General Speed

Deliberate practice is a crucial coaching tool for the development of speed in athletes. Unlike regular practice, which may involve repetitive execution of skills, deliberate practice is purposeful and systematic. It focuses on specific goals, immediate feedback, and constant refinement of technique. This method is particularly effective in enhancing general speed, as it addresses both the physical and technical aspects of performance.

Key Elements of Deliberate Practice

1. Specific Goals:
Deliberate practice involves setting clear, specific goals for each session. In the context of general speed development, this can include mastering a specific exercise, improving stride length, optimising ground contact times, or refining running mechanics. These focused objectives help athletes concentrate their efforts on precise aspects of their speed training. This helps coaches understand the path of specialisation and the transfer of training.

2. Immediate Feedback:
Providing immediate feedback is essential for deliberate practice. Coaches must observe athletes closely and offer constructive critiques on their form, technique, and performance. This real-time feedback allows athletes to make quick adjustments and understand the impact of their changes, leading to faster improvement.

3. Repetition and Refinement:
Deliberate practice involves repetitive execution of specific drills and exercises with a focus on refinement. For general speed development, this might include repeated technique drills designed to enhance specific components of speed. The goal is not just to perform the drills but to continually refine and perfect the movements.

4. Mental Engagement:
Athletes must be mentally engaged and focused during deliberate practice. This means paying close attention to the feedback, actively thinking about their technique, and being aware of their movements. Mental engagement ensures that athletes are not just going through the motions but are consciously working towards improvement. The role of deliberate practice features heavily within the learn load and execute framework.

At its heart the development of general speed completely revolves around deliberate practice. This phase of preparation is specifically and deliberately designed to enhance the biomotor and bioenergetic attributes of athletes. There can be direct correlation determined from training interventions and outcomes.

Displacement and Sprinting

In team sports, there is a mixture of horizontal and vertical displacement, which changes constantly with our gait cycle. The low to high process during acceleration is key to successful sprinting. The goal of this process is to push and drive the centre of mass into a position where we can express speed in the context of maximum velocity. Here the mechanics will morph from our acceleration favoured technique to a more cyclic maximum velocity one. This refers to the athlete's centre of mass rising and growing through every step as they gain speed. In team sports, the displacement relationship has more elements than the track and field events, where an athlete runs down a straight track.

To improve acceleration, it is necessary to improve the horizontal displacement achieved in each step, and improve all the supporting qualities. A change in displacement of the centre of mass horizontally and vertically must occur for any sprinting action to overcome the forces of gravity. During initial acceleration, the athlete's centre of mass is low, and ahead of their base of support, allowing them to push backwards, creating horizontal forces and horizontal displacement. When the athlete reaches top speed, their centre of mass is higher up, and vertically above the base of support, allowing them to create large vertical forces, and vertical displacements. and During deceleration, the centre of mass drops and goes behind the base of support, allowing the athlete to create force opposite to their direction of travel, slowing them down. The lower the athlete gets, the further out in front they can contact the ground, allowing them to create braking force for longer during each step. In order to create evasion movements, an athlete has to push their centre of mass laterally outside their base of support, so they can push in the direction they need to go.

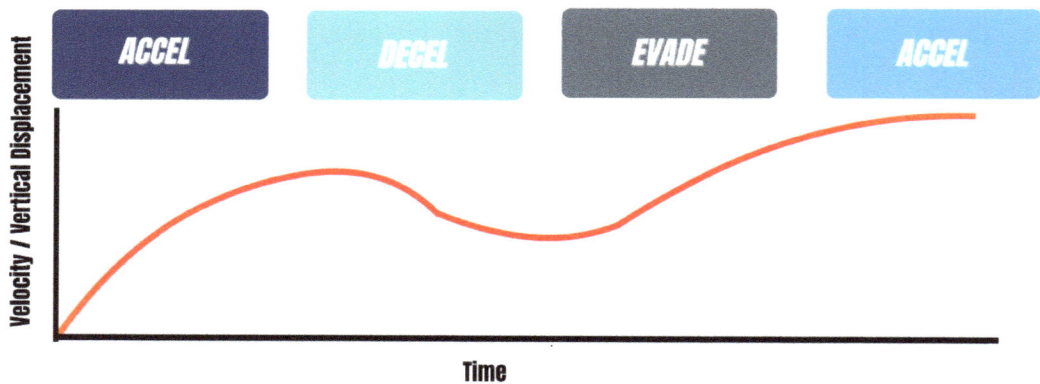

When athletes "drop" too fast during deceleration, they cannot create "exit" speed. This is due to the lack of physical capacity to tolerate such rapid increases in force. Decelerating rapidly from high speeds creates a tremendous amount of force. This requires a lot of fast eccentric strength to manipulate the stretch shortening cycle efficiently to convert that eccentric load into concentric movement. When creating exit speed we are looking to understand how much of our speed going into the movement we can conserve and use to evade the opponent. When an athlete struggles with this it can seem as if they get "stuck" on the ground when slowing down or cutting. This is also where we see a lot of injuries can occur, if there is a lack of capacity to handle those forces in deeper positions athletes can become a high injury risk. High level performers are able to do this repeatedly but also effectively anticipate the requirement for this and plan their movement effectively. This is a element of specialised speed that we will discuss later in this book.

Use this table to help you follow the basic rules of displacement and speed. I have included summaries and descriptors of each variable for further understanding.

VARIABLE	ACCELERATION	MAXIMUM VELOCITY
Ground Contact Time	Long	Short
Stride Length	Shorter	Longer
Horizontal Displacement	Low	High
Vertical Displacement	Minimal	Low
Stride Frequency	Low	High
Gait Emphasis	Back Side	Frontside

1. **Ground Contact Time**

   - **Definition**: Ground contact time refers to the duration an athlete's foot is in contact with the ground during each stride or step.
   - **Description**: In speed training, efficient ground contact times are desired. GCT must be longer during acceleration as there is an increased requirement to create force to overcome inertia and shorter at maximum velocity because we are no longer trying to accelerate and thus don't need to spend time pushing at the ground. Ground contact times in acceleration are longer as we need more time to produce force to overcome inertia. During maximum velocity this is the opposite as we have created all of our momentum and therefore do not need to spend much time "pushing" on the ground.
   - **Training Example:** Sprinters typically have shorter ground contact times compared to team sports athletes, this is due to the environmental constraints placed upon them. Athletics tracks are designed specifically to be hard, increasing ground contact forces demanding more stiffness produces faster speeds, whereas most team sport athletes play and train on grass synthetic pitches that do not facilitate higher ground reaction forces when compared to athletics tracks. This is also important in winter months when pitches can become softer. Being able to still move faster on soft surfaces is essential for any team sport sprinter. A focus on explosive and powerful movements, such as plyometric drills, can help minimise ground contact time.

2. **Stride Length**

   - **Definition:** Stride length is the distance covered with one full stride, measured from the point of initial contact of one foot to the next contact of the same foot.
   - **Description:** Improving stride length is essential for enhancing overall speed as the goal of running fast is to cover as much ground as possible per step at high speeds. It is achieved through increased power and force generation during each stride, allowing athletes to cover more ground with each step. This is the expected change in stride length we wish to see from acceleration to maximum velocity running.
   - **Training Example:** Drills that emphasise explosive leg movements and dynamic stretching can contribute to increased stride length. Dynamic stretching will help athletes extend their active range of motion to which then can be attained at higher speeds.

3. **Horizontal Displacement**

    - **Definition:** Horizontal displacement refers to the forward movement of the body during each stride or step.
    - **Description:** Maximising horizontal displacement of centre of mass is vital in the development of acceleration. Through this athletes overcome their inertia effectively and create momentum. As sprinting progresses through to maximum velocity horizontal displacement is at its greatest as velocity is at its highest and therefore athletes cover the most ground per step.
    - **Training Example:** Sprint drills such as 1 step pushes or kneeling wall shoots which focus on pushing off forcefully and maintaining a strong forward lean, can enhance horizontal displacement during acceleration.

4. **Vertical Displacement**

    - **Definition:** Vertical displacement is the upward movement of the centre of mass during each stride.
    - **Description:** While some vertical displacement is inherent in running, excessive upward movement can be detrimental to speed as we will spend an excessive amount of time in the air increasing the time it takes to complete a step. Efficiency in maintaining horizontal motion is crucial. During acceleration athletes need to push themselves forwards and "upward" gradually to raise the height of the centre of mass to make space for effective maximum speed mechanics.
    - **Training Example:** Exercises like long accelerations can aid in developing explosive power without creating excessive vertical movement as they give the athlete time to build their speed and not compromise on technique.

5. **Stride Frequency**

    - **Definition:** Stride frequency, or cadence, is the number of strides or steps an athlete takes in a given time, usually measured in strides per second.
    - **Description:** Increasing stride frequency can contribute to higher running speeds, and it is achieved through increasing the speed to which we alternate our legs in to complete faster gait cycles.
    - **Training Example:** Sprint drills that focus on rapid leg turnover, such as fast-paced high knees or condensed wickets, can enhance stride frequency.

6. **Gait Emphasis - Frontside vs Backside:**

    - **Definition:** Gait emphasis refers to the distribution of focus between the frontside (actions with the leg ahead of the centre of mass) and backside (actions with the leg behind the centre of mass) mechanics during running.
    - **Description:** Striking a balance between frontside and backside mechanics is crucial for optimising running biomechanics and speed. During acceleration athletes will spend more time in backside positions due to the angular action of acceleration, which is typically 45 degrees. Therefore pushing to go forwards at that angle leads to the legs visually spending more time behind the body.

This supports acceleration ability, whereas in maximum velocity sprinting an excessive amount of backside gait emphasis is counter productive to high speed sprinting as the angular nature of maximum speed sprinting is more upright and therefore the gait cycle should represent this.

- **Training Example:** Frontside emphasis involves exercises that emphasise knee drive and quick ground recovery, while backside emphasis involves powerful hip extension. Drills targeting each aspect help achieve a harmonious gait *(see appendix)*.

Considerations for Change of Direction and Deceleration

As sprinting in team sports is certainly not a linear speed endeavour I have included how displacement and other kinematic factors are expressed in change of direction and deceleration actions. In the table below I have weighted deceleration and change of direction against acceleration as they typically fit into the category of acceleration based movement. I have provided supporting summaries to further help your understanding.

VARIABLE	ACCELERATION	DECELERATION	CHANGE OF DIRECTION
Ground Contact Time	Long	Longer than Acceleration	Longer than Acceleration
Stride Length	Shorter	Shorter than Acceleration	Shorter than Acceleration
Horizontal Displacement	Low	Increasing Negatively	Lower than Acceleration
Vertical Displacement	Minimal	Increasing Negatively	Minimal
Stride Frequency	Low	Low	Low
Gait Emphasis	Back Side	Frontside	Backside

1. **Ground Contact Time**

    - **Definition**: Ground contact time refers to the duration an athlete's foot is in contact with the ground during each stride or step.
    - **Description**: During deceleration we see longer ground contact times than in acceleration based movements due to the nature of slowing down and we are reorientating an already established speed. This can be the same in change of direction as we are overcoming momentum.
    - **Training Example:** Managing ground contacts is deceleration and change of direction is essential for field sport performance. Drills that can help athletes develop effective mechanics, and gradually increase the speeds at which these are executed will enhance the athletes effectiveness of managing changing ground contact times.

2. **Stride Length**

    - **Definition:** Stride length is the distance covered with one full stride, measured from the point of initial contact of one foot to the next contact of the same foot.
    - **Description:** Improving stride length efficiency in change of direction and deceleration is essential for enhancing multidirectional movement. During deceleration we shorten stride length to gradually decrease momentum in relation to the required stopping distance. This is similar in change of direction

as we are looking to utilise deceleration to then reorientate the body position and reaccelerate. This requires shorter and more frequent strides at a gradual rate to optimise speed maintenance through movements.

- **Training Example:** Drills that emphasise preplanned stopping distances and predictable changes of direction will help teach the athletes and condition the rate at which stride length needs to change.

3. **Horizontal Displacement**

    - **Definition:** Horizontal displacement refers to the forward movement of the body during each stride or step.
    - **Description:** During deceleration there is zero horizontal displacement as we are decreasing the already existing displacement this constitutes negative horizontal displacement. During change of direction typically there is some horizontal displacement as you are changing direction whilst moving forward.
    - **Training Example:** Training Drills such as controlled stopping over resisted stopping can help encourage athletes to maximise decreasing horizontal displacement. Drills to help athletes focus on slowing down to maximise speed of change of direction will help optimise horizontal displacement in change of direction.

4. **Vertical Displacement**

    - **Definition:** Vertical displacement is the upward movement of the centre of mass during each stride.
    - **Description:** During deceleration there needs to be large amounts of negative vertical displacement. Having the ability to rapidly drop hip height is important for effective deceleration. During change of direction there is a reacceleration component and athletes need to push themselves forwards and "upward" gradually to raise the height of the centre of mass to make space for effective maximum speed mechanics.
    - **Training Example:** Drills that emphasis lowering the centre of mass will help train this quality in the context of sport. Including a change of direction and re-acceleration will help blend the qualities together as commonly seen in sport.

5. **Stride Frequency**

    - **Definition:** Stride frequency, or cadence, is the number of strides or steps an athlete takes in a given time, usually measured in strides per second.
    - **Description:** Increasing stride frequency can contribute to higher running speeds, and it is achieved through increasing the speed to which we alternate our legs in to complete faster gait cycles.
    - **Training Example:** Sprint drills that help athletes improve the ability to manipulate their stride frequency to slow down such as low incline downhill running or basic stopping distance drills can enhance this quality. This can be replicated with change of direction training to emphasise the powerful leg actions driving the athlete to change direction.

6. **Gait Emphasis - Frontside vs Backside:**

    - **Definition:** Gait emphasis refers to the distribution of focus between the frontside (actions with the leg ahead of the centre of mass) and backside (actions with the leg behind the centre of mass) mechanics during running.
    - **Description:** Striking a balance between frontside and backside mechanics is crucial for optimising running biomechanics and speed. During deceleration athletes will spend more time with their feet in front of their hips as they are actively breaking to slow down. During change of direction actions as you will see in the next section athletes spend a majority of their time in backside positions.
    - **Training Example:** Deceleration gait drills focus on learning to sit back into a low position and rapidly absorb ground reaction force whereas backside emphasis involves powerful hip extension. Drills targeting each aspect help achieve a harmonious gait.

Error Detection In Speed Training

This section delves into the concept of error detection within the context of speed training, highlighting the significance of the Learn-Load-Execute model and its role in facilitating skill acquisition and refining technique.

When it comes to error detection, the guiding principle is that "good is good enough." However, it is essential to evaluate whether the executed movements align with the desired technical model and most importantly speed of movement. focus is not only on the end result but also on achieving it through precise and effective movements. The rate of adaptation in the motor learning process should be balanced with preparedness, ensuring that fundamental skill levels are established before maximising force application. We will now examine this further.

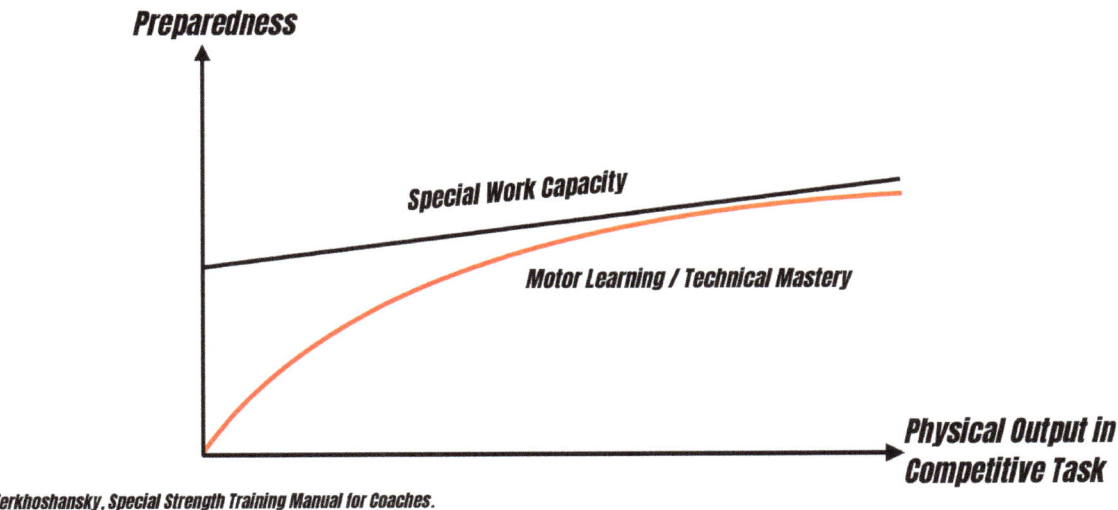

Verkhoshansky, Special Strength Training Manual for Coaches.

The integration of motor learning processes with the athlete's level of physical preparedness stands as a critical determinant of success. This delicate balance, often underscored by Yuri Verkhoshansky's principles, shapes the rate of adaptation and, consequently, the efficacy of speed development. Verkhoshansky's approach advocates for a harmonious integration of both elements. It's not just about pushing the boundaries of physical fitness but ensuring that every increase in physical preparedness is met with a corresponding refinement in motor skills. The shock method aligns with this philosophy, demanding that athletes not only develop strength and power but do so in a manner intricately connected to the demands of their sport. I have broken this process down to illustrate the image above.

1. Physical Output in Competitive Task:

To begin, it's essential to contextualise the physical output of the competitive task at hand. Whether it's effective acceleration or any other specific skill, coaches must clearly define the competitive task they aim to improve. By identifying the target skill, coaches can design training programs tailored to enhance performance in that particular area. Motor learning, the process through which skills are acquired and refined, is a complex aspect of speed training. It involves the interplay between the nervous system, biomechanics, and muscle memory. However, the rate at which an athlete can adapt and refine these skills is closely linked to their level of physical preparedness. This is where the learn-load-execute framework is a paramount driver for coaching as it deliberately breaks down competitive tasks into their key movements and trains them according to this principle. The athletes develop the motor quality whilst simultaneously developing the specific physical qualities required. Combined with the framework Stable - Unstable motor learning accelerates drastically as within the stable to unstable framework we can structure training to increase stability so we can intensify motor learning and physical development whilst increasing the task specificity of the exercises used.

2. Special Work Capacity:

A significant aspect of the training process is understanding the concept of adaptation. As pictured above in relation to developing the competitive task we are looking to understand the adaptation of an athlete's motor potential that is represented in the level of special work capacity. With regards to the development of Speed here we must understand that the special work capacity is with respect to exercises that directly stress the components required by the competitive task. This is where we will prescribe exercises in conjunction to special strength characteristics or that of higher classification. This will be expanded upon in the chapter exercise classification for speed. At the outset, athletes typically exhibit low proficiency in the targeted skill, resulting in a considerable gap between their initial output and the desired performance level and a large gap in preparation of special work capacity. This phase is akin to unconscious incompetence, where athletes lack awareness of their deficiencies. Within the Sports Speed System this would identify the athlete in the "Learning to Sprint" phase of development.

3. Motor Learning / Technical Mastery:

The process of motor learning as represented on the graph shows the improvement of the athletes skill to effectively use the motor potential with respect to the competitive task identified. Over a period of time as a coach we must be able to observe a decrease between the athletes level of special work capacity and their technical mastery of the competitive exercise. thus intern creating a high level of performance. Coaches must adopt a deliberate coaching approach focused on creating sustainable transfer and purposeful adaptation. This involves compartmentalising the coaching process to ensure that every training session contributes meaningfully to the athlete's development. Deliberate practice, characterised by focused, repetitive efforts aimed at skill improvement, lies at the heart of this approach. For example, if the competitive task has been identified as the improvement of initial acceleration then focusing on steps 0-3 is of paramount importance. In this instance we would use variations of static starts to challenge the skill of initial acceleration with deliberate attention placed on the specific motor skills of this skill. As athletes progress through the learning process, they transition through phases akin to those proposed in skill acquisition models—cognitive, associative, and autonomous. Through deliberate practice and structured training, athletes move towards closing the gap between their initial output and the desired performance level.

The ultimate goal is to bridge the disparity between initial output and desired performance through targeted training interventions. As athletes improve, the ratio between their proficiency and the desired performance level decreases. This progression towards specificity ensures that training efforts translate effectively to on-field performance. While the principles of motor learning remain consistent, an athlete's physical preparedness accelerates or decelerates the learning curve. Verkhoshansky's shock method, emphasising specific preparedness, becomes pivotal here. When an athlete is physically primed for the demands of speed, the motor learning process gains momentum.

Practical implementation hinges on recognising that athletes frequently forget new skills during the early stages of skill acquisition. To address this, coaches must keep training protocols simple, basic, and consistent, while gradually increasing training volumes. An imbalance between the rate of motor learning and physical preparedness can lead to suboptimal results. If an athlete's physical conditioning surpasses their motor learning adaptations, they may exhibit impressive physical attributes but struggle with the nuanced and intricate aspects of speed technique, which is very prevalent within the team sport athlete.

It's crucial to acknowledge the contributions of pioneers like Yuri Verkhoshansky, whose methodologies have significantly influenced modern speed training paradigms. By embracing these principles, coaches can optimise training outcomes and empower athletes to achieve their full potential on the field.

Throughout this book, the symbiotic relationship between motor learning and physical preparedness will continually surface. The goal is not just to make athletes faster but to enable them to seamlessly integrate their heightened physical capacity with the technical mastery required for top-tier speed performance. This is where the frameworks integrate with training to enhance the transfer of training.

To facilitate error detection and skill refinement, the Learn-Load-Execute model is introduced. This model provides a faster learning experience by associating specific movements with desired outcomes. Employ this approach to teach athletes key movements and directly link them to the execution of essential actions, such as the first and second steps of acceleration. By understanding and reinforcing these key movements, athletes develop a deeper understanding of proper technique and actively seek to apply it in various speed-related activities. This helps aid error detection as we are able to focus on the specific segment of the targeted skill and decrease the speed of execution to create a supporting coaching environment.

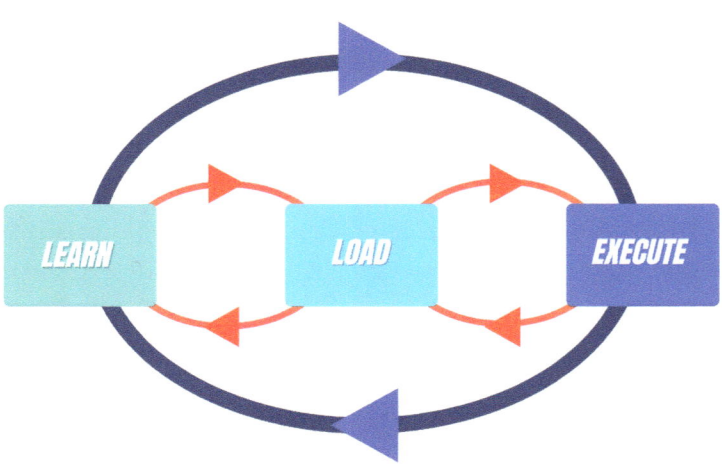

The implementation of the Learn-Load-Execute model involves utilising specialised exercises with defined technical criteria. It is based on the two ways in which transfer can be created in training. Transfer of training refers to the application of skills or physical adaptations gained in one context to another. In the realm of speed training for team sports, this transfer can occur through the learning and refinement of specific speed-related skills, ensuring that improvements made in technique directly translate to on-field performance. Alternatively, transfer can manifest as an increase in physical outputs, where gains in strength, power, and speed generated in training are seamlessly integrated into the demands of the sport. This is why the Learn-Load-Execute model is such a powerful tool.

These exercises serve as tools to psychologically condition athletes by showing them the step by step process to improving their speed while enhancing motor learning and association. The framework allows an athlete to complete the skill part of the key movement in the learn phase, the physical output part of the movement in the load phase and then the whole movement in the execute phase of the framework. Here is an example of this, refer to the appendix for exercise examples and images:

Aim: Improve Initial Acceleration. Steps 0-3.

- **Learn** - Bilateral Wall Hold

- **Load** - Single Leg Load and Smash

- **Execute** - Kneeling Wall Shoot

Observe the athlete's execution efforts, focusing on specific relationships and identifying deviations from effective technique. Each phase of the framework will help you identify where to focus your attention. This meticulous observation allows coaches to provide targeted feedback and guidance, facilitating error detection and correction.

The Learn-Load-Execute framework not only benefits athletes but also grows with the coach's expertise. As pictured the framework encourages you to create cycles and form feedback loops of the training. Revisiting learn-load-execute multiple times. You might start with basic drills like the wall drills to guide athletes to understand fundamental movement patterns, such as proper hip and knee positioning. However as athletes progress, resisted variations are introduced, providing additional challenges that promote skill acquisition and error detection. The athlete's speed age will dictate where they need to start their training. The model builds a coach's proficiency, enabling them to identify key relationships and technique nuances, ensuring continuous improvement and optimal program development. The lists of exercises provided in this book will help you utilise the framework and error detect efficiently.

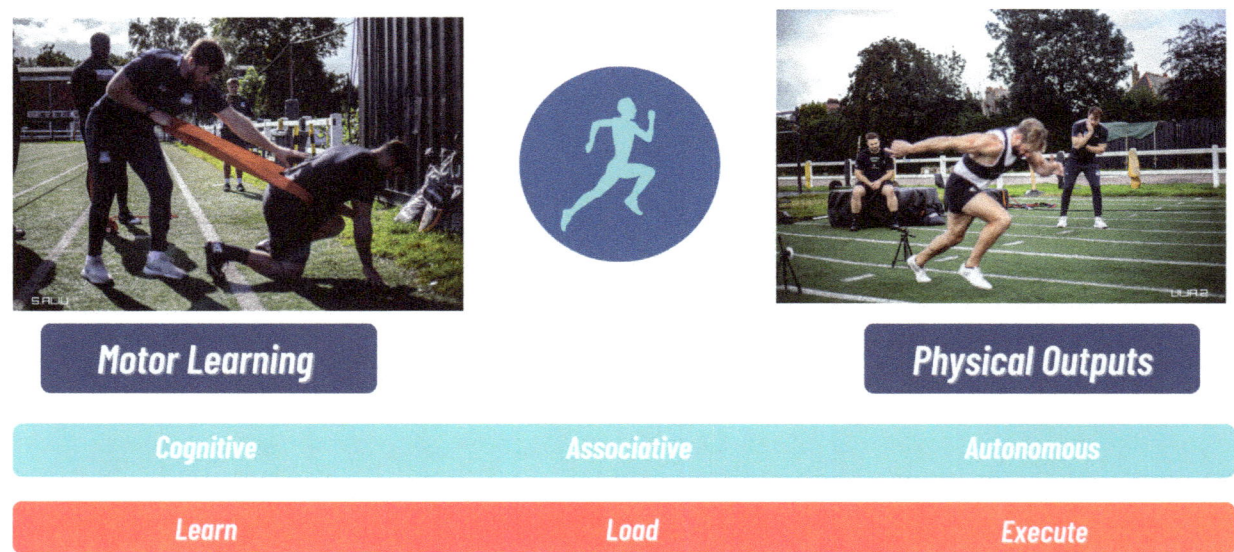

Throughout the training journey, a balance between motor learning and physical output must be maintained. By focusing on transferable skills and incorporating cognitive, associative, and autonomous stages of learning, coaches ensure a comprehensive development process. The weaving of transfer and learning principles within the Learn-Load-Execute model creates a holistic approach that fosters continual growth and improvement.

By embracing this model and emphasising the balance between transfer and learning, coaches can guide athletes towards enhanced speed, agility, and overall performance. As coaches embed the Learn-Load-Execute model into their programs, they cultivate their own expertise, contributing to the growth and success of both themselves and their athletes.

Technical Models in Sprinting Movements

Now we understand the process of error detection and how we can use the sports speed frameworks to coach these errors. It is important to look at some of the key technical points within acceleration, maximum velocity and change of direction movements. All in the attempt to find effective technique. Please refer to the appendix for links to detailed videos and demonstrations.

Understanding the Gait Cycle

A common issue faced by coaches and athletes alike is the gait cycle. It creates many discussions and can really cloud the process of developing speed and movement. In order to coach speed effectively it's important to understand gait. Gait is a simple concept and helps us understand the key biomechanical aspects of placing one foot in front of the other to propel an athlete in the direction they choose to go. Gait is the heart of sprinting mechanics. Let's explore each phase of the gait cycle in sprinting, along with coaching points and technical advice for acceleration and maximum speed.

Within the Gait Cycle there are two main phases and these are the Stance phase and the Swing phase. The stance phase is the period of the gait cycle from when the initial ground contact is created (touch down) through to the point at which the foot leaves the ground (toe off) Within these there are more detailed sub phases representing key movement signatures. The Swing phase lasts from the point of toe off until that leg touches down again as the opposite leg is going through its stance phases of the gait cycle. The images below outline the phases. Highlighted is the left foot of the athlete passing through one full gait cycle.

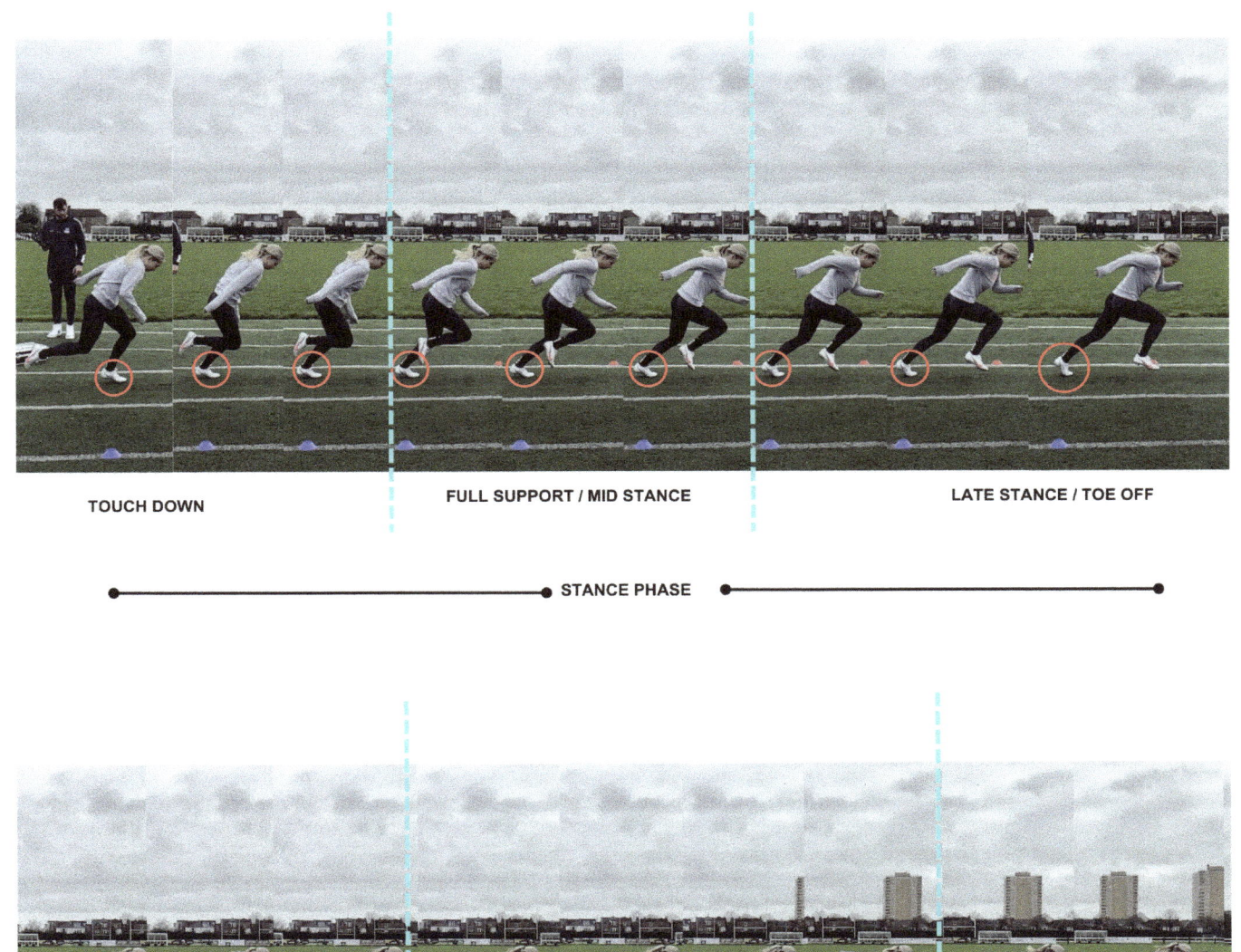

Emma Uren: Olympian, England and Great Britain Rugby Sevens

These have now been broken down for you in the most simple form for ease of understanding.

Macro Phase	Sub Phase	Definition
Stance	Touch down	The point of initial contact of the foot with the ground.
	Mid Stance	Where the athlete starts to propel the weight of the body forwards.
	Toe Off	The point at which the foot leaves the ground.
Swing	Early Swing	The point at which the foot leaves the ground but is not under the body. This is the point at which the hip and knee start to flex.
	Mid Swing	The point at which the non weight bearing leg passes directly beneath the body. The point at which the hip and knee reach maximal flexion.
	Late Swing	The point at which the non weight bearing leg is in front of the body in preparation for a subsequent touch down. No more flexion is needed and the process of extending the leg begins.

In speed coaching you might often hear reference to front side or backside mechanics. To put this simply, frontside mechanics refers to anything happening in front of the midline of the body and back side mechanics refers to anything happening behind the midline of the body.

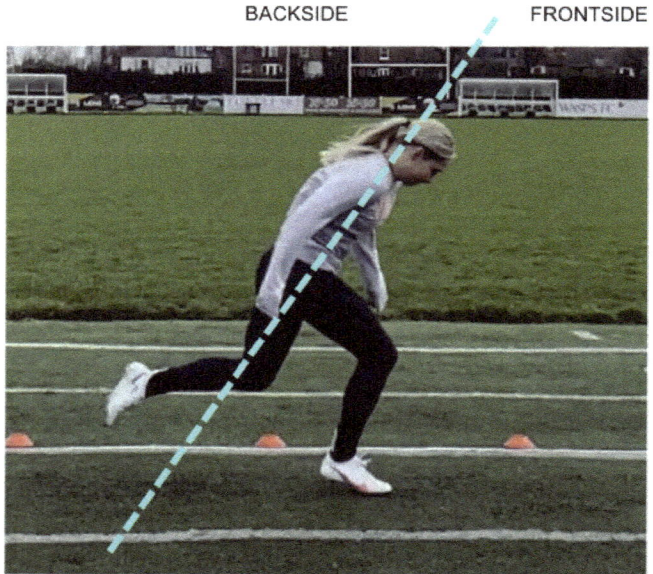

Coaching the Phases of Gait in Speed Movements.

Now there is an understanding of gait. It is important to understand how we coach athletes through these phases. I have broken down this into the main movements as follows:

- Early Acceleration
- Late Acceleration
- Maximum Velocity

- Shuffle
- Crossover
- Open Step

Before we go any further I would like to address and clarify a simple concept for you. If you refer back to the physics chapter we discussed projectiles and their motion. When coaching speed it is always important to remember the nature of a projectile. During acceleration based movements (Early, late, Maximum Velocity or our non linear sprinting movements) our priority is going to be maximising horizontal projection. During our transition phases and building to maximum speed variations our goal is to maximise vertical impulse. However these do not occur in isolation. Maximal vertical projection is a byproduct of maximal horizontal projection. The image provided is an illustration of this.

The point at which these two occur is slightly different. Maximum horizontal projection typically occurs during the midstance to toe-off phase whereas maximum vertical projection reaches its highest point of elevation between the sprinting strides.

Effective Acceleration

To achieve optimal acceleration, athletes must focus on technical aspects and understand the individual steps involved in early and late acceleration. By analysing these steps, coaches can effectively identify and address specific areas for development, leading to enhanced performance on the field. It is helpful to watch slow motion footage of both elite sprinters and elite team sports athletes, as well as athletes of other levels to build your technical model of what effective sprinting looks like on athletes of different shapes and sizes in different contexts.

Early Acceleration (Steps 1-3):

Technical Model Early Acceleration

Early acceleration refers to the initial phase of sprinting, where athletes transition from a stationary position into a full sprint. In this phase, athletes focus on generating explosive power and driving themselves forward in a controlled manner. Let's examine the key elements of early acceleration and the technical considerations involved.

1. Set-Up: Proper positioning is crucial for an effective start. Athletes should begin in a low stance, feet no more than a foot's length apart, hips width apart, with a forward lean. The weight should be predominantly distributed on the front foot. You should feel the weight through the balls of your feet and in a position where you want to drive forward, you will feel this as you are just at the point where you want to fall forward and the ball of your front foot is taking alot of your body weight. This will help emphasise a powerful push-off. However, common errors may include over-rotation and excessive forward lean, resulting in an imbalanced start. Furthermore it is important that when you are working with different levels of athletes the emphasis can slightly change. The key differences are through the early levels of speed age.

- **Learning to Sprint** - Focus on finding a comfortable position that will allow a good push off.
- **Training to Sprint** - The task is to refine the position to enhance the development of an explosive start.

2. Initial Step: The first step sets the foundation for subsequent movements. Athletes should learn to create large horizontal forces in this phase, ensuring that their centre of mass is in front of them. At the point of toe off, a correct foot placement applies pressure to the ground through the back of the ball of the foot. Optimal point of contact should be directly under or slightly behind the centre of mass. Contact should minimise any movement in the ankle to maximise efficiency as the force is transferred from the body to the ground. Correct ankle position is 90 degrees directly to the shank (shin). This plays an essential role in maintaining stability and generating force, through creating a strong ankle joint so force can transfer efficiently without dissipating.

Pictured below, the example on the left is much more flexed, which is the less optimal position. There are several reasons why a 90 degree angle is preferred. It optimises the length - tension relationship of the calf muscles, it allows for the best possible energy storage in the achilles tendon, and allows favourable alignment of the tibia at the knee.

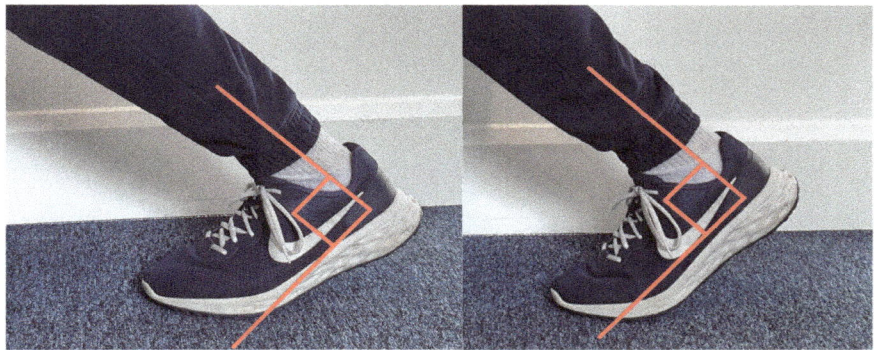

Optimal Ankle Positioning During Acceleration

3. Leg Movements: During early acceleration, athletes strive for a smooth leg pattern and controlled thigh movement. A controlled thigh movement is one where the athlete is able to pass through the swing phases without overextending or letting the thigh rotate upward too much, bringing the thigh closer to the body. Over-rotation can lead to compensatory actions, such as exaggerated thigh swing and increased shank velocity, this will cause the lower leg to accelerate too fast forward and in turn we will not be able to retract the leg ensuring we create an effective ground contact that keeps the athlete accelerating. A fatal flaw in acceleration is not creating a balanced leg exchange. This is created by ensuring stride length is consistent between the sides of the body. Over striding on one side of the body to compensate for a lack of power is a common occurrence. This occurs as a consequence to counteract the lack of displacement created by the subsequent ground contact. This will force the athlete to reach forward in an attempt to maintain or increase speed. This will only lead to an inability to create explosive acceleration and increase the risk of soft tissue injury.

Optimal Frontside Position in Acceleration

4. Counterbalancing: In order for an athlete to create speed in any direction. The arms and legs must work together to counter balance one another. This in turn cancels out the rotational inertia created by the limb actions. Athletes need to manage counter-rotations to maintain stability and alignment. Coaches should observe the positioning of the arms, ensuring they contribute to forward momentum rather than counteracting it. If we see a flaring arm action for example as in the arm flapping out to the side of the body this is an indicator of the arm balancing the body as opposed to contributing forward momentum. An effective arm action mimics the action of the leg.

Late Acceleration and Displacement (Steps 4-7):

Technical Model Late Acceleration

As athletes progress beyond the initial steps of acceleration, they enter a transitional phase where their movements evolve. Here, we focus on the late acceleration phase, emphasising the key technical aspects that facilitate seamless transition and continued momentum.

1. Ankle Flexion: Maintaining the previously mentioned ankle flexion allows athletes to maintain balance and generate power. Insufficient ankle stiffness can lead to instability and reduce propulsion. Coaches should emphasise having a "stiff" ankle by anticipating the ground contact to optimise late acceleration.

2. Pushing and Thigh Positioning: Athletes must push through their steps, finding a frontside position with the thigh at around 90 degrees to the torso to create continued forward propulsion the athlete must rapidly extend the contralateral hip to attack the ground and create large ground reaction forces. If we see a thigh that travels higher the athlete will be losing speed and power. This is because the thigh will be upwardly rotating forcing the athlete upwards and rotating the torso backwards. The aim here is to apply those forces to create the largest possible horizontal impulse from each step.

3. Chest Forward and Attack: During this phase (steps 4-7) we need to see the athlete's chest gradually rise with the hips. The torso angle should be roughly parallel to the angle of the frontside shin. If we bring the chest up too early, relative to the hips, then we compromise the integrity of the pelvic position causing an increased space between the ribcage and pelvis, rotating the pelvis forward. This will in turn limit the ability to accelerate effectively and increase the likelihood of injuries. Whilst this pattern may produce a fast short acceleration (0-5m) this will not produce faster speeds during a longer run.

Late acceleration is characterised by the gradual rise of the athlete's centre of mass.

Mastering the technical aspects of early and late acceleration is essential for athletes aiming to optimise their sprinting performance. By breaking down the individual steps and highlighting common errors, coaches can implement targeted interventions to enhance an athlete's acceleration abilities. Through a combination of specialised preparatory exercises, motor learning techniques, and focused coaching, athletes can improve their technique and achieve their speed goals. Later chapters in the book will examine this in greater detail.

Over Rotation in Sprinting

Over rotation can significantly impact an athlete's performance and increase the risk of injury. Here we will explore the concept of over rotation. By understanding the mechanics involved, coaches can better address and correct over rotation to optimise their athletes' movement efficiency.

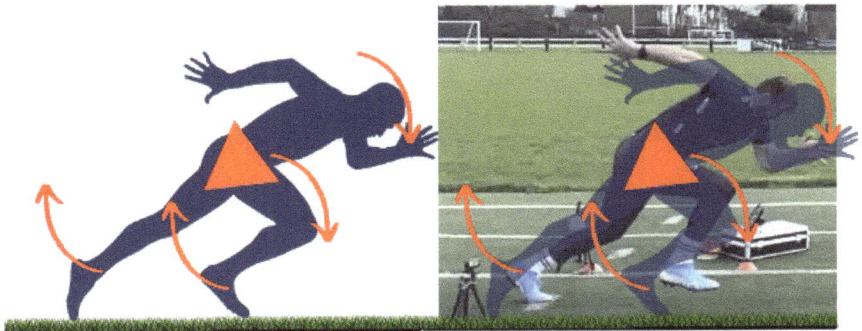

1. Balancing Act and Tipping Points: Over rotation occurs when the body exceeds its optimal rotational range, affecting balance and stability. This happens when the athlete's hips rotate too far forward causing the athlete's momentum to drive the athlete towards the ground. Optimal range as pictured above is the front edge of the triangle is directing the athlete forwards and upwards. The head's position plays a crucial role, as tipping the straight line formed by the head, shoulders, and hips forward or backward disrupts the body's equilibrium. Coaches must focus on identifying these tipping points to address over rotation effectively.

2. Strength vs. Speed: Over rotation can be linked to a strength versus speed issue. Athletes who possess significant strength but lack coordination in limb movements may push themselves too far forward, leading to over rotation. This creates a big problem as they will decrease their acceleration ability because they cannot exchange their legs quick enough underneath them to beat the pull of gravity to the ground. This is very common with athletes who are typically "gym strong" but not fast. Recognising this balance issue is essential, and coaches should consider a comprehensive approach that combines strength development with coordinated limb movement training.

3. Coordination and Pelvic Role: The pelvis plays a vital role in balancing the body's centre of mass during movement. Excessive forward rotation of the pelvis (anterior pelvic tilt) can lead to compensatory movements throughout the body, affecting performance and increasing injury risk. Athletes must learn to counterbalance rotational forces through coordinating and mastering the desired positions of sprinting.

4. Sporting Movements and Gait: Over rotation is prevalent in various sporting movements, particularly those involving complex coordination and gait patterns. Coaches must observe athletes during cutting, turning, and ball-handling situations, noting how hip movement, shoulder rotation, and ball position influence overall rotation. As a coach, identifying over rotation in these movements commonly can be seen when the athlete shows a lack of balance in their movement. They might stumble or tip over in their torso. This is a great place to start with developing your coaching eye for these movements. Understanding the interplay between these factors helps coaches develop appropriate training strategies.

5. Avoiding Training-Specific Activities: Coaches should exercise caution to prevent sport-specific activities from overshadowing general movement preparation. While technical coaches focus on specific skills, coaches specialising in speed and movement should prioritise training elements that prepare athletes for optimal acceleration angles, efficient gait patterns, and rotational control. This approach ensures a well-rounded training program within time constraints.

Over rotation poses challenges in sprinting and sporting movements, affecting performance and increasing injury risk. By understanding the mechanics behind over rotation and implementing appropriate coaching strategies, coaches can guide athletes to move with optimal efficiency and minimise the negative effects of over rotation. Recognising the balance between strength and coordination, coordinating pelvic movements, and considering the demands of specific sporting activities are essential aspects of coaching athletes to achieve their full potential.

Rotation and Compensation Combined with Axis and Planes of motion

Effective speed coaching requires a nuanced understanding of the biomechanics of rotation and compensation during running, especially in team sports where athletes often carry a ball. Let's start to unpack the complex interplay between different body planes and axes during sprinting and agility drills.

The Importance of Biomechanical Axes and Planes

When coaching athletes, it's essential to recognise the role of the body's three primary axes: the frontal, longitudinal, and sagittal axes. Each axis corresponds to specific movements and rotations:

- **Frontal Axis:** Involves movements such as lateral tilts.
- **Longitudinal Axis:** Encompasses rotational movements around the body's vertical axis.
- **Sagittal Axis:** Includes forward and backward movements.

Athletes typically rotate through all these planes simultaneously when sprinting, and should be made a necessary consideration to a comprehensive approach to coaching speed multi directional movements.

Ball Handling and Body Mechanics

To deepen the understanding of this concept. Let's break down this ball handling as pictured. A critical aspect of sprinting with a ball is understanding how the ball's position affects the athlete's balance and movement efficiency. The ball often counterbalances the body's movements:

- **Counterbalance:** In this example the athlete is counterbalancing himself by placing the ball on the outside of the hip that is in the front side position of sprinting. This will emphasise the flexed shoulder position we will naturally see in sprinting without the a ball.
- **Hip and Shoulder Rotation:** The hips and shoulders rotate to counterbalance each other, ensuring the athlete remains stable and efficient. This is going to help maintain the direction of speed. The shortening of the torso here creates strength and helps to offset and the overrotation that might occur otherwise.

Coaches should observe how athletes manage ball handling, particularly when cutting or changing direction. The ball's position relative to the body can significantly impact the athlete's ability to maintain speed and control.

Compensatory Mechanisms in Running

When there is limited rotation available in the body when holding a ball or carrying an implement other body parts must compensate to maintain speed and direction due to the lack of range of motion the ball or stick etc creates. For instance:

- **Increased Leg Speed:** To offset limited upper body rotation, athletes may need to increase their leg speed.
- **Enhanced Leg Work:** More effort from the legs is required to maintain momentum and direction.

Understanding these compensatory mechanisms allows coaches to tailor their training to enhance the athlete's natural compensations and improve overall performance. When working towards this level of details do not over emphasise the "technical model", be more productive with creating more fluid movements as these will yield greater results.

Understanding the interplay between rotation, compensation, and efficient movement is vital for effective speed coaching in team sports. By focusing on fundamental biomechanics, utilising scenario-based drills, and avoiding over-coaching, coaches can enhance their athletes' performance and prepare them for the dynamic demands of their sport. This approach not only improves speed and agility but also ensures athletes can apply these skills effectively in game situations.

Maximum Velocity Sprinting

Achieving maximum velocity in sprinting requires a solid technical foundation that optimises biomechanics and leverages the principles of physics. While team sport athletes may not resemble sprinters in their form, they can still benefit from understanding and applying key coaching points to enhance their speed. We will focus on the technical model of maximum velocity sprinting, exploring the individual elements and steps involved. We will examine a real-life example of Alex Gray, a remarkable athlete with impressive speed despite his unique body proportions. When observing the technical model of maximum velocity sprinting, it becomes evident how important displacement and stride efficiency are. Alex Gray's performance provides an excellent example of these principles in action. With his significant height and weight, he manages to achieve a speed of ten metres per second, a remarkable feat for an athlete of his size. It is important to recognise that team sport athletes may not exhibit the same sprinting form as elite sprinters like Usain Bolt. Each athlete has unique body proportions and biomechanics, influenced by their sport-specific demands. Coaches should prioritise optimising an athlete's potential within their specific context rather than striving for a perfect sprinting technique.

1. Transition and Leg Exchange: During the transition phase, as the athlete is in the air, one crucial aspect is the reorganisation of the legs. While airborne, the focus shifts to finding the ground and actively preparing for touchdown. As the foot comes into contact with the ground, the thighs align, setting up a strong foundation for maximum propulsive velocity.

2. Figure-Four Position and Ground Reaction Force: As the athlete reaches full support, the figure-four position becomes crucial. This alignment allows for efficient unfolding of the leg as it has travelled through the shortest but most efficient path, which enables optimal timing with the movement of the centre of mass.

This allows for effective utilisation of the ground reaction force, as the hip passes over the stance legs at the most appropriate time to enable forward propulsion.

Technical coaching for maximum velocity sprinting involves understanding and applying the fundamental principles of displacement, leg exchange, figure-four position, and ground reaction force. While team sport athletes may not resemble elite sprinters, they can still achieve impressive speeds by implementing these technical coaching points. By embracing an athlete's individuality and focusing on optimising their potential within their sport-specific demands, coaches can help athletes improve their sprinting performance.

Technical Model Maximum Velocity

Max Speed Mechanics - Key Positions:

1. Touch-down:
- The point where the foot makes contact with the ground.
- Plays a crucial role in generating propulsion and absorbing impact forces as this point initiates impulse to create speed.

2. Stance Phase:
- The weight-bearing phase of the gait cycle.
- Foot acts as a shock absorber and lever. This lever as pictured is recognised as a second class lever which plays a crucial role in the creation of speed and force

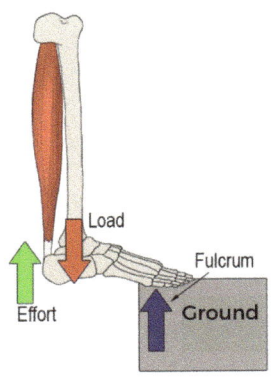

transference. As the ball of the foot strikes the ground the ankle joint receives load from the athlete's mass creating ground reaction force to which the achilles complex and posterior chain must stiffen to preserve and enhance speed.
- Supports the body as it passes over the support leg.
- Stance phase ends when the foot leaves the ground.

3. Toe-off:
- Marks the beginning of the swing phase of the gait cycle.
- The foot lifts off the ground, preparing for the next stride.

4. Swing Phase:
- The phase where the foot is not in contact with the ground.
- The free leg recovers forward in preparation for the next ground touch-down. Throughout this phase the athlete should simultaneously flex the hip and knee bringing the foot upward and forwards into the figure 4 position by the time the opposing leg makes contact with the ground. At this point we do not want to see any athlete leaning too far forward as this will increase the time of the swing phase as the pelvis will rotate forwards and the leg will take longer to go through the cycle. The torso should be in an upright or nearly upright position and not having an overextended lower back.

5. Flight Phase:
- Specific to running, this phase occurs when neither foot is in contact with the ground.
- It includes the swing phase mentioned above.
- During this phase, the body is airborne and not supported by the ground.

Understanding these key positions in max speed mechanics provides valuable insights into the mechanics and sequence of movements involved in sprinting. Coaches and athletes can analyse and optimise each phase to improve efficiency, stride length, and overall sprint performance. However it is important to always remember the goal is to improve effective technique to increase speed.

Technical Models of the Shuffle, Open Step, and Crossover

Sprinting involves various technical models for different scenarios, including transitional and non-linear sprint variations. In this chapter, we will dissect the technical models of the shuffle, open step, and crossover, focusing on the key elements and their significance in sprinting. Understanding these models can help athletes, particularly those involved in team sports like rugby or football, improve their lateral movements and acceleration.

1. The Shuffle Technical Model: The shuffle is a lateral weight shift of the hip, commonly used in low amplitude acceleration cutting or escape movements where the feet stay very close to the ground at all times. The primary objective is to achieve a lateral displacement of the hip while maintaining a close alignment of the shoulders with the feet. By mastering the shuffle, athletes can effectively transition from one position to another laterally minimising the time that the foot spends in the air and maximum displacement. This technique sets the foundation for subsequent movements.

Technical Model Shuffle

2. The Open Step Technical Model: The open step is a critical technique for athletes requiring lateral agility. In the example below It primarily focuses on the movement of the right hip, which plays a significant role in executing the shuffle. The initial shuffle movement emphasises the lateral displacement of body mass, encouraging athletes to shift their body weight to the left or right. By opening the torso in the direction it wants to go the hip can move through and facilitate the subsequent movements by activating the posterior oblique lines of the fascial system. This is enabled by aggressive arm action and forceful leg drive. The open step creates a lateral sling effect, setting the stage for a powerful snap-back motion that propels athletes into their crossovers.

Technical Model Open Step

3. The Crossover Technical Model: The crossover is a fundamental technique used to transition from lateral movement to linear acceleration. In this model, maximum lateral displacement is essential. Athletes generate a strong push, resulting in a large lateral extension. Unlike linear acceleration, where triple extension (ankle, knee, hip) is critical, the crossover relies more on counter-rotation. The push generates an equal and opposite reaction, closing off the body and directing the athlete in the desired direction. As the leg comes down, the shoulders rotate, creating space for the foot to touch down. This space is created by the rotational movement of the upper body created by the violent leg action and the shoulder extension of the contralateral arm (opposite side). The rotational movement continues until the thigh pops up, transitioning into the linear acceleration model. Arm movement plays a crucial role in splitting the body to stop excessive rotation of the torso which is created by the aggressive leg action. This allows a gradual rotational movement to occur just before foot contact.

Technical Model Cross Over

The technical models of the shuffle, open step, and crossover provide valuable insights into the mechanics of lateral movements and transitions in sprinting. Mastering these techniques can greatly enhance an athlete's ability to execute effective cuts, escapes, and changes of direction. Coaches and athletes should focus on developing proper weight shifts, hip displacement, and rotational movements to optimise performance in team sports. Understanding and implementing these technical models will contribute to improved agility, acceleration, and overall sprinting proficiency.

Training and Development of Deceleration Abilities in Team Sport Athletes

Deceleration, or the ability to rapidly reduce speed, is as crucial as acceleration in team sports. Effective deceleration not only prevents injuries but also enhances overall performance by allowing athletes to change direction quickly, stop suddenly, and reposition themselves efficiently. Deceleration whilst important is not heavily emphasised inside the sports speed system due to its general classification, meaning that trained in isolation will not provide much transfer to higher specialised speed qualities. However due to its general classification it is still a quality that should be given some attention. The reason why this isn't heavily emphasised is that during training we get an indirect transfer of deceleration when training our non linear speed movements and change of direction, we are always considering what action comes after we decelerate as opposed to the ability to stop. As we will touch on later in the book, understanding how the brain and body create deceleration is more important than the development of "stopping distance" in isolation. Deceleration involves eccentric muscle contractions, where muscles lengthen under tension to absorb force and reduce momentum. There is one slight exception to this rule when training receivers in American football. The demands of route running require high braking forces therefore special consideration to this quality should be addressed in off-season periods to prepare the athletes for the specific demands of their position.

Key components of deceleration include:

1. **Eccentric Strength and Rate of Force Development:** The ability to produce force while muscles lengthen at high rates.
2. **Reactive Strength:** The capacity to transition quickly from eccentric to concentric contractions. This is required when using short decelerations to offset an opponent and opposed to rapid braking.
3. **Neuromuscular Control:** The coordination between the nervous system and muscles to execute controlled movements.
4. **Body Positioning:** Proper alignment and posture to distribute forces efficiently and reduce the risk of injury.

Mechanical Effect of Deceleration

When decelerating, an athlete's body undergoes significant mechanical stress. The forces involved in deceleration can be up to five times the athlete's body weight, particularly during high-speed stops. When coaching athletes I always encourage my athletes to imagine that when you try to stop your body still wants to keep travelling in the direction you have pushed it in. Therefore you have to pull it into the next direction you want to take it, this can be either stopping at a desired position or linked directly to change of direction ability as we are reorientating the centre of mass towards a new trajectory. . Proper technique is essential to manage these forces effectively:

– **Foot Placement:** The foot should strike the ground in front of the body's centre of mass to create a braking force.

– **Centre of Mass:** The centre of mass must drop during deceleration, as this allows longer ground contacts, so that braking forces can be applied for longer. It also allows the braking leg to approach the ground more horizontally, and apply forces from a more efficient angle.

- **Knee Flexion:** During deceleration the knee should gradually flex more and more though each step, this is to take advantage of how strong we are in outer range positions and manage the rate at which we can control the speed of deceleration.

Hip Hinge: Engaging the hips during deceleration helps distribute forces across larger muscle groups, reducing the strain on the lower limbs.

- **Core Stability:** A strong core maintains balance and control, allowing for efficient force transfer and reducing the risk of injury.

Types of Deceleration

As we know team sports are incredibly chaotic and can demand a lot of our athletes to make successful tactical speed decisions. There are many ways in which an athlete can decelerate. Therefore we need to prepare for various types of deceleration scenarios:

1. **Linear Deceleration:** Slowing down while moving straight ahead. This type of deceleration is common when an athlete needs to stop quickly after sprinting.
2. **Lateral Deceleration:** Reducing speed while moving sideways. Essential for sports like basketball and soccer, where athletes frequently change directions.
3. **Rotational Deceleration:** Slowing down during a turn or pivot. Important for maintaining control and balance during rapid changes in direction. Also includes fakes, feints, and jukes, where the body turns to face one direction and then goes back the other way.
4. **Deceleration with a Change of Direction:** Combining deceleration with an immediate change in direction, often seen in agility drills and game situations.

Training for Deceleration Abilities

When we look at the training and development of acceleration ability. The sports speed frameworks all apply. As previously stated deceleration is a general quality in sport as coaches we must not over emphasis this too much. As we have discussed previously, deceleration ability is trained indirectly through weight room and jump training. Also athletes are prepared physically just from sprinting alone due to the high amounts of forces produced in these actions. It has been identified that the best decelerators possess great eccentric rate of force development. Eccentric rate of force development is the ability to produce force quickly as the muscles are lengthening. In your profiling of athletes it is strongly suggested to consider this as an area of attention if you notice that your athlete has difficulty controlling momentum, breaking down to a stop or changing direction fast at steep angles.

When we look at the classification of deceleration in the general speed phases of training these all arise from pre-planned movement. Later in the book in the section on specific speed development we will look at how vision is an important component in the development of deceleration.

To train and develop general deceleration abilities there are some fundamental technical principles that should be adhered too. Unsurprisingly these are close to the direct opposite of developing acceleration. However there is one slight difference. The preparation distance or period will dictate the way deceleration occurs. If we look at a gradual deceleration then the athletes will be able to maintain a more upright position. Conversely if the stopping distance is shorter then the athlete will need to create much deeper angles to create greater breaking forces. See the example below of a commonly used test 5-0-5. A general test to understand deceleration and change of direction.

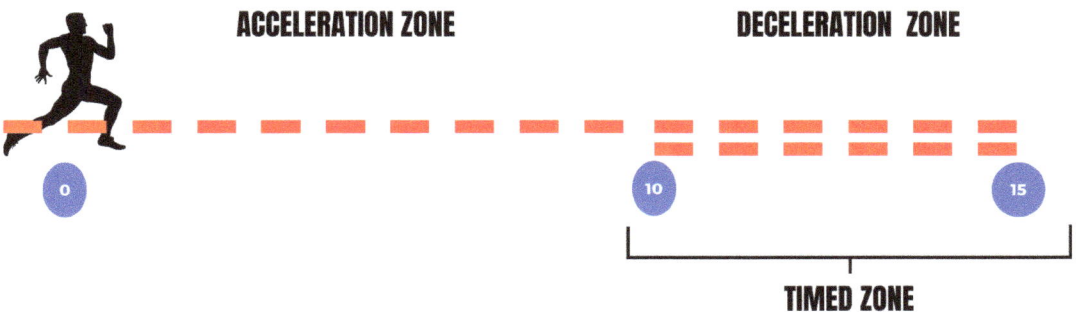

The 5-0-5 test is a measure of change of direction ability that requires a lot of rapid deceleration. The athlete must generate as much speed as they can over the first 10 metres then decelerate, change direction and reaccelerate back through the timed zone. The time taken is assessed by the 10-15m shuttle time. This requires a lot of deceleration. These images below are provided by a slow motion video capture software and demonstrate the mechanical process that an athlete has to go through to effectively navigate the Timed zone. You will observe the mechanical changes as previously described.

The data provided illustrates just how much deceleration goes into this test and in very few steps. This is an important consideration when determining what type of deceleration you are looking to train and in what context it will be used later within the sports speed system.

METRIC	VALUE
Total Time 10-0-5 (s)	3.52
Time 5-0-5 (s)	2.35
Time 5-0 (s)	1.13
Time 0-5 (s)	1.22
Peak Velocity (m/s)	5.81
Time to Stop (s)	*1.22*
Distance to Stop (m)	*4.81*
Average Deceleration (m/s^2)	*-4*
Average Early Deceleration (m/s^2)	*-3.23*
Average Late Deceleration (m/s^2)	*-6.23*

The data demonstrates the high mechanical load that deceleration creates in this test over the 4.81m stopping distance of this athlete. When planning or considering to plan deceleration training with your athletes ensure that you appreciate the acute training effect that this can have and ensure you use the programming principles and guidelines in this book to manage the athletes stress.

Team Sport Athlete Archetypes: Understanding Physical Biases

When working with athletes, it is essential to recognise the unique characteristics and biases that shape their performance. In this section we delve into the archetypes commonly observed in team sports. These are the archetypes that as a coach I have faced over and over again. Understanding these archetypes is crucial for designing effective training programs that address individual physical biases while enhancing overall athletic performance. But first I want to introduce you to the "MMA" fighter and what we can learn from the evolution of this historic sport.

The "MMA" Fighter

We can learn so much from outside team sports and the one place that I use in conversation over and over again is Mixed Martial Arts. The UFC was formed in 1993 and was made up by a collection of fighters who all had specialised in one type of combat discipline. What became apparent quite shortly after the popularity of this sport grew was that over-specialisation was a common downfall, in MMA you had to become an MMA fighter in order to excel in the sport. In field sports we can learn so much from this in the way that we prepare our athletes. Within this book hopefully you are learning to create the team sport sprinter and the possibilities this can have for on field performance.

Gym Strong Movement Weak

The concept of "Gym strong movement weak" provides a valuable framework for understanding athlete archetypes. It emphasises the dominance of weight room experience and strength training bias, often accompanied by a lack of exposure to sequential training. This raises an important question: have coaches adequately sequenced their training programs to optimise athlete development?

Archetype Breakdown

1) **Bodybuilder:** These athletes prioritise aesthetics over performance. While they possess significant strength, they often lack speed, reactive strength qualities, and efficient movement. Fragility and poor skill capabilities are also notable characteristics.
2) **Powerlifter:** Strength is paramount for powerlifters, resulting in a low rate of force development and a focus on heavy lifting. However, the transfer of these qualities to the field may be limited. They tend to exhibit tense and one-dimensional movement patterns, have limited eccentric capacity, minimal lower limb strength, poor skill capacities, and an increased risk of injury.
3) **Games Player:** Games players excel in their specific sport due to outstanding game-specific skills and tactical prowess. While they may not possess exceptional physical profiles, they compensate through game knowledge and strategic play. They rely on teammates to compensate for their physical deficiencies.
4) **Sprinter:** Former track athletes transitioning to team sports often exhibit exceptional speed but struggle with game-specific movements, lateral agility, and repeatability. While their sprinting capabilities may be impressive, they may lack other essential qualities required for team sports.
5) **Crossfitter:** Crossfitters thrive on continuous training without much rest. Their high general fitness levels may overshadow specific fitness for their sport. They often lack tendinous response and elastic properties, leading to one-paced performance and an increased risk of injury.

Understanding the archetypes prevalent in team sports provides valuable insights into individual physical biases. Coaches and trainers must tailor training programs to address these biases while developing well-rounded athletes. By acknowledging the strengths and limitations of each archetype, the path to optimising performance becomes clearer. Striking a balance between specialisation and comprehensive training is key to unlocking the full potential of athletes in team sports.

Anthropometrics and Team Sport Sprinting

When it comes to team sport athletes, the wide array of anthropometric characteristics cannot be overlooked. From towering props and linemen to lean and agile wingers and receivers, athletes come in various shapes, sizes, limb lengths, and mass distributions. Understanding these anthropometric differences is crucial for coaches and trainers in optimising sprinting performance. This chapter explores the impact of anthropometrics on team sport sprinting and the need for tailored training approaches.

The Diversity of Anthropometric Profiles

Team sport athletes exhibit remarkable diversity in their anthropometric profiles. Examples include Joe Launchbury's height and physicality, Pocock's compact and muscular build, and Cristiano Ronaldo's athleticism and lean physique. Each athlete's unique characteristics contribute to their performance, and coaches must consider these factors when designing training programs.

Leveraging Physics and Understanding Anthropometrics

Anthropometrics play a significant role in sprinting performance by affecting lever lengths. Coaches should recognize that each athlete's height, weight, and body shape influence their acceleration patterns. While athletes like Joe Launchbury may not follow a textbook acceleration pattern, the goal remains the same: to achieve rapid rates of change in velocity. However, the approach to reaching that goal may differ significantly between athletes.

Pushers and Pullers: Embracing Individual Differences

Coaches often categorise athletes as pushers or pullers based on their anthropometric dimensions. This is typically where we find that pushers are more shorter muscular driven sprinters and pullers are more taller elastic driven sprinters. However these loose categories can be lost in team sports as the athletes do come in varying anthropometric proportions. While these categories can provide guidance, they should not limit an athlete's potential or movement capabilities. Coaches must understand how an athlete's unique build affects their job requirements and adapt training accordingly. By embracing individual dimensions, coaches can optimise performance while avoiding unnecessary restrictions.

Anthropometric Categories

Taller Athletes

Athletes with above-average height, such as Joe Launchbury tend to exhibit lower relative strength and excel in posterior chain dominance. They possess longer levers, conserve momentum well, and find it easier to maintain speed once attained. However, acceleration may be more challenging for them. Here are 5 key differentiating factors to consider with taller athletes.

- Lower Relative Strength
- Longer Levers
- "Poor" Accelerators
- Posterior Chain Dominant
- Easier to maintain top speed due to longer stride lengths.

Middle-of-the-Road Athletes

Athletes with relatively balanced anthropometric characteristics, like Pocock and Marcus Smith, face a mix of advantages and challenges. Their force-velocity profiles are well-balanced, allowing them to respond effectively to general speed training. However, they must work through all phases of speed development and do not excel in any specific area naturally. Here are 5 key differentiating factors to consider with middle of the road athletes.

- Best of Both
- Worst of Both
- Relatively balanced F-V profile
- Responds well to general speed training
- Have to work for all phases of sprinting

Shorter Athletes

Shorter athletes, such as Raheem Sterling and Christian Wade, possess higher relative strength, shorter levers, and better initial acceleration. They may struggle with top-end speed and require high-frequency movements to maintain their speed due to their shorter leg length. These athletes excel in deceleration, change of direction, and cutting manoeuvres. Here are 5 key differentiating factors to consider with middle of the road athletes.

- High relative strength
- Shorter levers like pushing
- Better initial accelerators
- Struggle with top end speed duration
- Need high levels of frequency to maintain speed.
- Very Good Deceleration and COD

Anthropometrics play a significant role in team sport sprinting, shaping an athlete's unique characteristics and capabilities. Coaches and trainers must embrace the diversity of anthropometric profiles within their teams. By understanding the strengths and challenges associated with different body types, coaches can tailor training programs to optimise sprinting performance. A holistic and efficient approach that bridges the gap between gym work and running is essential in maximising the limited time available for training. Ultimately, acknowledging and leveraging anthropometrics will help athletes reach their full potential in team sport sprinting.

Tailoring Training for Different Height Athletes

Anthropometrics play a huge part in the training and development of speed as a skill. With all different shapes, sizes and positional requirements it can be a minefield for effective coaching. This is where I strongly suggest you initially implement the frameworks as dictated. This is because your first job is to restructure training to engineer speed development as the primary general objective of training. Then you can identify speed age. From here you will know and understand how you are best to generate transfer from your training.

When considering different anthropometrics with athletes the place I started to create associations was to think of the athletes in the form of their animal counterparts. Whilst slightly abstract this concept has helped me tailor training to suit their different needs. The trick is to accommodate training to their strengths and not their weaknesses. This is how they will find speed on the field of play and probably why they play the positions they do.

The chimpanzee whilst small is springy and agile in nature is great at short speed and change of direction. Training when developing the chimpanzee knows that short speed is their domain and will be able to master these techniques quickly. However when looking to develop the ability to accelerate for long distances or reach maximum speed this type of training will come at a heavy cost to them.

The cheetah, wiry, light and the most elastic animal there is. Can produce serious amounts of speed and has great lever distribution. They only have one gear and its max out. Volume is not the cheetahs friend and can struggle with reactive change of direction. This is where they will lose out on the field of play.

The lion, big, strong, powerful and fast. But not the fastest. Unlike the cheetah the lion is muscular and gladiatorial in its approach to sport. You do not want to be anywhere near a lion inside 20m. The lion is a force applicator and drives hard and aggressively. Resisted speed training will be where the lion loves to train.

The gorilla, one of the strongest there is. Big and a huge physical presence can be devastating to stop. Again another animal that likes to push and pull heavy objects and throw heavy objects. Its size can make them a risk to top speed but this can be developed in small doses. If the gorilla gets you, there is no getting away.

The rhino, now are stepping into the big boy club. Taller, heavier and a little slower off the mark than the rest. To get a rhino moving takes a lot of work and a lot of force. A rhino can spend a ton of time in stable conditions developing specific and special strength. Give a rhino a stable platform to push hard and fast on and they will fly.

The elephant, equally as powerful but a little more rangy with its longer legs. Taller and heavier an elephant will take a lot of time to learn how to coordinate all its limbs along with the additional mass. With a ton of strength an elephant but not alot of capacity they will find the most basic of work challenging. Keep their training more extensive in nature and they will be fine.

The giraffe, long, rangy and slightly awkward looking when in motion. While possessing better relative strength than the elephant its long limbs make it challenging for them to accelerate and also hit top speed. Get a giraffe working on their coordination and rhythm and they will improve speed very quickly.

Mastering the Process of Sports Speed

Achieving technical change in sports speed requires a deep understanding of the process of mastery. Coaches play a crucial role in guiding athletes from unconscious incompetence to conscious competence. By applying principles from coaching science and utilising effective coaching strategies, coaches can help athletes master the skills necessary for optimal speed performance. We will now explore the process of mastery, coaching cues, deliberate practice, constraints, affordances, and the stages of qualification in sprinting.

1. The Process of Mastery within the Sports Speed System: Mastery involves progressing through cognitive, associative, and autonomous stages, accompanied by the experiences of learning, loading, and executing. Coaches must recognize where athletes are in their technical journey to coach effectively. Understanding the role of each stage and implementing appropriate coaching methods allows athletes to develop conscious competence.

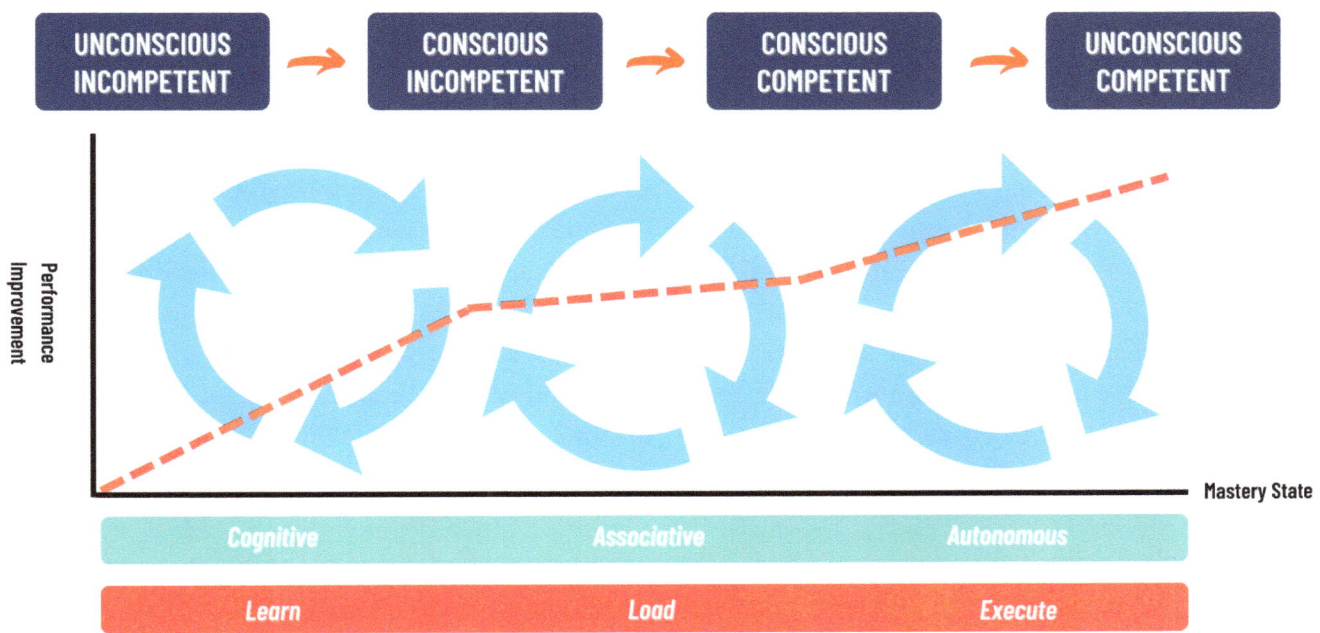

2. Educate and Simplify: To create technical change, coaches should prioritise educating athletes and providing associative learning, anchoring technical cues to relatable concepts enhances learning and helps athletes appreciate the coaching process. Keeping coaching cues simple and concise improves understanding and facilitates effective skill execution. For example, using three cues for effective acceleration—throw your body forward, attack the ground, and keep your thighs in front—simplifies the coaching process while cleaning up acceleration technique.

3. Deliberate Practice and Stretch Goals: Deliberate practice involves deconstructing movements, focusing on key body links, and setting stretch goals to push athletes beyond their current capabilities. Coaches should encourage athletes to project future achievements and create stretch goals that challenge and motivate them. By incorporating deliberate practice into training sessions, coaches provide opportunities for athletes to improve their skills and enhance performance. To apply these stretch goals use the flowchart below.

Deliberate Practice (where you can)

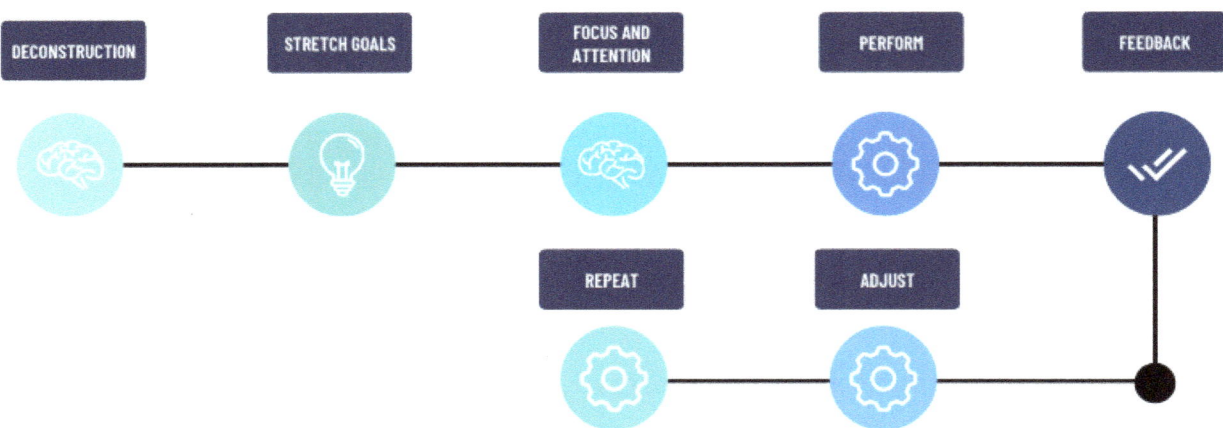

4. Constraints and Affordances: Coaches can use constraints and affordances to shape the training environment. Constraints involve limiting tasks based on objectives, equipment, and area, while physical constraints encompass factors like height, weight, strength, power, speed, and motivation. Task based constraint manipulation is the quickest way to manipulate training, whereas the adaptation you create from task manipulation will alter the physical constraints. This is a positive training tool for coaches as it can help us shape the training for the stimulus required. For example distance is a constraint of speed training, a 5m acceleration will provide an acceleration based constraint. Task based manipulation can provide an athlete a targeted but also varied stimulus of training. Affordances refer to the opportunities for action that the environment offers to an individual, based on their capabilities and skills. In speed coaching, affordances are the possibilities for action that arise within the training environment, influenced by the interaction between the athlete and the specific context in which they are performing. For example when training reaction speed using unpredictable stimuli, such as a coach's signal or a moving target, can train athletes to quickly recognise and react to affordances in real-time, enhancing their decision-making speed and agility. Or an even more simple example is how different surfaces (grass, turf, track) help athletes develop the ability to adjust their speed and stride patterns according to the affordances of each surface.

Constraints vs Affordances
Good Coaching Relies on both

CONSTRAINTS

Task based constraints - objectives, equipment, area to work within.

Physical Constraints - Height, weight, strength, power, speed, motivation, knowledge

AFFORDANCES

Exist in an environment based on a learners physical and mental constraints.

Use these to help guide your coaching

5. Stages of Qualification: Coaching speed involves guiding athletes through the cognitive, associative, and autonomous stages of learning. Coaches should provide a structured progression, incorporating learn, skill, drill, practice, and perform phases. Understanding and applying coaching strategies within these stages enable athletes to develop and refine their speed skills effectively.

The final piece of the process is to understand how speed age fits into mastering the process of sports speed. Below I have given you an image that shows the preferred path of implementation with regards to the layering of speed age and motor learning. Through my experience I have learned with minimal time it is important to deliver the most appropriate intervention that facilitates the learner. The initial goal of any sports speed program is to learn to sprint and there can be no time wasted on this. It is a general quality and therefore as coaches this has to be delivered fast and accurately. As the competency of the athlete progresses more sophisticated drills and broader motor learning principles can be applied.

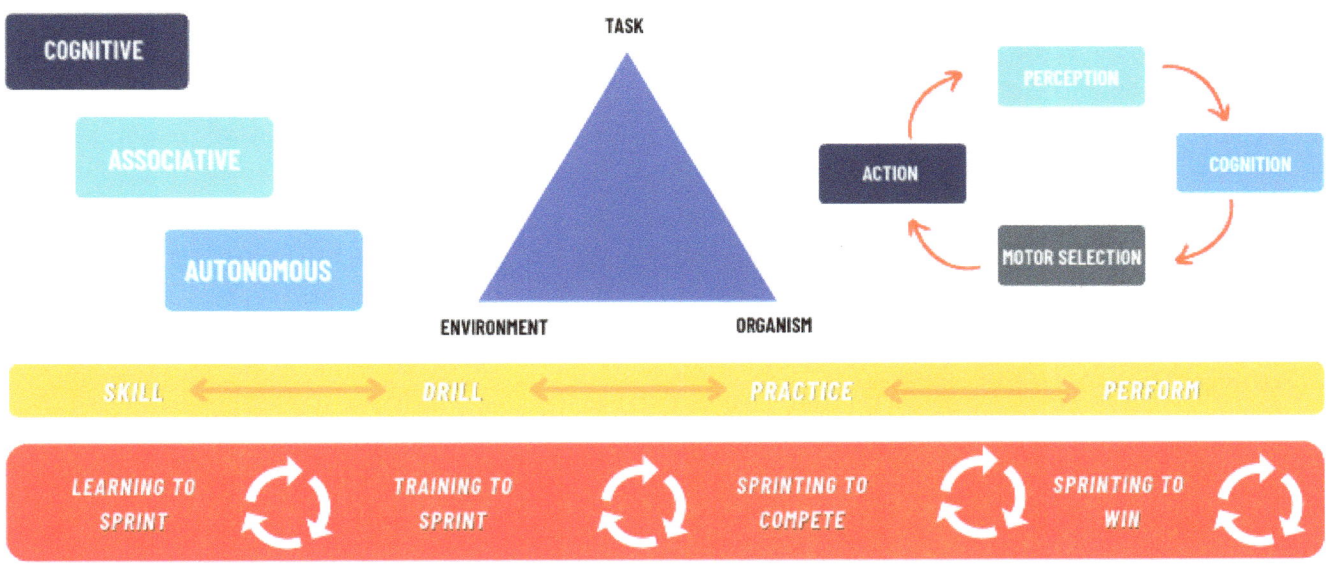

Mastering the process of sports speed requires coaches to employ effective coaching strategies and draw on coaching science principles. By educating athletes, simplifying coaching cues, incorporating deliberate practice and stretch goals, utilising constraints and affordances, and guiding athletes through the stages of qualification, coaches can facilitate technical change and help athletes achieve their speed performance goals. Embracing the coaching process and maintaining a focus on individual progression will contribute to coaching success and athlete development.

EXERCISE CLASSIFICATION FOR SPEED

In this chapter, we delve into the concept of utilising exercise classifications for speed training. The first part of it will cover the theories and principles around my interpretation of the subject. As a coach, my journey in creating exercise classifications for speed training has been a significant part of my evolution. In this chapter, I aim to equip you with the necessary tools and frameworks required to utilise exercises for speed development.

I aim to challenge conventional wisdom and debunk the myths around exercises necessary for speed training and to develop the ability to produce speed. My personal experience as an athlete shaped my bias around exercise classification. As someone who was naturally fast, I assumed that lifting weights to put on mass would help improve my speed. However, I discovered that my speed remained stagnant, despite my weightlifting efforts. I then had to re-evaluate my entire approach to speed training, realising that sprinting was the most effective method for me. This conscious incompetence is common among many individuals, and my personal experience is a testament to this. I knew I was wrong but I didn't have the skill set yet to make the changes. I had to learn it.

The turning point in my approach to speed training came when I decided to observe and study sprinters to understand how to deconstruct optimal ways to create speed specific qualities. This led to an epiphany, and I became acutely aware of the gap between my current approach and the optimal approach. Once I had seen the difference, I could not unsee it.

The "Specificity gap" of team sports speed training and the sequential effect of training are essential for speed development. The Specificity gap in the development of team sport speed training exists in the over emphasis of general weight and jump training ignoring the requirement for more specialised training to develop the specific qualities of team sport speed. The sequential effect refers to how the tread of exercise selection compliments the overall goal and how each proceeding exercise enables the development of the following exercise. To simplify in rugby most players lift weights a lot, do some jump training, some wall drills and expect to run faster. This is not a well thought out training process. Once you see this gap, there is no turning back. It is essential to look at the base theory around exercise classification because it is often missed, and this is why it doesn't get applied in the right way. Firstly in order to understand correct classification, we must look at the concept of reductive thinking.

Reductionism is a philosophical and scientific approach that seeks to explain complex phenomena by reducing them to simpler, more fundamental elements. It originated from the works of philosophers such as René Descartes and Isaac Newton, who believed that understanding the basic building blocks of a system would lead to a comprehensive understanding of its functioning. Reductionist thinking is a crucial concept in exercise classification. By breaking down complex movements into their fundamental components, reductionist thinking provides a logical rationale for designing targeted exercises that enhance speed performance.

When applied to speed training, reductionist thinking helps coaches identify the key components and underlying factors contributing to speed performance. By breaking down the running motion into its constituent parts, such as stride length, stride frequency, ground contact time, and joint angles, coaches can design exercises that specifically target and improve these elements. Research has shown that stride length and stride frequency, for example, significantly relate to sprint performance. By designing exercises that directly address these factors, coaches can optimise an athlete's speed potential.

Furthermore, biomechanical analysis has revealed the critical role of joint angles and muscle activation patterns in sprinting. Reductionist thinking allows coaches to focus on improving specific joint angles, muscle activation sequences, and force production capabilities through targeted exercises and drills. This approach enables athletes to develop the necessary biomechanical efficiency and coordination required for enhanced speed performance.

The application of reductionist thinking in exercise selection for speed training offers several benefits. Firstly, it provides a systematic approach to address the specific needs and weaknesses of individual athletes. By identifying and targeting key components, coaches can tailor training programs to optimise each athlete's speed potential.

Secondly, reductionist thinking allows for progress tracking and evaluation. By isolating and focusing on specific elements of speed performance, coaches can measure and assess an athlete's improvement in each component. This data-driven approach enables more accurate monitoring of progress and the ability to adjust training protocols accordingly.

Embracing reductionist principles in exercise selection can help coaches optimise training outcomes and enhance athletes' speed capabilities. This concept is significant in strength and conditioning because of the attachment coaches possess to the "strength" side of the athletic development paradigm. However, there is a problem when we continue to use simple training methods and exercises in the pursuit of improvement of specific and complex actions. We need to know how strong is strong enough. **You are strong enough once the metric that you're measuring improvement with stops showing transfer**. You then need to become stronger in a different way with more complexity and specificity. For example, with an athlete in the very early stages of development, improving their squat consistently seems to be driving improvements in their 10m time. Once improving the squat seems to stop improving their 10m time, they might be strong enough at squatting and now we need to improve their strength in a more complex and/or specific task. We might then try to improve the strength of the athlete in a single leg box squat at some relevant joint angle. This gets the 10m time moving downwards again. Once progress stalls out here, we need to rotate to a new exercise, once again addressing capacities at a higher level of specificity and complexity.

The task demand of running or moving fast is simple and adaptation arrives from a form of stimulus and response. Coaches need to learn to break things down to stimulus and response in the context of a series of stimulus response chains. What great coaches do is constantly test and observe the change in the human body to what they do.

A great coach can create training programs that have exercises progressions that complement one another and a training direction that does not interfere with the sport. If done appropriately our athletes will reap the benefits of continual adaptation and performance increases. This is where we will start to assess that specificity gap and the sequential effect of training. This is where we start to apply reductionist thinking to exercise classification.

Bondarchuk's Exercise Classification

Anatoly Bondachuk is one of my biggest influences. An Olympic medalist, shot put coach and the leading researcher in the transfer of training. Bondarchuk's exercise classification system categorises exercises based on their specific training effect and intended outcome. He identified four main exercise classifications: special preparatory exercises, special developmental exercises, specific preparatory exercises, and competitive exercises. Each classification serves a distinct purpose in the training process and contributes to overall performance enhancement.

Bondarchuck's exercise classification system can be effectively applied to speed training, facilitating a structured and systematic approach to improving an athlete's speed capabilities.

1. General Preparatory Exercises:

These exercises focus on developing general physical qualities and foundational attributes required for speed training. They aim to enhance an athlete's strength, power, mobility, and overall athleticism. Examples of general preparatory exercises for speed training include resistance training, plyometrics, agility drills, and general conditioning exercises. By incorporating these exercises into the training program, coaches can lay a solid foundation for subsequent speed-specific training.

2. Special Developmental Exercises:

Special developmental exercises target and overload specific muscle groups and movement patterns directly related to speed performance. These exercises aim to improve stride mechanics, leg power, and coordination. Examples of special developmental exercises for speed training include explosive jumps, bounds, and resisted sprinting. By incorporating these exercises, athletes can refine their technique, optimise muscle activation, and enhance the specific qualities necessary for sprinting at maximum speed.

3. Specific Preparatory Exercises:

Specific preparatory exercises simulate competitive or sport-specific movements while still emphasising speed development. These exercises bridge the gap between general speed training and sport-specific actions. In the context of speed training, specific preparatory exercises may involve simulated starts, acceleration drills, and change of direction exercises tailored to the athlete's sport. These exercises help athletes develop the necessary skills and movement patterns required for their specific speed demands.

4. Competitive Exercises:

Competitive exercises closely resemble the actual sporting actions and involve race simulations, competitive drills, and sport-specific speed challenges. These exercises replicate the high-intensity, game-like conditions athletes encounter during competitions. By incorporating competitive exercises into speed training, athletes can improve their ability to perform at maximum speed in a competitive setting, enhancing their race-specific skills, mental resilience, and decision-making abilities.

Bondarchuk's exercise classification system provides a valuable framework for organising and selecting exercises in speed training. By incorporating special developmental exercises, specific preparatory exercises, and competitive exercises, coaches can systematically enhance an athlete's speed capabilities. This structured approach ensures a comprehensive and progressive training program, targeting both general physical qualities and specific speed-related attributes. By utilising Bondarchuk's exercise classification, coaches and athletes can optimise their speed training strategies and ultimately achieve peak performance on the field or track.

Simultaneously to this work, we have the work of Verkoshansky in the area of dynamic correspondence. Yuri Verkhoshansky, renowned sports scientists and coaches, introduced the concept of Dynamic Correspondence, which has revolutionised training methodologies, particularly in the realm of sprinting for team sports.

Dynamic Correspondence

Dynamic Correspondence is a training principle that emphasises the match between training exercises and the specific demands of the sport or activity. Verkhoshansky proposed that for optimal performance enhancement, training exercises should closely resemble the biomechanical patterns, intensities, and dynamics required during competition. By applying the following five criteria, coaches can design effective sprint training programs for team sports. Exercises that fulfil all five criteria are known as special strength exercises.

1. Amplitude/Direction of Movement:

The exercise should take into consideration the specific joints used, the proper motion of the body segments, the regions of muscular work and the direction and planes of motion through which movement is created. Simply put, the exercises we use should train in the way we move in sport. For example linear speed should be developed with linear exercises and rotational speed should be developed through rotational exercises. This is where the power of drill stacking comes into play as the segment stage represents the criteria of dynamic correspondence. The foundation of drill stacking is targeting the segment portion of the key movement identified training it specifically. For example when training hip extension for acceleration we are able to specifically target this action in wall drills to meet this criteria of dynamic correspondence.

2. Accentuated Region of Force Production:

Understanding the regions of force production in sprinting is essential for effective training. Coaches should focus on exercises that target the muscle groups and joint actions predominantly utilised during sprinting in team sports. This criterion enables athletes to develop the necessary strength, power, and explosiveness in the specific regions of force production relevant to their sport. For example, the leg swing and ground contact both occur during hip extension, but the swing is high velocity-low force, and the contact is low velocity-high force.

3. Dynamics of Effort:

The dynamics of effort refer to the intensity and speed of movement during sprinting. Training exercises should replicate the high-intensity bursts and explosive efforts required in team sports. By incorporating drills and intervals that match the dynamics of effort during competition, athletes can improve their sprinting abilities and adapt to the specific demands of their sport. This applies at a global and segmental level.

4. Rate and Time of Maximum Force Production:

Maximising force production within specific time frames is crucial in sprinting for team sports. Training exercises should target the rate at which athletes can generate maximum force and the time window within which force needs to be applied effectively (the duration of a ground contact). This criterion enhances an athlete's ability to accelerate, change direction, and generate explosive power during sprints within game contexts. This criteria often is confused with **Accentuated Region of Force Production** which is where the maximum dynamic force occurs close to a specific joint angle as opposed to the rate at which the force is produced which compliments the dynamics of effort.

5. Regime of Muscular Work:

The regime of muscular work refers to the specific energy systems and metabolic demands encountered during sprinting in team sports. Training exercises should reflect the duration, rest intervals, and work-to-rest ratios experienced in competition. This criterion ensures the appropriate development of energy systems, allowing athletes to sustain high-intensity efforts and recover efficiently during sprints in team sports.

Application in Sprinting for Team Sports:

Yuri Verkhoshansky's Dynamic Correspondence principle provides a valuable framework for optimising sprint training in team sports. By considering the five criteria—amplitude/direction of movement, accentuated region of force production, dynamics of effort, rate and time of maximum force production, and regime of muscular work—coaches can design training programs that closely match the demands of speed training and sprinting for team sports.

As we are building the theoretical layers of exercise classification and exercise selection it is imperative to address the outcome of these principles which is the transfer of training.

Transfer of Training

THE USE OF TRAINING MEANS FOR DEVELOPING PHYSICAL ABILITIES AND IMPROVING TECHNICAL MASTERY IN ACCORDANCE WITH THIS PRINCIPLE.

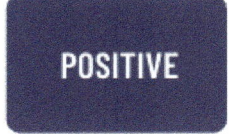 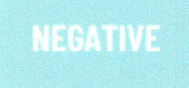 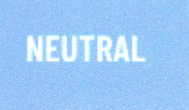

The transfer of training is a crucial concept in speed training, as coaches aim to maximise the transfer of improvements from training exercises to actual sprinting performance. Anatoliy Bondarchuk, a renowned Soviet and Ukrainian coach, has provided valuable insights into optimising the transfer of training in the context of speed development.

Bondarchuk emphasises the principles of similarity and specificity when designing speed training programs. Similarity refers to the degree of resemblance between the training exercises and the actual sprinting movements. To enhance transfer, coaches should select exercises that closely mimic the biomechanics, muscle actions, and energy systems involved in sprinting. This can include drills such as acceleration runs, resisted sprints, and plyometric exercises that replicate the explosive nature of sprinting.

Specificity is another key principle, focusing on tailoring the training stimulus to match the specific demands of sprinting. Training exercises should target the specific muscle groups, movement patterns, and energy demands required for sprinting. By incorporating exercises that closely mirror the sprinting mechanics and energy systems, coaches can enhance the transfer of training effects to sprint performance.

Individualisation is also essential in speed training. Each athlete has unique strengths, weaknesses, and technical characteristics that require individual attention. Coaches should consider an athlete's biomechanics, stride length, stride frequency, and any technical deficiencies when selecting exercises and training methods. By customising the training program to address the individual needs of each athlete, coaches can optimise the transfer of training in speed development.

Bondarchuk's approach to the transfer of training in speed training underscores the importance of selecting exercises that closely resemble the sprinting movements and are specific to the demands of the sport. By prioritising similarity, specificity, and individualisation, coaches can enhance the transfer of training and maximise the athlete's speed development. Ultimately, this approach can lead to improved sprint performance and success in competitive team sports.

Conjugated Training Effects (CTE)

Conjugated Training Effects (CTE) goes beyond focusing on a single training modality, such as strength training or speed training, and encourages the concurrent development of various physical attributes. CTE is a training concept that holds immense importance in speed training for team sports. Adapted from the work of U.V. Menkhin, a Russian sports scientist and coach, CTE emphasises the strategic integration of different training methods and modalities to maximise training adaptations and enhance athletic performance. The core principle of CTE is the combination of various training stimuli that target different physiological systems and motor abilities. In team sports, speed is a critical factor, and athletes need to develop multiple physical qualities simultaneously.

By incorporating both strength and speed training in a coordinated manner, athletes can benefit from the complementary interaction between these modalities. Strength training enhances explosive power (because power is force x velocity), and strength training enhances force production, while training velocity represents sprint actions improves acceleration and top speed. Through the integration of these modalities, athletes can achieve greater overall improvements and enhance their performance on the field.

CTE also emphasises the significance of careful planning and periodisation in training. Different training methods may have varying impacts on specific physiological systems or motor abilities. Coaches must strategically organise training phases and design a well-structured training program to capitalise on the cumulative effects of different modalities and optimise athletes' progress.

Moreover, individualisation plays a vital role in CTE. Coaches must tailor training programs to meet the specific needs and characteristics of each athlete. Factors such as sport, position, skill requirements, strengths, weaknesses, and injury history should be considered. By personalising the training approach, coaches can address individual requirements and optimise athletes' development and performance. The image below illustrates how coaches need to prioritise training.

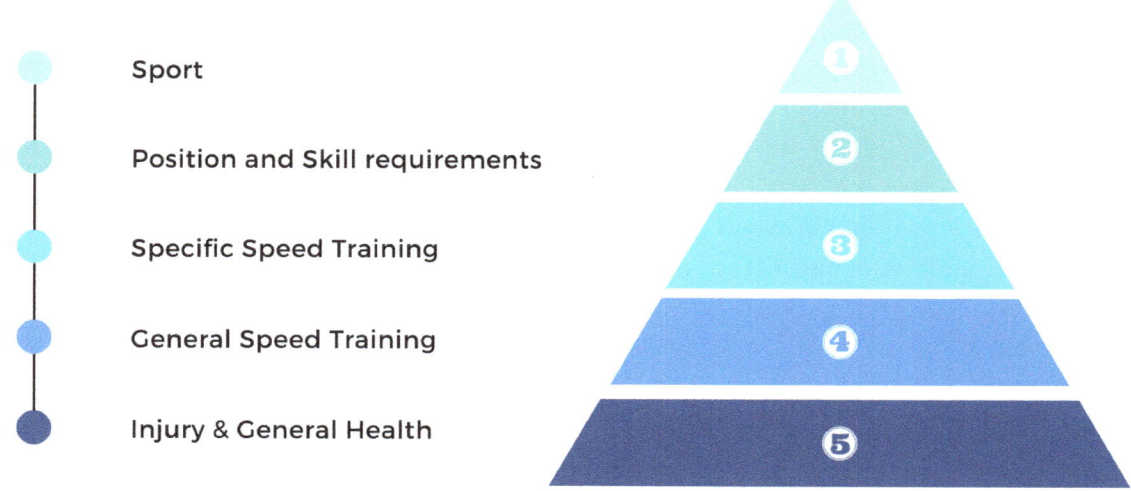

CTE provides a framework for integrating different training modalities and optimising athletic performance in speed training for team sports. This will be demonstrated in great detail later in the book. By structuring training appropriately using CTE training methods, coaches can enhance athletes' physical qualities, improve their speed and agility, and ultimately achieve long-term success. Strategic planning, individualisation, and the synergistic interaction between different training stimuli are key elements in maximising the benefits of CTE.

Body Links

To maximise speed training, coaches can incorporate the concept of body links, as emphasised by renowned sports scientist Yuri Verkhoshansky. Body links refer to the interconnectedness and coordination of different body parts during movement. As discussed in the previous chapter a great example of this is how the arms counterbalance the rotation of the hips during sprinting actions. By understanding and optimising body links, athletes can enhance their speed and overall athletic performance.

Efficient and powerful movement relies on the proper functioning and coordination of various body segments. In speed training, athletes need to generate force, transfer it through the body, and apply it to the ground to propel themselves forward. Body links play a crucial role in this process as they determine the efficiency of force transmission and movement coordination. When the body is properly coordinated, it is able to find the correct timing of relaxation and stiffness which will allow for the highest speed of movement. The leg must generate maximum stiffness as it transfers force into the ground and then relax to enable it to whip through and recover. If the leg is stiff for too long, the whippiness and recovery are compromised, and if the stiffness does not start at the correct moment, and proceed in the correct sequence, it will not be able to store energy elastically on ground contact.

Exercise classification is an important aspect of speed training as it helps coaches and trainers select appropriate exercises to target specific physiological systems and motor abilities. When considering exercise classification in the context of body links, the focus is on exercises that enhance the coordination and integration of different body parts involved in sprinting and acceleration.

Exercises that promote body links typically involve multi-joint movements that engage multiple muscle groups and require coordination between the upper and lower body. Examples include various forms of special strength exercises, plyometrics, such as bounding, skipping, and depth jumps, which involve coordinated movements of the arms, legs, and core.

Additionally, strength training exercises like squats, deadlifts, and Olympic lifts can enhance body links by developing overall strength and coordination between the upper and lower body in the most general form.

Benefits of Optimising Body Links in Speed Training:

By incorporating exercises that target body links, athletes can experience several benefits in their speed training:

1. Improved Movement Efficiency: Enhancing body links helps athletes develop more fluid and efficient movement patterns, reducing energy wastage and enhancing speed and agility.

2. Increased Force Transmission: Strong and well-coordinated body links allow for effective transfer of forces generated by the muscles, leading to more powerful and explosive movements.

3. Injury Prevention: Optimising body links helps distribute forces evenly throughout the body, reducing the risk of imbalances and overuse injuries commonly associated with speed training.

4. Transferability to Sports Performance: The improved coordination and integration of body links developed through speed training can directly translate to enhanced performance in team sports that require sprinting, acceleration, and quick changes of direction.

When designing speed training programs, coaches and trainers should consider the concept of body links and exercise classification. By selecting exercises that promote the coordination and integration of different body parts, athletes can optimise their movement efficiency, force transmission, and overall speed performance. Incorporating body links into speed training enhances athletic abilities, reduces the risk of injuries, and helps athletes excel in team sports.

Exploring Part, Whole, and Mixed Methods of Motor Learning with respect to Exercise Classification

To optimise speed training, coaches and trainers employ various motor learning strategies. Three prominent approaches in motor learning are the part method, the whole method, and the mixed method. Understanding the characteristics and benefits of each method can help coaches design effective training programs for enhancing speed skills in team sports.

Part Method:

The part method involves breaking down complex skills into smaller, more manageable components or "parts." Athletes focus on mastering each component individually before integrating them into the whole skill. In the context of speed training, the part method can be applied by isolating specific aspects of sprinting or acceleration technique, such as arm swing, leg drive, or body posture.

Benefits of the Part Method in Speed Training:

1. Skill Mastery: By isolating specific components, athletes can develop a deeper understanding and mastery of each element, leading to improved overall technique and efficiency. Athletes are able to focus on a single element at a time, allowing their full concentration to be devoted to what they are trying to improve.

2. Targeted Feedback: Coaches can provide specific feedback and corrections for each part, enabling athletes to address weaknesses or technical errors more effectively. This is because it is fundamentally easier to coach these movements.

3. Progressive Skill Acquisition: Athletes gradually build their skills by mastering each part, facilitating a smoother progression toward executing the entire skill with greater proficiency.

Whole Method:

The whole method focuses on practising skills in their entirety, without breaking them down into smaller parts. Athletes engage in full-speed sprinting or acceleration drills, aiming to replicate game-like conditions.

In speed training, the whole method involves performing complete sprinting or acceleration movements without interruption or segmentation.

Benefits of the Whole Method in Speed Training:

1. Skill Integration: By practising the entire skill, athletes can develop a better sense of rhythm, timing, and coordination necessary for executing fast and fluid movements.

2. Contextualization: The whole method allows athletes to experience the demands of speed in a realistic and game-specific setting, enhancing their ability to transfer skills directly to team sports performance.

3. Improved Decision-Making: Practising skills as a whole helps athletes develop effective decision-making abilities, such as identifying opportunities for acceleration, adjusting speed, or reacting to game situations.

Mixed Method:

The mixed method combines elements of both the part and whole methods. Athletes alternate between practising the whole skill and isolating specific parts or aspects for focused training. This method provides a balance between skill integration and targeted refinement. Here we would look to contrast modalities. For example a stable prowler push into an unstable acceleration.

Benefits of the Mixed Method in Speed Training:

1. Comprehensive Skill Development: The mixed method allows athletes to refine specific components while also practising the skill as a whole, promoting a well-rounded and versatile skill set.

2. Transferability: By training both isolated parts and integrated whole movements, athletes enhance their ability to transfer skills to dynamic game situations, where they must adapt and react quickly.

3. Individualisation: The mixed method allows coaches to tailor training programs based on athletes' specific needs, addressing weaknesses or technical deficiencies while maintaining overall skill development.

In speed training for team sports, the part method, whole method, and mixed method each offer unique advantages. Coaches should consider the specific requirements of their sport, individual athlete characteristics, and the desired training outcomes when selecting an appropriate method or a combination thereof. When constructing session designs it is important to consider the speed age of the athlete. This will dictate the amount of time spent in each method of coaching. Framework 2: learn load, execute encapsulates this well. The below image illustrates how you will shift emphasis on coaching methods as your athlete increases competency.

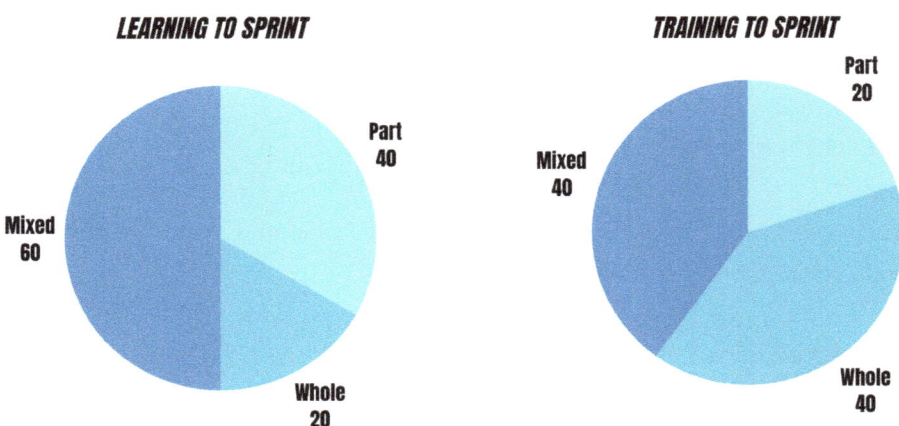

A well-designed training program that incorporates elements of all three methods can effectively enhance speed skills, promote motor learning, and contribute to improved performance on the field or court.

The Law of Accommodation

The Law of Accommodation states that the human body adapts to a specific training stimulus over time, leading to a reduced response and diminishing returns. Understanding this law and its relevance to exercise classification is crucial in optimising speed training and achieving performance goals.

The Law of Accommodation emphasises the importance of varying training stimuli to continually challenge the body and prevent the accommodation effect. In the context of speed training, this principle plays a vital role in designing progressive and effective training programs. There are 4 main areas to consider when applying the law of accommodation to speed training.

1. Avoiding Plateaus: The Law of Accommodation highlights the necessity of regularly modifying training variables in speed training to prevent performance plateaus. Athletes who continuously perform the same training routines without variation are more likely to experience a diminished training response over time. By incorporating diverse training methods, intensities, volumes, and rest intervals, coaches can stimulate ongoing adaptations and optimise speed gains.

2. Periodisation: The Law of Accommodation aligns with the concept of periodisation, which involves planned variations in training stimuli to elicit specific adaptations during different training phases. In speed training, periodisation allows athletes to experience different intensities, distances, and sprinting techniques throughout the training cycle. This strategic approach helps athletes avoid accommodation and facilitates continuous progress.

3. Exercise Selection and Variation: Exercise classification plays a crucial role in speed training by providing a framework for selecting and varying training exercises. By employing a variety of sprinting drills, resistance training exercises, plyometrics, and agility drills, coaches can target different physiological systems, movement patterns, and energy systems. This diversity of exercises helps counter the accommodation effect, keeping athletes engaged and continually challenging their bodies.

4. Progressive Overload: The Law of Accommodation reinforces the importance of progressive overload in speed training. To elicit ongoing adaptations, athletes must gradually increase training volume, intensity, or complexity over time. By progressively challenging the body with incremental changes, athletes can continue to stimulate improvements in speed, power, and acceleration.

5. Progessing in Specilisation: One often overlooked factor when applying the law of accomodation to training is the desire to achevie it. When trying to realise a new level of performance athletes must accomodate to a new level of training in order to create and utlise more specific training means. We often are faced with reluctance to remove barbell loading in team sports through fear of maladaptation where if we have applied to law of accomdation correctly and introduced more specific means the stimulus provided by those traditional movements will not create the adaptation we need. We must accommodate to training to ascend the level of specificity.

The Law of Accommodation serves as a guiding principle in exercise classification and speed training. Coaches and trainers must recognize the body's tendency to adapt, and adjust training variables to maintain continual progress. By incorporating periodisation, exercise variation, and progressive overload, coaches can design effective training programs that optimise speed gains and enhance overall performance. Understanding and applying the Law of Accommodation empowers athletes to continually push their limits, achieve new milestones, and unlock their full speed potential.

SAID Principle

The SAID (Specific Adaptations to Imposed Demands) principle underscores the notion that the human body adapts specifically to the demands placed upon it during training. Understanding this principle and its relevance to speed training and exercise classification is essential for designing targeted and effective training programs.

The SAID principle guides the process of exercise classification by emphasising the importance of tailoring exercises to elicit specific adaptations. By selecting exercises that closely mimic the demands of the desired skill or performance outcome, athletes can maximise their training potential. There are four main areas to consider when applying SAID principle to speed training and how it is used in the Sports Speed System.

1. Specificity of Training: The SAID principle highlights the importance of specificity in speed training. To improve speed, athletes must engage in exercises and drills that directly target the specific aspects of sprinting, such as acceleration, top speed, agility, and technique. By designing training programs that closely resemble the movement patterns and energy systems involved in sprinting, athletes can enhance their speed-related adaptations.

2. Exercise Selection: Exercise classification based on the SAID principle helps coaches select appropriate exercises for speed training. By identifying exercises that mimic the neuromuscular demands of sprinting, such as resisted sprints, plyometrics, and sprint-specific drills, coaches can create training programs that elicit the desired adaptations. This approach ensures that athletes are exposed to training stimuli that directly translate to improved speed performance.

3. Progressive Overload: The SAID principle emphasises the need for progressive overload in speed training. Athletes must gradually increase the demands placed on their bodies to continually challenge and stimulate adaptations. By incrementally increasing training volume, intensity, or complexity over time, coaches can ensure that athletes experience a progressive overload, leading to improved speed capabilities.

4. Skill Acquisition: The SAID principle extends to skill acquisition in speed training. Athletes must practise and refine the specific skills required for sprinting, such as proper sprinting technique, body positioning, and coordination. By incorporating skill-focused drills and exercises into training sessions, coaches can help athletes develop the necessary motor patterns and neuromuscular control, leading to improved speed performance.

The SAID principle is a foundational concept in exercise classification and speed training. By aligning training exercises and modalities with the specific demands of speed-related movements, coaches can optimise the adaptations and improvements in speed performance. By focusing on specificity, exercise selection, progressive overload, and skill acquisition, athletes can develop the necessary physiological and technical foundations to excel in sprinting and enhance their overall speed capabilities. Understanding and applying the SAID principle empowers coaches and athletes to design targeted and effective speed training programs that yield desired results.

Exercise Classification for Team Sports Speed Training: Bridging the Practical Gaps

When it comes to speed training in team sports, a comprehensive exercise classification model is essential to bridge the practical gaps and optimise performance. By categorising exercises based on their specific objectives and qualities, coaches can design effective training programs that enhance speed, agility, and overall athletic performance. Let's delve into the exercise classification model and explore its practical application.

Exercise Classification Model:

To serve as a reminder, the exercise classification model for team sports speed training involves a hierarchical approach, starting from competition exercises and working backwards through specialised developmental exercises and general preparatory exercises. Each category serves a unique purpose and contributes to the athlete's speed development journey.

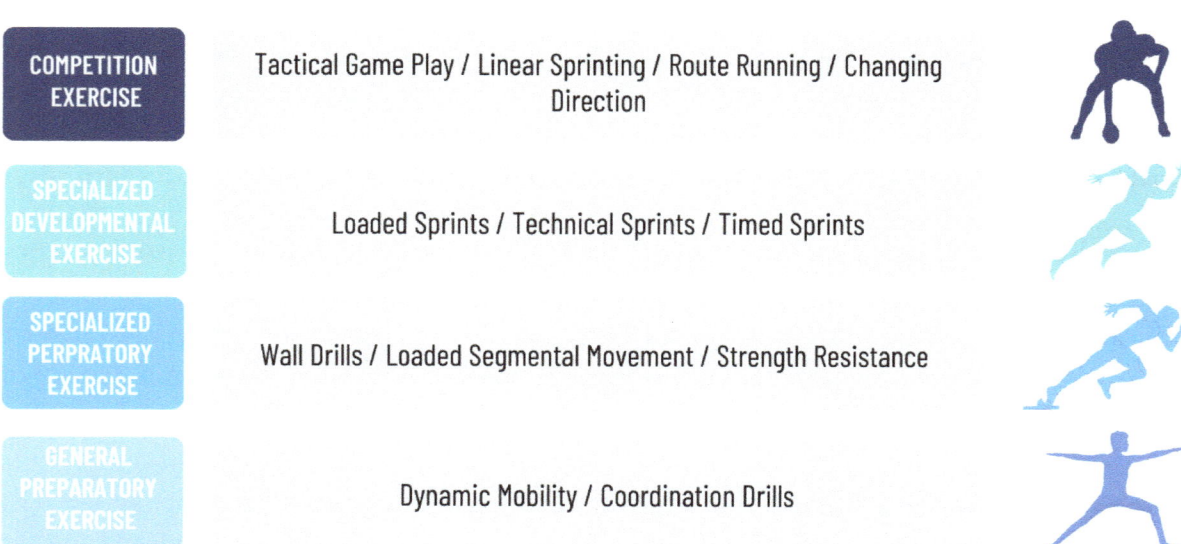

1. Competition Exercises:

At the top of the classification model are competition exercises. These exercises mimic the demands of actual gameplay, focusing on tactical awareness, decision-making, and executing skills at maximum velocity. Examples include game simulations, sport-specific drills, linear sprinting, and route running. Competition exercises replicate the real-world scenarios athletes face during matches, enhancing their ability to perform under game-specific conditions.

2. Specialised Developmental Exercises:

Specialised developmental exercises form the next tier in the exercise classification model. These exercises target specific aspects of speed development, such as loaded sprints (running with additional resistance), technical sprints (running with an emphasis on technique over speed), and timed sprints (sprinting to attain a certain time). They provide a progressive overload to challenge the neuromuscular system and enhance speed, acceleration, and power.

3. Specialised Preparatory Exercises:

Moving further down the classification model, specialised preparatory exercises focus on developing the foundational qualities necessary for speed. This category includes various drills that improve body links, dynamic mobility, coordination, and strength. Body links exercises promote efficient movement patterns, while dynamic mobility drills enhance flexibility, joint mobility, and coordination. Strength exercises target specific muscle groups and movements related to speed performance.

4. General Preparatory Exercises:

The base of the exercise classification model comprises general preparatory exercises. These exercises serve as the foundation for speed training, emphasising dynamic mobility, coordination drills, and general conditioning. They improve overall athleticism, movement quality, and physical preparedness. Examples include running drills, plyometrics, agility ladder drills, and general strength training.

Practical Considerations:

When applying the exercise classification model, coaches must consider several practical aspects:

1. **Technical Capacity:** Exercises should align with the athlete's technical abilities and ensure proper execution of movement patterns. Technically complex exercises need to be chosen judiciously when coaching large groups.
2. **Velocity:** Exercises should be classified based on the velocity or intent at which they are performed, whether it's maximum velocity, submaximal, or acceleration-focused.
3. **Repeatability:** Assessing how repeatable an exercise is for an athlete is crucial for progressive training and building depth of speed capacity.

4. **Reverse periodisation:** Reverse periodisation, a valuable preparatory tool, involves focusing on power development before building capacity. Coaches should incorporate this concept strategically into their training plans.

Applying exercise classification to the development of speed isn't as complex as you may think. Exercise classification is a powerful framework for structuring speed training in team sports. By understanding the hierarchy of exercises, you can design targeted programs that address specific aspects of speed development, from competition exercises to specialised developmental and preparatory exercises. This approach allows athletes to progress systematically, improve technical capacity, and enhance their ability to perform at maximum velocity during competitive situations.

Layering the Force-Velocity Curve to Build Sprint Training Programs

The force velocity curve is incredibly important to sprinting and needs to be considered within programming. By understanding the relationship between force and velocity and considering the complexity of movements, coaches can create structured programs that lead to desired results. Let's explore how this concept can be applied to sprint training.

The Force-Velocity Curve

When examining the force-velocity curve from a sprinting perspective, it becomes clear that different types of exercises should be incorporated to target specific aspects of sprint performance. Starting with walk variations or heavy resisted walks focuses on building force production and overcoming resistance. Progressing along the curve, projection patterns and exercises that enhance the ability to drive and overcome gravitational forces come into play. Finally, sprinting itself emphasises maximum velocity and execution of complex movement, therefore the inherent understanding is that the higher the velocity of movement the more complex it becomes.

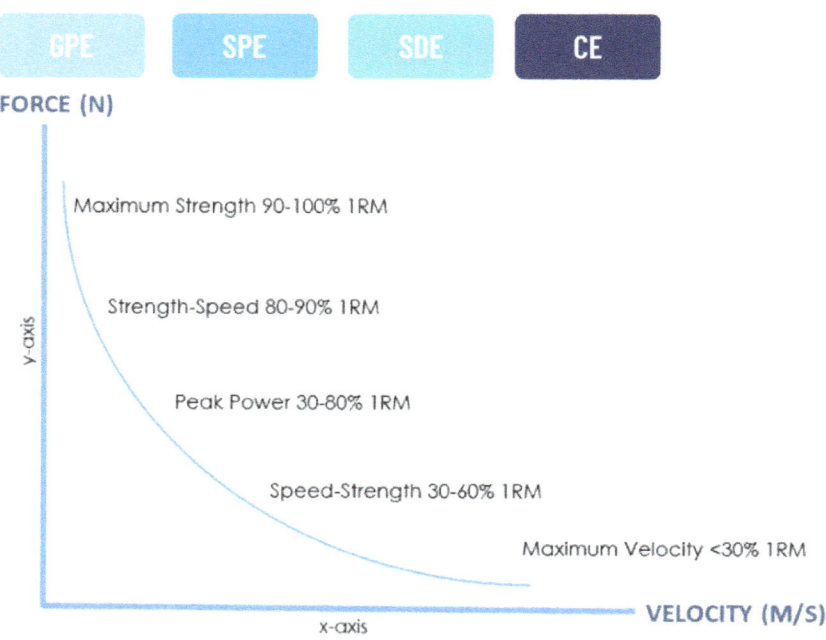

The image below illustrates the coachability of the general speed exercises. It is important to understand as a coach where the most impact can be had. As speed increases within speed classification it becomes harder and almost impossible to directly influence the movement via concurrent coaching or modelling. This is where other elements of skill acquisition become more important.

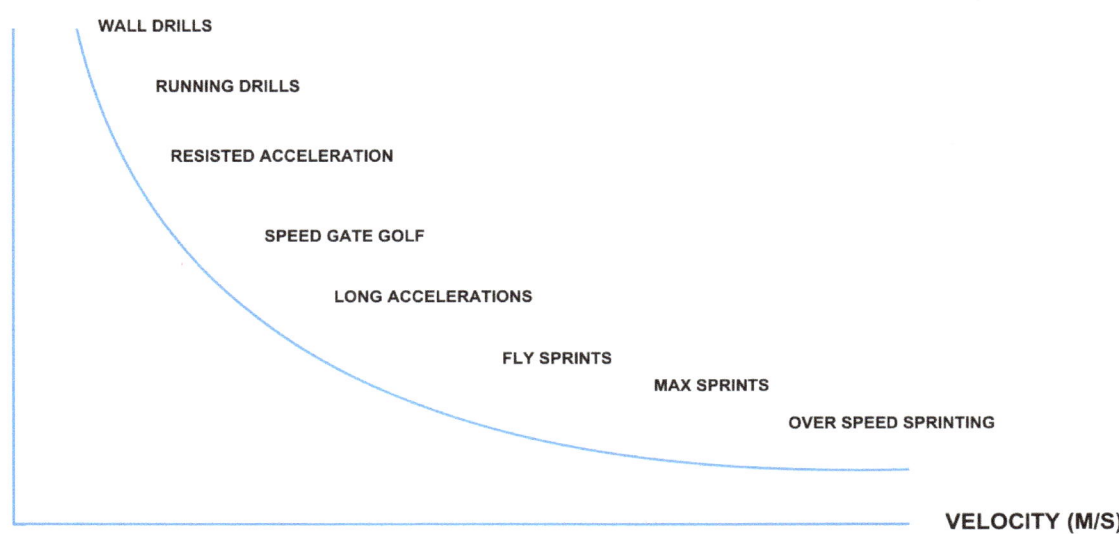

Creating Continuity:

As athletes progress through the different stages of the force-velocity curve, the goal is to establish continuity and a seamless transition within the training program. Linking exercises and progressively increasing the demands placed on athletes helps them adapt and improve. Pictured in the graph below is how we can view the relationship between technique of movement, velocity and their place within the exercise classification model. This allows us as coaches to emphasise and complement certain training means at the correct point in the training cycle. In turn this creates continuity within our exercise progressions and our intensity.

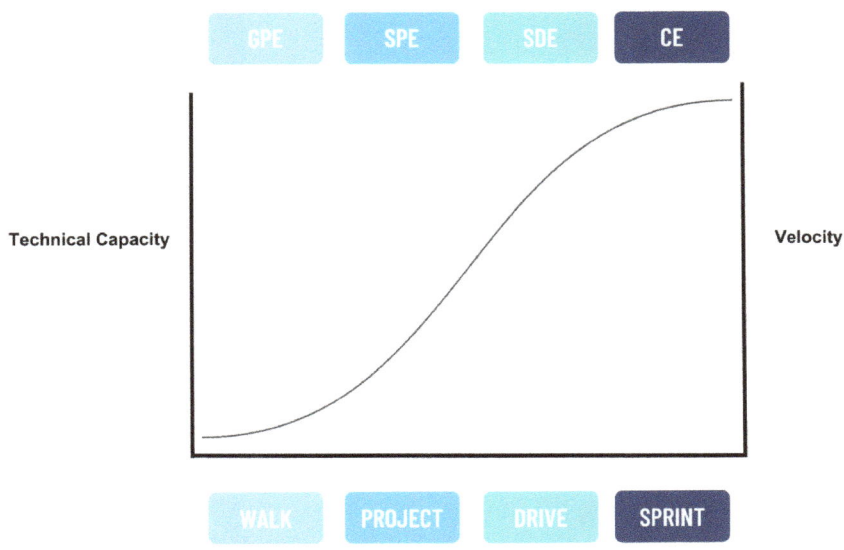

This continuity ensures that the program effectively bridges the gap between force production and velocity development, leading to enhanced sprint performance. The x axis of the modified graph demonstrates how different versions of locomotion connect. When we for example rush from walk to sprint the athletes suffer due to the massive change of intensity and complexity. That is why we must consider this relationship carefully when creating classification.

Layering Exercise Classification and Dynamic Correspondence:

To further optimise sprint training programs, coaches should integrate the five factors of dynamic correspondence into their exercise classification. This combination allows for a comprehensive evaluation and categorisation of exercises based on their specific objectives and impacts on performance. By ranking and ordering training exercises, coaches can create a structured and targeted approach that aligns with the principles of dynamic correspondence.

Achieving Dynamic Correspondence:

In sprint training, achieving dynamic correspondence means designing and implementing exercises that directly correlate with the specific demands of competitive sprinting. By focusing on key movements and addressing the criteria of dynamic correspondence, coaches ensure that athletes are prepared for the challenges they will face during competition. Dynamic correspondence is achieved through the sequential chaining of appropriate specialised exercises

DYNAMIC CORREPSONDANCE	GPE	SPE	SDE	CE
Amplitude and direction of movement	↑	↑	↑	↑
Regime of Muscular Work	DYNAMIC MOVMENT	WALL DRILLS	↑	↑
Accentuated Region of Force Production			LOADED AND CONTEXTUAL SPRINTING	↑
Rate of and time of Maximum Force Production				↑
Dynamics Of Effort				SPRINTING

Utilising the force-velocity curve as a foundation for building sprint training programs offers a structured and effective approach to enhancing speed and performance. This does not mean that athletes are excluded from running at certain speeds or using certain exercise classifications, but it helps to guide where the bulk of the programming needs to be. By progressing through various exercise categories aligned with the curve, athletes develop the necessary force production and velocity capabilities required for sprinting. Incorporating exercise classification and the principles of dynamic correspondence further enhances the training process, ensuring that athletes are adequately prepared for competitive situations.

Utilising Exercise Classification and Strength Types in Speed Training Programs

When designing a speed training program, it is crucial to consider exercise classification and its relevance to specific movements and performance goals. By categorising exercises based on their purpose and impact, coaches can ensure that each exercise serves a specific function within the training program. Understanding the different strength types involved in speed development further enhances exercise selection and training specificity.

1. Starting Strength:

Starting strength refers to the maximum amount of force an individual can exert at the beginning of a contraction. Traditionally these are seen only in the context of weight room exercises such as pin squats. However, our ability to overcome our own body mass as fast as possible allows us to utilise our own mass to build starting strength. Exercises that enhance starting strength include one-step projections, kneeling starts, block starts, and wall drives. These exercises focus on developing explosive power from a static position, making them ideal for improving acceleration and initial bursts. All of these movements are concentric only, with no eccentric phase preceding the contraction. As such, the body is forced to generate force and rapidly activate motor units without help from the stretch shortening cycle.

2. Speed Strength:

Speed strength involves the ability to exert maximal force during high-speed movements. Exercises that target speed strength include resisted drives and power speed drills such as A skips, high knees, egg crackers etc. These exercises aim to improve force production and transfer of strength into rapid movement, particularly during the acceleration phase.

3. Reactive Strength:

Reactive strength is the ability to overcome momentum via eccentric muscle action and convert it to concentric force. It plays a vital role in quick and efficient force production during sprinting. Exercises such as high-speed bounding, reactive strength drills, and leg frequency work focus on developing reactive strength and optimising leg turnover. Examples of these can be found in the appendix.

4. Special Strength:

Special strength exercises are designed to address specific weaknesses or technical aspects of an athlete's sprinting mechanics. They target isolated muscle actions and movements, helping to improve hip integrity, muscle coordination, and overall sprinting performance. Examples of special strength exercises include wall drill variations and isolated muscle actions.

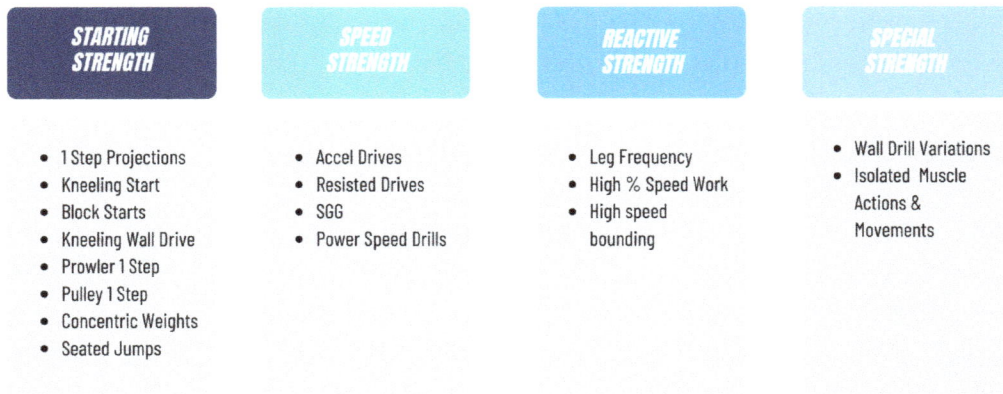

Organising the Training Program:

Once exercises are classified and strength types are identified, organising the training program becomes essential. Coaches must define a clear path for progression and ensure exercises are aligned with the desired outcomes. Consider whether an exercise aims to create biomotor output such as speed, power, strength or improve motor learning specificity for example deliberately refining the skill of a specific action related to sprinting. This principle of specificity helps create a focused and purposeful training program.

Exercise classification and strength types play a crucial role in the development of effective speed training programs. By categorising exercises and targeting specific areas of strength, coaches can create structured and progressive training programs that lead to improved sprint performance. Understanding the purpose and impact of each exercise allows coaches to maximise the benefits of training while focusing on the individual needs of athletes. With a well-organised training program that incorporates exercise classification and strength types, athletes can reach their full speed potential and achieve their performance goals.

Organising Speed Training: Defining Progression within Exercise Qualification

In this section we are going to delve into the importance of defining a progression plan and exercise qualification, highlighting the significance of specificity in motor learning and bio motor output. By understanding where each exercise fits and its purpose, coaches can optimise training programs and achieve desired outcomes.

Defining Progression and Exercise Qualification:

Exercise qualification refers to the suitability of an exercise or training modality to create stress and adaptation to an athlete. To develop a well-structured speed training program, coaches must establish a clear path for progression. This progression plan is closely linked with the principles of programming, emphasising the need for specificity in training. By determining the purpose of each exercise, coaches can align them with either bio motor output or motor learning specificity. This understanding forms the basis for organising the training program effectively.

Exercise Qualification and Placement:

Proper exercise qualification is crucial in ensuring that exercises are suitable for athletes at different stages of training. As athletes progress and their qualification improves, exercises need to be tailored to their specific needs. The reason for this is something known as the dose-load response. Utilising the fundamental principle of training known as progressive overload, it is important to strive for the least amount of training stimulus that robustly improves performance. When an athlete is in the Learn to Sprint phases of training every part of speed training will possess a high stress load, as opposed to when that athlete progresses into the Training to Sprint phases, the original exercises will not have as much effect on them. For instance, static wall holds can serve as motor learning activities for beginners, gradually transitioning into physical development exercises for conditioning and hip speed enhancement. Similarly, exercises such as resisted sled marches and sprinting occupy different positions on the qualification continuum, offering distinct benefits. Sled marches offer a high load exercise with moderate stability which allows an athlete to increase specific force and power with an opportunity to refine motor learning. Sprinting creates high velocity load that is the most specific task to improve speed, challenging the athlete to the highest level.

The Relative Proportion of Total Motor Units:

An important aspect of exercise qualification lies in understanding the relative proportion of total motor units involved in different training activities. This knowledge helps coaches identify the appropriate placement of exercises within the training program. By considering the total motor units involved in sprinting activities, coaches can determine where exercises like isometrics and supplementary lifts should be incorporated. This is hypothesised based on the nature in which these actions are performed and based upon Size Principle. Size principle is a fundamental concept in motor unit recruitment, guides how our bodies utilise muscle fibres during exercise which is discussed to create detail in the next chapter.

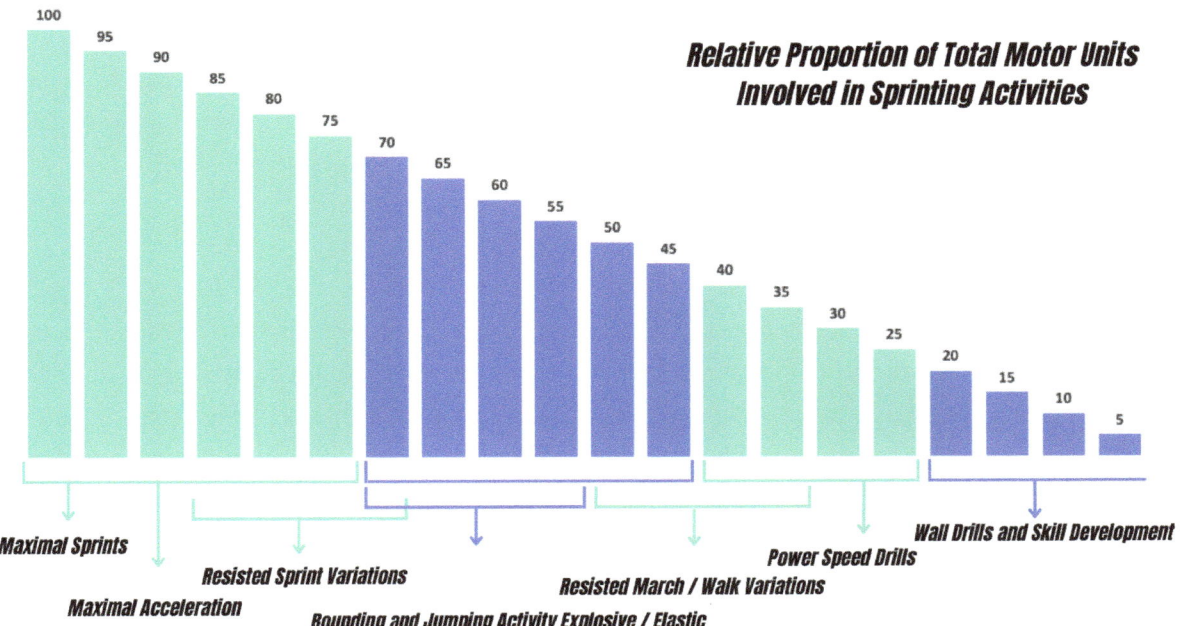

Strategic Exercise Placement:

Coaches must strategically place exercises to optimise training and adaptability. The placement of exercises depends on the athlete's qualification level and the desired training outcomes. It is crucial to strike a balance between exercises that target specific aspects of strength and power, such as resisted sprints or bounding and jumping activities. This is because they are training similar qualities (explosive strength), therefore it is important to prioritise the most specific elements of training.

Defining a path for progression and exercise qualification is key to organising an efficient speed training program. Coaches must carefully consider the purpose and impact of each exercise, ensuring alignment with the desired outcomes of motor learning specificity and bio motor output. By strategically placing exercises and understanding the relative proportion of total motor units involved, coaches can optimise training programs to maximise progress and enhance sprinting performance. With a well-organised and tailored training program, athletes can achieve their full potential in speed development.

The Thought Process of Speed Training: From Problem Solving to Execution

In the realm of speed training, it is essential for coaches to have a well-defined thought process that guides their training decisions. This section explores the series of questions and considerations coaches should go through when organising speed training programs. From understanding the problem they aim to solve to exercise qualification and progression, this systematic approach helps coaches optimise training outcomes and improve athlete performance.

Identifying the Problem:

Coaches begin by asking themselves fundamental questions to identify the problem at hand. They ponder whether the athlete is learning to sprint, training to sprint, sprinting to compete, or sprinting to win. By categorising the purpose (how we use an exercise) and objective (what we want it to achieve), coaches gain valuable insights such as athletes qualification, biomotor and motor skill competency into the athlete's developmental stage and training focus.

Exercise Intensity and Adaptive Reserves:

After determining the problem, coaches consider the appropriate exercise intensity and adaptive reserves for the athlete. At this point it is important to define the term adaptive reserve as it is not commonly used or considered. Adaptive reserve is the resource or capacity set aside for an athlete to make change. When we progress specificity of training we must invert volume and intensity to ensure we maintain the health of our athletes. For example performing 3 x 50m long accelerations creates an adaptive reserve for 3 x 30m acceleration. In this example we have reduced the total volume of work and increased the intensity of the training. This also involves assessing the athlete's prior experience and capabilities. For beginners in learning to sprint, low physical intensity and high cognitive learning drills are suitable, with adaptive reserves being relatively low. This doesn't mean that the athletes training at this point is deemed as "low output", this is purely relative to repeated maximal speed sprinting. When the specialised exercises are performed appropriately they are very taxing and require lots of intent. Furthermore as an athlete progresses through the speed ages and increases specificity of training, their inherent ability to tolerate higher training intensities and volumes increase. Thus increasing the qualification and adaptive reserve. This is a by-product of appropriate long term training.

General Speed

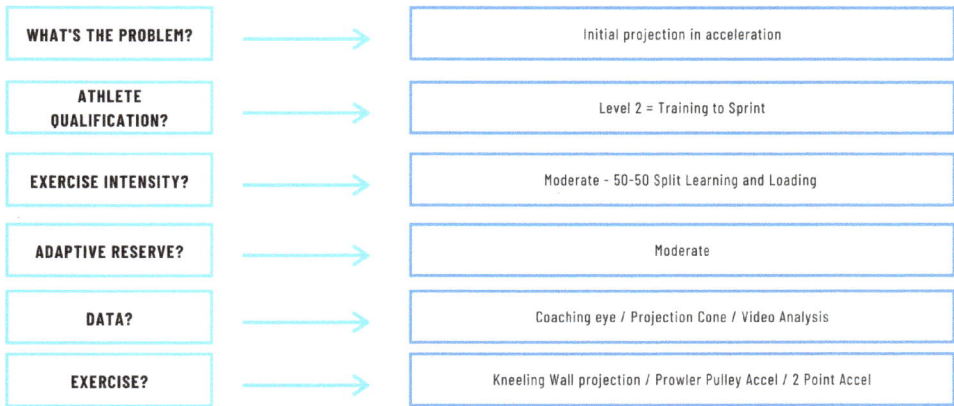

Exercise Selection and Measurement:

Coaches then select exercises that align with the athlete's level and specific needs. For example, in learning to sprint, exercises like bilateral wall projection and prowler pulley are suitable. Coaches measure progress using simple yet effective tools like broad jump distances, bound distances or sled loads used, providing tangible feedback on the athlete's development. This allows coaches to track improvements and project future performance levels. When considering exercise selection please adhere to the laws of specificity. You will see how this is utilised within the sample programs provided in the appendix and error correction cheat sheet.

The Drill Buckets Approach:

Categorising athletes into "drill buckets" based on their characteristics and needs proves valuable, particularly when working with diverse groups or team sports. By understanding these buckets, coaches can structure their training programs to include appropriate drills that address specific requirements. The drill buckets approach ensures that athletes receive targeted training to enhance their performance in their respective positions. As a reminder we centre our focus around here on Speed Age. This becomes the reference point as to where we focus our classification from. This table below illustrates some of the things to look for when identifying speed age and when to progress into later stages.

Speed Age	Entry KPI	Exit KPI	Means of Training
Learn to Sprint	0-2 years of Sports Speed Training	Rate of Progress stagnates	Heavy resisted sleds, highly stable training. Technical Sprinting
Train to Sprint	2-4 years of Sports Speed Training		Light resistance, moderate stability training.
Sprint to Compete	4-6 Years of Sports Speed Training	No exit criteria - this is 90+% of potential is exhausted and performance optimisation is the priority.	Max Speed, Overspeed Sprinting variations
Sprint to Win			

When you consider this table for application please understand that The Sports Speed System is not a "track sprint system" it is a system for the development of the team sport sprinter. With that in mind please understand that 90% of the high velocity and high effort sprinting is done in sport practice and games.

Applying the Learn-Load-Execute Process:

Coaches leverage the learn-load-execute process, adapting it to each athlete's progression level. As athletes advance from level one to level four, the focus shifts from stable movements to more specific and force-dominant exercises. This is where framework 4, stable to unstable, plays a crucial role (see image below for a refresher).

Stable		Stable - Unstable		Unstable - Stable			Unstable	
Segmented	Connected Movement	Segmented	Connected Movement	Hand Supported	Hand Supported Hip Resisted	Hip Resisted	Sprinting	Overspeed Sprinting
Ankle / Knee / Hip Emphasis	Full Range Joint or Multi Joint Action	Single Leg Ankle Flexion Extension	Single Exchange Pattern	Prowler March	Prowler March with Hip Resistance	Resisted Sled March	Long Acceleration	Assisted Max Speed
Overcoming Isometrics	Unilateral Load and Smash	Single Leg Hip Flexion Extension	Kneeling Wall Shoot	One Step Push	Prowler Prance with Hip Resistance	Resisted Sled Prance	Fly Sprints	Assisted Drills

If progressed properly and as described the subsequent exercise modalities compound to support the next. Here we are constantly switching between the transfer of motor control and biomotor development. Therefore in one cycle an ankle isometric drill will be prioritised as a learning drill will then be sequenced out and replaced by a more complex movement. This process, allows athletes to learn, load, and execute speed in a comprehensive manner. The image below outlines this process and shows visual representation of how we can also utilise the drill stacking framework.

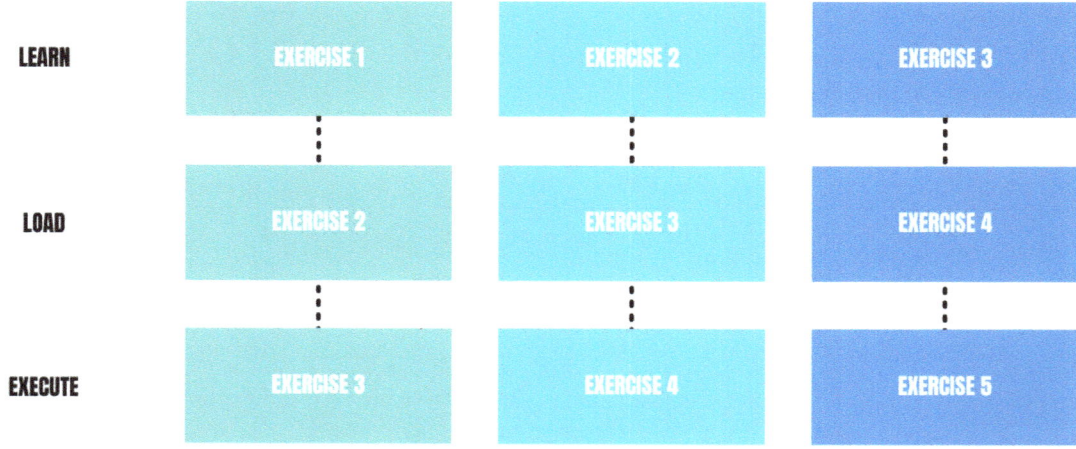

Order	Experience Level / Speed Age	Learn	Load	Execute
LEVEL 1	Novice to speed training / Learning to Sprint	Fixed Wall Drills / Segmented Movement/ Stable Movement	Slow	Speed Gate Golf Level 1 / Long Accelerations
LEVEL 2	Late Learning to Sprint Phases	Wall Drills Segmented Movement / Connected Movement / Stable - Unstable-Stable	Slow High Force	Speed Gate Golf Level 2 / Long Accelerations
LEVEL 3	Initial Training to Sprint Phases	Gait Drills Connected Movement / Unstable Stable	Fast Low Force	Task Specific Training - Sprinting to Load
LEVEL 4	Advanced Training to Sprint	Gait Drills Connected Movement / Unstable	Fast High Force	Task Specific Training - Sprinting to Load

Task specific training - loading the sprint based movements of the chosen sport.

Balancing Force Dominance and Supporting Strength:

When working with more advanced athletes, understanding an athlete's force dominance and force deficit is crucial for optimising their performance. Force dominance is knowing and understanding how an athlete prefers to express their force and the deficit of this force is how far away from optimal the force expression is. This is based upon ground reaction force in sprinting. Many athletes struggle to express force fast enough into the ground initially due to lack of specific speed training. Therefore these athletes will have a deficit in rate of force development. This can be seen still in some of the fastests team sport athletes in relation to elite sprinters. Optimal force application in sprinting is defined by the amount of force expressed that leads to positive changes in velocity during a ground contact. A mistake many coaches make is focussing too much on this advanced investigation when the athlete does not meet that level of qualification. The reality in most cases is that these athletes need more time to learn to sprint and naturally these force characteristics shift over time with the inclusion of specialised exercises as more specific training prepares the athletes for the desired attributes of sprint performance. If we look into the optimal ground contact times in acceleration and maximum velocity sprinting when you have an athlete who has progressed to a higher level of training to sprint and sprinting to compete you can take a deeper look at these characteristics to fine tune your athlete performances.

Optimal Ground Contact Times for Sprint and Movement Skills

Acceleration

- **Initial Acceleration Phase:**
- **Optimal Ground Contact Time (GCT):** Approximately 0.18 to 0.25 seconds.
- **Characteristics:** During the initial steps of acceleration, athletes need to generate significant force to overcome inertia. This requires longer ground contact times to produce the necessary force.

Maximum Velocity Sprinting

- **Maximum Velocity Phase:**
- **Optimal Ground Contact Time (GCT):** Approximately 0.08 to 0.12 seconds.

- **Characteristics:** At maximum velocity, the goal is to maintain high speeds with minimal ground contact time. Efficient and rapid leg turnover is crucial, with a focus on maintaining speed and minimising deceleration.

Research Support

- **Acceleration Phase:** Research by Weyand et al. (2000) demonstrates that higher ground reaction forces are necessary during initial acceleration, necessitating longer ground contact times.
- **Maximum Velocity Phase:** Studies by Clark and Weyand (2014) indicate that maintaining maximum velocity requires minimal ground contact time, efficient force production, and optimal running mechanics.

Change of Direction (COD)

- **Characteristics**: Change of direction involves a quick deceleration followed by an acceleration in a new direction. Optimal ground contact times in COD movements are typically longer than in straight-line sprinting due to the need to decelerate and then reaccelerate.
- **Optimal Ground Contact Time (GCT)**: Approximately 0.20 to 0.40 seconds.
- **Examples**: A football player making a quick cut to evade a defender or a basketball player performing a crossover dribble.

Agility Movements

- **Characteristics**: Agility involves rapid, precise movements often requiring a combination of speed, balance, and coordination. Ground contact times can vary widely depending on the specific agility drill.
- **Optimal Ground Contact Time (GCT)**: Approximately 0.15 to 0.35 seconds.
- **Examples**: An athlete performing ladder drills or shuttle runs where quick, multidirectional movements are essential.

Research Support

- **Change of Direction (COD):** Studies by Spiteri et al. (2013) demonstrate that effective COD performance is strongly related to an athlete's ability to decelerate and reaccelerate efficiently, highlighting the importance of optimal ground contact times.
- **Agility Movements:** Research by Young and Farrow (2006) indicates that agility performance is linked to the ability to execute rapid, coordinated movements with minimal ground contact time, underscoring the importance of quick, efficient footwork

By following a systematic thought process, coaches can design effective speed training programs that address specific problems and enhance athlete performance. From problem-solving to exercise qualification, intensity selection, and drill bucket categorisation, this approach ensures that athletes receive targeted and progressive training. With careful planning and execution, coaches can guide athletes towards achieving their speed development goals and maximising their potential.

A SYSTEMATIC APPROACH TO EXERCISE CLASSIFICATION OF SPEED

Exercise classification for speed is essential to the successful development of the team sport sprinter. Knowing and understanding how and where to place exercises, their intended outcome and stress on an athlete is of paramount importance to the training process. As we move into further discussion in this book, we will explore weight training and programming considerations. Here you will clearly be able to see the usefulness of exercise classification.

WEIGHT TRAINING FOR SPEED

In this chapter, we will provide you with a framework to enhance sprint performance by addressing the specificity gap between weight training and sprinting. By understanding the nature of physical development and optimising training methodologies, you can unlock the full potential of your athletes' speed capabilities.

"The ability to generate maximum strength and the ability to produce high speeds are different motor abilities, so that it is inappropriate to assume that development of great strength will necessarily enhance sporting speed."
- Supertraining

This phrase highlights the transformative effects of weight room work on speed. However, it's crucial to recognise that excessive weightlifting can hinder speed development. We need to bridge the gap between maximal effort weightlifting and sprinting to ensure weight room training enhances an athlete's ability to run fast. By the end of this chapter you will be able to construct weight training programs that intentionally develop speed.

The Role of Strength Training and Transfer

Our focus lies in supporting and nurturing the growth of speed. To what extent does strength truly matter? The answer is nuanced. Strength is crucial, but only as long as it serves its purpose. If an athlete has a low training age when we introduce strength training there will be rapid initial adaptation to that exercise. They will improve their strength within that exercise. This strength will then create some positive transfer to sprint ability. Over time as that strength increases, within the squat for example, there is an inherent decline in transfer to sprint ability. Taking the athlete from squatting 80kg to 120kg might make them much faster. Taking them from 120kg to 160kg might not noticeably change their speed at all. Taking them from 160kg to 170kg might well make them slower. This is because the adaptations that have been created are more specific to squatting than sprinting. Initially just being able to produce more force was enough to improve sprinting ability, but after this, the other adaptations we make to squatting, such as changing nervous system firing patterns can outweigh the benefits of enhanced force production. At this point in training, we need to emphasise exercises with greater dynamic correspondence to sprinting. Therefore these traditional and conventional lifting movements become less useful and our programming and exercise selection should represent that. We must plot a well-defined path that aligns with the athlete's level and goals.

Maximising Training Efficiency:

The ultimate goal when working towards a specific speed target is to minimise the need for strength training as quickly as possible. General strength training can be time-consuming and divert attention and recovery resources away from speed development. By optimising your training program and aligning it with specific speed goals, you can free up valuable time for targeted speed training. Not to mention that speed training will improve an athlete's strength through the improvements of the nervous system.

Understanding the Specificity Gap:

To grasp the hierarchy of training needs and priorities, we must acknowledge the distinct roles of skill development, physical conditioning, and speed improvement. In the context of sports preparation our primary role is to develop the skills of the sport then secondary to that is the role of developing the physical qualities to perform those skills. Here I must remind you that speed and strength are different motor abilities but they both rely on similar underlying abilities. This is where many coaches make the mistake of utilising strength exercises for too long as covered in the discussion on adaptation. The goal of physical development work is to ensure we enhance the speed and repeatability of execution of the tasks presented by the sport.

Adaptations to Strength Training

In the book "Supertraining" by Yuri Verkhoshansky and Mel C. Siff, the structural and functional training effects refer to distinct physiological adaptations that occur in response to different types of training stimuli. Differentiating these as a coach is incredibly important when we want to consider the choice of training modality, as different modalities will have different structural and functional effects, specific to their demands.

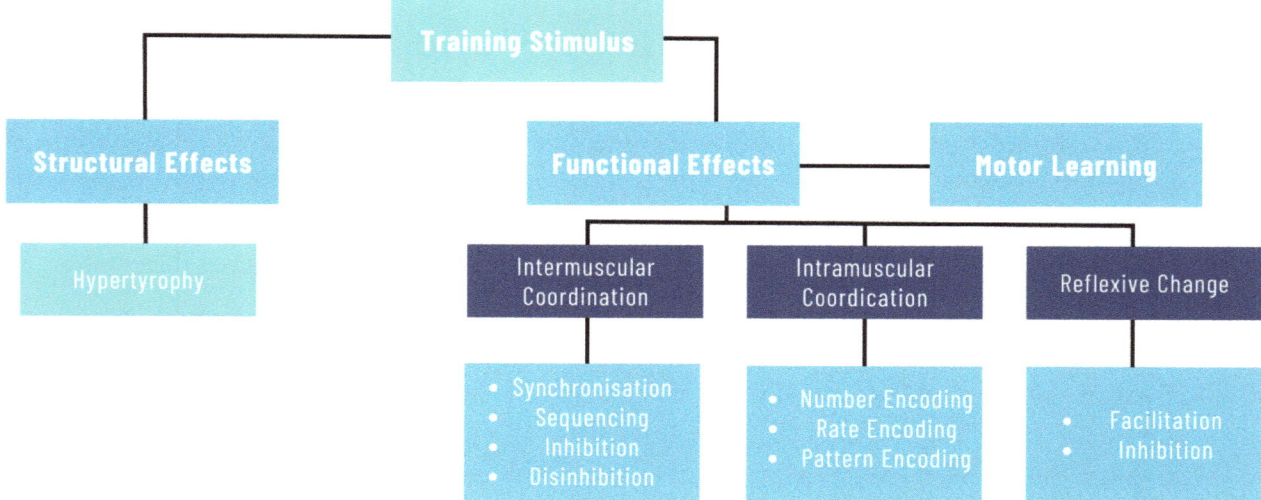

1. Structural Training Effects:

- Structural training effects primarily involve changes in the anatomical structures of the body, such as muscles, bones, tendons, and ligaments.
- These adaptations often result from resistance training, including exercises with weights or other forms of resistance, which stimulate muscle hypertrophy (growth) and increase bone density.
- Examples of structural training effects include increases in muscle cross-sectional area, tendon stiffness, bone mineral density, and connective tissue strength.
- These adaptations are crucial for athletic performance and injury prevention.

2. Functional Training Effects:

- Functional training effects pertain to improvements in the neuromuscular system's efficiency and coordination, leading to enhanced athletic performance.
- Unlike structural adaptations, which involve changes in the physical structures of the body, functional adaptations primarily involve neural adaptations and coordination patterns.
- Functional training focuses on developing movement patterns, motor skills, balance, agility, and proprioception, all of which contribute to athletic proficiency and movement efficiency.
- Examples of functional training effects include increased motor unit recruitment, improved intermuscular coordination, enhanced rate of force development, and improved movement biomechanics.
- Functional adaptations are crucial for translating increases in muscle size and strength into practical improvements in athletic performance, such as speed, power, agility, and skill execution.

As you can see it is important to understand the role of the strength training you are doing and the adaptations you are trying to create. These examples show when we might choose to target these different training effects. These examples are isolated for clarity, any given exercise will have some level of both structural and functional effects.

Training Effect	Weakness	Targeted Adaptation	Exercise
Structural	Poorly Developed Hamstring	Increase cross sectional area of the hamstring	Lying Hamstring Curls
Functional Intermuscular coordination	Inability to perform wall drills correctly	Increase coordination of movement	Tempo Wall Drills
Functional Intramuscular coordination	Slow speed of movement	Increase starting and explosive strength	Kneeling Wall Shoots

When writing strength training programs in accordance with speed development for the purpose of sport performance it is imperative that you do not lose sight of the context which you are developing strength within. Make sure it continually supports the overall goal of speed improvement. Even if that means not performing strength training.

Consideration of Size Principle and Intent When Programming Weight for Speed Development

Two crucial aspects to focus on are the Size Principle and intent in weight training programming for speed development. By understanding and incorporating these principles into training protocols, coaches and athletes can optimise their efforts to achieve superior speed gains. In this chapter, we delve into the significance of the Size Principle and intent when programming weight for speed development.

The Size Principle:

The Size Principle, a fundamental concept in motor unit recruitment, guides how our bodies utilise muscle fibres during exercise. According to this principle, under load, the body recruits muscle fibres from smallest to largest, choosing the smallest fibres necessary to perform a task. It begins with the small, slow-twitch fibres before engaging the large, fast-twitch fibres. By understanding the Size Principle, coaches can design training programs that systematically activate the desired muscle fibres, leading to improved speed performance. However when we manipulate the intent of the movement we are able to activate fast-twitch muscle fibres much earlier in the contractile process. The best example of this is for maximum velocity running in this exercise we want as many fast twitch fibres as possible activated as quickly and as often as possible, and ideally to selectively not recruit slow twitch fibres. This is a stimuli that forces selective activation of fast twitch fibres unlike conventional training activities.

Intent in Weight Training Programming:

Intent refers to the level of effort and focus put into each movement during weight training. By increasing the intent of movement, athletes can enhance neuromuscular activation, thereby recruiting the higher threshold motor units responsible for generating explosive power and speed. This can be achieved through modalities such as plyometrics, sprinting, and specific weightlifting movements that emphasise speed and explosiveness. Competition is also a great way to maintain intent with athletes. Facilitating an environment that fosters healthy competition makes a huge difference to intent. This is where we are able to create competition within training to heighten the nervous system and drive more powerful contraction.

Strategic Programming and Weight training optimisation for Speed Development:

When programming weight training for speed development, it is important to strike a balance between strength development and speed-specific adaptations. This is where exercise classification comes into its own. As discussed in the previous chapter we have General, Specific and Special exercises that help us to create a clear path of training to maximise positive transfer at all levels of athlete. Within those classifications there are some key considerations:

1. Progressive Overload: Gradually increasing the training stimulus over time is crucial for continuous progress. Athletes should aim to challenge themselves with incremental increases in weight to stimulate adaptations in both strength and speed. In the early stages of an athlete's training these incremental increases should be determined by the coach and not selected by the athletes.

2. Specificity: To enhance speed, the weight programming should align with the specific demands of the sport or activity. This is where we start to emphasise more ballistic movements and explosive movements, such as Olympic lifts, jump squats, or medicine ball throws, with greater dynamic correspondence to speed-related actions.

3. Periodisation: Implementing periodisation techniques, such as incorporating phases of high-intensity and low-intensity training, can help prevent plateaus and optimise performance gains. Periodisation enhances fatigue management, and will allow weight training to complement speed training, rather than competing with it.

4. Individualisation: Recognise that athletes have varying levels of strength and speed development. Tailor weight programming to suit individual needs, taking into account factors such as training age, current abilities, and injury history. Training can be individualised to as a best fit for the needs of a cohort as well as to fit an individual athlete

5. Monitoring and Adjusting: Regularly assess and track athletes' progress to ensure the weight programming remains effective. Adjustments can be made based on individual responses, performance outcomes, and feedback from athletes.

Complimentary Weight Room Programming for Speed

Developing speed is a crucial aspect of athletic performance, particularly for sprinters and athletes participating in sports that require quick bursts of acceleration. While track and field training focuses primarily on improving speed through specific running drills and workouts, complementary weight room programming can play a significant role in enhancing an athlete's speed development. This chapter explores the hierarchy of needs in speed development, the importance of stimulus rotation, and the progression of weight room exercises to support speed training.

Understanding Hierarchy of Needs

When designing a complementary program for speed development, it is essential to understand the hierarchy of needs. The primary focus should be on speed development itself, followed by technical and physical adjustments. Questions to consider include what technical changes are necessary, what physical adaptations are required, how much plyometric and jump training should be incorporated, and what ballistic training exercises should be utilised. It is also vital to recognise which qualities athletes will develop from playing their sport, and during sports practice, and which qualities need to be enhanced outside of sport practice. It's important to note that complementary programming doesn't have to be limited to the weight room but can extend to specialised exercises using various resistance methods. Consider these three broad categories.

1. Speed Development: The primary focus is on improving speed through technical and physical changes. Consider modifications in technique and the incorporation of plyometric, jump training, and ballistic exercises to enhance speed development. While these exercises are not confined to the weight room, specialised resistive variations can be utilised for maximum effectiveness.

2. **Strength Training:** Once speed development is addressed, strength training becomes supplementary. Prioritise accelerative strength over maximal strength to support and enhance speed development. Gradually progress through different strength training phases, including accelerative strength, maximal strength, and ballistic exercises.
3. **Energy System Development:** Recognize that effective aerobic metabolism underlies all aspects of training. Conditioning the energy system is crucial for overall performance. Design a program that encompasses aerobic and lactic tolerance work, adjusting the intensity and volume based on specific goals and percentages.

Modality	Specificity	Fatigue Cost	Rate of Transfer
Speed	High	High	Slow
Jump Training	Moderate / High	High / Moderate	Slow / Moderate
Ballistic Training	Moderate	Moderate	Moderate
Strength Training	Low / Moderate	Low / Moderate	Moderate / Fast
ESD	Low	Lo	Fast

The Rotation of Stimulus

Rotating stimulus is crucial for an effective speed development program. By carefully planning and rotating exercises, athletes can maximise their training adaptations. Strength training is an integral part of the program, with a focus on accelerative strength during the initial phase. As the program progresses, a rotation occurs, incorporating maximal strength, ballistic exercises, intensive jumps, and extensive jumps. The goal is to emphasise speed while gradually tapering off on plyometric and jump variations over time, to integrate intensive speed work effectively.

	PRE-SEASON PHASE			COMPETITION PHASE
	ACCUMULATION	*INTENSIFICATION*	*REALISATION*	*IN-SEASON 1*
SPEED	ACCELERATION, TEMPO + CHANGE OF DIRECTION	LONG ACCELERATION, TEMPOS + CHANGE OF DIRECTION	FLY 10'S + REACTIVE CHANGE OF DIRECTION	MINIMAL DOSE - OBSERVE EXPOSURE IN TEAM SPORT PRACTICE
PLYOMETRIC	EXTENSIVE	EXTENSIVE + INTENSIVE	INTENSIVE + EXTENSIVE	LOW DOSAGE - INTENSIVE
BALLISTICS	MED BALLS (STARTING STRENGTH) + GYM BASED (ACCELERATIVE STRENGTH)	MED BALLS (STARTING STRENGTH) + GYM BASED (STRENGTH -SPEED)	WEIGHTED JUMPS (STARTING STRENGTH)- GYM BASED (SPEED STRENGTH)	WEIGHTED JUMPS + GYM BASED (SPEED STRENGTH)
STRENGTH	ACCELERATIVE STRENGTH	ACCOMMODATIVE MAXIMAL STRENGTH	ACCOMMODATIVE ACCELERATIVE STRENGTH	STRENGTH SPEED

*Recommended training structure for a **training to sprint** athlete.*

Residual Training Effect and Adaptive Reserve

Understanding the residual training effect and adaptive reserve is essential for programming speed development. The accumulation phase, which focuses on building adaptive reserves, tissue quality, and motor learning, is followed by intensification phase which allows athletes to turn the fitness adaptations they've gained into sport-specific skills and realisation phases which allow athletes to peak those sport specific skills to establish a new level of training.

Accumulation Phase:

This phase focuses on building adaptive reserves, tissue quality, and motor learning. It emphasises foundational work, including hypertrophy, basic strength, and technical skills. Well-trained athletes can expect a net return 25 to 35 days after the initial accumulation phase has ended. As they have experienced this phase of training before the body we respond quickly adapting back to a previously trained state. Untrained individuals also experience significant improvements during this phase as their bodies will adapt very quickly to the motor learning aspect of training. As the training provides a novel stimulus the adaptation curve is much steeper than for the well trained individual.

Intensification Phase:

Following the accumulation phase, the intensification phase aims to increase the intensity of training. This phase is characterised by heavier loads, lower volumes, and a focus on developing maximal strength and power. The goal is to convert the foundational work done in the accumulation phase into higher levels of performance. To create optimal conversion in the context of speed training this is where we must remove load that "slows" down the body. All training must be fast and explosive. An easy example of this is that If we have been using heavy sled pushes in the accumulation phase we transition to very light sleds and focus on how fast we are moving as opposed to how heavy the load is. This will allow for the current accumulation of fatigue in the athletes to subside whilst stimulating higher levels of neuromuscular activity.

Realisation Phase:

The realisation phase, sometimes referred to as the peaking or competition phase, is designed to translate the gains from the previous phases into sport-specific performance. This phase of training is usually very short lasting no longer than 12-14 days. This phase includes high-intensity, sport-specific exercises with reduced volume to ensure athletes are at their peak for competition.

By rotating stimuli effectively through these phases, athletes can maintain freshness and build upon their previous training cycles, maximising their progress. This is an extremely overlooked part of training. Rotating stimuli allows us to avoid the law of accommodation as previously discussed. When the body is faced with a new stimulus, rapid progress can be achieved without high volumes and intensities. As the body begins to accommodate to the stimulus, higher volumes are needed to continue driving progress. This would be very fatiguing to the athlete, so instead we switch stimuli again. This allows the body to repeatedly benefit from the rapid adaptation to a new stimulus, and avoid paying the fatigue and staleness costs of staying with one stimulus for too long. This structured approach allows for systematic development and optimal performance when it matters most.

The Impact of Gym Programming on Speed

When training sprinters in the gym, it's crucial to consider athlete qualification, relevant metrics, and muscle-sling dynamics. Rather than fixating on specific barbell lifts, it is important to prioritise movements that engage muscles and aid movement through the use of slings. Avoiding exercises that only train one plane of movement and minimal access to rotation is vital. Understanding compensation patterns and their impact on acceleration properties is also essential. For example, a lower back-dominant squatting technique may hinder acceleration due to an imbalance between the lower back and glutes/hamstrings. By making programming adjustments based on athlete data and leading indicators, coaches can optimise gym programming to support speed development effectively.

Exercise Progressions and Specificity

Exercise progressions should be designed based on specificity, energy system demand, range of motion, and contractile ability. Specificity should not be ignored, as it plays a significant role in optimising training adaptations. Understanding the energy system demands of different applications of exercises, whether they emphasise hypertrophy, lactic tolerance, alactic capacity, or a lactic power, is crucial. The reason for this is that you might be spending too much time training for the wrong adaptations without knowing. For example, lots of gym programs use too much volume and inadequate rest for the neuromuscular adaptations we are aiming to make. A traditional prescription such as 4 sets of 8 repetitions with 60-90 seconds rest; leads to the excessive accumulation of lactate, and insufficient rest for the nervous system. Beyond this, too much fatigue occurs within each set due to the number of repetitions, meaning the body sends increasingly imperfect, and less forceful, activation patterns to the muscles as the set goes on. In the attempt to improve strength to therefore improve speed we find we must do the opposite. We need long rest periods to allow for neuromuscular system recovery, and we only want to train the body with good signals. This is a fundamental application of specificity.

Range of motion, whether full, partial, or specific, should also be considered in exercise progressions. As touched on in the previous chapter, transfer of training is largely dependent on creating specific forces in specific times at specific angles. Full range movements in the gym are advised in early stages of preparation, for the general strength and hypertrophy they create, as well as their positive influence on joint health, however as we progress training partial ranges become more appropriate. Partial ranges facilitate greater external load and force, and allow us to train at joint angles with much greater correspondence to speed. For example an athlete performing a half squat (to parallel) would be able to move the same load more quickly in a quarter squat. The weight room provides us with tools to support the development of speed, but we have to use them in a way that meets the specific needs of speed development.

Additionally, coaches should take into account the contractile ability and reflexive/reactive elements of training to develop a well-rounded program. Further to support the role of specificity in the training process, avoiding heavy grinding movements in favour of fast, bouncy and explosive movements will ensure that there is not a dampening of reactive ability. Many athletes who focus on strength too much end up lifting heavier weights but they become slow in the process as the type of strength required to lift massive amounts of weight is different from that needed to develop speed.

Here is a table as to how you could progress the back squat throughout the course of an 8 week training plan to maintain the development of speed.

Week	Phase	Squat Variation	Sets x Reps	% of Training Max Full Squat (90% of Max)
1	Accumulation	Full Squat	3 x 5	65
2		Full Squat	3 x 3	75
3		Half Squat	3 x 3	80
4	Intensification	Half Squat	3 x 2	85
5		¼ Squat	3 x 2	100
6		¼ Squat	2 x 2	110
7	Realisation	¼ Squat from Pins	3 x 2	120
8		¼ Squat from Pins	2 x 2	120

This cycle maintains a low volume strength training approach, and decreases the range of motion, increasing the specificity and forces imposed.

Supportive Training Elements

Understanding the strength continuum for speed provides a framework for supportive training elements. The central idea behind this continuum is to understand the types of strength that might be lacking when we see our athletes move. For example many team sport sprinters struggle to put together 15-20 steps of acceleration from a static start. This is crucial to master in virtually all sports. With most team sport athletes being very high force-low speed in the way they create movement they tend to get stuck low to the ground. This is because they are unable to apply force more quickly throughout the stages of acceleration. Supporting your speed training focusing on the development of these different types of strength will improve your chances of developing effective acceleration. Starting strength, accelerating strength, strength speed, and speed strength are the key components. It's important to observe what is seen on the field and in the collected data to determine the appropriate training solutions. The data you can obtain here doesn't need to be sophisticated at all. As we will discuss later in the book, your eye is your most valuable weapon. Focus on seeing what the body does as a result of the steps taken. Once you start to see the gaps as this system will reveal to you; you can focus on the specific needs of the athlete's speed development.

Strength in the Context of Sprinting

When it comes to optimising athletic performance, understanding the specific strength requirements of an athlete is crucial. By tailoring training programs to address individual needs, coaches can help athletes achieve their ultimate goal of excelling in their sport. In this section, we explore the different strength qualities relevant to sprinting and how they can be harnessed to unlock an athlete's speed potential.

Identifying Strength Qualities:

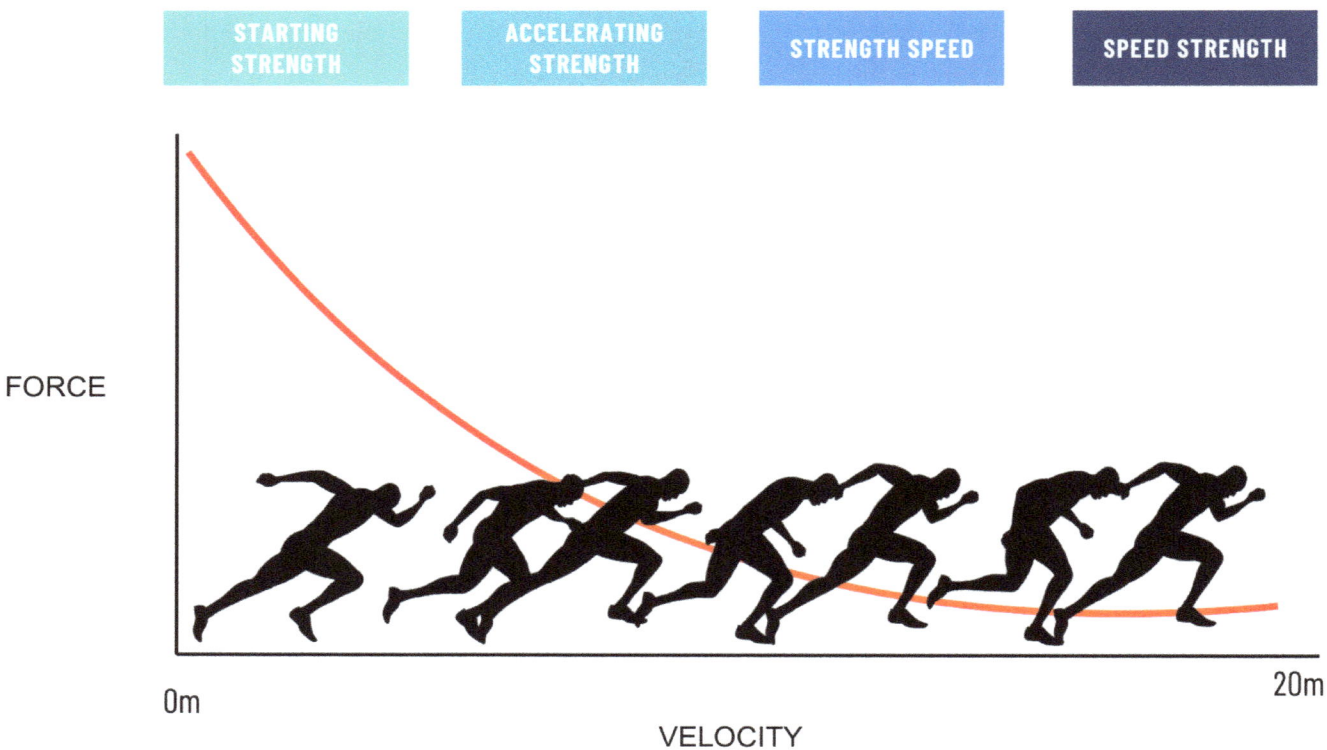

To comprehend an athlete's strength needs, it is essential to recognise the various strength qualities that contribute to sprinting performance. These include supra maximal strength, maximal strength, explosive strength, starting strength, accelerating strength, speed strength, and strength speed. As we have previously discussed, the transfer of training is the most important aspect of training all coaches need to focus on. Speed age is an important lens to view these strength qualities through. Early in the training of the athlete, improving one of these aspects will improve each of the others. Further into the training career, these elements must be trained in a sequence tailored to the athlete. As the athlete grows more advanced, general strength training will display diminishing transfer to speed. Once this early transfer has ceased it is important to consider other types of strength. Let's delve into each of these qualities, ensure you refer to the table provided to support these explanations:

1. Supra Maximal Strength: This refers to generating an extremely high force output, beyond what can even be generated under maximal isometric conditions. It involves handling the maximum load possible during eccentric movements. For example, lowering a back squat to pins with loads greater than your 1 rep max.

Forces 50-100% greater than maximal isometric forces are also generated during the imposed yielding of plyometric actions.

2. Maximal Strength: It represents the ability to produce the greatest voluntary force, such as in isometric static strength exercises like mid-thigh pulls. Developing maximal strength contributes to overall force production capabilities.

3. Explosive Strength: This quality involves achieving maximal force production in the shortest possible time. It is highly desirable for sprinting performance as it allows athletes to generate rapid and explosive movements. To develop explosive strength I like to use trap bar jumps with moderate loads.

4. Starting Strength: Starting strength is characterised by rapid force production at the onset of muscular tension. It plays a significant role in quick acceleration and explosive starts, making it crucial for sprinters. Moving your body weight or light weights from static positions is my favourite way to train this quality. Kneeling wall shoots or jump squats from pins are great for this.

5. Accelerating Strength: This quality focuses on achieving rapid maximum force effort during the final phase of muscular tension. This is where we are focussing on moving the weights or ourselves as fast as we can through the whole movement. It contributes to the acceleration phase of sprinting, particularly in the later steps. Conventional weight training does not train this quality well as the force required to move a weight drops as the weight gains momentum. My favourite exercise to develop this in the weight room is banded trap bar deadlifts. Using bands really emphasises this type of strength, as the resistance from the bands works to prevent the bar from gaining momentum, so you have to push harder and harder through the motion.

6. Speed Strength: Speed strength entails performing high-speed movements against minimal resistance. It aims to increase velocity and emphasises the rate of change of velocity, a key factor in sprinting performance. Any form of light resisted acceleration is going to target this quality the best. I prefer to start with prowler drives and then switch to sleds later utilising the stable to unstable framework.

7. Strength Speed: Strength speed relates to power generation in sports where force predominates over velocity. It involves activities like weightlifting and track bar jumps, which enhance force-dominant movements. This is most relevant to early acceleration.

Throughout sprinting movements certain strength qualities are expressed at certain times. This is why exercise classification and the previous discussed categorisation of training is so imperative to successful weight training for speed. There is considerable overlap between these qualities, and for athletes in the earlier stages of training, enhancing any one of these qualities will improve the others. Beginners do not need to separately train supra maximal strength and maximal strength, as any type of strength stimulus is sufficient for them to improve. In the following table you will see that "Bar Speed / Velocity" has been identified. This is measured using a bar speed measuring device. This will be explained in greater detail in a later section.

Strength Type	% of 1RM	Bar Speed/ Velocity	Suitable Exercises	Description
Supramaximal	> 100% (eccentric only)	Negative	Eccentric Squats, Eccentric Deadlifts	Training with loads exceeding 100% of 1RM, typically during the eccentric (lowering) phase.
Maximal Strength	85-100%	≤ 0.3 m/s	Squats, Deadlifts, Bench Press, Overhead Press	Developing the highest level of force a muscle can produce in a single maximal effort.
Explosive Strength	70-85%	0.75-1.0 m/s	Power Cleans, Snatches, Jump Squats	Focus on producing maximal force in minimal time, typically through Olympic lifts and jumps.
Starting Strength	50-70%	1.0-1.3 m/s	Box Jumps, Medicine Ball Throws, Sprints	Enhancing the ability to generate force rapidly from a stationary position.
Accelerating Strength	30-50%	1.3-1.6 m/s	Speed Deadlifts, Speed Squats, Band-Resisted Movements	Improving the ability to accelerate weights or one's body mass effectively.
Speed Strength	20-30%	1.6-2.0 m/s	Plyometrics, Medicine Ball Slams, Band-Resisted Sprints	Emphasising quick, explosive movements with lighter loads to maximise speed.
Strength Speed	50-70%	1.0-1.3 m/s	Loaded Jumps, Push Presses, Heavy Medicine Ball Throws	Balancing strength and speed, important for movements requiring both power and velocity.

In sprinting, strength training plays a crucial role in enhancing speed performance. By understanding the different strength qualities required for sprinting and designing training programs that address specific deficiencies, coaches can unlock an athlete's full potential. Tailoring programming to target areas such as starting strength, accelerating strength, and speed strength can lead to significant improvements in sprinting performance. This will now be discussed with the integration of ballistic training means.

Ballistic Training for Speed: Programming and Progressions

Ballistic training is a powerful tool that can revolutionise the way athletes train for speed. Ballistic exercises involve an initial impulse generated by the agonist muscle group, followed by a state of relaxation where limb motion continues due to the build-up of momentum. Understanding the true essence of ballistic exercises and their programming considerations can take training effectiveness to new heights. In this section, we delve into the definition of ballistic exercises, their impact on training outcomes, and the importance of timing. We also explore the role of medicine balls and categorise ballistic modalities for effective programming. Additionally, we examine how ballistic training can be incorporated into athlete qualification and hierarchy, leading to enhanced speed development.

Defining Ballistic Exercises:

As previously stated, ballistic exercises involve an initial impulse generated by the agonist muscle group, followed by a state of relaxation where limb motion continues due to the build-up of momentum. By embracing the true nature of ballistic exercises, coaches can maximise their training impact. In the previous section I presented a similar table demonstrating how you can create these specific strength adaptations in the weightroom. Here we will start to look at how you can implement these in a more specific way that will target speed more. This is where we will shift from our classification focus from general preparatory exercises to more specific preparatory and specific developmental exercise.

Strength Type	Description	Speed Specific Ballistic Modalities
Accelerative Strength	Achieve a rapid maximum force effort in the final phase of muscular tension.	• Band resisted wall drill variations. • Moderately heavy resisted sprints. • Hill Sprints
Strength-Speed	Power capability in sporting actions with force dominating velocity	• Early Acceleration • Medicine Ball Accelerations
Speed-Strength	High speed movements applied against small resistance	• Lightly resisted sprints.
Starting Strength	Produce a rapid increases of force effort at the beginning of muscular tension	• Static Start variations.

When choosing resistance loads for weighted sprint modalities. Without incredibly expensive technology it is challenging to be highly accurate. Therefore the best advice I can give you is to judge it by the execution of the movement based on the descriptions provided. Load the movement to how you want it to behave.

The Power of Medicine Balls:

Medicine balls are an underutilised yet highly effective tool for ballistic training. The reason why they are so effective is that they can be thrown. This throwing action facilitates the acceleration and tension followed by relaxation and weightlessness required to be categorised as a ballistic movement. For example when you throw a medicine ball in the air as high as you can you express force throughout the whole movement and become weightless and relaxed at the end when the ball is in the air.

Categorising Ballistic Modalities:

To streamline programming and ensure targeted training, it is beneficial to categorise ballistic modalities based on specific strength qualities and velocity ranges, however overall they fit into the category of general physical preparation and general preparatory exercises. By using tools like Tendo units or velocity measurement devices, coaches can determine the appropriate percentage of training max and work within the desired velocity ranges. To identify the strength deficit an athlete has is quite a simple process that does require some specialist equipment. This flexible approach allows for precise adjustments in training stress and complements various areas of an athlete's overall development, supporting their speed journey. I will now walk you through a couple of ways to identify individualised training approaches.

Conducting a Force-Velocity Profile Using Barbell Movements

Objective:
To assess an athlete's force-velocity profile using the barbell lifts to tailor training programs for optimal performance improvements.

Equipment Needed:
– Barbell and weight plates
– Squat rack
– Linear position transducer OR velocity-based training device (e.g., GymAware, Tendo Unit) OR velocity measuring app
– Calculator or software for data analysis - Google Sheet Calculator included in the Appendix

Steps:

1. Preparation:
– Ensure the athlete is thoroughly warmed up.
– Familiarise the athlete with the testing protocol and equipment.
– Load the barbell with an appropriate starting weight (usually 30-40% of the athlete's estimated 1RM).

2. Determine Maximum Load (1RM):
– Calculate the athlete's 1RM through testing or estimation.
– For safety, it's often best to use a predictive method to estimate 1RM rather than testing it directly, especially with athletes not accustomed to maximal lifts.

3. Conduct the Test:
– The athlete performs multiple sets of the barbell squat at different loads, ranging from light (30-40% 1RM) to heavy (85-90% 1RM).
– For each load, the athlete should perform a single repetition with maximal effort focusing on lifting the bar as explosively as possible.
– Measure and record the barbell velocity for each lift using the velocity-based training device.

Sample Protocol:
– 30% of 1RM: 1 rep, record velocity
– 50% of 1RM: 1 rep, record velocity
– 70% of 1RM: 1 rep, record velocity
– 85% of 1RM: 1 rep, record velocity
– 90% of 1RM: 1 rep, record velocity

Important:
— Ensure adequate rest between sets (2-3 minutes) to prevent fatigue from affecting performance.
— Use consistent technique for each lift to ensure accuracy.

4. Data Collection:
— For each load, note the weight (force) and the corresponding mean barbell velocity.
— Collect at least 5 data points across the range of loads.

5. Data Analysis:
— Plot the data points on a graph with Force (Load) on the Y-axis and Velocity on the X-axis.
— Fit a linear regression line to the data points. The slope of this line represents the athlete's force-velocity relationship.

6. Interpretation:

Understanding the Slope:
— **Steep Slope:** Indicates the athlete has a high capacity for force production but lower velocity capabilities. This suggests a strength-oriented profile.
— **Shallow Slope:** Indicates the athlete has higher velocity capabilities but lower force production capacity. This suggests a speed-oriented profile.

Tailoring Training:
— **Strength-Oriented Athletes (Steep Slope):** Focus on developing velocity. Incorporate more explosive strength and speed-strength training (e.g., plyometrics, lighter load high-velocity lifts).
— **Speed-Oriented Athletes (Shallow Slope):** Focus on increasing maximal force production. Incorporate more maximal strength and hypertrophy training (e.g., heavy squats, deadlifts).

Adjusting Training Loads:
— Use the force-velocity profile to determine optimal training loads for different training focuses.
— For example, if the goal is to improve explosive strength, identify the load corresponding to 70-85% of 1RM and focus on maximising bar speed at those loads.

Example Interpretation:

Sample Data

Load (% of 1RM)	Weight (kg)	Velocity (m/s)
30%	60	1.2
50%	100	0.9
70%	140	0.6
85%	170	0.4
90%	180	0.3

Analysis:
- Plot the data points: (60 kg, 1.2 m/s), (100 kg, 0.9 m/s), (140 kg, 0.6 m/s), (170 kg, 0.4 m/s), (180 kg, 0.3 m/s).
- Fit a linear regression line to these points.
- Determine the slope and y-intercept to define the force-velocity relationship.

Conclusion:
- Based on the slope of the line, you can determine if the athlete needs more focus on developing force or velocity.
- This helps in customising training programs to target specific adaptations needed for improving performance.

Practical Application:

Strengthening Weaknesses:
- If the athlete shows a strength-oriented profile, incorporate more velocity-based training, such as:
  - Light weighted Jump squats
  - Power Snatches
  - Plyometric exercises

(Note: these are non exhaustive but for the purpose of the book I wanted to give examples most athletes would have access to).

Enhancing Strength:
- If the athlete shows a speed-oriented profile, incorporate more strength-based training, such as:
- Heavy squats
- Deadlifts
- Heavy sled pushes

Optimising Training Programs:
- Regularly reassess the force-velocity profile to adjust training loads and ensure continuous improvement.
- Use the profile to periodise training, alternating between strength-focused and velocity-focused phases.

By following this guide, you can accurately assess and interpret an athlete's force-velocity profile, allowing for precise and individualised training interventions that maximise athletic performance.

Dynamic Strength Index (DSI) Test

Another test that can be used is the Dynamic Strength Index test. The Dynamic Strength Index (DSI) measures an athlete's ability to transfer their maximal strength capacity into explosive power. This index is useful for identifying imbalances between maximal strength and explosive strength, guiding individualised training interventions.

Equipment Needed:
- Force plate (for measuring jump forces)
- Barbell and weights (for measuring maximal strength)
- Smith machine or squat rack
- Vertical jump mat or a device to measure jump height (if force plate not available)

Testing Components:
1. Isometric Mid-Thigh Pull (IMTP): Measures maximal strength.
2. Countermovement Jump (CMJ): Measures explosive strength.

Testing Protocol

Step 1: Preparation
1. Warm-Up:
   - Perform a general warm-up consisting of 5-10 minutes of light aerobic activity (e.g., jogging).
   - Follow with a dynamic warm-up focusing on major muscle groups involved in jumping and pulling exercises (e.g., leg swings, bodyweight squats, lunges).

2. Set Up the Equipment:
   - Ensure the force plate is properly calibrated and positioned for both the IMTP and CMJ.
   - Set up the barbell for the IMTP in a squat rack at mid-thigh height when the athlete is in a standing position.

Step 2: Isometric Mid-Thigh Pull (IMTP)

1. Positioning:
   - The athlete stands on the force plate with their feet hip-width apart.
   - The barbell is placed at mid-thigh height, and the athlete grabs the bar with a shoulder-width grip.
   - Ensure the athlete's back is neutral, and the hips and knees are slightly bent.

2. Execution:
   - Instruct the athlete to pull the bar upwards as forcefully as possible without actually lifting it, maintaining the position.
   - Hold the maximal effort for 3-5 seconds.
   - Record the peak force output.

3. Repeat:
   - Perform 2-3 trials with adequate rest (2-3 minutes) between attempts to ensure maximal effort.

Step 3: Countermovement Jump (CMJ)

1. Positioning:
   - The athlete stands on the force plate or jump mat with feet hip-width apart.

2. Execution:
   – The athlete performs a quick downward movement followed by an explosive jump as high as possible, using their arms for momentum.
   – Ensure a consistent technique for all jumps.

3. Recording:
   – Measure the peak force output
   – Perform 2-3 trials with adequate rest (1-2 minutes) between attempts.

Calculation of DSI *(Google Sheet Provided in Appendix)*
The Dynamic Strength Index is calculated as the ratio of CMJ peak force to IMTP peak force.

DSI= IMTP Peak Force (N) / CMJ Peak Force (N)

Interpretation of Results

– **DSI < 0.6:**
– Indicates the athlete has a high level of maximal strength relative to their explosive strength.
– Training Focus: Emphasise explosive and speed-strength exercises (e.g., plyometrics, Olympic lifts).

– **DSI between 0.6 and 0.8:**
– Indicates a balanced relationship between maximal and explosive strength.
– Training Focus: Maintain a balanced training regimen including both strength and power exercises.

– **DSI > 0.8:**
– Indicates the athlete has high explosive strength relative to their maximal strength.
– Training Focus: Emphasise maximal strength development (e.g., heavy squats, deadlifts).

These two tests are the most commonly used to assess strength capabilities within athletes. However if you don't have specialist equipment do not be put off. We will now look into what training and exercises should be used in conjunction with speed age. This will help you pick the most appropriate and easiest ways to improve your athletes performance.

Incorporating Ballistic Training in Athlete Qualification:

Speed Age is a valuable framework for applying ballistic training effectively. By understanding an athlete's skill level, coaches can prescribe the appropriate level of ballistic exercises. Athletes who fall into the Learning to Sprint Speed Age may focus on executing loaded heavy walks to develop foundational strength and speed. As athletes advance, they can progress to more complex and resisted movements, emphasising starting strength and speed-strength. Athletes who are sprinting to win can explore advanced assisted movements, enhancing accelerative strength. The provided qualification framework helps coaches stack training qualities systematically, resulting in optimal performance gains. Time and results dictate the progression through the stages of speed age. Do not rush to advanced modalities of training purely based on the results gained. Adhere to the laws of transfer to assure that you are progressing training at the appropriate rate.

Speed Age	Speed	Plyometrics	Ballistics	Strength
Learning To Sprint	Learning to execute – Loaded Heavy Walks	Bodyweight Extensive to intensive	Medicine Ball light resistance to heavy resistance	Development of submaximal strength to Accelerative Strength
Training To Sprint	Increase complexity + Speed Resisted movements Starting Strength to Speed-Strength	Weighted Extensive to Intensive	Introduction of Gym based exercises Accelerative Strength + Weighted Jumps Starting Strength	Maximal Strength to Strength-Speed
Sprinting to Compete	Resisted movements Strength-Speed to Accelerative Strength	Depth Jumps	Gym based exercises progress from Strength-Speed to Speed-Strength + Weighted Jumps Speed-Strength to Strength-Speed	Partial Range / Increase Speed and Power in SDE
Sprinting To Win	Progress to utilise Assisted sprint variations Variations	Over Speed Depth Jumps		

Programming Progressions and Integration:

To ensure continuous improvement, coaches should utilise progressions as outlined based on exercise classification and integrate different training modalities. For example referring to the previous table a coach could focus on developing general strength in the weight room with traditional barbell movements. Then use heavy sleds to create specific strength for acceleration whilst utilising heavier medicine balls to develop explosive strength through ballistic throws and jump training. This could encompass a whole program and even a season (see appendix for examples). Plyometric exercises, categorised based on body weight, weighted, and depth jumps, offer a valuable means to enhance speed development. By analysing athletes' responses to training and strategically stacking ballistics and strength, coaches can optimise programming for exceptional results.

Maximising Speed with Jump and Plyometric Training

Jump and plyometric training are essential components for enhancing speed and athletic performance. Understanding the intricacies of these training methods and their progressive programming can lead to significant improvements in speed development. In this section, we delve into the significance of jumps and plyometrics, explore their sequencing, and highlight the importance of understanding contact time and intensity. By following a systematic approach and leveraging data, coaches can optimise jump and plyometric training to achieve remarkable results.

The Power of Jumps and Plyometrics:

Jumps and plyometrics play a crucial role in speed development. These training methods have the potential to revolutionise an athlete's performance by bridging the specificity gap and unlocking new levels of explosiveness. When properly incorporated into training programs, jumps and plyometrics provide unique benefits that extend beyond mere warm-ups or skill-building exercises. Understanding the distinction between jumps and plyometrics lies in the critical factor of contact time, which determines the type of movement and the specific adaptations achieved.

Differences Between Jumps and Plyometrics

A common mistake made by coaches is confusing the difference between a jump and a plyometric activity. Both are crucial components to training but they do serve different purposes. A true plyometric such as depth jumps or bounding, emphasise the rapid transition from eccentric to concentric muscle actions, known as the stretch-shortening cycle (SSC). This cycle enhances the muscle's elastic properties and neuromuscular efficiency, leading to shorter ground contact times and a more explosive response. Plyometric exercises exploit the pre-stretching of muscles to generate greater force and power in a shorter period, making them highly effective for improving speed, agility, and reactive strength. Plyometrics are categorised based on the time spent on the ground and for an exercise to be considered a true plyometric the ground contact time must be less than 0.2 second. While jumps build foundational power, true plyometrics specifically train the body to react quickly and forcefully, a key requirement in many athletic scenarios.

Benefits of plyometrics for athletes

Having plyometrics in an athletes' training programme is an absolute must! This will develop the ability to produce explosive power and reflexive actions such as sprinting and changing direction. The following list gives an overview of the positive effects plyometric training has on performance:

— Training to utilise the stretch shortening cycle
— Elicits greater elastic recoil of muscle and tendons
— Improves coordination and timing
— Greater muscle fibre firing rates
— Creates tendon stiffness to reduce ground contact time
— Stimulates to enhances the Central nervous system signalling outputs
— Allows you to effectively produce more force into the ground
— Reduces non-contact injuries through better preparedness
— Reduce metabolic energy being produced through muscular contraction by increasing the use of elastic energy

Jumping as a skill

Jumping is a skill and as with any skill, it can be taught, practised, and improved. Like sprinting and changing direction, jumping involves colliding with the ground, creating a landing and rebounding movement. With the right methods, applied in the correct sequence, plyometric training can enhance essential motor abilities, promoting appropriate muscle activation and efficient contraction-relaxation patterns. To teach this motor skill, two key categories of jumping are implemented to elicit different training effects:

- Long Coupling Jumps (Longer ground contacts)
- Short Coupling Jumps (Shorter ground contacts)

Long coupling jumps are predominantly hip and knee dominant movements. Long coupling jumps will have a longer ground contact time (>0.2s) and typically greater displacement of the person centre of mass. This covers actions such as countermovement jumps and broad jumps. These movements use a slow stretch shortening cycle, and high degrees of muscle activation and force production. There is time for greater tension to develop before the concentric phase begins, allowing for large concentric forces and powerful jumping actions.

Short coupling jumps are predominantly ankle dominant movements which are performed with much shorter ground contact times (<0.2s) through shorter joint ranges. The fast stretch shortening cycle is active here. The elastic components of the muscle and tendon stretch and rebound, complemented by involuntary muscle contractions from the stretch reflex. This movement should look and feel bouncy due to the short ground contact times mentioned previously.

Sequential Order of Jumps and Plyometric Training:

To ensure a progressive and effective training program, it is vital to follow a systematic approach to jumps and plyometric exercises. This allows athletes to build a solid foundation and gradually intensify their training. The journey begins with landing and non-countermovement jumps, focusing on developing proper landing mechanics and explosive power. Next, extensive jumps, akin to running drills, are introduced to further refine technique and timing. These discrete jumps serve as building blocks for more advanced exercises.

Progressive Intensity and Qualification:

As athletes progress, the training intensity can be progressively increased. Weighted variations of jumps and plyometrics are introduced to challenge the musculoskeletal system and enhance power output. Moving forward, athletes can engage in short coupling activities that involve rapid stretch-shortening cycle actions. These exercises are followed by intensified versions, which demand a high level of explosiveness and coordination. The table below shows a recommended progression when utilising jump training. This 3 phase checklist explains when to progress to different jumps and the right time to move onto the next method:

1. Establish the correct technique
2. Apply higher force efforts using the correct technique
3. Build a higher level of work capacity and skill with a more complex variation

If this process is adhered to well and athletes have adequately prepared their bodies and adapted to the progressively higher intensities, depth jumps can be incorporated, giving access to the potent stimulus of this advanced plyometric exercise.

Progression Phase	Landing and Non Counter Movement Jumps	Extensive Jumps	Intensive Jumps	Introduction to weighted jumps	Extensive weighted jumps	Intensive weighted jumps	Supramaximal Jumps
1 - Technique	Drop Landings	Pogo Series	Long Coupling	Weighted NCMJ	Medicine Ball Pogo Series	Long Coupling	Depth Jumps
2 - Apply Force	Non-Countermovement Jump	Extensive Series	Short Coupling	Weighted Eccentric Focus	Weighted Extensive	Short Coupling	Overspeed Depth Jumps
3 - Build Capacity	Countermovement Jump	Advanced Extensive	Altitude Landings		Overspeed Jumps	Drop Jumps	

Note: Full Definitions and Examples can be found in the appendix.

PROGRAMMING FOR SPEED

In this chapter we will delve into the practical application of speed training in the real world. The key lies in understanding the specific needs of individuals, establishing a sequence of progression, and incorporating elements of motor learning and physical development. This creates a structured framework that fosters order, progression, and effective sequencing, putting you in an advantageous position as a coach or trainer.

As you consider these aspects, you may find yourself realising that many of these components are already within your reach. You have the ability to identify what athletes need to focus on, using the learn load execute framework to assess athletes ability and speed age by gauging the athlete's ability to perform basic sprint drills and specific strength exercises. Structure a logical progression using the drill stacking and stable to unstable frameworks, and ensure both motor learning and physical development are addressed implementing the stable to unstable framework. Supported with a comprehensive understanding of exercise classification and the transfer of training, with a well-organised system and a strategic stacking of training elements, there should be no reason for progress not to occur.

The data serves as a validating tool that supports the work being done. As we examine the factors that impact progress in speed development, we can break it down into four key parts: qualification, training stages, sports specificity, and the physical profile. These components provide a comprehensive framework for understanding the various aspects of speed training. From the stages of learning to sprint, training to sprint, sprinting to compete, and sprinting to win, to the training phases of off-season, pre-season, in-season, and injury recovery, we can tailor our approach accordingly. Additionally, considering the athlete's physical profile, including anthropometric and morphological profiling data, further enhances the specificity of training. By incorporating these factors, we can create a well-structured program that aligns with the unique demands of each athlete's sport.

Fundamental Principles of Constructing Training Programs, Periodisation, and Training Organisation

Developing a successful training program for team sport athletes requires an understanding of several fundamental principles and periodisation strategies. This section will explore General Adaptation Syndrome (GAS), progressive overload, the principle of specificity, block periodisation, vertical integration, and agile periodisation. We'll discuss how these can be utilised within a holistic approach to developing speed and provide practical examples. This section can be an entire book in itself therefore I have recommended further reading in the appendix and provided brief applied summaries of each principle. This section lays the foundation to some of the more nuanced considerations we will discuss. However it is important to understand the structures of which you will outline your programs with.

Progressive Overload

Progressive overload involves gradually increasing the stress placed on the body during training to stimulate adaptation and improve performance. When developing speed this can be done in many ways. Incremental increases in intensity, volume, or complexity are ways to do this. Here are a couple of examples:

Intensity Increases: In this example we are using the percentage of max speed typically attained at a given distance when sprinting from a static start.

– Week 1: 3 x 10m - 60% Max Speed
– Week 2: 3 x 20m - 80% Max Speed
– Week 3: 3 x 30m - 90% Max Speed
– Week 4: 3 x 40m - 100% Max Speed

Volume Increases: In this example we are increasing the volume of runs completed at a given distance each week.

– Week 1: 3 x 20m sprints = 60m
– Week 2: 3 x 30m sprints = 90m
– Week 3: 4 x 30m sprints = 120m
– Week 4: 4 x 40m sprints = 160m

Note: These are for demonstration purposes only and not recommended volume loading parameters.

Complexity Increases: In this example we have manipulated a flying start distance (build distance) to challenge the athletes ability to accelerate at different rates to achieve a designed sprint speed. All runs are required to be completed at 80% speed for the allocated distance.

– Week 1: 20m build in 20m Sprint
– Week 2: 15m build in 15m Sprint
– Week 3: 10m build in 20m Sprint
– Week 4: 10m build in 30m Sprint

Principle of Specificity

The principle of specificity states that training should be relevant and appropriate to the sport for which the individual is training. Training drills and exercises should closely mimic the movements and energy systems used in the athlete's sport. For a rugby player, speed training should include acceleration, maximum speed, change of direction and deceleration training that help support the demands of the game.

Block Periodisation

Block periodisation involves dividing the training program into distinct blocks or phases, each focusing on a specific aspect of performance maximings the athletes ability to peak at a specific time. A speed development program might include blocks for foundational strength, explosive power, and sport-specific speed.

Block	Focus	Duration	Example Speed Work	Example Strength Work
1	Foundational Strength	4 weeks	Wall Drills / Heavy Resisted Sled / Extensive Jumps	Squats, Deadlifts, Calf raises.
2	Explosive Power	4 weeks	Loaded Wall Drills Light Sled Training / Intensive Jumps	Power cleans, Snatches
3	Sport-Specific Speed	4 weeks	Sprint drills, Agility work, Reaction drills	Single Joint Health

Vertical Integration

Vertical integration involves training multiple fitness qualities simultaneously but with varying emphasis over different phases. Athletes continuously work on speed, strength, and endurance, but the focus shifts depending on the training phase.

Phase	Primary Focus	Secondary Focus	Maintenance
Pre-Season	Endurance	Strength	Speed
Early Season	Speed	Strength	Endurance
Mid-Season	Accelerative Strength	Speed	Endurance
Late Season	Speed	Endurance	Strength

Conjugate Method

The conjugate method involves training multiple fitness qualities concurrently, with emphasis shifting weekly or biweekly. This method allows for continuous development without overtraining any single aspect. For speed development, this might mean incorporating elements of maximal strength, explosive power, and specific speed drills in the same training week. It is important to note here that this table is reference to off-season periods of training.

Week	Maximal Strength Focus	Dynamic Effort Focus	Speed Work Focus
1	Heavy Squats, Deadlifts	Power Cleans, Box Jumps	Maximum Speed Build Ups
2	Heavy Deadlifts, Squats	Snatches, Plyometrics	Agility Drills
3	Heavy Squats, Deadlifts	Power Cleans, Depth Jumps	30m Acceleration Sprints
4	Heavy Deadlifts, Squats	Snatches, Hurdle Hops	Reaction Drills

Agile Periodisation

Agile periodisation is a flexible approach that allows for adjustments based on the athlete's progress and feedback. This approach adapts to the athlete's response to training and external factors such as competition schedule and injury status. If an athlete shows signs of overtraining or plateaus in speed development, the coach may adjust the training load or switch the focus to recovery and regeneration.

Holistic Approach to Speed Development

By combining these principles and periodisation strategies, coaches can create a well-rounded and adaptable training program that meets the needs of team sport athletes.

Example Speed Development Program

Macrocycle: 12 weeks

Week	Focus	Main Training Activities
1-4	Accumulation	Foundational strength, basic sprint drills, low-intensity plyometrics
5-8	Intensification	Explosive power, high-intensity sprints, advanced plyometrics
9-12	Realisation	Sport-specific speed, agility drills, reaction time exercises

Weekly Microcycle Example:

Day	Focus	Example Workout
Monday	Strength	Squats, deadlifts, core stability
Tuesday	Speed	30m sprints, acceleration drills, agility ladder
Wednesday	Recovery	Light jog, stretching, mobility work
Thursday	Power	Power cleans, snatches, box jumps
Friday	Speed	Reaction drills, sport-specific sprinting
Saturday	Game Simulation	Small-sided games, tactical drills
Sunday	Rest	Active recovery, rest

Utilising principles such as GAS, progressive overload, specificity, and various periodisation strategies can significantly enhance the effectiveness of a training program. By integrating block periodisation, vertical integration, and agile periodisation within a holistic approach, coaches can ensure that team sport athletes develop speed efficiently and sustainably. This structured yet flexible framework allows for continuous progress and optimal performance throughout the competitive season.

Training Cycle Layout: Macrocycle, Mesocycles, and Microcycles

Understanding the structure of training cycles—macrocycles, mesocycles, and microcycles—is essential for effective program design. These cycles work together to ensure athletes peak at the right times and maintain optimal performance throughout their competitive season. This structured approach is especially important in team sports, where consistent performance and adaptation to varying competition schedules are crucial.

Macrocycle

The macrocycle is the longest training period, typically encompassing an entire season, year, or the time between major competitions. It outlines the overarching goals and phases of the training program.

Purpose:
— To provide a long-term framework for training
— To ensure athletes peak for major competitions
— To balance periods of high-intensity training with adequate recovery

A 12-month macrocycle for a football team might include pre-season, in-season, and off-season phases.

Duration	Main Goals	Period
3 months	Build foundational strength and fitness	Pre-Season
6 months	Maintain performance, peak for key games	In-Season
3 months	Recovery, address weaknesses	Off-Season

Mesocycles

Mesocycles are intermediate training cycles within the macrocycle, typically lasting 4-8 weeks. Each mesocycle focuses on specific training objectives that build upon each other.

Purpose:
— To target specific fitness components (e.g., strength, power, speed)
— To allow for systematic progression and variation in training
— To facilitate adaptations and prevent overtraining

A mesocycle in the preseason for a rugby team might focus on strength development.

Week	Focus	Main Training Activities
1-4	Strength	Heavy squats, deadlifts, hypertrophy work
5-8	Power	Power cleans, snatches, plyometrics

Microcycles

Microcycles are the shortest training cycles, usually lasting one week. They detail the specific daily training sessions and recovery periods.
- To manage day-to-day training loads and recovery
- To implement the training objectives of the mesocycle
- To monitor and adjust training based on athlete feedback

A microcycle for a team sport athlete during the power mesocycle.

Day	Focus	Example Workout
Monday	Speed Strength	Squats, bench press, core stability
Tuesday	Speed	40m sprints, agility drills
Wednesday	Recovery	Light jog, stretching, mobility work
Thursday	Power	Power cleans, box jumps, med ball throws
Friday	Speed	Reaction drills, sport-specific sprints
Saturday	Game Simulation	Small-sided games, tactical drills
Sunday	Rest	Active recovery, rest

How They Work Together

The macrocycle, mesocycles, and microcycles are interconnected, each serving a specific purpose within the overall training plan:

- **Macrocycle:** Provides the long-term roadmap, ensuring athletes peak at the right times and maintain overall progress.
- **Mesocycles:** Break down the macrocycle into manageable segments, each focusing on specific aspects of performance. Organises systemic aspects of fatigue and recovery.
- **Microcycles:** Organise daily and weekly training activities, ensuring the goals of the mesocycle are met while managing fatigue and recovery.

Macro	1											
Meso	1				2				3			
Micro	1	2	3	4	5	6	7	8	9	10	11	12

Importance of Structured Training

Having your training structured and laid out ahead of time ensures that you can plot the changes in training you want to make and ensure you are able to provide adequate recovery. This boils down to five key benefits.

1. Systematic Progression: Structured training ensures a systematic progression from general preparation to specific performance, enhancing overall athletic development.

2. Optimal Performance: By peaking at the right times, athletes can perform at their best during long seasons of competition.

3. Injury Prevention: Properly planned recovery phases within mesocycles and microcycles help prevent overtraining and reduce the risk of injuries.

4. Adaptation: Structured training allows for continuous adaptation to training stimuli, ensuring that athletes are constantly improving.

5. Flexibility: Structured but flexible planning, such as agile periodisation, allows for adjustments based on athlete feedback and unexpected changes (e.g., injuries, game rescheduling).

Example Training Cycle for a Team Sport Athlete

Below I have provided a rough outline of what a typical 12 month training cycle could look like using a progression block approach.

Macrocycle: 12 Months

Period	Duration	Main Goals
Pre-Season	3 months	Build fitness, strength, and tactical skills
In-Season	6 months	Maintain performance, peak for key matches
Post-Season	1 month	Active recovery, address injuries
Off-Season	2 months	General conditioning, technical skills

Mesocycle Example (Pre-Season)

Week	Focus	Main Training Activities
1-4	General Conditioning	Endurance runs, aerobic drills
5-8	Strength	Gym sessions (squats, deadlifts), plyometrics
9-12	Speed & Power	Sprint intervals, power cleans, agility drills

Microcycle Example (Week 5 of Pre-Season)

Day	Focus	Example Workout
Monday	Strength	Squats, deadlifts, core stability
Tuesday	Speed	30m sprints, agility ladder drills
Wednesday	Recovery	Light jog, stretching, mobility work
Thursday	Strength	Bench press, pull-ups, plyometric jumps
Friday	Speed	Reaction drills, sport-specific sprinting
Saturday	Game Simulation	Small-sided games, tactical drills
Sunday	Rest	Active recovery, rest

This structured approach ensures that team sport athletes develop speed, strength, and endurance effectively, allowing them to perform optimally during their competitive season.

Tools and Modalities for Speed Development

When designing a program for speed, it is crucial to choose the right tools and modalities that will enhance an athlete's development rather than hinder it. It's important to remember the law of accommodation – if we don't progress, we don't ascend.

One must be mindful that a training tool or modality, once relied upon excessively, can become an athlete's worst enemy. It can actually slow down their progress and impede their performance.

In the realm of programming, there are key metrics to consider: volume, intensity, density, and qualification. Volume, in particular, deserves careful attention. Many coaches make the mistake of misjudging volume, where by there isn't enough awareness that in sprinting one step is a repetition as opposed to a run of a specific distance. When this mistake is made athletes tend to accumulate too much fatigue leading to suboptimal results. Understanding the two types of volume – extensive and intensive – is crucial, and it should always be relative to an athlete's qualification level.

Inside the Sports Speed System qualification is the guiding variable that allows coaches to be able to select the most appropriate training means to generate adaptation. Through the ascending levels of Speed age the goal within the Sports Speed System is to be able to use the least amount of volume, intensity, and density to create the greatest amount of improvement. As the athlete progresses through their training and at different stages of preparation, we as coaches should manipulate these variables to specifically create the adaptation that we need in conjunction to the type of programming and periodisation that we have selected and deemed most appropriate for the athlete at that time.

It is not uncommon to come across recommendations suggesting 240 metres of acceleration work to improve acceleration. While it may seem reasonable, this represents a very significant total volume. Breaking it down, this could translate to 24 sets of 10-metre sprints. However, if we were to equate this to 170 intensive single-leg plyometric contacts, it would likely raise eyebrows.

This highlights the importance of considering the appropriateness of volume based on an athlete's qualification level. Extensive volume, involving longer distances and lower intensity, may be suitable for individuals with a lower level of physical preparation. On the other hand, intensive volume, characterised by shorter distances and higher intensity, may be more appropriate for athletes in the later stages of their training journey.

When designing a speed development program, it is crucial to strike a balance between volume and intensity, ensuring that the workload is appropriate for the athlete's current level of qualification. It is important to note here that in sprinting intensity is categorised based on the percentage of maximum speed. Therefore we categorise training in those terms. By understanding that in order to create overload from volume you need to add a single extra step, coaches can optimise training programs and help athletes reach their full potential. For example in the development of maximum speed adding an additional step at 90% sprint speed per run will create a signification overload. Take these simple workings below to understand big impact small increases can make in a training program:

Steps 90%	Total Runs	Total Steps	% Increase
4	3	12	
5	3	15	22
6	3	18	18

Where great coaches set themselves apart from the rest is the understanding of frequency in a training program. We define training frequency as the amount of training sessions we have within a specific window of time relative to non training days. This is where we can understand the density of loading. Most coaches will plan their training around the traditional seven day week. whereas coaches with a greater understanding of training adaptation consider the greater picture. Working from a standard seven day week creates a lot of problems when we consider team training schedules and the ability for the athlete to recover within specific windows of time. It has been documented that high stress activities can take up to 72 hours before complete recovery can be made and in some cases maybe longer. During off-season coaches can create a more favourable distribution of training sessions with their athletes. In season for example this becomes a lot more challenging. If you play on a Saturday 72 hours later from there you are only able to start to perform intensive activity, and this is typically consumed by sport practice. Therefore we have to target adaptations through the accumulation of successful small workouts or specific individual workouts will create greatest success for athletes in the long term. As previously discussed the effect of density is driven by the intensity of training. I have included some tables below that demonstrate ways in which you can manipulate density to create a high level of coaching effectiveness.

This table indicated speed training sessions every 72 hours for 28 days in an off season period. Within this evenly balanced example there are 10 speed training sessions and 18 recovery days. As you can see trying to maximise time based on a standard 7 day week loses effectiveness in training. I have also included where gym based training can be programmed to completed to maximise the training opportunity.

1	2	3	4	5	6	7
Speed Session	GYM		Speed Session	GYM		Speed Session
8	**9**	**10**	**11**	**12**	**13**	**14**
		Speed Session	GYM		Speed Session	
15	**16**	**17**	**18**	**19**	**20**	**21**
	Speed Session	GYM		Speed Session	GYM	
22	**23**	**24**	**25**	**26**	**27**	**28**
Speed Session	GYM		Speed Session	GYM		Speed Session

As we are prioriting speed as the main stressor in the program gym training always proceeds this as it is not the priority. This training is supportive in nature. Emplyoing the asynchronous approach allows for the athlete to have a more equal distribution of training to maximise performance. As this is an off-season example we would consider this an accumilation phase of training.

If we were to apply this to an inseason fixture schdeule training will look very differently. A part time rugby team for example will train on a tuesday and thurday night. Not too dissimilar within the progessional ranks where tuesday and thursday are the most stressful days of training in a majority of teams. Therefore I have placed training with respect to these two days being the most intensive training days of the week. Within this scenario we identify the training days in relation to the game as indicated in the table.

GD	**GD+1**	**GD+2**	**GD+3**	**GD-3**	**GD-2**	**GD-1**
MATCH	Recovery		TEAM & SPEED		TEAM & SPEED	
GD	**GD+1**	**GD+2**	**GD+3**	**GD-3**	**GD-2**	**GD-1**
MATCH	Recovery	Supportive Weights	TEAM & SPEED		TEAM	
GD	**GD+1**	**GD+2**	**GD+3**	**GD-3**	**GD-2**	**GD-1**
MATCH	Recovery		TEAM& SPEED		TEAM & SPEED	
GD	**GD+1**	**GD+2**	**GD+3**	**GD-3**	**GD-2**	**GD-1**
MATCH	Recovery	Supportive Weights	TEAM & SPEED		TEAM	

What you will notice in this table is that there is a lack of gym based training. This is due to the role of copetition. In competitive periods of training the priority should be focussed on sporting tactical and technical abilities and speed of execution. For all team based sports weight training is a general means of training and inseason can be used to maintain joint integrity through more closed chain movements and facilitate recovery.

Volume Considerations for Speed Training Programs

When designing speed training programs, coaches need to consider various factors, including volume, intensity, density, and qualification. Understanding an athlete's qualification level is particularly important for locomotive activities like sprinting. In this section, we will focus on volume and its significance in training programs. Coaches often make mistakes in this area, so it is crucial to grasp the distinctions between extensive and intensive volume.

Extensive Volume and Qualification

Extensive volume comprises exercises with high repeatability and minimal fatigue to the athlete. These exercises can align with aerobic developmental principles and can include striding, bounce runs, running drills, wall drills, resisted walks, extensive tempo runs, and linear movements. As we have discussed in previous chapters the importance of aerobic development from a central perspective is greatly important as we will increase the overall recovery abilities of the athlete. Also when using specific activities such as striding bounce runs, wall drills and the like we will develop peripheral adaptation of the working tissues therefore as touched on previously we can utilise this work in an accumulation phase of training. This will in turn create a more specifically conditioned athlete that will then possess a higher level of adaptive reserve for when we transition to more intensive aspects of training. Exercises within the extensive volume category provide a solid foundation for training programs, especially for athletes with a low level of physical preparation. The classification of exercises is important when determining the way in which you want to accumulate extensive volume. This is where the athlete's speed age comes into question. The level of qualification an athlete possesses will dictate what is simple versus complex. A complex exercise will carry a higher level of cognitive demand and therefore be unlikely to be utilised as a good exercise to accumulate extensive volumes. Please keep in mind that athlete qualification will determine the level of complexity an exercise is.

Intensive Volume and Qualification

Intensive volume consists of exercises with low repeatability and a higher cost to the athlete's state of readiness. These exercises focus on high-intensity activities that promote ground contact time, frequency, velocity, and intent. Examples include intensive bounding and jumping, resisted high-speed runs, maximum accelerations, fly sprints, long accelerations, and intensive tempo running. It is essential to carefully integrate intensive volume exercises based on an athlete's qualification level. This can be achieved by apply step load to understand the cost of intensive speed training.

Categorising Volume and Balancing Complexity and Intensity

To optimise skill acquisition and performance gains, coaches can categorise exercises into four quadrants. This classification helps identify the relationship between physical development and motor learning. To fully understand this quadrant we need to break it down to its individual parts. the reason why this quadrant has been produced is that coaches tend to overload intensity and complexity with too much volume more often than not. this quadrant will help you understand how to place volume alongside complexity and intensity. As previously discussed an excessive amount of volume with too much either complexity or intensity will create and negative adaptation to the athlete. Also please consider that athlete qualification is paramount here so gague your complexity / intensity indexes based on your athletes speed age.

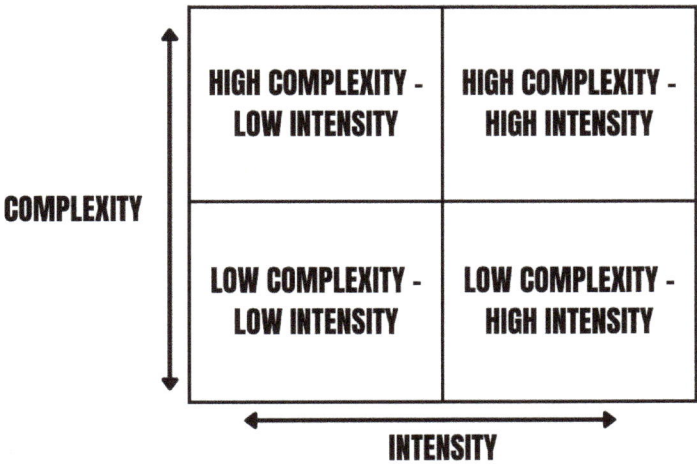

Low Complexity / Low Intensity: This is where we are able to get the bulk of extensive training performed. This can be performed at high volumes at minimal cost to the athlete.

High Complexity/ Low intensity: When using low intensity and high complexity exercises we are able to utilise a lot of extensive volume. The goal of this training is to develop the skill associated to the movement.

High Intensity / Low Complexity: If the priority of training is to utilise high intensity training then the complexity demands placed on the athlete should be limited as the priority of this training is to generate adaptation based from intensity as opposed to skill mastery.

High Complexity / High Intesity : Volume here should be allocated sparingly and only used for the most specific of training scenarios in latre stages of preparation cycles. This possesses a great cost to the athlete.

Intensity Considerations in Speed Training Programs

Speed training programs play a crucial role in enhancing athletic performance. When designing these programs, one must carefully consider the intensity levels to ensure optimal results. In this chapter, we will delve into the various aspects of intensity in speed training programs and explore how they can be effectively implemented.

Qualification, Specificity, and Accommodation

In any speed training program, it is essential to apply the rules of qualification, specificity, and accommodation. Qualification involves determining the athlete's readiness and ability to perform specific exercises or drills. Specificity emphasises tailoring training to closely resemble the demands of the target activity. Accommodation addresses the need for progressive adjustments in training to avoid stagnation and optimise results. By adhering to these principles, coaches and trainers can create a solid foundation for effective speed training.

Building Levels of Intensity

Creating levels of intensity within a training program opens up a world of possibilities. By combining ideas and methodologies from various sources, trainers can design innovative and effective training protocols. However, it is crucial not to rush the process and to use appropriate data for exercise selection and classification. By following a plan-do-review approach and making necessary adjustments, coaches can fine-tune the intensity levels in the program.

The Low-Hanging Fruit: Level 1 Movement and Drills

To achieve significant improvements in team sport speed, it is vital to focus on level 1 movement and drills (see appendix). This level primarily involves stable force application and expression, such as extensive ballistics, extensive jumps, and plyometrics. By integrating these exercises effectively, coaches can help athletes shave off precious tenths of a second and push their speed to new levels. It is important to recognise that complexity and excessive training volume can hinder progress and lead to fatigue, so it is crucial to strike a balance. I will now go into these further and explain how they can look in your training programs.

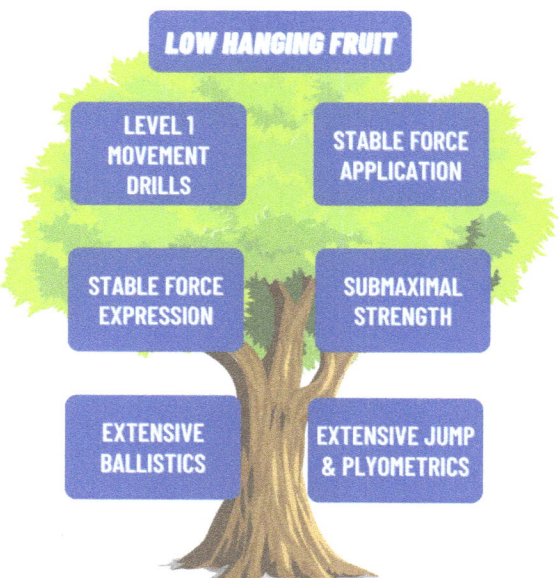

Level 1 movement drills encompass the basic running drill movements that have been utilised for years with sprinters. Exercises such as Skips and Marches offer great teaching opportunities for coaches and learning environments for athletes. Skills can suffer through lack of cognitive capacity when they have recently been introduced, therefore the athlete will improve substantially by rehearsing these movements at low speed, before then adding velocity and increasing exercise complexity over time. Another important factor to consider in this is understanding what each drill is being used for and how it helps improve the likelihood of increasing speed over the long term.

Stable force application provides athletes with specific preparatory exercises. They create and help transfer general strength qualities into the actions of sprinting. For the development of acceleration utilising General strength training exercises such as the Trap bar deadlift and then taking that Force production ability and utilising it with more specificity for acceleration. This can be done by overloading the wall drill variations you can see in the appendix, in which an athlete has two fixed surfaces into which they can express high amounts of force. After this, utilising the stable to unstable continuum, we would then look to use heavy marches with a sled or a Prowler that allow the athlete to continue to learn how to use the forces created in the general strength condition of the track bar deadlift. This is how we continue to move from stable Force expression (producing force in non specific environments) to stable Force application (attempting to apply previously attained force in spedcifci environment) as we are increasing the specificity by including the pattern of acceleration.

Submaximal strength training offers significant benefits over maximal strength training when it comes to enhancing athletic performance and speed. Unlike maximal strength training, which focuses on lifting the heaviest weights possible, submaximal strength training emphasises lifting moderate weights at higher velocities and with greater control. This approach is particularly advantageous for athletes as it promotes the development of power and speed-strength, crucial components for explosive movements required in many sports. As we have already identified in the classification chapter, general strength exercises do not create the greatest transfer to speed. By training at submaximal loads, athletes can perform more repetitions with better technique, reducing fatigue and risk of injury while improving neuromuscular efficiency and muscular endurance. Additionally, submaximal strength training allows for more frequent training sessions without overloading the central nervous system, leading to better recovery and sustained performance gains. This makes it a practical and effective strategy for athletes aiming to enhance their speed and overall athletic capabilities.

When we look at extensive means of ballistic strength production, jump training and plyometrics it is important to consider the specificity this type of training provides and the general lack of it within existing means of athletic development. When we consider the functional adaptations of strength training; intermuscular and intramuscular coordination, and reflex change are the most important variables when we are looking to develop explosive power and speed. Most training programs naturally tend to gravitate to the more intensive variations of this type of training without reaping the benefits of the submaximal extensive variations to support motor learning and local tissue adaptations.

You will find examples of these progressions within the appendix of this book.

The Shiny Objects: Load Velocity Profiling and Overspeed Work

As coaches we can become drawn to "shiny objects" and think they will solve all of our coaching issues. This couldn't be further way from the truth. The shiny object is patience and having a system. For example Load velocity profiling and overspeed work are often considered "shiny objects" in speed training programs. Load velocity profiling involves understanding the force and load relationship at different velocities. Taken from how you would perform this with a barbell. Exciting but completely misses the mark on creating step by step speed due to its average brackets of load pescription. This research has now been proven incorrect along with force velocity profiling. Overspeed work aims to improve speed by training in unstable and high-velocity conditions. However, these techniques can be complex and may not always be suitable for every athlete or training phase. Coaches should prioritise understanding their athletes' developmental cycles and focus on using the right methods for the individual or group.

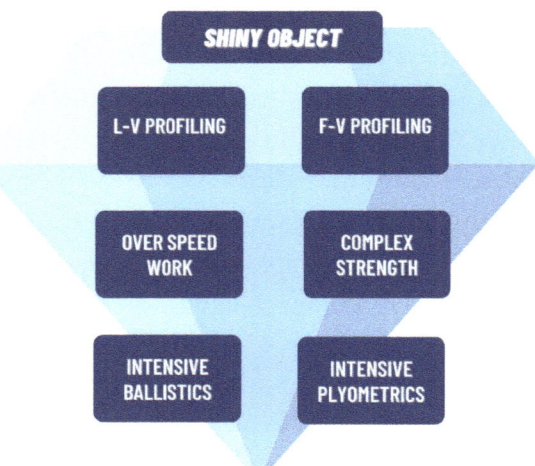

Modifying Track and Field Models for Team Sports

There are glaring differences between track sprinting and field sports. If you are reading this book I am sure I do not need to outline these for you. When loading speed inside the sports speed system I have modified a well known track speed loading protocol. The Short to long or long to short approach popularised by the late Charlie Francis. We are able to do this by understanding the typical acceleration profiles of team sport athletes and plot this against the maximum distances used to develop aerobic abilities.

The short to long training approach, focuses on developing speed through the progressive increase of training distances. This method starts with short, high-intensity sprints and gradually extends the distance over time. The philosophy behind this approach is that by initially focusing on short sprints, athletes can maximise their acceleration and top speed early in the training cycle. This helps to establish a strong speed foundation, which can then be extended to longer distances as the training progresses. The key benefit of this approach is the prioritisation of quality over quantity; athletes learn to run fast first and then sustain that speed over longer distances.

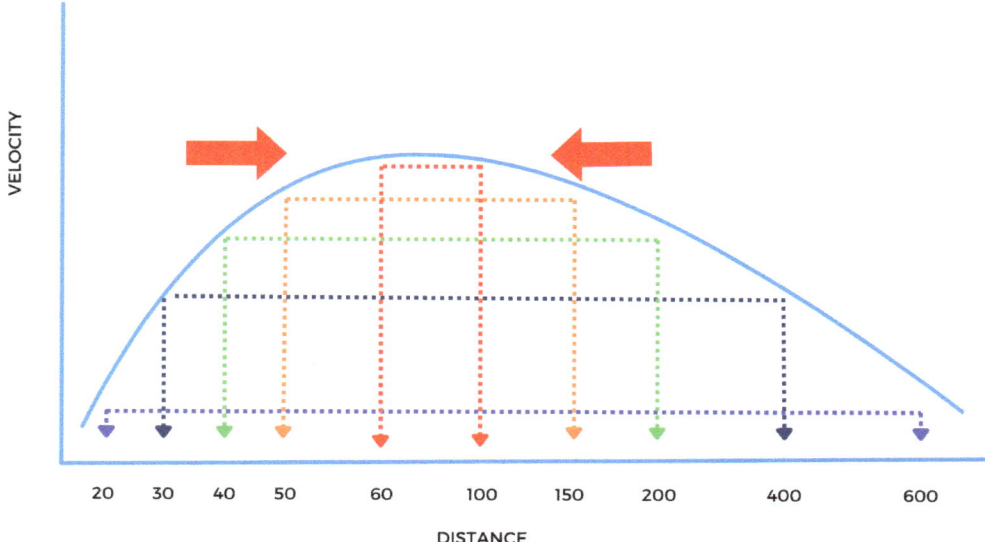

Comparining short to long an long to short approaces in attaining velocity.

In practice, the short to long approach begins with distances as short as 30 metres, emphasising explosive starts and rapid acceleration. As the training cycle advances, the distances increase incrementally to 60 metres, 100 metres, and beyond, maintaining the high-intensity effort. This method is particularly effective for sprinters, as it mirrors the demands of competitive races where the ability to reach and maintain maximum velocity is crucial. Moreover, by focusing on short sprints initially, athletes can develop neuromuscular efficiency, improve their running mechanics, and enhance their overall power output without the excessive fatigue associated with longer distances. However whilst a sound approach to sprinters 30 metres in a field sport setting is considered a long sprint. Therefore we must consider redistributing the distances. A long distance in within team sport is considered 100 metres based on the demand of most team sports whereas a short distance is considered to be 5 mertres. With this condensed view we are able to successfully manipulte the approach specifically to team sports.

Conversely, the long to short training approach takes the opposite path. This method starts with longer, lower-intensity runs and progressively decreases the distance while increasing the intensity. The rationale here is to build a solid aerobic and speed endurance base early in the training cycle, which can then be sharpened into peak speed and explosive power as the competitive season approaches. This approach is particularly useful for athletes who need to develop endurance for longer sprint events or team sports requiring sustained high-intensity efforts.

In the long to short approach, athletes might begin with distances such as 200 or 400 metres at a moderate intensity (60-70% Max Sprint Speed). Over time, as the athlete's endurance and strength improve, the training distances are reduced, but the intensity and speed of the runs are increased. This gradual reduction in distance while ramping up the intensity helps athletes peak at the right time, ensuring they are both fast and resilient. This method can be beneficial for athletes who need to maintain high performance over longer periods or distances, providing a balanced approach that addresses both the aerobic and anaerobic systems. As you can see from the image below we are able to adjust the distances to ensure representation for field sport athletes.

Both approaches are integral to Charlie Francis's overall training philosophy and can be tailored to the specific needs of the athlete, depending on their event, goals, and physiological characteristics. Combining elements of both approaches can also be beneficial, ensuring that athletes develop a comprehensive range of speed, power, and endurance capabilities. When aplpying this ensure that you are developing speed technique and conditioning over longer distances and explosive power and speed over shorter distances. This can be seen in the programs provided in the appendix.

Speed Zones

When planning intensity of running and sprinting I adhere to basic principles, as coaches we are initially taught these modalities through the means of weight training by never through the context of sprinting. Whilst it is slightly more complex the principles still apply. In any modality of training intensity is always prescribed form the maximal capabilities of our athletes. As a reminder we have three different maxima we can work off of. The Image below illustrates these.

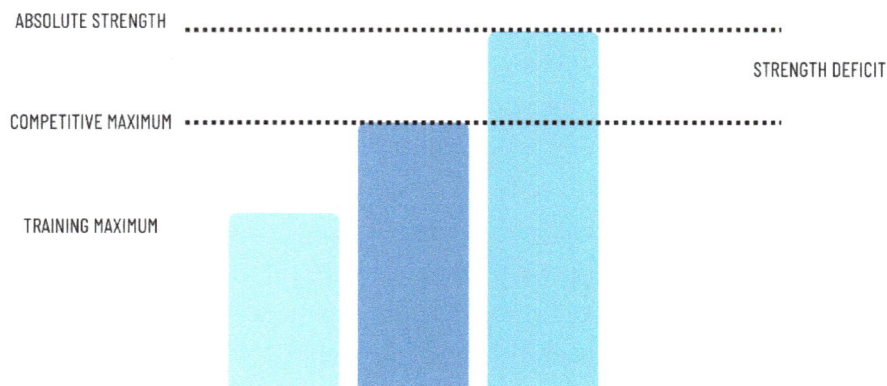

Within the context of sprinting and creating intensity that an athlete can adapt from, I have slightly modified this model for you to understand how you can prescribe training speeds. It is important to note that training maximum is in place to help prevent the accumulation of fatigue athletes will face during the training block. As mentioned many times within this book if the motor skill of the athlete isn't mastered then the relative cost of an exercise is greater. This is why we see great progress from simply learning how to sprint with field sport athletes.

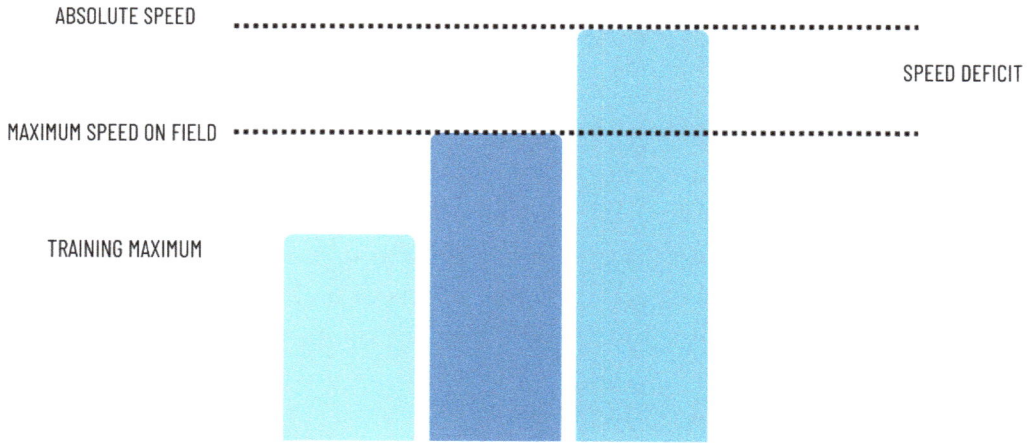

Highlighting speed zones is an important way to ensure that you manage intensity. How I choose to do it is based on maximum acceleration and maximum velocity. In track, athletes continue to accelerate up to 60 metres in many cases. However in team sports, athletes will do most of their accelerating inside 20m. As they are a less skilled and prepared athlete there is a much greater cost to this work. Therefore when we look at the development of acceleration we build acceleration based on their intent to accelerate over a series of steps.

For example to develop initial acceleration (steps 0-3) we will use the following step principles to progressively overload acceleration. The first number is the step we are creating load with and the second is the steps we are coasting/technically refining:

- 1+2
- 2+1
- 3

A Systematic Approach to Exercise Classification of Speed

This is then built out over late acceleration from steps 0-7 and then up to 15 steps *(recommended loading table in the appendix)*. By 15 steps most team sport athletes have accelerated close to their maximum velocity. Below I have calculated an example data set based on the NFL 40-yard Combine.

Hypothetical Dataset

Assume we have a data set for a group of athletes running the 40-yard dash. We measure their times at each 10-yard segment and observe the change in time per segment.

Key Assumptions

1. The maximum acceleration occurs at the start and decreases as the athlete approaches top speed.
2. We analyse the different to yard segments to establish speed (0-10 yards).

Example Data Set

Athlete	0-10 Yards (s)	10-20 Yards (s)	20-30 Yards (s)	30-40 Yards (s)	40-Yard Time (s)
A	1.6	1	0.9	0.8	4.3
Drop Off		0.6	0.1	0.1	
B	1.6	1	0.98	0.85	4.43
Drop Off		0.6	0.02	0.13	
C	1.55	1	0.88	0.77	4.2
Drop Off		0.55	0.12	0.11	

Looking at each individual athlete we are able to determine how they continue to accelerate over the 40 yards. As acceleration is greatest inside the initial 10 yard segment we can see big drop offs inside the 10-20 yard range. However what is interesting athlete B when compared to A struggles to maintain acceleration through the later segments of the run whilst having the same initial 10 yard time. This is not uncommon for team sport athletes due to the nature of their game. This is why it is important to teach and train acceleration as a special exercise. The curve loading framework and step by step become valuable tools when encountering this problem. As a coach please use this simple method with your athletes to help direct your training approach.

When we consider intensity zones in relation to maximum speed we use the same formula but extend the distances covered. This is where long accelerations become integral in the development of maximum speed especially in the learning to sprint phases of training. This is because they are categorised as extensive speed training. This will be covered in greater detail in later sections. As we progress from learning to sprint to training to sprint we need to consider the use of velocity zones to train speed. Here I always work from the concept popularised by the late Charlie Francis.

Classification of Running Velocity - Charlie Francis

HIGH INTENSITY - 95-100% of Best Time
- High Central Nervous system demand
- Enhances muscle fibre recruitment
- Requires complete recovery between repetitions
- Requires minimum of 48 hours recovery between sessions
- Non - circulatory.

MEDIUM INTENSITY - 76-94% of Best Time
- Too slow to be specific to the training objective
- Too high to recover adequately within 24 hours
- CNS recovery limited by lack of circulatory response

LOW INTENSITY - 75% of Best Time and Slower
- Circulatory response (active recovery)
- Speed Enhancement through the effect of increased capillary density (i.e. heating of muscle motor neurons, lowering electrical resistance
- Increased capillary density slows blood flow through tissue allowing more time for nutrient transfer and waste removal
- Enhances CNS recovery through improved parasympathetic response.

It is important to note here that this classification of running velocity has been deliberately designed for world class sprinters. however we are able to adapt and recreate this based on its fundamental principles to suit and fit the mould of the field sport athlete. In the creation of intensity alone I feel it is important to adjust the high intensity zone based on the previous discussion on the creation of maximum outputs. Team sport athletes inherently possess a lack of specific physical preperation with regards to tolerating high intensity, therefore submaximal velocity exposures will help develop skill and specific strength to withstand higher speed running. Therefore I recommend working from 80-85% of maximal speed initially and then progression to higher intensities as you would with an untrained performer with any new training means. We also need to consider the medium intensities zone as a zone we can exploit in the specific preparation of repeat ability. Repeatability in field sports is incredibly important and as we move into the specific and specialised areas of speed creation for field sports we will explore this area a lot more. However, it does not serve the purpose of developing maximum qualities; it only helps to reproduce higher percentages of submaximal qualities. Lastly, understanding the way that we can utilise the low intensity zone is incredibly important as for the field sport athletes modalities such as extensive tempo running and extensive running drill activities serve a great purpose for specific tissue adaptation for speed and power improvements. We will now discuss and look into how motor learning plays into the role of intensity.

The Motor Learning Response and Exercise Exposure

When we consider motor learning and it applies to the development of specific exercises there are three phases of exposure. Phase one focuses on exercises that an athlete is still unable to execute correctly, providing limited stimuli for functional improvement. Phase two marks the point where exercises begin to produce adequate stimuli for desired improvements. This is when we can add more intensity to the current training regime. Rushing into phase two without allowing sufficient time for phase one can hinder progress due to the rates of learning as discussed within our skill acquisition sections. Finally, phase three occurs when an exercise no longer provides adequate stimuli, indicating that the athlete has reached their training potential for that specific exercise. It is now a fully learned skill that the athlete can use reflexively. Understanding these phases helps trainers create hierarchies of exercises and ensures appropriate training progressions.

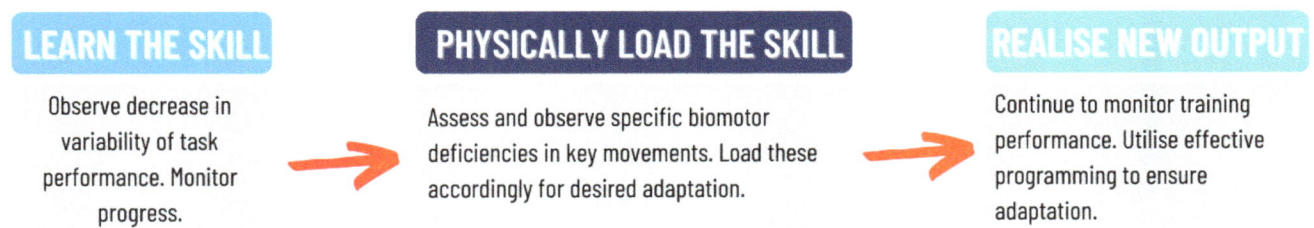

The work of Verkhoshansky offers valuable insights into the motor learning response and exercise exposure and developing the competitive task. The competitive task in this context is the next level of specialisation we are seeking out in training. The improvement in this competitive task is directly dependant on the increases in athletes motor potential and the athletes ability to execute the motor skill of the competitive task. This concept forms the foundation for increasing an individual's specialisation over time and is one of the guiding principles of speed age.

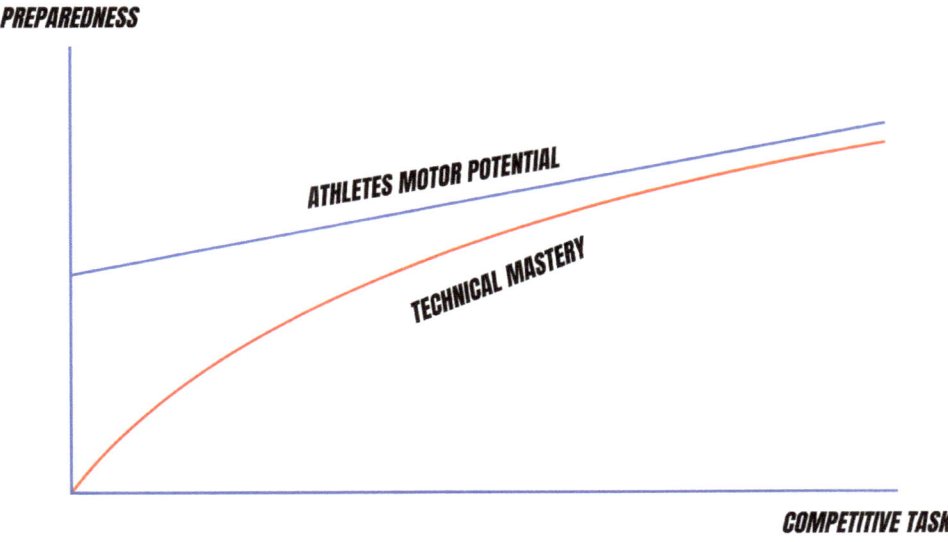

As an athlete increases their working capacity and competency and most importantly outputs in the competitive task, coaches are able to introduce more complex and intense training stimulus. This is a vital part of the journey of training. Identifying and acknowledging that a specific training modality generated one result to elicit a specific adaptation at one part of the training cycle is an important distinction to make when looking to increase specificity of training. Also when as coaches we are looking to prolong and extend windows of adaptation and preparedness. This combines very well with the law of accommodation. Here we aim to adapt to the competitive task (e.g. new speed training exercise) therefore we must focus training on technical mastery to realise nee levels of motor potential in the chosen competitive task.

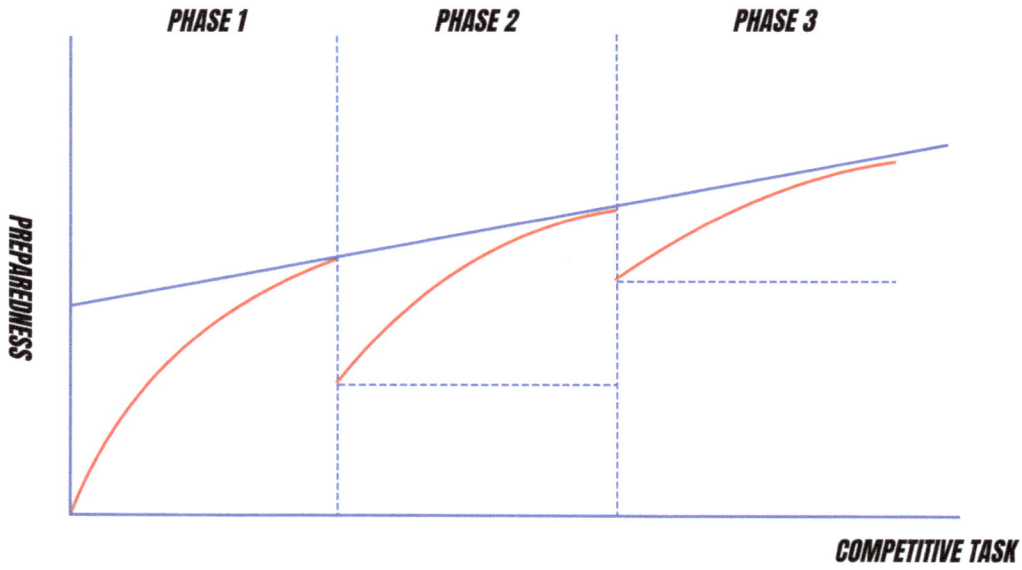

As you now know through reading this book we highlight the specific actions of sprinting and various other movements as the competitive task in general speed. This is how we have created exercise progression and sequencing of training. This relationship changes as we progress to the more specific phases of sport preparation but as physical preparation specialists, it is important to acknowledge and understand the parameters we want to support and change. Below is an example of how the Sports Speed System integrates with the preparations of a rugby winger. As you can see if we effectively change the competitive exercise (the way in which we assess affective transfer) then as coaches we can target training and specialise performance at the most appropriate times. What is most important about this is that where the coach has minimal direct contact with players these adaptations can be observed in training and games.

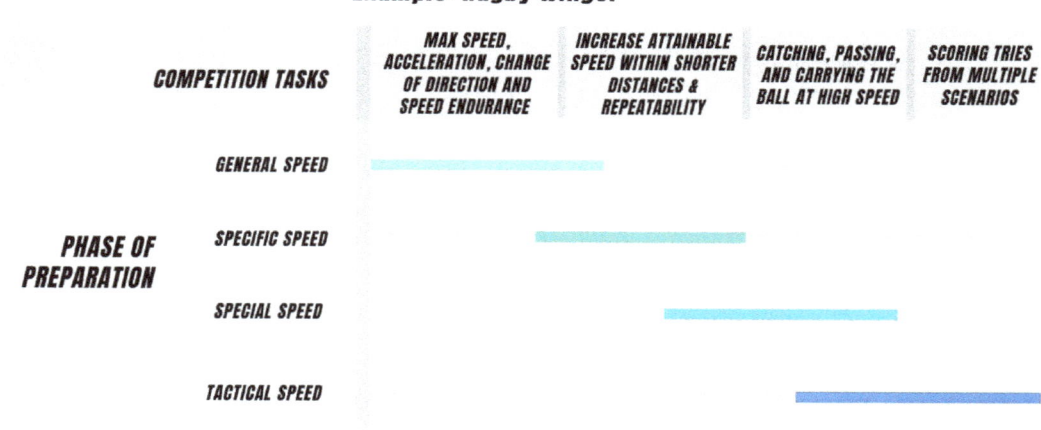

Within the realm of motor learning and skill acquisition this type of training would constitute deliberate practice. We are pre-determining the task and the skills in order to increase the output of that specific exercise to create transfer. As we progress through the system the ways in which we use skill acquisition change to meet the overall outcome of the speed we are trying to create.

Conjugate Sequencing applied to Speed Training

Utilising intensity to create adaptation for Speed training is a vital tool for any coach. However, many coaches try to use as much intensity as possible as soon as possible, when we need to be doing the complete opposite. The goal of effective intensity allocation in training is to find the intensity that creates adaptation but does not negatively affect the athletes performance. This foundational principle of training ensures that we are able to maximise the effects of training and minimise the detraining effect that excessive exposure can create. A common example of this is when an individual in their offseason starts to perform repeated maximum sprints having not done that for almost a year, and ends up massively fatigued and frequently injured. I have witnessed this first hand in the professional rugby environment. One of the best players in the English Premiership was exposed to multiple cross field Kicks as a tactical adjustment to the training program. Over the past six weeks of training and games he had not exceeded over 80% of his maximum speed. In this session he broke 90% of his current maximum speed 8 times. Unfortunately he did not complete the session as he had a reactive hamstring and did not play that week. This was simply more volume and intensity than he was prepared for, and this demonstrates how training intensity can negatively impact performance. We must prepare our athletes intelligently to negotiate the fine line between stimulus and injury. As athletes get more advanced, this must be done with ever greater precision.

The diagram below illustrates the effect that intensity can have on the rate of adaptation. This ties in very well to many of the other training principles that we have discussed such as the law of accommodation. As you look at the diagram from the left hand side you will find that there is a steady gradual increase in performance at low intensities which require minimal effort. For example, this is where we find many team sport athletes experiencing increases in Speed by improving their maximum strength. Here we are utilising general non-specific training but generating a specific result because of the current level of athlete specialisation. For example creating adaptation in speed performance from the use of barbell based movement. As we progress and introduce more specific and intense stimuli you can see that the slope of the intensity-adaptation curve drastically starts to increase. This means that as we increase intensity the rate of adaptation actually slows down and the time it takes to create adaptation becomes longer. This is because the percentage increases at higher levels of performance become much harder to attain. This is because we are at a level where we are pushing the athlete to their absolute limits.

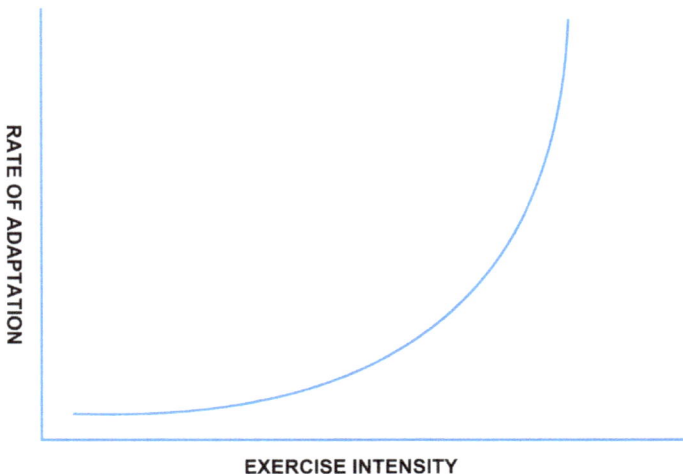

Having clearly defined parameters of intensity make training program design and prescription incredibly easy and, to an extent, predictable. I have included below an image that indicates typically what most coaches will do when they try to increase intensity of training. The image on the left shows a significant jump in intensity which will lead to poor adaptation and if not injury.

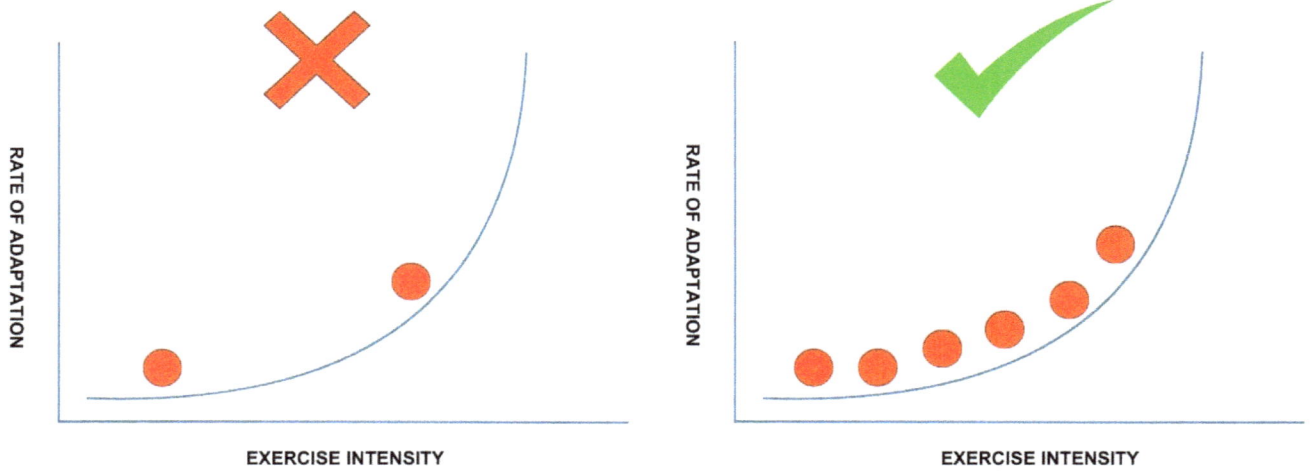

As we know from previously discussing the law of accommodation, an athlete's body must gradually adapt to a stressor over a period of time, before using a more potent stimulus. This is why it is important not to jump too fast in specialisation. The image on the right illustrates the type of progression of intensity that we will look for and is desired. This ensures that throughout the training process and the career of the athlete we are maximising the continuity between training stresses. This is very important for two main reasons. The first reason is that in the diagram on the left the athlete will experience high levels of shock from the training leading to what we will call a missed opportunity of adaptation. This means that the body will reject the straining stimulus and not adapt to it and should be revisited when the athlete is ready according to SAID principle. The second reason is that as we gradually progress in training intensity, the athlete's body does not resist the new intensity of training so we are able to continue to progress training cycles without having to change the distribution of training too aggressively, to accommodate for the mismanagement of intensity. Conjugate sequencing is the most appropriate way to do this and we will now discuss this further.

Conjugate sequencing is a training methodology that is vital to the success of speed training programs. Conjugate sequencing creates levels of intensity in training and categorisation of exercises. This lends itself perfectly as an extension to the previous work of Verkhoshansky as discussed with regards to motor learning. It provides a programming pathway for the desire of specificity and intensity within training programs.

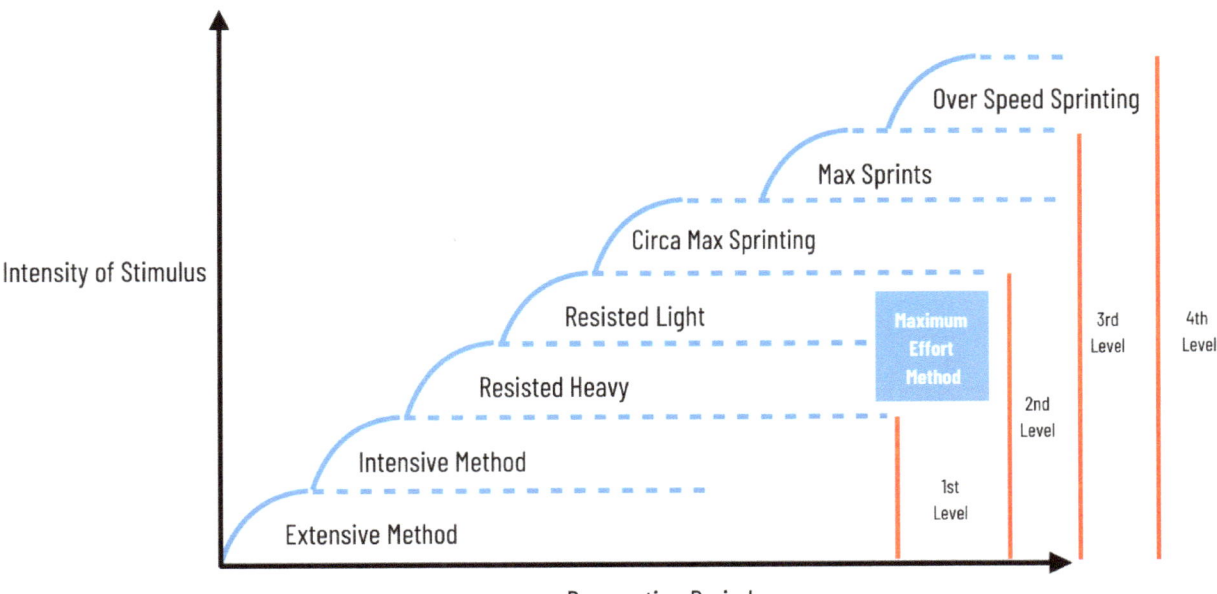

It is important to discuss here the parameter of intensity. With the specific application of conjugate sequencing of speed, I have chosen the most intensive method of improving sporting qualities is the use of overspeed training. This is where an athlete is accelerated by an external force to make them run faster than they can normally run.

The extensive method represents the initial levels, followed by progressive increases in intensity. Level two includes maximum effort method exercises, while level three involves circa max sprinting and maximum sprints. The fourth level encompasses all previous levels and introduces overspeed training. Coaches must recognise the importance of adaptive reserves and adjust training intensity accordingly to sustain desired adaptations. In this case the most general volumes of training must be removed otherwise our athletes will not be able to tolerate this additional stress and create negative adaptation or injury.

As previously discussed the utilisation of conjugate sequencing allows us to gradually and specifically increase intensity in order to continue to create performance increases via adaptations that are not too aggressive for the athlete. There are a couple of ways in which you can look at this, however I would urge you to take the view that each stage can represent a phase of training, for example offseason, preseason etc, which can be revisited year on year. However the goal of increased specialisation is that each time we revisit these phases we utilise them less and less. This means we will spend less time in each phase as the athlete progresses their level of performance. This is because we as coaches know that in order to make adaptations with athletes who possess high levels of output we need to utilise more intense means of training for longer periods of time. Athletes must frequently rotate exercises, variations, and training methods to continually challenge the body and avoid adaptation plateaus. This also stops athletes from progressing too fast and exposing themselves to excessive amounts of intensity too early in the preparation period.

I have Included a tables below that define the specific levels and illustrate the exercises and their intensity which can be utilised within the sports speed system.

Level	Intensity Stimulus	Definition
1st Level Learning to Sprint	Extensive	Submaximal higher volume training that develops motor learning and specific capacities of the exercises.
	Intensive	Higher intent and lower volume execution of previously used exercises.
2nd Level Learning to Sprint / Training to Sprint	Resisted Heavy	Sprinting with external loads that exceed 50% of an athlete's body mass.
	Resisted Light	Sprinting with external loads that do not exceed 50% of an athlete's body mass.
3rd Level Training to Sprint / Sprinting to Compete	Circa Max Sprinting	Sprinting from static or rolling conditions between 80% - 90% through all phases of sprinting - Acceleration, transition, maximum velocity in a single effort.
	Max Sprinting	Sprinting from static or rolling conditions maximally through all phases of sprinting - Acceleration, transition, maximum velocity in a single effort.
4th Level Sprinting to Compete / Sprinting to Win	Over Speed Sprinting	Being assisted to produce speed that is typically unattainable when otherwise unassisted.

As you can see there is definite sequential order to the gradual intensification of movement. In the table below I have outlined how you would do this for acceleration and maximum speed.

Level	Intensity	Variation One - Acceleration Bias	Variation 2 - Max Speed Bias
1st Level Learning to Sprint	Extensive	Unresisted Wall Drills	70% 50m Tempo Runs
	Intensive	Resisted Wall Drills	85% 50m Intensive Tempo Runs
2nd Level Learning to Sprint / Training to Sprint	Resisted Heavy	Heavy Prowler March	N/A
	Resisted Light	Sled Acceleration	
3rd Level Training to Sprint / Sprinting to Compete	Circa Max Sprinting	30m Technical Acceleration	Long Accelerations
	Max Sprinting	30m Max Acceleration	Fly Sprint
4th Level Sprinting to Compete / Sprinting to Win	Over Speed Sprinting	Assisted Acceleration	Assisted Max Speed Sprints

During this process I think it is important to mention certain details. As we have discussed intensity is defined by the absolute maximums of exposure an athlete can be subjected to. This also means that no athlete is the same and will respond differently to stressors placed on them due to their training history. This is where specialisation and training qualification become paramount. As you will see in the programs provided in this book for an athlete learning to sprint we will use the first three levels consistently. However the time spent in each level will differ based on what the athlete needs the most. The following image demonstrates the relationship between speed age and relative intensity of training stimulus needed. The motor control and motor learning elements of speed in the early speed ages far exceed the gains that occur from excessively intense means of loading.

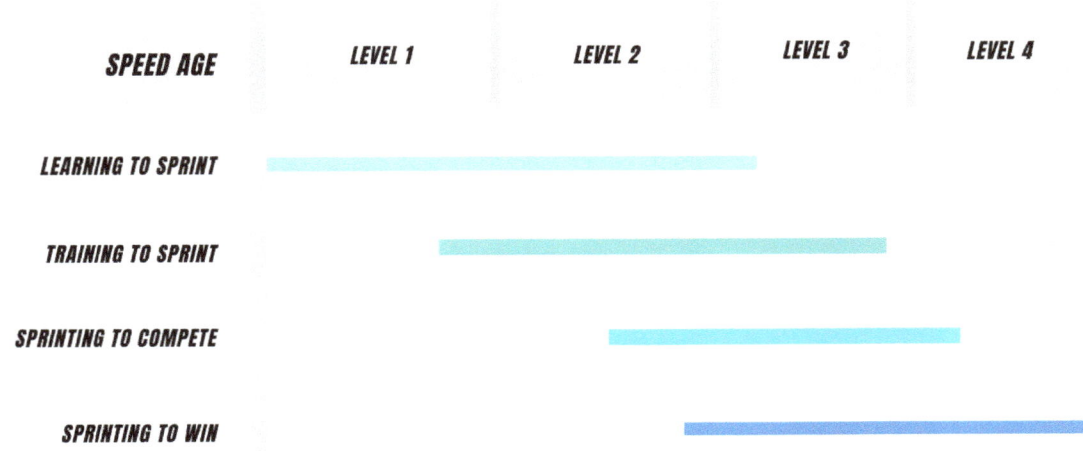

Exit Criteria and Monitoring Progress

In speed training programs, exit criteria play a vital role in evaluating progress and determining the readiness to move on to the next level of intensity. Skill performance assessment, identification of bio-motor deficiencies, and appropriate adjustment of loading parameters are essential for effective program design. Continuous monitoring of training performance allows for timely adjustments and ensures that athletes progress in a safe and effective manner. At the heart of this is understanding two simple principles. The first is the process of phased exercise exposure. Initially presented by Yuri Verkhoshasnky; the relationship between learning how to do the exercise before the exercises becomes a learned skill to create functional changes in performance. When this is attained in phase 2 there is an actual opportunity to create functional improvements within the athlete. Then finally as mastery of the exercise at a given intensity is attained it then stops creating stimulus for the athlete to improve. This is when an exercise needs to be changed. A simple example of this is using horizontal jumps. Just by learning how to jump forward, athletes will increase their jump distance. However once that initial rate of adaptation has occurred there is then a need to change in stimulus. This is where we would exit extensive jumps and incorporate intensive jumps.

PHASE 1

The exercise is still not able to induce an adequate stimuli for the needed functional improvement of athlete's body because the athlete is still not able to execute the exercise the in correct way

PHASE 2

The exercise begins to produce an adequate stimuli for the needed functional improvement of athlete's body because the athlete becomes able to execute the exercise in the correct way.

PHASE 3

The exercise ceases to produce adequate stimuli for the needed functional improvement of athlete's body because the training potential of exercise is exhausted

This initial phase of learning the skill is really important in the athletes training. It is the blend between learning the skill and existing biomotor abilities trained through other general means of training that can unlock speed improvements relatively quickly for athletes.

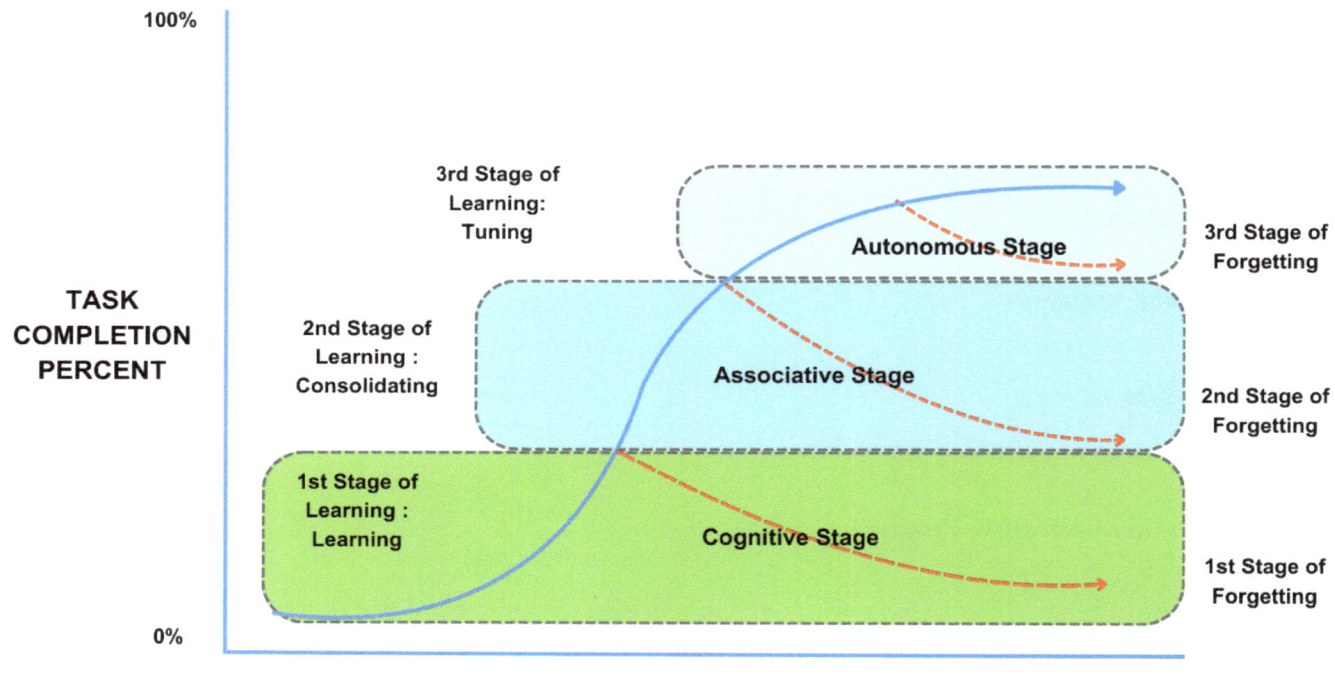

One often overlooked factor in the process of skill acquisition is the rate at which a new skill is retained in the learner. Often I see coaches make the mistake of not giving the athlete time to consolidate a new exercise. Even if they have shown they are capable of performing a movement correctly in one set or a session it doesn't necessarily mean they will be able to repeat that the following session. Defining exit criteria for a training stimulus should be largely dependent on this simple fact. We will be taking a deeper look at skill acquisition later in this book. However for the purpose of this section consolidated motor learning is paramount before progressing training intensity. Throughout all stages of learning athletes can and will forget what they have been taught. This is specifically important when creating programs and sessions. During sessions an athlete will only have a finite capacity for learning and memory. Do not overload this with lots of exercises or complexity. This is why learn load execute as a framework combined with drill stacking compounds the learning experience and reduces rates of forgetting. Ultimately because there is a constant thread throught out training process. Over a succession of training sessions a coach should judge retention by changing the coaching style to a more athlete lead approach. Instead of coaching drills just ask the athlete to perform them. This is where you will be able to determine what if any changes need to be made.

From an understanding of change in physical output. I have brought back an image previously used in the book. Tracking simple variables such as distance and speed it is important for a coach to highlight the competitive exercises that all training is being measured against and plot the progress to ensure there is maximum efficiency of training. This is how we establish exit criteria and continuity within our training progressions.

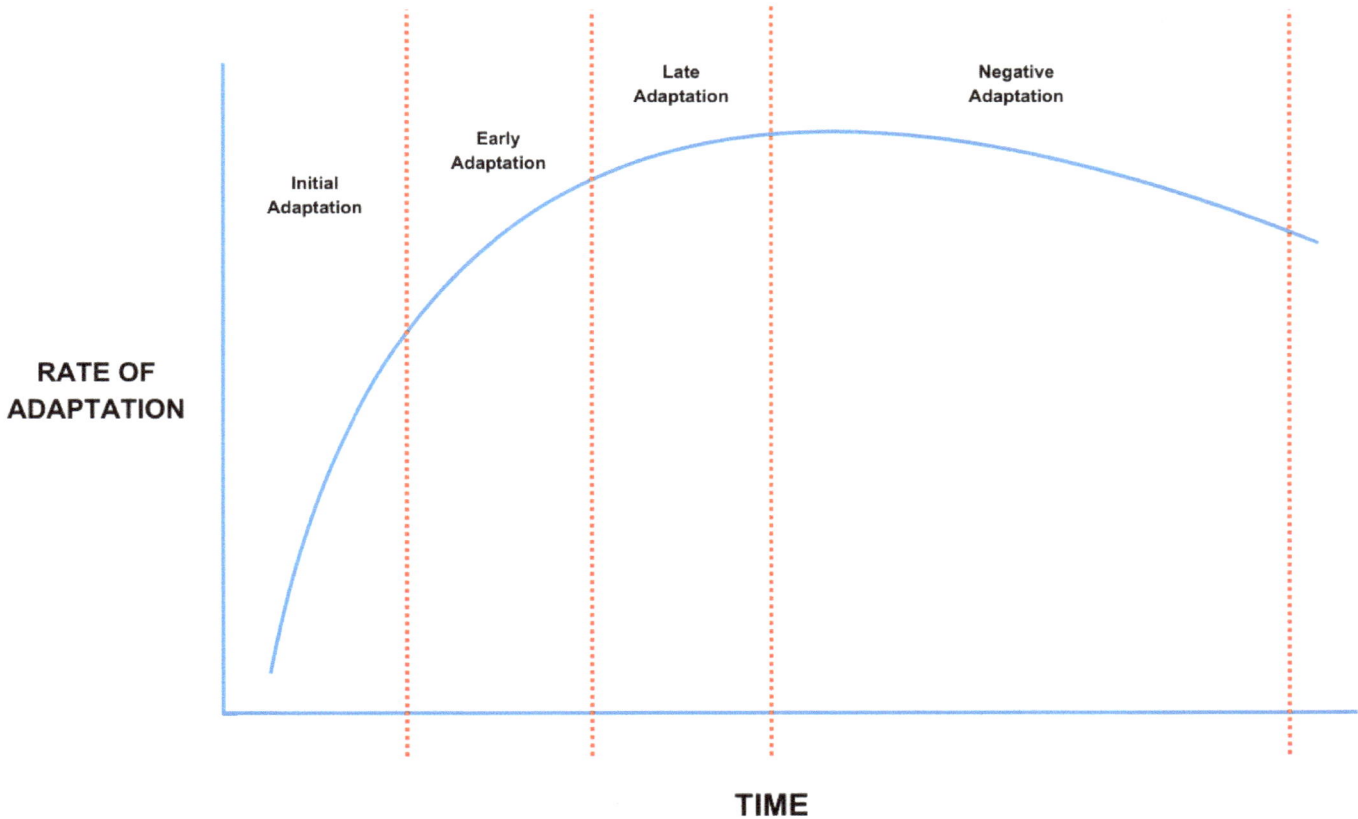

Effort and Intensity Considerations in Different Speed Training Methods

Effort and intensity considerations vary across different speed training methods. Linear velocity training focuses on front-end acceleration, transition, and maintaining maximum velocity. Non-linear speed training, which involves cuts, crossovers, and swerving, requires specific attention to movement patterns and associated intensity levels. Coaches must tailor the training program to the specific demands of the chosen sport and movement patterns involved. This is where the sports speed system comes into its own. In the Specific and Specialised speed sections of the book we will explore how you can deconstruct your sport to establish these patterns.

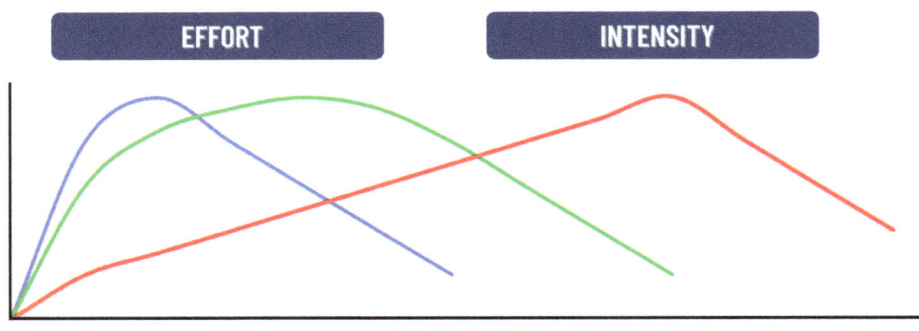

By understanding the principles of intensity and implementing them effectively, coaches can design comprehensive training programs that optimise performance gains while minimising the risk of excessive fatigue. As we previously highlighted, intensity in speed is based on maximum velocity. This means that any training that contains acceleration is high effort training and any training that targets maximum speed is high intensity training. To create specific intensity the coach needs to decide what quality of sprinting they are trying to positively affect and then what percentage of maximum they are going to train at. This is the same logic as applied to creating changes in barbell movements, by using the principle of progressive overload. By considering the scientific aspects, such as motor learning response, and exercise exposure, coaches can fine-tune their programs and help athletes reach new levels of speed and performance. This is where tracking progress becomes of paramount importance.Creating Levels within Your Speed Training Program

In speed training, qualification levels within your training program is essential to guide athletes through their journey of skill development and performance improvement. By understanding the stages of learning and progression, coaches can design effective programs that prioritise speed and address individual needs. This section explores the concept of creating levels within a speed training program and highlights the importance of prioritising speed over traditional strength training.

The Journey from Learning to Winning

The athlete's journey in speed training can be categorised into four stages: learning to sprint, training to sprint, sprinting to compete, and sprinting to win. The transition from one stage to another represents a shift from unconscious incompetence to unconscious competence. The initial jumps in skill acquisition are significant, but the progress slows down as athletes reach higher levels of competence. Here I feel it is important to remind you that the skills of sprinting are simple and perfection is not the goal, being effective is, as identified in the coaching speed section. Understanding this progression is crucial for designing effective training programs.

The Importance of Prioritising Speed

A common misconception in training programs is placing more emphasis on strength training over speed development. However, it is vital to recognise that speed holds greater significance than gym work. As we have previously discussed the principal is specificity dictates our choice in training methodologies. It is important to prioritise speed over strength related movements purely because the gym training is in place to support the development of speed. If we favour gym related training over speed we will actually decrease the rate of transfer of training as opposed to increase the rate of transfer. This is why it is so important to understand the classification of training and exercises used in order to support the overall goal. As we know within the sports speed system, speed is a general quality that needs to be nurtured in order to see successful transfer on the pitch.

Creating a Matrix for Qualification Levels

To create effective levels within a speed training program, coaches can use a matrix approach. This matrix includes two dimensions: physical variance (qualifications related to physical output) and motor variance (qualifications related to sprinting skills). The assumed scenario is that athletes and coaches aim for the winning category, but the reality is that most athletes fall under the competing category in terms of physical output. This highlights the need to focus on skill development and exploit the window of opportunity for improvement aggressively.

PHYSICAL OUTPUT

	LEARNING	TRAINING	COMPETING	WINNING
LEARNING			Typical Sport Athlete	
TRAINING				
COMPETING				
WINNING				

MOTOR LEARNING

Most team sport athletes do possess very high levels of general physical output, meaning that they have a high level of specialisation in gym based movements. They are usually able to produce and express strength and power within the context of barbell movements, however they are unable to put that expression of strength and power to use within the specific motor task of sprinting. These athletes have a low level of specialisation with respect to speed training and the development of speed therefore our initial qualification should be based on their ability to learn and retain the motor qualities of the skills of sprinting in an attempt to maximise the pre-existing ability to express strength and power. This simple model can serve as a great mental model for you to optimise and prioritise training.

Identifying Gaps and Promoting Transfer

Analysing the training program requires identifying gaps and promoting transfer between physical and motor qualifications. As a basic rule of training, prioritising motoring learning is paramount to accelerated development in speed. Coaches must observe the level of transfer within their athletes to ensure they are producing the required speed and training in a way that fosters skill development.

Example Level Execution

The creation of levels within a successful training program is dependent upon the athletes current readiness to train, their current specialisation of performance and their ability to perform the competitive task that has been identified. As a coach it is your primary job to create the successful transfer of training. One of the most effective aspects of the sport speed system lies within the unique methodology of how training and exercises are blended with one another over time. As we have discussed extensively, the concept of speed age is based upon the prioritisation of motor transfer over the transfer of physical development in order to maximise and maintain a continual rate of progress with our athletes. Meaning the athletes ability to execute the motor skill demands of the task of speed and movement guide the assertion in speed age. I have included a table below that demonstrates how you are able to insert the learn load and execute framework in conjunction with speed age.

This is the power of understanding qualification and creating levels. At the Learning to Sprint speed age you will find, as you can see in the table, what constitutes an execution exercise becomes a learning exercise as you progress into the Training to Sprint speed age. This is where we are able to continue to maximise the rate of adaptation and create seamless interchange between performance enhancements from motor learning as opposed to the sole reliance on physical development. This ensures that the potency of a training stimulus remains high at all times and does not lose its potency due to overexposure. This is in keeping with the law of accommodation and SAID principle which we have previously discussed. What I think is most important is that you can now see it being brought to life and how you will apply it in a day-to-day coaching environment.

	Learning To Sprint	Training to Sprint	Sprinting to Compete	Sprinting to Win
Learn	Stable Wall Drills Projection / Retraction Long Accelerations	Stable - Unstable Wall Drills / SPE Medium Curve Accelerations	Unstable -Stable Drills and SPE All Curve Accelerations	Circa Maximal Constrained Running
Load	Resisted Walks Sub Maximal Long Sprints	Resisted Accelerations Circa Maximal Long Sprints	Profiled Accelerations Maximal Long Sprints	Assisted Accelerations Assisted Long Sprints
Execute	Constrained Accelerations	Constrained Runs of all Variety	Maximal Runs of all Variety	Competitive Racing

If we isolate this top row of the table and how it corresponds with the speed ages I want you to understand and see how we are able to create a complimentary training effect by the increase of complexity without the need for increasing intensity. What I mean by a complimentary training effect is having a foundation in the development of a specific movement. For example, in the development of acceleration, creating a stable environment where we learn to develop competency and retain the ability to express the fundamental movements of early acceleration provides an important foundation as we progress through the speed ages. The next logical step from a highly stable environment is to gradually reduce the stability. This will drastically increase the complexity of movement as the athlete has to negotiate and re-stabilise the positions. In this condition we are trying to take the learned behaviours that we have developed previously and then utilise them in more specific conditions. This is how we integrate the frameworks across the speed ages to create seamless continuity.

	Learning To Sprint	Training to Sprint	Sprinting to Compete	Sprinting to Win
Learn	Stable Wall Drills Projection / Retraction Long Accelerations	Stable - Unstable Wall Drills / SPE Medium Curve Accelerations	Unstable -Stable Drills and SPE All Curve Accelerations	Circa Maximal Constrained Running

Furthermore if we isolate the learning to sprint speed age and examine it closely against the learn load and execute framework we are able to see how we can progress a low level of specialisation but create highly specific training. In the learn phase again we have a high degree of stability focusing on the development of forward displacement of the centre of mass and the ability to minimise the error in the naturally occurring scissors motion of acceleration. Also within this phase, in the context of maximum velocity speed development, we would utilise long accelerations that help athletes learn to slowly build to high percentage velocity running with minimal effort. This allows the athlete to have a much higher cognitive load when sprinting to support the learning of the new skill as they can think more about their technique as they build there speed as opposed to just running flat out fast. Remember as previously discussed in these phases there is a high rate of forgetting so therefore it is important to maintain a high volume of learn based training.

	Learning To Sprint
Learn	Stable Wall Drills Projection / Retraction Long Accelerations
Load	Resisted Walks Sub Maximal Long Sprints
Execute	Constrained Accelerations

As we look to highlight the load phase, I want to remind you that the learn load and execution model of work does not isolate itself to a single element only covered at one time. For example only doing learn based work for a single session is not how the framework is intended to be utilised. it is intended to be utilised as a complementary structure of which you use in a complete session. A session will start with a learn-based movement, then introduce load to that movement, and then challenge the athlete to execute that movement. This helps you as a coach understand the rate at which your athlete learns. So when we look at the load-based work for acceleration in the learning to sprint phase we will complement highly stable drills with highly stable locomotion via the means of heavy resisted walks. These variations are fantastic as they slow the athlete down enough to develop the appropriate mechanics required in a dynamic fashion whilst applying force in the most appropriate way. These serve as a fantastic teaching tool as they provide immediate feedback, if you do not get in the right positions, the load simply will not move. As we look at the other end of the spectrum and turn our attention to loading variations of maximum velocity sprinting, here we try to accumulate an increased number of steps of higher percentage running. Our long acceleration variations provide a minimal amount of high velocity running whereas our sub maximal longer sprints will dedicate specific zones or distances to cover at a specific speed. Over time we can increase the number of steps at a given percentage of maximum velocity in order to create a larger stimulus, which will in turn yield greater speed adaptations.

Lastly we look at this from the perspective of Execution. This is where we will task the athlete to create acceleration in different scenarios. If we are focused on acceleration then we will task the athlete with increasing the number of short distance acceleration efforts they are capable of, and giving them more difficult acceleration tasks, rather than increasing the distance which would emphasise top speed. This ultimately will be the litmus test to see whether the coaching and the constraints we have placed on the athlete have worked. The litmus test here is either improved technique or improved speed or a combination of both. Sometimes we can improve technique and not speed due to the time it takes to realise a new level of output with refined technique.

Planning for Speed Training Programs

When it comes to designing effective speed training programs, proper planning is essential. By understanding the athletes' readiness to train, their qualification level, available time, and body type, coaches can create a comprehensive and tailored approach to speed development. This section explores the key elements involved in planning for speed training programs and provides insights into how coaches can optimise their coaching strategies to achieve significant improvements in team sport speed.

1. Assessing Readiness to Train:

Before diving into speed training, coaches must assess the athletes' readiness to train. This involves evaluating their overall physical condition, injury history, and current fitness levels. By understanding the athletes' readiness, coaches can determine the appropriate starting point and progression for their speed training programs.

2. Understanding Athlete Qualification:

Athlete qualification refers to identifying the specific speed components that require development based on the athlete's individual strengths and weaknesses. This can be done through performance testing, video analysis, and feedback from the athletes themselves. By identifying areas of improvement, coaches can focus on targeting specific aspects of speed development within their training programs.

3. Time Management:

Optimising training time is crucial in speed training programs. Coaches need to allocate sufficient time for each training session, taking into account warm-up, skill development, conditioning, and recovery. Efficient time management ensures that athletes can dedicate enough time to each aspect of their speed training, leading to improved results.

4. Body Type Considerations:

Body type plays a significant role in speed development. Athletes with different body types may have varying strengths and limitations when it comes to speed. The biomechanics of how speed is created is dependent on the athlete to utilise their levers. An athlete with a short body and long legs has a greater potential to run fast than an athlete with a long body and long legs. This is due to the overall distance and limb distribution from the foot to the head. Coaches should consider these factors when designing training programs, incorporating exercises and drills that maximise the athletes' strengths while addressing any weaknesses associated with their body type.

5. Creating Variation within training:

Variation in training is a really important principle of training that can also be applied to speed training. Using the learn load and execute formula it is advised to create variance within the load and execution stages. Coaches can rotate training stimuli based on variations in distance, intensity, and change of direction. By utilising this method, coaches can create a diverse training program that targets different aspects of speed development, keeping athletes engaged and progressing.

6. Execution and Monitoring:

To ensure the effectiveness of speed training programs, coaches need to pay attention to execution and monitoring. Proper coaching and feedback are crucial in teaching athletes correct techniques, improving sprint mechanics, and addressing specific weaknesses. Additionally, monitoring performance and progress through data analysis, video feedback, and regular assessments can help coaches gauge improvements and make necessary adjustments to the training program.

7. Exercise Selection:

Exercise selection plays a vital role in speed training. Coaches should carefully choose exercises that align with the goals of the training program and address the specific needs of the athletes. This may include incorporating acceleration drills, change of direction exercises, plyometric workouts, and sports-specific drills that simulate game situations. Exercises are implemented based on specificity and intensity, but they can also be utilised based on athletes preferences. For example during gym related training the difference between a squat and a deadlift is not much. They are both general exercises to produce force and axial loading. On the other end of the spectrum, during field based work we would use different exercises to reinforce more specific adaptations. This is where we would place exercises in our training program that improve technique and speed related qualities. This book provides you a list of troubleshooting exercises specifically for this purpose.

Effective planning is the foundation of successful speed training programs. By considering factors such as readiness to train, athlete qualification, time management, body type considerations, execution and monitoring, and exercise selection, coaches can design comprehensive and tailored speed training programs that yield significant improvements in team sport speed. By implementing these strategies and continuously evaluating and adjusting the program as needed, coaches can guide athletes towards achieving their full speed potential and excelling in their respective sports.

Throughout this chapter you have been provided with the essential strategies, frameworks, and specific tools that you need in order to create speed training programs that deliver results. We have discussed the varying individual differences that need to be overcome but also shown how you can appreciate the long-term process of a speed train program. There is no one size fits all answer however there are proven frameworks that support your coaching. This chapter should have opened your eyes to how effective speed train programs are built, how you load speed and how you structure your training to focus on the development of Speed. In the appendix you have been provided with cheat sheets and intensity gauges for specific exercises that will shortcut your process for writing training programs for stop if you follow the rules that have been put in place and apply the methodologies discussed you will reap the benefits of the sports speed system and much much more.

Multi-Year Periodisation Considerations for Team Sport Athletes using the Sports Speed System

Developing speed in team sport athletes requires a nuanced approach that balances the cultivation of various physical qualities over an extended period. Drawing on the work of Anatoliy Bondarchuk, principles of block periodization, and the concept of vertical integration, coaches can craft multi-year periodization plans that progressively enhance speed and overall athletic performance. As all of these principles were not directly designed for team sport, we have to carefully pick the most suited parts of their logic to devise training programs that enable peak performance for multi peak sports. The continuous nature of competition in team sports where being at our "best" is needed every week in season changes the choice of preparation modality we can use.

Track and Field Peaking Model

Most of the traditionally sited periodisation work was developed with olympic sports where the athletes really only needed to peak once a year (outdoor seasons) and every 4 years for an olympic cycle.

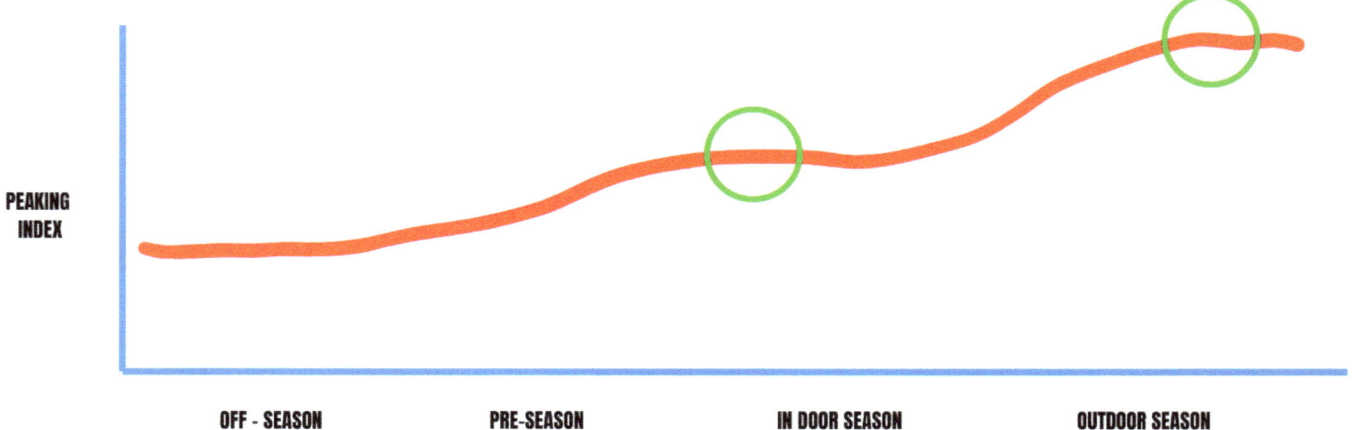

Team Sport Peaking Model

A key difference between Olympic sport disciplined and teams for disciplines is the seasonal nature of competition and the extended schedules of competition. As you will be well aware, team sport athletes can play over 50 competitive games in one season. Therefore the consideration of how we peak out athletes to maintain a high level of performance is incredibly important. Through the image below you can see that during the year we need to create many micro Peaks during the season and can choose strategic peaks during the offseason and preseason preparation periods. This is where the focus needs to be on the development of general and specific speed qualities and we can consider the use of block periodisation to peak the qualities of general speed most effectively. However in season our goal is to maintain recovery and peak specialised and tactical speed. This is where vertically integrated approaches to speed training can be implemented.

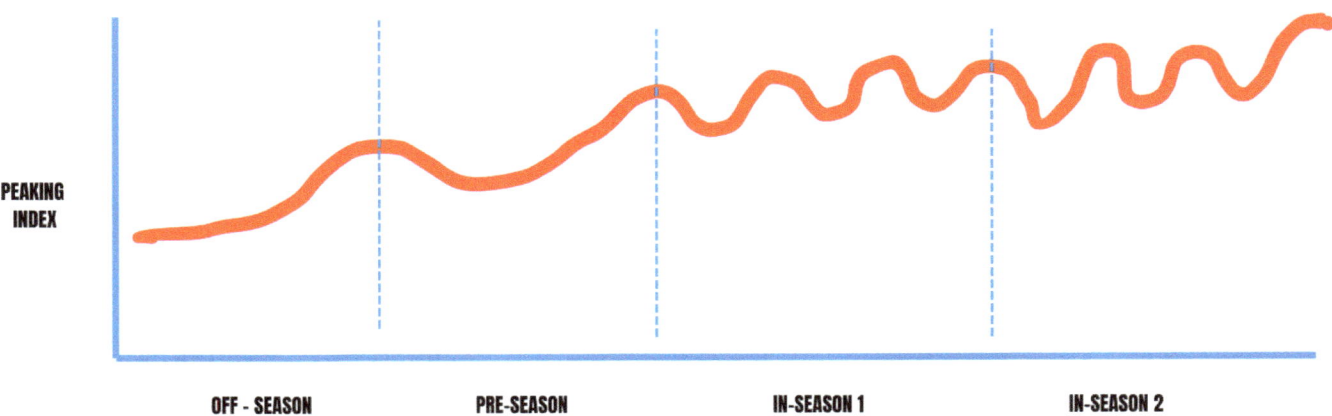

Principles of Multi-Year Periodization

Bondarchuk's methodology

When we consider Bondarchuk's methodology emphasising the transfer of training effects from general to specific exercises we know that there is a preset sequence of exercises based on their specific relationships to the competitive task. In our case this is general speed. In a multi-year plan, the initial focus on GPE and SPE lays a solid foundation. As athletes progress, the emphasis shifts towards SDE and CE, ensuring that improvements in general qualities translate effectively to specific performance gains.

Block Periodisation: Focused Blocks of Training

Block periodisation structures training into distinct blocks, each targeting a specific physical quality. In a multi-year framework, the duration of the accumulation phase decreases as athletes advance, making room for longer transmutation and realisation phases. This ensures that more specialised and sport-specific qualities receive greater attention as the athlete's foundation solidifies. For example an athlete who has an established history of senior sport would not need to have an extended accumulation phase of general training such as six weeks. This could be decreased to 2-3 weeks in a multi year approach as the athlete will not need more time to improve general capacities as they already possess them, and can regain them very quickly when detrained.

Vertical Integration: Concurrent Development

Vertical integration involves concurrently developing various physical qualities throughout the training cycle but prioritising them based on the competitive calendar. This method ensures that no quality is ever completely neglected, allowing for continuous, albeit varied, emphasis on different aspects of performance. This is incredibly important when implementing training during the season. With careful monitoring of our "competitive exercises" we can track specific qualities to ensure they do not diminish and sport remains the highest trained quality.

There are a couple of ways we can utlise a vertically integrated approach in the sport speed system. If we look at the at how we would progress the speed classifications over a season cycle it would take the form of the graph provided below. As we progress towards competition periods the goal is the execution of tactical speed which is the ability to combine the motor taks of movement and speed with the skills of the game.

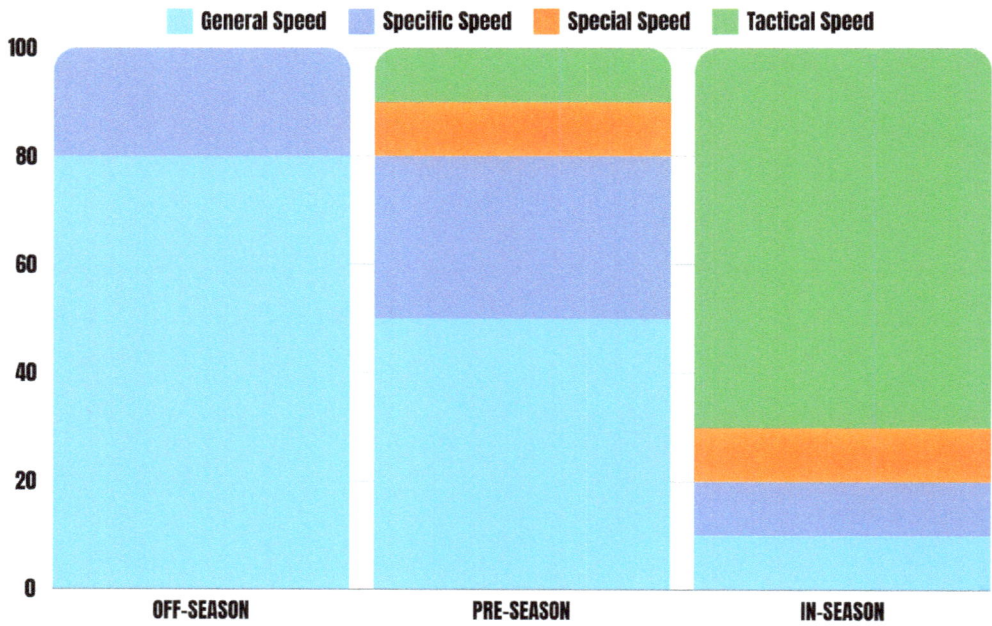

Then if we take a deeper look into the role of speed in the bigger picture the distribution of training takes a different view. Understanding the distribution of total work throughout these cycles is the key to effective vertical integration. A mistake often made by coaches is to not consider the wider volumes and demands of the sport during competitive cycles. When consider your training volumes as a the lowest priority when managing in season load. This is how you will create effective transfer and optimise performance.

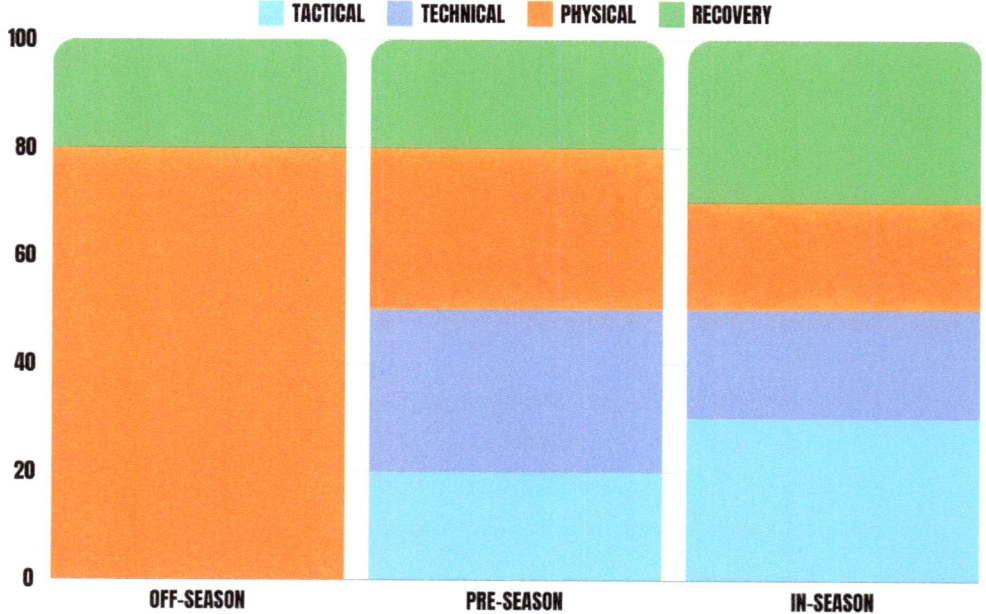

A Systematic Approach to Exercise Classification of Speed

Application to Multi-Year Periodisation using the Sports Speed System

Below I have outlined a hypothetical multi-year approach utilising the sports speed system. However I feel that it is important to make an essential comment regarding the progression of Speed age in a linear fashion. The progression of Speed age and the type of training conducted is a direct reflection of the level of specific training history that the athlete possesses full stop therefore you could theoretically, and this is something I have seen, keep an athlete in the learning to sprint phases of training for two to three years before further specialisation. The reason for this is even with some of the most "gifted athletes" in the context of team sports they haven't build to working capacity to tolerate specialised speed training. Therefore this simple paradigm shift reshapes their preparation for sport and we continue to see performance increases from the foundations of the sports speed system. To explain further, many team sport athletes have prepared for sport by playing the sport and spending a significant time in the gym developing general strength and power qualities. Therefore included more volume of speed in place of general strength and power will yield greater results for an extended period of time as this is stil a novel stimulus. This is for you to determine for your athletes, based on close tracking of the rates of improvement that the athlete is showing. This is examined closer in a subsequent section of the book on data. However, for this example I wanted to show you how you can blend multiple approaches to training organisation and periodization that will directly influence the role of developing the team sports sprinter. Remember that the rate at which the athlete is improving at the assessed exercises is the barometer for progression.

Year 1: Learning to Sprint

- **Focus:** General Speed Development.
- **GPE and SPE:** High priority on building strength, endurance, and basic motor skills.
- **Training Blocks:** Longer accumulation phases with shorter transmutation and realisation phases.
- **Speed Development:** Basic sprint mechanics, Primarily long acceleration and specific preparatory exercises.

Period	Phase	Focus
Pre-Season	Accumulation	General Speed - Max Speed Focus / Relative Strength
Early Season	Transmutation	Specific Speed, agility
In-Season	Realisation	Sport-specific speed, tactics

Year 2: Training to Sprint

- **Focus**: Enhanced specific speed and specific power
- **SPE and SDE:** Greater emphasis on exercises that closely relate to sport performance.
- **Training Blocks:** Balanced duration of accumulation, transmutation, and realisation phases.
- **Speed Development:** Shortened max velocity training, acceleration development and specialised change of direction / agility training.

Period	Phase	Focus
Pre-Season	Accumulation	Strength and power foundations
Early Season	Transmutation	Speed and agility drills
In-Season	Realisation	High-intensity sport-specific drills

Year 3: Sprinting to Compete

- **Focus:** Improve capacity of general/specific speed outputs and refinement of specific skills.
- **SDE and CE:** Predominantly sport-specific and competitive exercises.
- **Training Blocks**: Shorter accumulation phases, with extended transmutation and realisation phases to ensure peak performance.
- **Speed Development:** High-intensity sprinting, competition simulations, and recovery strategies.

Period	Phase	Focus
Pre-Season	Accumulation	Maintain strength, injury prevention
Early Season	Transmutation	High-intensity speed and agility
In-Season	Realisation	Sport-specific performance peaks

As you can see, the multi-year approach to preparation of team sport athletes requires a strategic integration of Bondarchuk's classification with block periodisation and vertical integration. By gradually shifting focus from general speed to specific speed training, and ensuring a seamless transition between different phases, coaches can optimise the long-term development of their athletes. With this we can utilise special speed strategies and modalities within team training sessions. This approach not only maximises performance gains within the available time but also ensures that athletes are well-prepared for the demands of their sport as they progress through different stages of their athletic careers.

SPEED GATE GOLF

It's time we delve into the fascinating world of Speed Gate Golf. We will explore how the counterintuitive concept of learning to run slowly can actually make athletes faster than ever before. It may sound absurd, but trust me when I say it works, and in this chapter, I will reveal the reasons why.

The birth of this methodology and game came from a place of necessity, and it has continued to evolve and deliver impressive results. Initially, while working with a professional club, I sought a way to use speed as the defining metric of my program's effectiveness. After all, in sports preparation, speed is the cornerstone that underpins everything which reminds me of a great quote from Yuri Verkhoshasnky "the ultimate aim of sport preparation is to increase the speed of movement". I no longer needed to rely solely on one-rep max measurements; I wanted to prioritise speed. However, convincing those in control to integrate speed gates into our training regimen posed a significant challenge.

To overcome the resistance and behaviour modification issues associated with introducing speed gates, I embarked on a path of motor learning, behaviourism (the idea that all behaviours are acquired through conditioning), and training qualification. This journey ultimately led to the development of Speed Gate Golf, a game that would transform the way we approach speed training in team sports.

In team sports, speed training is often flawed and insufficiently prioritised. I firmly believe that we need to invest more time in coaching speed, making it the central focus of our programs. Athletes, when asked whether they want to be slower or faster, will always opt for speed. It's a simple outcome that aligns with their aspirations. However, using speed gates can come with certain challenges, such as negative associations with testing, punishment-oriented behaviour, limited understanding of speed monitoring, time-consuming processes, and increased injury risks.

But we are determined to break these barriers. We recognize that time-consuming procedures can be streamlined with an efficient processing system. Furthermore, we understand the importance of addressing the psychological aspects associated with speed training. By creating psychological change, we can overcome resistance and pave the way for a more effective training system. This chapter will explore the fundamental psychology that underpins the success of the Speed Gate Golf training system.

The Psychology of Speed Gate Golf: Unlocking Peak Performance

The innovative approach of Speed Gate Golf starts the conversation between psychology and speed training. This section explores the fascinating psychology behind this training method and its profound impact on athlete performance. Through the lens of psychological principles and conditioning techniques, we unravel the transformative power of Speed Gate Golf.

Rewriting the Rules: The Psychology of Performance

When introducing Speed Gate Golf to athletes, it was crucial to approach it from a psychological perspective. Recognising the importance of psychology in performance, we understood that the athlete's perception of their environment greatly influenced their performance. It was crucial to create an environment that challenged their physical and psychological resources while ensuring their well-being.

Stress and Performance: A Delicate Balance

For the purpose of this section I would like you to consider this definition of stress;

> "a particular relationship between the person and the environment that is appraised by them person as taxing or exceeding his or her resources and endangering his or her well being"
> – *Lazarus & Folkman (1984)*

Performance testing is often very stressful for athletes. However, to maximise performance, we need to remove the sense of threat and redefine the rules. By reframing the association with speed testing, we aimed to alleviate the emotional and psychological stress athletes experienced and create more accurate data from their subsequent tests.

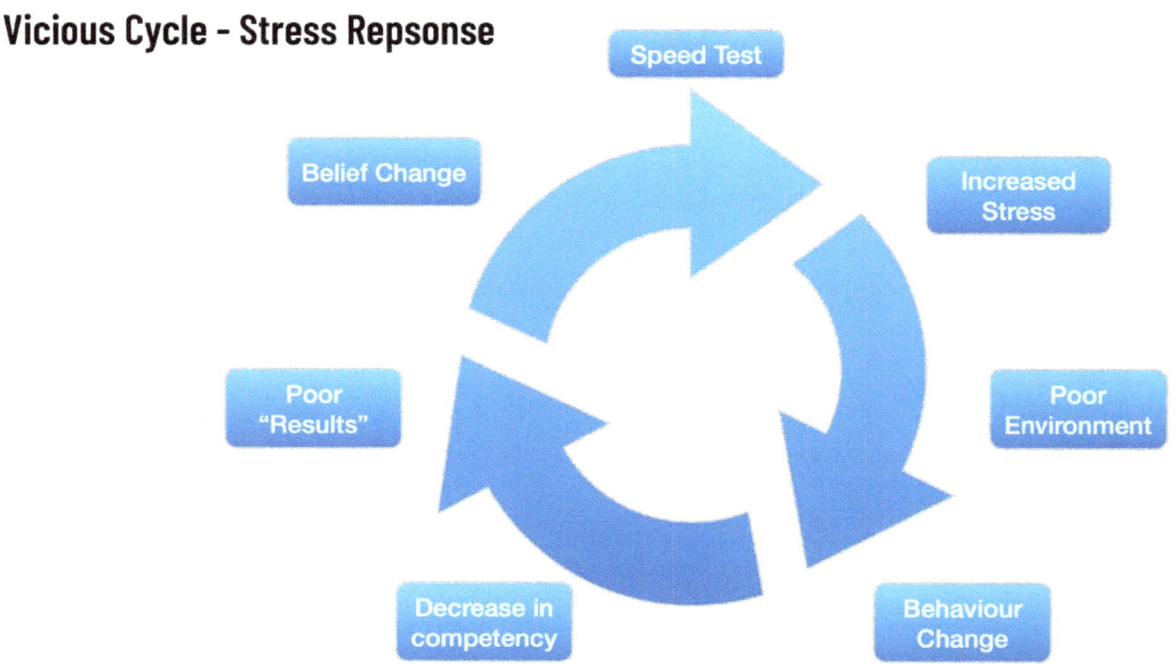

The Multifaceted Stress Response

The stress response manifests itself in various forms: emotional, behavioural, physical, and cognitive. Athletes may experience fear, anxiety, apprehension, or even withdrawal. Some may exhibit fight, flight, or freeze responses. Physically, increased stress levels can lead to tension and reduced task execution meaning slower speed times. Cognitively, emergency stress can enhance concentration but decrease attention span and increase error rates, meaning decreased ability to execute technique. The image below illustrates these responses.

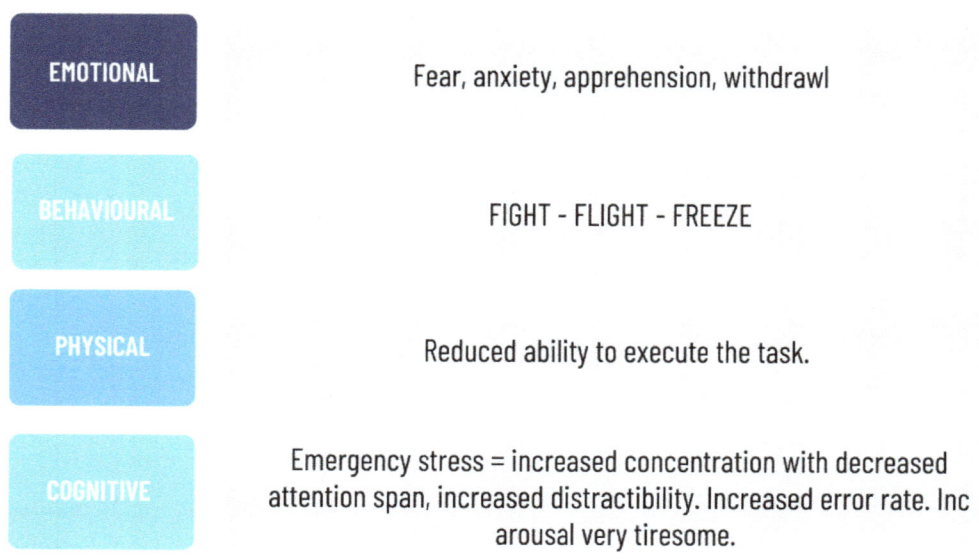

Creating a Positive Shift: Optimal Stress Levels

The Yerkes Dodson Law, 1908

- Positive Shift
- Normalise
- Engage
- Succeed

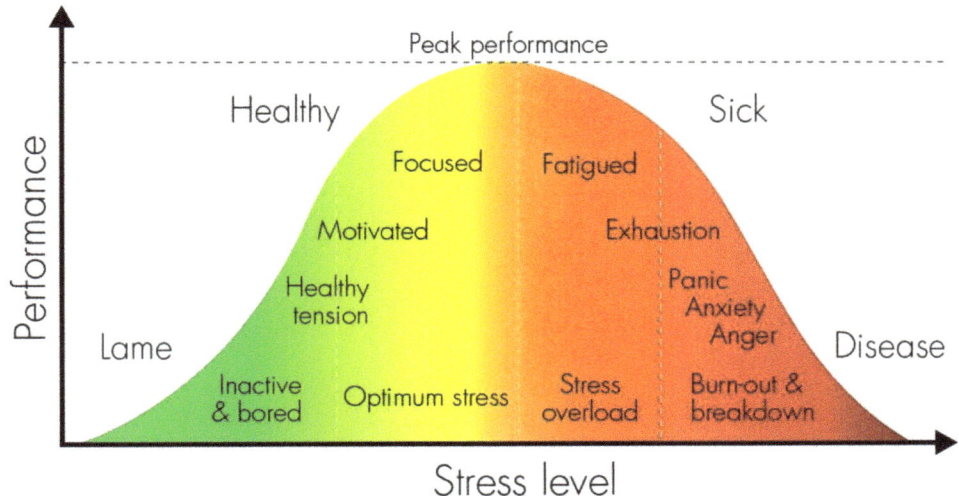

According to the Yerkes-Dodson law, performance is related to an optimal level of stress. As observed in the general adaptation syndrome it is vital to keep the nervous system on our side. If we over expose it to stress then the body will shut down to protect ourselves as we over introduced too much of a threat response. Our goal was to keep athletes within this optimal stress range, where they could thrive.

To achieve this we have to change the association with performance testing and speed gates that the athletes can have a preconditioned response to. We found that when speed gates were presented to athletes their arousal increased; players would shy away from the gates and others would just run through them when they weren't even on, demonstrating the stress they felt. We had to change the pre-existing association that the athletes had to speed gates in order to change their behaviour. In many team sport environments speed gates are not used that often, typically only for testing, and some clubs do not even have them. Many athletes have a history of being judged and either rewarded or scolded for their performance scores, hurting our goal of using the speed gates as a training tool to improve performance. We created healthy stress within the environment by learning to run through the gates at sub maximal speeds and there was a reward linked to not running as fast as you can but to running the time at which I had set for the players. This created a massive shift from the negative associations and negative stress responses the athletes had, to a much more positive training environment. This way I was able to make a significant change in the environment and was able to engage the athletes in a more deliberate practice approach to using the speed Gates. Pictured below myself with players who "Won" the competition to run the time I had decided for the day.

Behavioural Psychology: Conditioning Success

In Speed Gate Golf, principles of behavioural psychology played a vital role. The law of effect, classical conditioning, and operant conditioning helped shape athletes' responses and associations. The consequences of previous responses influenced future behaviours. We reinforced desired behaviours through positive and negative feedback, while minimising negative associations. Clear rules and boundaries are vital, ensuring a positive training environment. Submaximal running is required to engrain efficient movement patterns and remove the frantic tension created in athletes from the desire to "run fast". The athletes were expelled if they ran too fast, if they did they were excluded from the session and I would not read out their time. This reinforced the boundaries of the exercises and demonstrated to the group the expected behaviours. The positivity that was reinforced was better than expected. As the athletes were exposed to more repetitions the variance of times within the group minimised which created excitement and joy this was because of learning via Osmosis. This is where the athletes learn just by being exposed to one another. As one individual got closer to the desired time, so did the others. This made using the speed gates fun as the "winning" was defined by the time to run not the fastest time. Therefore motivation was redirected but harnessed all the same.

Gamification and the Fun Factor

By leveraging gamification and turning speed testing into a highly specific game, we transformed the speed gates into a positive and engaging experience. This strategic approach influenced athletes' mood and associations, facilitating peak performance.

The psychology of Speed Gate Golf unveils the intricate relationship between an athlete's mindset and their performance. By understanding and applying psychological principles, we have revolutionised the training approach, reshaping athletes' associations and unlocking their full potential. Speed Gate Golf stands as a testament to the profound impact psychology can have on athletic performance, paving the way for a new era in speed training.

Gamification of Speed Gate Golf: Igniting Competence and Motivation

In the realm of speed coaching, gamification has emerged as a powerful tool to drive engagement and motivation. This section explores the application of gamification principles in the context of Speed Gate Golf. Gamification is a powerful engagement tool that stimulates the reward centre in our brains. Reducing the speed that the athletes run at maximises the number of exposures to good technical sprinting we can perform in a session, giving them more opportunities to learn how to run faster. By leveraging behavioural perspectives, reinforcing environments, and cultivating a desire for improvement, coaches can tap into the transformative potential of gamification to enhance athlete performance.

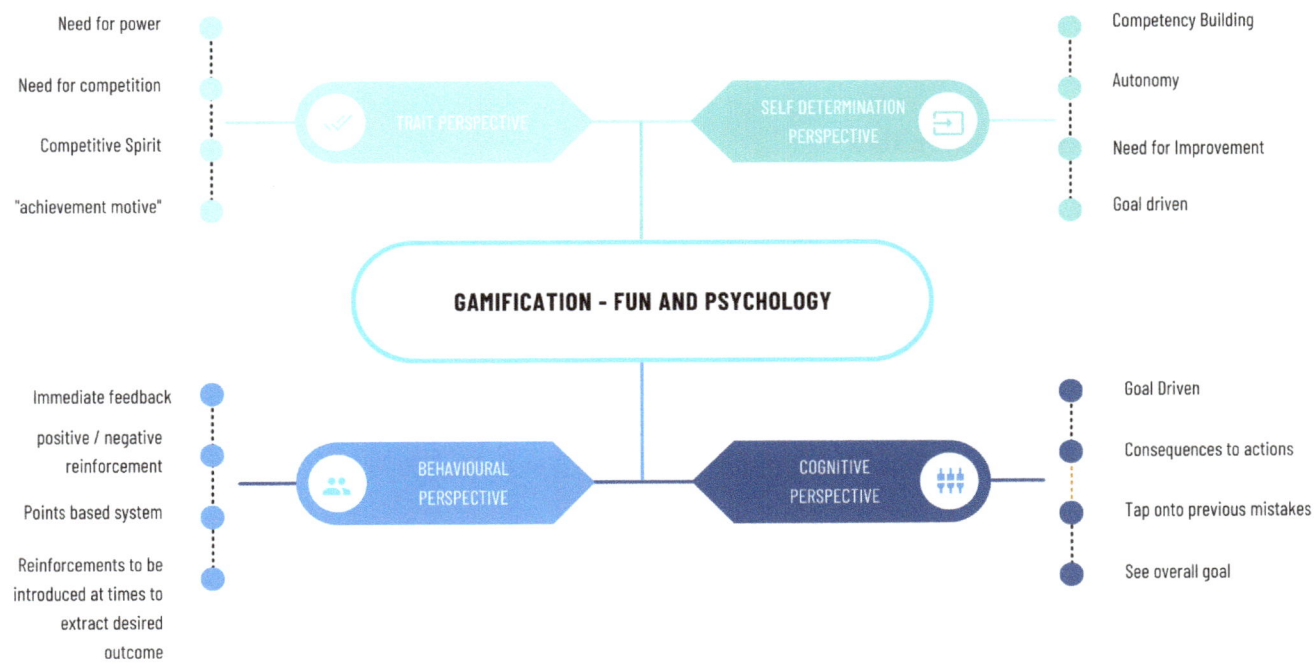

Behavioural Perspectives: Reinforcing the Environment

Coaching and programming strategies play a crucial role in driving the gamification of Speed Gate Golf. By adopting a behavioural perspective, coaches can create a point-based system that reinforces desired behaviours and outcomes. Below is a simple point based system for speed gate golf. Where the highest points achieved over the session is the winner. This approach allows athletes to engage in the training process and shift their focus away from mundane repetitions, creating a more dynamic and motivating experience.

Time	Points
Desired Time Achieved	3
Within 0.3 of desired time	2
Within 0.4-0.7 of desired time	1

Cognitive Perspective: Goal-Driven Gamification

Cognitive gamification involves setting goals and associating them with consequences. In Speed Gate Golf, athletes are rewarded for running a prescribed time set by the coach. This creates an associated experience that taps into the self-determination perspective. Athletes feel a desire and need for improvement, building competency, and experiencing a sense of autonomy. By understanding the power of consequences and goal orientation, coaches can effectively drive motivation and performance.

Unleashing the Competitive Spirit

The gamification of Speed Gate Golf taps into the inherent human desire for competition and achievement. By combining the elements of gamification, athletes are motivated to compete against themselves and others. The achievement motive, combined with the desire for improvement, creates a powerful system that propels athletes to push their limits and continuously strive for excellence. The gamified approach becomes a catalyst for growth and advancement.

Building Competence and Autonomy

Speed Gate Golf employs stages of competency to develop athletes' self-awareness and observation skills. By integrating timing and metronome practices where you can use a metronome to guide the cadence of movement, coaches create an environment that fosters competence. Applying the principles Yerkes and Dodson Law, coaches aim to keep athletes in a motivated state. As athletes progress and become more competent, they recognise their areas of improvement and seek coaching guidance. This is where you as the coach can question formally or informally to engage the athlete. This awareness is created by not being able to hit the time required even though it is within their grasp. Then the coach is able to educate and coach the athlete to the desired standard. Here the value of the coach becomes incredibly important. As the athlete is unable to execute the task required the coach can step in with the right training intervention to achieve the desired result. This can be technical coaching on a micro level but on a macro scale this is implementing the sports speed system.

Testing, Observing, and Progressing

Speed Gate Golf serves as a powerful tool for testing and observation. By incorporating speed gate sessions into training routines, coaches can assess athletes' progress regularly. The continuous utilisation of speed gates instils confidence the athletes will continue to receive real time feedback of their speed and train with a high degree of specificity.

Cognitive Behavioral Techniques and Speed Gate Golf: A Path to Performance Enhancement

Cognitive behavioural techniques offer a multifaceted approach to addressing human problems, encompassing various perspectives such as philosophical, theoretical, methodological assessment, orientated, and technological. In the context of Speed Gate Golf, the application of Cognitive behavioural principles becomes evident in three key areas: stress inoculation, systematic desensitisation, and positive attention. By understanding and implementing these techniques, coaches can enhance athletes' performance and mental resilience.

Stress Inoculation: Constructive Coping

To introduce athletes to the challenges of Speed Gate Golf, stress inoculation employs a constructive coping approach. Gradual exposure is utilised. Coaches assess athletes' initial associations with the activity by presenting them with a visual representation, such as a piece of paper with "gate" written on it. This non-threatening exposure sets the foundation for constructive coping. Through gradual exposure, imagery, rehearsal, and fostering a sense of mastery, athletes develop the skills necessary to navigate the challenges of Speed Gate Golf. Visualisation and imagery techniques play a crucial role in this process, along with education and rehearsal within the training cycles.

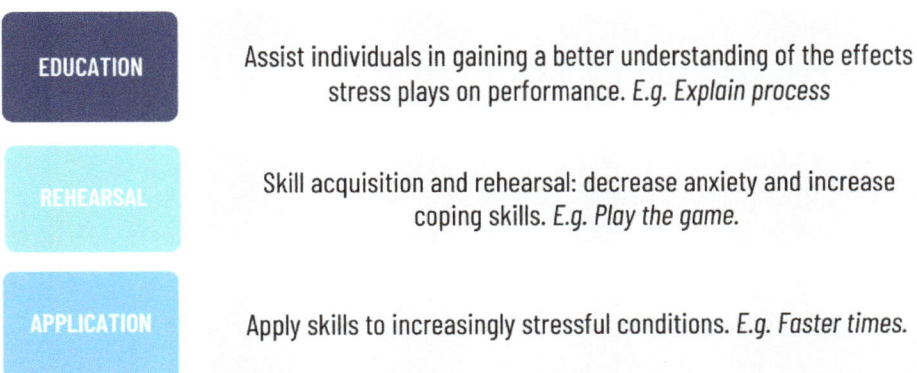

Systematic Desensitisation: Reciprocal Inhibition

Reciprocal inhibition was a concept derived from classical conditioning that formed the basis for the Joseph Wolpe theory of systematic desensitisation. In psychology, reciprocal inhibition refers to a technique in which a desired behavioural response is gradually introduced to a stimulus that causes an undesired response. Systematic desensitisation is a vital component of the cognitive behavioural techniques used in Speed Gate Golf. It aims to counter-condition athletes' responses of stress and anxiety associated with the gates. The process begins with relaxation techniques, creating an environment that fosters suggestion and familiarity with the upcoming challenges. The gradual stages of exposure to speed gates helps coaches gauge the stress response and adapt interventions accordingly. Imaginary exposure, presents a stress of the gates while athletes are in a relaxed state, further reinforces the process. The goal is for athletes to become desensitised to the gates, enabling them to approach the activity with reduced anxiety and increased coping abilities.

Positive Attention: Reinforcing Success

Positive attention serves as a powerful tool in the cognitive behavioural framework of Speed Gate Golf. Coaches can employ strategies such as praise, reflection, imitation, enthusiasm, and active ignoring to reinforce desirable behaviours and foster a success-driven environment. By providing positive social feedback, athletes associate their achievements with the desired behaviour and strive to imitate successful demonstrations. Ignoring faults while maintaining enthusiasm, tonality, and body language further reinforces a positive feedback loop and cultivates a culture of success within the program.

Implementing Cognitive Behavioral Techniques in Speed Gate Golf

The application of cognitive behavioural techniques in Speed Gate Golf follows a progressive and strategic approach. Over the course of seven sessions, coaches can guide athletes through the following stages:

1. Verbally introduce speed gates assessments during training sessions to familiarise athletes with the concept.
2. Place the gates near the training area to make athletes aware of their presence.
3. Set up gates in a nonspecific manner to test athletes' initial responses.
4. Gradually decrease the distance between gates to ten metres, allowing athletes to jog through them and become accustomed to the process.
5. Introduce the game element, challenging athletes to complete a ten-metre run in two seconds.
6. Incorporate the game into regular training sessions, making it a part of the execution phase.
7. Manipulate the game and progress the rules, incorporating points and prizes to increase engagement and competition.

Cognitive behavioural techniques provide coaches with a powerful framework to enhance athletes' performance and mental fortitude in Speed Gate Golf. By employing stress inoculation, systematic desensitisation, and positive attention, coaches can help athletes overcome anxiety, develop coping skills, and create a success-driven training environment. The progressive implementation of these techniques paves the way for improved performance and a heightened sense of achievement.

Unleashing Positive Feedback Loops in Speed Gate Golf for Optimal Performance

Cognitive behavioural techniques are instrumental in enhancing performance and overcoming challenges in various domains. In the context of a sport that combines speed, agility, and movement precision, cognitive behavioural techniques can play a crucial role in optimising athletes' performance. One of the key aspects of these techniques is the establishment of feedback loops, which serve as a catalyst for improvement and growth. By understanding and harnessing the power of feedback loops, athletes can unlock their full potential and achieve exceptional results in speed gate golf.

Creating Positive Feedback Loops

Feedback loops are essential mechanisms that facilitate learning and behaviour change. In speed gate golf, two types of feedback loops are particularly relevant: reinforcing loops and balancing loops. Reinforcing loops involve operant conditioning, where desired behaviours are reinforced through positive consequences, for example praising better technique and encouraging the use of it to control speed. To achieve positive loop dominance, it is crucial to establish a series of feedback cycles that gradually compound momentum and strengthen associations with high performance.

Speed monitoring becomes an integral part of the feedback loop, but the approach is reframed to emphasise improvement and progress. Athletes continually measure their speed, receive positive feedback for meeting or surpassing expectations, and then strive for further improvement. This cycle creates a self-reinforcing loop where athletes associate themselves with being fast, further boosting their belief in their abilities.

Measuring, Comparing, and Adjusting

The core principle of feedback loops in speed gate golf lies in the measurement, comparison, and adjustment process. Athletes set measurable goals, such as completing a 10-metre run in 2 seconds, and then compare their actual performance to these expectations. Having a coach identify the gaps between expectation and reality, athletes can focus on specific aspects, such as timing, rhythm, and loading, to initiate an associative learning experience.

Rapid adjustments based on actionable information, such as the athlete time and technical feedback are crucial to reinforce positive feedback dominance. Athletes can progress to the next level once they consistently achieve the desired outcome, ensuring that the adjustments are not merely a fluke. This process fosters a belief change, leading athletes to associate themselves with success and competence.

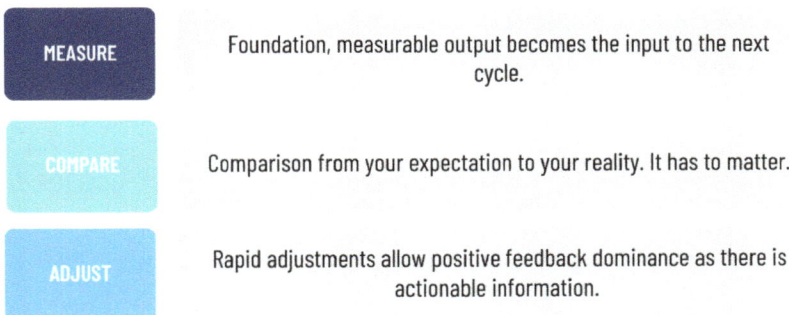

Harnessing Positive Feedback Loops

Incorporating gate therapy (speed gate golf) which involves stress inoculation, desensitisation, and positive attention toward speed gates, is an effective approach to nurture positive feedback loops in speed gate golf. By gradually exposing athletes to speed gate-related stimuli and providing positive reinforcement for desired performance, athletes develop a belief system rooted in continuous success. Below is an image demonstrating how the positive feedback loop is manipulated with speed gate golf.

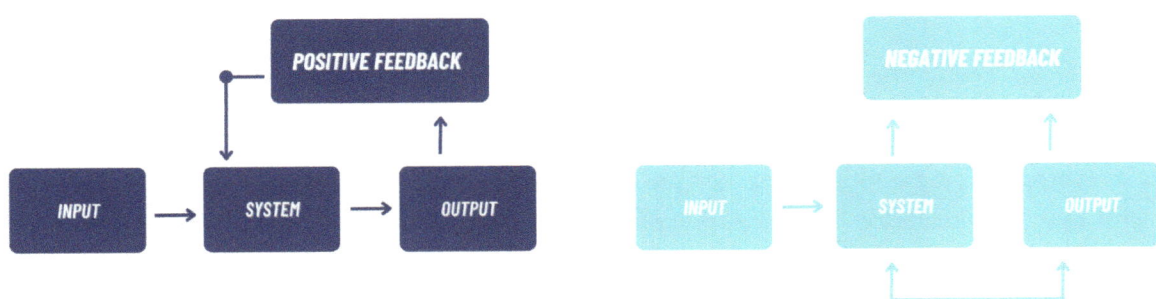

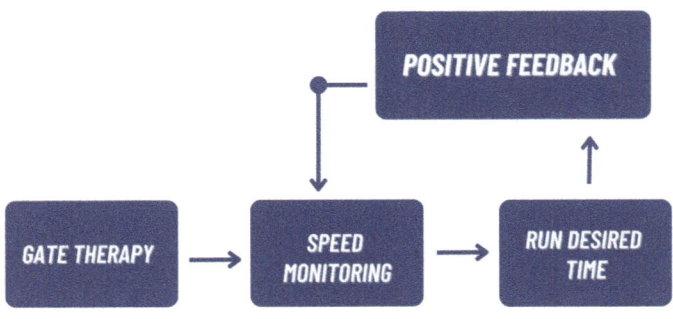

The Power of Habituation and Behavior Stacking

Habituation plays a significant role in cementing positive associations with speed. By consistently running at sub-maximal velocities and receiving rewards for their performance, athletes develop suitable habits and behaviours such as prioritising speed and the value of technical and physical development at submaximal speed. This fundamental habituation allows athletes to stack further performance habits, ultimately translating into enhanced speed and agility. As athletes experience improvements in their speed gate golf performance, the entire training environment becomes infused with a focus on speed, creating a powerful feedback loop.

Changing Belief Systems

The interrelation of ideas and experiential influence shapes athletes' belief systems in speed gate golf. By initiating positive feedback loops, building and stacking performance habits, and providing regular objective support, coaches and trainers can help athletes transform their belief systems. Over time, athletes begin to associate themselves with being fast, fostering a positive mindset that fuels continued growth and success.

Playing the Ace Card

In the pursuit of optimal performance, there comes a time to play the ace card—the moment when athletes have accumulated a solid foundation of sub-maximal steps, bridging the specificity gap between specialised preparatory and developmental exercises. This is the opportune time to unleash maximum effort and witness remarkable results. By strategically timing and executing this ace card, athletes can achieve extraordinary speed and surpass their previous limits. A perfect time to do this is once the athletes are playing the game well and consistently hitting the times prescribed. Then let them "run fast" and enjoy the personal bests.

Enhancing Motor Learning in Speed Gate Golf

Motor learning plays a vital role in developing expertise and proficiency in sports such as rugby. By understanding the stages of motor learning and applying key principles, athletes can reach the autonomous stage where they perform with ease and efficiency. This section explores the motor learning process in speed gate golf, focusing on the cognitive, associative, and autonomous stages. Additionally, we delve into Nikolai Bernstein's degrees of freedom and the importance of minimising bandwidth to optimise performance consistency.

The Motor Learning Process

Motor learning is a progressive journey that athletes undertake as they develop their skills and refine their movements. Athletes progress through three key stages: cognitive, associative, and autonomous.

During the cognitive stage, athletes are introduced to the fundamentals of speed gate golf. They learn the basic techniques and movements involved, acquiring an initial understanding of the game. Coaches emphasise minimising variability in movement patterns and ensuring consistent average velocity throughout the run. This gradual physical speed conditioning lays the foundation for future proficiency.

In the associative stage, athletes refine their skills and improve their performance. They become more comfortable with the game's demands and begin to develop a sense of control and consistency in their movements. Complexity and cognitive demand gradually decrease, accelerating the learning process.

The ultimate goal is to reach the autonomous stage, where athletes perform skillfully and effortlessly. At this stage, athletes have internalised the necessary movements and strategies, allowing them to execute with minimal conscious effort. In speed gate golf, athletes should be able to navigate the gates without stress or hesitation, performing consistently at a high level.

Understanding Bernstein's Degrees of Freedom

Nikolai Bernstein's concept of degrees of freedom highlights the inherent variability in movement execution. Regardless of skill level, there are numerous variables that can influence the execution of a movement. However, the end result remains the same. In the context of speed gate golf, minimising the bandwidth of movement becomes crucial as this is the first step in the process of adaptation, athletes must learn the skill. Athletes can run the course in various ways, emphasising speed at different sections. However, coaches should strive to condition a consistent average velocity throughout the entire run, but encouraging an equal and rhythmic cadence. This minimisation of variability helps athletes maintain precision and control, leading to improved performance.

The Process of Motor Learning

Motor learning is an evolutionary process that aligns with an athlete's stage of competence, meaning that task required to elicit motor adaptation will only be as complex as needed and should only increase with the competency of the athlete. As athletes become more proficient and autonomous in their skills, coaches can introduce additional technical information and coaching structures. This progression enhances complexity and overall learning speed.

By providing athletes with the appropriate level of challenge at each stage, coaches can foster continuous growth and skill development. Athletes gradually adapt to the increasing demands, expanding their capabilities and reaching new levels of performance.

Motor learning is a fundamental aspect of achieving excellence in speed gate golf. By progressing through the cognitive, associative, and autonomous stages, athletes refine their skills and reach a level of autonomous performance. Understanding Nikolai Bernstein's degrees of freedom allows coaches to minimise variability and maintain consistent performance. By applying effective motor learning strategies, athletes can unlock their full potential in speed gate golf and achieve exceptional results. Within the broader context speed gate golf fits as a whole task to which the athlete learns through consistent feedback from the environment via speed times.

Enhancing Motivation through Athlete Groupings in Speed Gate Golf

Motivation plays a crucial role in athletic performance, and in the exercise of speed gate golf, it is no exception. To optimise motivation and foster a supportive training environment, coaches often utilise athlete groupings. This chapter explores the significance of athlete groupings and their impact on motivation in speed gate golf. By understanding how different groupings can influence motivation levels, coaches can create an environment that enhances athlete engagement, performance, and overall enjoyment of the sport.

The Power of Athlete Groupings

Athlete groupings refer to the organisation of athletes into smaller units within the training program. These groups can be based on various criteria, such as skill level, experience, or specific training objectives. While the primary purpose of athlete groupings is to facilitate training and skill development, they also have a significant impact on motivation.

1. Homogeneous Groupings:

Homogeneous groupings involve grouping athletes with similar skill levels or performance abilities. This grouping strategy allows athletes to train alongside individuals who face similar challenges and possess comparable skill sets. Homogeneous groups create a sense of camaraderie and healthy competition among athletes, which can be highly motivating. Athletes within these groups can benchmark their progress against their peers, driving them to push their limits and strive for improvement.

2. Heterogeneous Groupings:

Heterogeneous groupings involve mixing athletes with varying skill levels and performance abilities. This grouping strategy promotes a supportive learning environment where more experienced athletes can mentor and inspire less experienced ones. For novice athletes, being surrounded by more skilled peers can ignite motivation, as they aspire to reach the same level of performance. Meanwhile, elite athletes benefit from the opportunity to showcase their skills and reinforce their expertise through teaching and leading by example.

3. Task-Specific Groupings:

Task-specific groupings involve grouping athletes based on specific training objectives or specialised skills. For example, athletes may be grouped based on their strengths in certain aspects of speed gate golf, such as acceleration. Task-specific groupings allow athletes to focus on refining specific skills and expertise, which can be highly motivating as they see tangible progress in their areas of specialisation. It also fosters a sense of shared purpose and camaraderie among athletes with similar training objectives.

Motivation and Training Environment

Creating a motivating training environment in speed gate golf involves more than just athlete groupings. Coaches should consider several key factors:

1. Positive Reinforcement: Encouragement and positive reinforcement from coaches and peers can significantly enhance motivation. Recognizing and celebrating individual and group achievements boosts confidence and fosters a sense of accomplishment, driving athletes to persist and excel.

2. Goal Setting: Setting realistic and challenging goals provides athletes with a sense of purpose and direction. Clear goals help athletes track their progress, feel a sense of achievement, and maintain their motivation throughout their speed gate golf journey.

3. Supportive Coaching: Coaches who foster a supportive and inclusive coaching style promote a positive training environment. By providing constructive feedback, addressing individual needs, and creating opportunities for growth, coaches can enhance motivation and commitment among athletes.

Motivation is a vital ingredient for success in speed gate golf. Athlete groupings offer coaches a powerful tool to enhance motivation levels within the training environment. Whether using homogeneous or heterogeneous groupings, or task-specific arrangements, coaches can foster healthy competition, mentorship, and a sense of shared purpose among athletes. By combining effective athlete groupings with positive reinforcement, goal setting, and supportive coaching, coaches can create an environment that cultivates motivation, maximises performance, and ensures an enjoyable speed gate golf experience for athletes at all skill levels.

STAGE	1	2	3	4	5
Gate Activity	Pitch Side	Set Up	Set 10m Apart	Rehearsal	70% Velocity Gate
Behavioural Approach	Classical Conditioning				Operant
Perceived Negative Stress	High	High	Med	Low	High
Compentancy	Unconscious Incompetence		Conscious Incompetence		Conscious Competence
Psychological Readiness	LOW	LOW	LOW/MED	MED	MED
Stress Inoculation	Education		Skill Acquisition and Consolidation		Application
Systematic Desensitisation	Relaxation		Gradual Exposure	Imaginal Exposure	
Motor Learning	Cognitive	Cognitive	Cognitive / Associative	Cognitive / Associative	Cognitive / Associative

Implementing Speed Gate Golf

Speed gate golf is a training modality that combines elements of sprinting, agility, and decision-making skills. Implementing this unique training method requires careful planning and consideration. In this chapter, we will provide a step-by-step guide on how to effectively introduce and incorporate speed gate golf into your training program. From initial exposure to structuring sessions within a training week, we will explore various strategies to maximise the benefits of this training approach.

1. Stages of Implementation:

To begin implementing speed gate golf, it is essential to follow a systematic approach. The following stages can guide you through the process:

a. Exposure: Start by introducing the concept of speed gate golf to your athletes. Familiarise them with the visual placement of the gates by setting them up on the side of the pitch next to each other on display.
b. Gate Setup: Gradually progress to setting up the gates ten metres apart. Test the gates to ensure they are working properly. Initially, have players jog through them at three-quarter pace before progressing to sub-maximal sprinting.
c. Subsequent Sessions: Incorporate speed gate golf early in your training program to increase the chances of success. Implement specific rules, such as running through the gates within a designated time frame. Provide clear consequences for rule violations, emphasising zero tolerance through immediate disqualification.
d. Accumulate Repetitions: Focus on consistency rather than improvement in the initial sessions. Encourage athletes to achieve the desired technique and reinforce it through consistent repetitions. Accumulating repetitions at a specific percentage of maximum speed reinforces proper technique and facilitates effective loading.

2. Structuring Speed Gate Golf in Training:

Integrating speed gate golf into your weekly training plan requires careful consideration. Here are two block variations to help you structure your training:

Block One Variation:

In this variation, incorporate speed gate golf on a Monday following a specific training sequence:
- Short Acceleration: Perform five-metre and ten-metre sprints to develop explosive power.
- Long Acceleration: Engage in 20-metre and 30-metre sprints to enhance maximum velocity capacities.
- Resisted Acceleration: Utilise sleds with 30% body weight to add resistance and build strength.
- Extensive Tempo: Implement speed gate golf as a conditioning tool to reinforce running times and pacing.

Advanced Variation:

For more advanced athletes, consider adjusting the sequence as follows:
- Long Acceleration: Perform longer sprints to target maximum velocity capacities.
- Short Acceleration: Follow up with shorter sprints, two days after the long acceleration session.

- Resisted Acceleration: Introduce resisted sprints before engaging in extensive tempo training.
- Extensive Tempo: Use speed gate golf for conditioning purposes, focusing on maintaining consistent pacing.

	MONDAY	TUESDAY	WEDNESDAY	THURSDAY	FRIDAY	SATURDAY	SUNDAY
BLOCK 1	SHORT ACCEL		LONG ACCEL		RESISTED ACCEL	EXT. TEMPO*	
BLOCK 2	LONG ACCEL		SHORT ACCEL		RESISTED ACCEL	EXT. TEMPO*	

Note: Use Speed Gates for all sessions if applicable. Hand timers are fine for extensive tempo.

3. Integrating Speed Gate Golf in Season:

To incorporate speed gate golf during the competitive season, consider the following example for a game day plus three scenario:
- Perform a long acceleration speed gate golf session on the third day after the game.
- Follow up with a short acceleration session on minus two days before the next game.
- Reserve the game day for rest and performance.

	GD +2	GD +3	GD+4	GD-2	GD-1	GD	GD+1
7 Day Example		LONG ACCEL*		LONG ACCEL*	SHORT ACCEL		

Implementing speed gate golf requires a strategic and gradual approach. By following the stages of exposure, gate setup, subsequent sessions, and accumulation of repetitions, coaches can effectively introduce this training modality. Structuring speed gate golf within the training week, either through block variations or advanced variations, allows for optimal integration into the overall training program.

USING DATA IN TEAM SPORT SPRINTING

Welcome to the final chapter of the book. Congratulations on reaching this milestone. I appreciate your dedication and I trust that your journey has been rewarding thus far. In this chapter, we will delve into the realm of data analysis and explore how it can be harnessed to drive performance and eliminate unnecessary complexities. As coaches, we often find ourselves overwhelmed by the multitude of metrics and the temptation to create new ones. However, the key lies in understanding existing metrics and their practical utility. By focusing on the essentials and embracing a hands-on coaching approach, we can unlock the true potential of our athletes and foster an environment of growth and enjoyment.

Embracing Data for Performance Enhancement

Data analysis has revolutionised the way we approach coaching in team sports. By utilising relevant data, coaches can gain valuable insights that contribute to informed decision-making and improved performance outcomes. However, it is essential to avoid getting caught up in the quest for excessive metrics or creating new ones without understanding their significance. Rather than running before we can walk, let us first explore the existing data landscape and identify its practical applications.

Striking a Balance: Coaching from the Field, Not the Desk

As coaches, our primary role is to be on the field, actively coaching and imparting knowledge. Sometimes, we may find ourselves trapped behind a desk, fixated on analysing training programs instead of engaging with our athletes. This chapter aims to dismantle that barrier, empowering coaches to break free from excessive computer-based analysis and refocus their efforts on face-to-face interaction with athletes. It is through this direct engagement that true coaching magic happens.

As we conclude the sports speed book, we enter the realm of data analysis with the goal of leveraging its power to drive performance in team sports. By prioritising existing metrics over creating new ones, coaches can access meaningful insights and make informed decisions that positively impact their athletes' growth and development.

Big Picture Thinking: Leveraging Data in Team Sports for Optimal Performance

When it comes to utilising data in team sports, taking a big picture approach and understanding the organisation of exposure is key. By focusing on leading indicators and their implications within the training process, coaches can predict future outcomes and streamline their data management strategies. This chapter explores the importance of big picture thinking when using data in team sports, emphasising the identification of leading indicators, the assessment-monitoring cycle, and the appropriate tools for data collection and analysis.

Leading Indicators: Unlocking Predictive Insights

Leading indicators serve as critical signposts within the athlete's qualification journey. They provide valuable information about areas that, when improved, have a direct impact on overall performance. By identifying and focusing on these leading indicators, coaches gain the ability to predict future outcomes and tailor their training interventions accordingly. Understanding the progression from learning to sprint, sprinting to compete, and sprinting to win is crucial in identifying the appropriate metrics for each phase.

Assessment and Monitoring: Two Paths to Data Utilisation

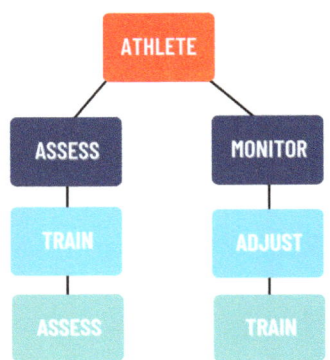

The effective use of data in team sports involves both assessment and monitoring processes. Assessments provide a snapshot of an athlete's current capabilities and serve as the basis for training interventions. Monitoring, on the other hand, involves continuous data collection during training sessions to guide adjustments and ensure progress. Balancing these two approaches is essential for maintaining a cohesive and effective training program.

Choosing the Right Tools for Data Collection

To obtain accurate and relevant data, coaches need to select appropriate tools for data collection. Starting with the "right eye-ometre," coaches train their observational skills and rely on basic measurement tools such as tape measures and stopwatches. For more detailed information, jump mats and apps can be utilised. However, it is crucial to remember that in team sport scenarios, the inclusion of technologies such as speed gates, force plates, GPS trackers, and motion analysis tools like high-speed video or wearable sensors can significantly enhance data insights.

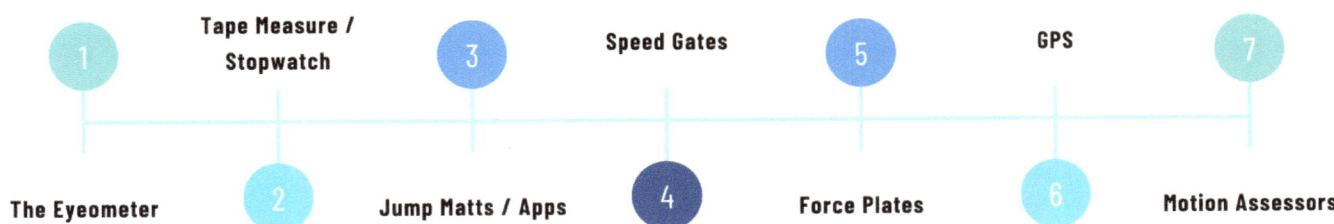

Balancing Data utilisation in Team Sport Contexts

While advanced data collection tools can provide valuable insights, it is important to maintain a balanced perspective in team sport environments. Coaches should consider the practicality and relevance of data collection methods in relation to the specific sport and athlete's needs. Striking the right balance between data utilisation and hands-on coaching ensures a congruent training process, where data serves as a supportive tool rather than dictating training decisions.

Adopting a big picture mindset when using data in team sports is crucial for optimising performance outcomes. By identifying leading indicators, coaches gain the ability to predict future performance improvements and tailor training interventions accordingly. Leading indicators are identified by the physical qualities that compound on one another through exercise classification. This is the process of layering general to specific qualities to create a spine of stimulus within your program. This ensures that you can start to identify where the potential issues are in your programming. For example in 10m acceleration we would use this as a stack of leading indicators.

- General - Trap Bar Deadlift Strength
- Specific - Standing Broad Jump
- Special - 0-5m Acceleration

In this example you might have a really strong deadlift but in comparison a short broad jump. Therefore more effort needs to be placed in the development of the broad jump with specific training to determine the effect on 0-5m acceleration speed.

Decision Making and Athlete Performance: Leveraging Data to Drive Success

Making informed decisions based on data is an essential aspect of coaching in team sports. By identifying the factors that limit performance and utilising a comprehensive coaching process, coaches can effectively analyse data, prioritise areas for improvement, and drive positive outcomes. This chapter delves into the importance of decision making when utilising data in team sports, highlighting the significance of understanding limiting performance factors, assessing metrics, and utilising a metric hierarchy to guide training interventions.

Identifying Limiting Performance Factors

Successful decision making begins with identifying the specific factors that hinder an athlete's performance. Initially I always advise using your eye before you start to introduce technology. When you introduce technology start very simple as outlined previously. Coaches must assess and collect data on these factors, observing their behaviour and impact. By understanding what aspects can be changed, coaches can focus their efforts on the most critical areas for improvement. prioritising these changes becomes crucial, taking into consideration the available time and resources for training.

Metrics Hierarchy for Speed Training

When measuring and evaluating metrics in speed training, coaches should prioritise maximum speed variation as the primary focus. Short acceleration and change of direction come next in importance, followed by sport-specific preparation for maximum speed. Jump variations, global force determinants, and isolated force determinants also play a significant role. Coaches should adapt their metric hierarchy according to the athlete's qualification and the specific demands of the sport.

Metric Hierarchy

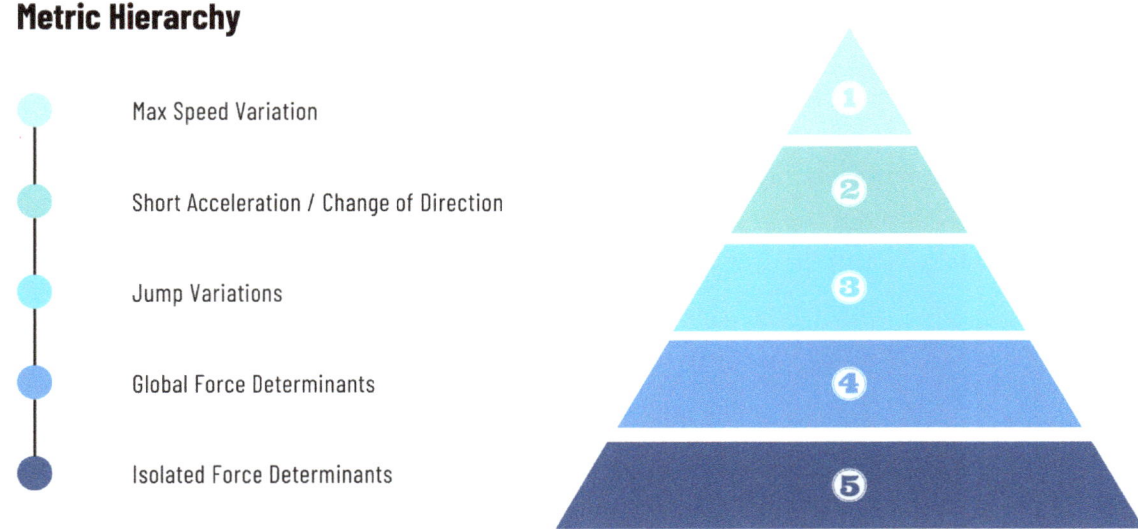

- Max Speed Variation
- Short Acceleration / Change of Direction
- Jump Variations
- Global Force Determinants
- Isolated Force Determinants

Metrics Assessment and Monitoring

To effectively utilise data, coaches should measure, track, and reference metrics within the training environment. It is important to understand that the effectiveness of certain metrics may vary depending on the athlete's stage of training. Metrics that have worked in previous stages may not yield the same results in future training, the most popular example is the initial effect on speed that general strength training has. As an athlete improves, general strength will not provide enough of a stimulus to further improve speed. Therefore, coaches must adapt and change metrics accordingly, ensuring they align with the athlete's progress and training goals.

Utilising Metrics for Qualification and Monitoring

A systematic approach to assessing athlete qualification and monitoring is crucial. Coaches can reference a qualification and monitoring table that outlines the specific metrics to focus on at each stage of speed training. This includes parameters such as sprint times, force-velocity profiles, jump height and distance, and reaction reactivity. By consistently examining these metrics and their variations, coaches can make data-driven decisions to optimise athlete performance.

Stage	Speed	Jumps	Ballistic	Strength
Learning to Sprint	Speed Gate Golf (time)	Jump Height & Distance	Medicine Ball (Distance)	Submaximal Strength (5RM)
Sprinting to Sprint	Short Sprint (time)	Jump Height / Distance / Reactivity	Weighted Jumps (Strength - Speed m/s)	Max Strength (1RM, Peak Force)
Sprinting to Compete	Short & Long Speed Times / GPS (m/s & Time)	Output Creation (Rate of force development)	Weighted Jumps (Speed-Strength m/s)	General Rate of Force Development
Sprinting to Win	Repeatability of high % Speed running.	Output Efficiency (RSI)	L-V Profiling	Specific Rate of Force Development (0-250ms)

Ignore the fluff

You might look at this table and wonder why there aren't many "advanced" metrics in it. This is because a systematic approach to training like the sport speed system which respects adaptation will surpass any metric that is considered in isolation. As coaches our job is to distil down training and the decisions made. With team sport sprinters these metrics whilst only providing advanced data to general speed qualities will often create more confusion than clarity. Simple is always more effective in these cases.

Sophistication and individualisation

As athletes progress in their training, the level of sophistication and individualisation increases. Coaches need to consider strength sub-maximal, maximal strength, general rate of force development, and specific rate of force development. This involves analysing force application during sprinting and tailoring training accordingly. Understanding the relationship between strength capabilities and maximum sprinting performance is crucial for designing effective training programs.

Speed Gates: Enhancing Performance Through Data Analysis

Speed gates have become the gold standard for measuring absolute time and velocity in athletic performance. Utilising speed gates and analysing the resulting data can provide valuable insights into an athlete's acceleration, velocity, and force performance. In this section, we will explore the benefits of speed gates in training, discuss data interpretation, and highlight how this information can drive necessary changes and improve performance.

Setting Up Speed Gates for Optimal Data Collection

When setting up speed gates, it is essential to consider the athlete's arm movements and foot carriage to ensure accurate timing. Placing the gates low during early acceleration prevents the arms from triggering the laser prematurely. Additionally, adjusting the gate height based on foot carriage ensures reliable testing and observation. Starting the athlete roughly 50 centimetres behind the gates allows for a static start in a favourable position, minimising potential issues caused by starting too close to the laser.

Interpreting Speed Gate Data

Speed gate data offers valuable metrics for analysis, including average maximum velocity, rate of acceleration. Evaluating the average times for fly tens, fly twenties, or similar intervals provides insights into an athlete's velocity capabilities. Furthermore, analysing the drop-off in acceleration between different gate distances helps identify areas that require improvement. Congruent drop-offs in split times (0-10m/10-20m/20-30m etc) indicate consistent acceleration, while variations highlight potential areas for focus and development, such as inconsistent times would question technical issues that need to be addresses where are an inability to keep accelerating would demonstrate the need for more specialised training.

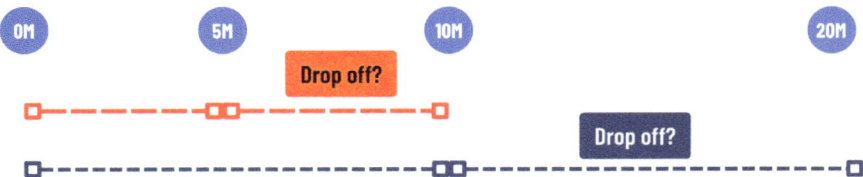

Individualisation and Training Adjustments

Speed gate data can be used to create load velocity profiles, allowing for individualised training and determination of maximum effort levels. By exposing athletes to specific loading drills and resisted sprinting at various percentages of body mass, coaches can identify optimal training maxes, this can be established by using a velocity decrement on loaded sprinting, creating a 90% of best 10m time for example for a loading range is optimal for team sport athletes. Again this is another reason why long accelerations work so well due to their submaximal nature.

Considering Auto-Regulation and Readiness

While speed gate data provides valuable insights, it is crucial to consider an athlete's readiness and daily variation in performance. Daily RPE (Rate of Perceived Exertion) and assessing an athlete's readiness play a vital role in understanding how they present in training. Individual responses to training loads can vary, emphasising the importance of auto-regulation. The readiness assessment can include submaximal loads to gauge an athlete's ability to produce speed and adjust training accordingly.

Using Force Platforms to Enhance Your Speed Training Program

In the realm of athletic training, the pursuit of speed and power is paramount. Coaches and trainers are constantly seeking tools and techniques to enhance their athletes' performance. One such tool that stands out as the gold standard in ground reaction force analysis for speed training is the force platform. This powerful device offers valuable insights into jump conditions and various other performance metrics. However, it's crucial to navigate the potential complexities of force platform data and focus on key performance indicators (KPIs) that truly matter for optimising speed training programs.

Understanding the Fundamental Metrics

When delving into force platform analysis, it is essential to break down the data into three core components: force, time, and displacement. These metrics mirror the crucial elements observed in sprinting, making force platforms highly relevant to speed training. By examining an athlete's ability to generate force, the time taken to do so, and the resulting displacement, coaches gain valuable insights into their performance.

Recommended Tests for Speed Training

Identifying what specific tests we would like to use as a coach is paramount. These tests should complement one another and follow the path of specificity. Here is how and why I use the tests highlighted in the image below.

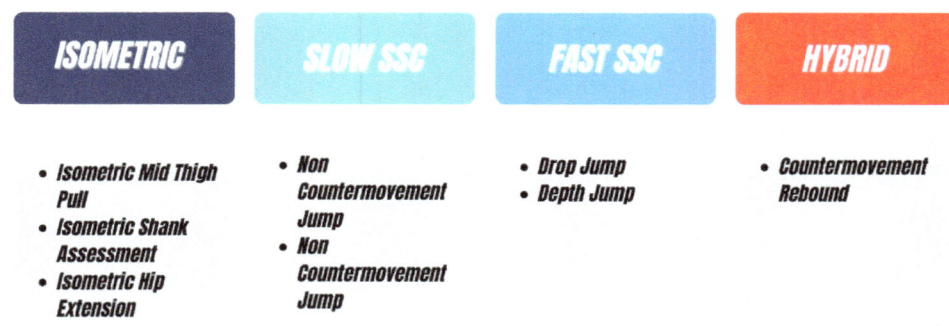

Isometric Mid-Thigh Pull (IMTP)

Explanation: The IMTP involves the athlete pulling against a fixed barbell from a mid-thigh position.

Benefits: This test assesses maximal isometric strength, providing insights into an athlete's overall strength and the ability to produce force. It is particularly useful for identifying strength deficits and monitoring training progress over time.

Isometric Shank Assessment

Explanation: This test measures the isometric force production of the lower leg muscles (shank), typically in a fixed position.

Benefits: It helps in evaluating the strength and stability of the lower leg muscles, which are crucial for running, jumping, and changing direction. Understanding the isometric strength of the shank can help in preventing injuries and improving performance.

Isometric Hip Extension

Explanation: This test measures the force produced during an isometric contraction of the hip extensors, usually performed supine with the hips weighted against the floor.

Benefits: Hip extensor strength is critical for sprinting, jumping, and explosive movements. Assessing this strength can help in identifying weaknesses that might limit performance or increase injury risk, allowing for targeted strength training interventions.

Non-Countermovement Jump (NCMJ)

Explanation: The NCMJ involves jumping from a static position without a preceding counter movement, typically measured using a force plate to assess jump height and force production.

Benefits: This test isolates the concentric phase of jumping, providing insights into an athlete's explosive strength and power without the influence of elastic energy stored during a counter movement. It is useful for evaluating pure concentric power output and monitoring training adaptations.

Drop Jump

Explanation: The drop jump involves stepping off a box 20-60cm high with hard landings to maximise stress on the connective tissues without arm swing and immediately jumping as high as possible. The aim is to produce maximal height with minimal ground contact during the ground contact phase with execution involving low magnitude of leg flexion and no use of the arms. By falling from a height, the exercise will improve the capabilities to utilise greater elastic energy recoil. This reactive strength improves the maximal force output expressed during the rebound segment of the ground contact phase.

Benefits: This test evaluates reactive strength, the ability to rapidly transition from an eccentric to a concentric muscle action. It is crucial for sports requiring quick, explosive movements, and helps in assessing an athlete's ability to utilise stored elastic energy efficiently.

Depth Jump

Explanation: Similar to the drop jump, the depth jump involves stepping off a higher box (75cm - 1.10cm), landing, and then jumping as high as possible. It is typically measured to assess the athlete's jump height and ground contact time.

Benefits: The depth jump is particularly useful for assessing an athlete's plyometric ability and reactive strength. It helps in understanding how well an athlete can handle high-intensity eccentric loads and convert them into powerful concentric actions, which is essential for sports requiring explosive power.

Leveraging Force Plates and Resources

Hawkin Dynamics provides an excellent resource for coaches and trainers utilising force plates. Their comprehensive table offers valuable guidance on assessing and analysing data, aiding in a deeper understanding of motion in relation to traditional jumping phases. Coaches can print and display this resource to enhance their comprehension of force platform data, empowering them to make informed training decisions. These can be found linked in the appendix.

Force platforms are an invaluable tool for optimising speed training programs. By dissecting force, time, and displacement metrics, coaches gain valuable insights into an athlete's performance and can target specific areas for improvement. However, it is essential to focus on KPIs and avoid getting lost in unnecessary deep metrics. With the aid of recommended tests and resources, coaches can leverage force platforms to unlock an athlete's full potential in speed training, ultimately propelling them to success in their athletic pursuits.

Categorisation and Decision-Making: Maximising the Potential of Force Platforms

Force platforms have revolutionised athletic performance analysis, providing valuable insights into an athlete's capabilities. Categorising and making decisions based on force platform data is a crucial aspect of optimising training programs. By focusing on specific categories and key metrics, coaches and trainers can drive informed decisions to enhance performance. This section explores the categorization process and its role in decision-making when utilising force platforms.

Categorisation for Initial Investigation

In the initial investigation phase, coaches typically categorise force platform data based on height, distance, and force. These fundamental metrics shed light on an athlete's jumping abilities, answering questions such as how high and far they can jump. By establishing these baselines, coaches can gauge an athlete's overall jumping capacity. This helps us as coaches know where to start implementing jump training and ensure that the athlete enters the program at the right level. See appendix for implementation of jump training.

Adding Reactivity

To delve deeper, coaches introduce the element of reactivity into the analysis. This involves examining an athlete's performance in reactive jumping conditions, considering how high and far they can jump with a reactive strategy. Understanding an athlete's reactive capabilities provides crucial insights into their dynamic performance and overall athletic prowess. Speed is all about reactivity, as discussed earlier in the book impulse plays a crucial factor in speed development. Understanding fundamental reactivity in controlled conditions such as an RSI test can highlight possible gaps in the athletes preparation. In team sport you often find players are not very reactive but very strong. This is a big problem when sprinting as they cannot utilise the force they can create effectively.

Strategy and Efficiency Assessment

In addition to evaluating an athlete's reactivity, coaches analyse their strategy and efficiency in executing jumps. The chosen strategy and its efficiency play a vital role in determining impulse, a high-level determinant of performance. Assessing an athlete's strategy and efficiency allows coaches to identify areas for improvement and make informed decisions regarding training interventions. Jump strategy can largely be defined by either anthropometric differences and power creation preferences. Femur length plays an important role in different jump strategies. An athlete with a longer femur will typically fold over in the hip creating a more posterior chain dominant jump. Athletes whose limbs are more equally distributed would jump with a more upright torso and use a more "balanced" jump strategy between anterior and posterior chain. When considering how athletes produce force, athletes who are more muscular or strength driven will favour longer times on the ground and deeper joint angles giving them more opportunity to create force. Whereas athletes who are more elastic and tendinous will favour shorter times and shallower joint angles to create and express their force. These profiles are the same as discussed in the differences between elastic and muscular driven sprinters.

Avoiding Overwhelm

It is important to note that while the in-depth analysis of force platform data is valuable, coaches should not get overwhelmed or feel limited by the absence of force plates. The focus should remain on using available information to inform higher qualification decisions. Coaches can still drive performance improvements by utilising other reliable assessment methods and integrating force platform insights where applicable.

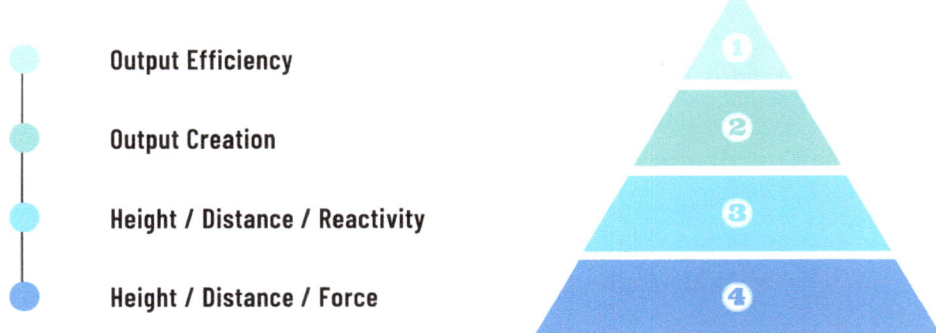

Combining Metrics for Powerful Data

In the realm of performance analysis, the combination of metrics plays a pivotal role in generating powerful data. By utilising force platforms, apps, or jump mats, coaches and trainers can gain valuable insights into an athlete's performance capabilities. This chapter explores the significance of combining metrics and highlights key metrics such as eccentric utilisation ratio, dynamic strength index, and reactive strength index in driving informed training decisions.

Eccentric Utilisation Ratio

The eccentric utilisation ratio evaluates the contribution of eccentric muscle actions in ballistic activities, reflecting the efficiency of the stretch-shortening cycle. This metric provides quick and easy insights into an athlete's performance level. By comparing the ratio of jumps with and without a countermovement, coaches can identify areas for improvement and prioritise training accordingly. Athletes with a well developed SSC should be able to jump at least 10% higher with a countermovement. If the athlete cannot pass this baseline, they must prioritise reactive and elastic adaptations via plyometrics, if the athlete is jumping 10% (ideally significantly higher) then they can likely continue to drive progress with a mixture of both strength training, ballistic training, and plyometrics.

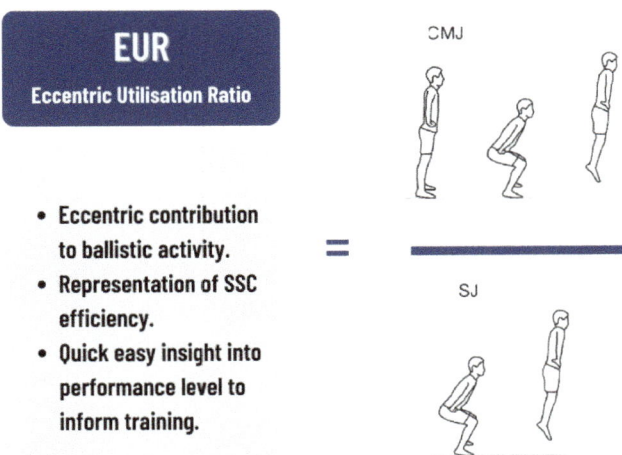

Dynamic Strength Index

The dynamic strength index compares an athlete's peak force production in an isometric mid-thigh pull to a counter movement jump. We calculate the ratio between force production with ample time versus limited time, highlighting an athlete's ability to convert strength into explosive power. Coaches can use this metric to guide training emphasis and bridge any technical gaps hindering performance. An athlete who can create a large fraction of their maximum possible force very quickly will likely be able to create further progress by raising the ceiling of strength. An athlete who cannot quickly access their strength must use ballistic means to enhance their rate of force development

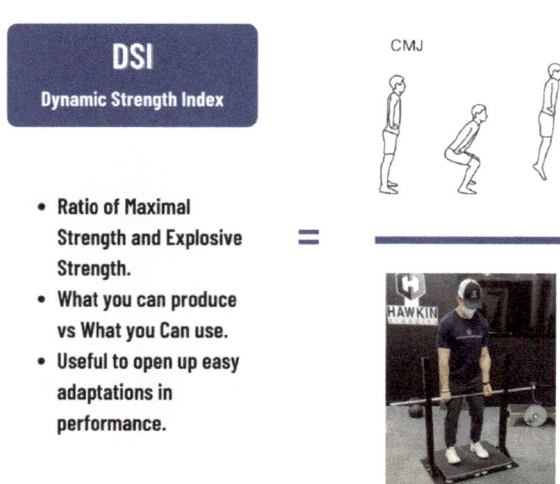

Reactive Strength Index

The reactive strength index combines jump height and contact time to assess an athlete's fast stretch-shortening cycle activity and qualify true plyometric movements. Ground contact time is a crucial component of plyometrics. Coaches can use this metric to determine the appropriate intensity and progression of jump variations, ensuring optimal training outcomes. Athletes who cannot bounce quickly and easily off the ground are not yet ready to benefit from more intensive means and must develop basic reactive abilities through extensive means.

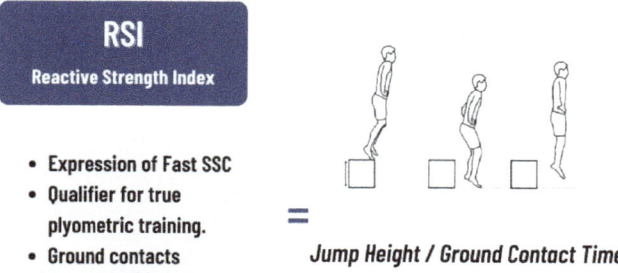

Data Comparison and Targeted Training

Utilising advanced systems like the Hawkin Dynamics system enables inter-data comparison and facilitates data-driven decision-making. Coaches can assign athletes to specific groups based on key metrics relative to desired positions, such as speed. This approach allows for targeted training programs that align with an athlete's unique profile, maximising the effectiveness of training interventions.

Utilising GPS Data to optimise Speed Programs

GPS technology has emerged as a valuable tool for coaches and trainers seeking to enhance their athletes' speed performance. While there may be variability between GPS units, understanding and harnessing its capabilities can significantly benefit training programs. This chapter explores the power of GPS data in informing speed training, allowing coaches to observe transferability and quantify load, while also providing insights into acceleration, velocity, and density metrics.

Quantifying Load and Informing Practice

GPS data enables coaches to break down training sessions based on percentage brackets of maximum velocity, offering a practical means to optimise training. By examining metrics such as maximum acceleration, peak acceleration, and accelerations above 90% of peak, coaches can gauge training load and density. Analysing metres covered within specific velocity ranges further aids in understanding step counts and contact loads, providing valuable insights for future training adaptations.

Expressing Speed in Context

GPS data not only allows for measuring speed in straight-line sprints but also facilitates evaluating an athlete's ability to express speed in dynamic contexts, such as evasion and change-of-direction scenarios. By integrating benchmark change-of-direction tests and other relevant drills, coaches can assess an athlete's speed capabilities within specific contexts, leading to targeted training interventions.

The Importance of Contextualizing Data

While maximum velocity is a valuable metric, coaches should remember that it is just one aspect of a comprehensive training program. utilising GPS data should focus on the practical adaptations required for an athlete's sport-specific demands. By contextualising the data and identifying key metrics aligned with training goals, coaches can optimise training programs effectively. The biggest understanding we can create is how the game affects individual players. Therefore looking at the players outputs as a % of their maximum speed is a great place to start. Secondly, understanding the distance it takes for that athlete to find their top speed is really important too. One of the most important metrics for team sport is speed exposures above 90% per game. Remember that your goal is preparation. If you are able to prepare your athlete to break 90% of their max speed multiple times per game you have created a team sport sprinter with tremendous capacity. In periods of preparation like pre season targeting acceleration volume or distance above 70% of max speed will help players prepare more intensive tactical training.

Going Beyond GPS

Coaches can further enhance their analysis by exporting raw velocity accelerometer data and conducting in-depth individual sprint analyses. This advanced approach provides the opportunity to track individual profiles over time, offering valuable insights into an athlete's progress. Here your attention needs to be placed on the distance it takes to achieve top speed. This where in training you can use standardised accelerations to determine if your acceleration training has worked. However, it is essential to prioritise such detailed analyses when necessary due to the time-consuming nature of the process.

GPS data offers a wealth of information for coaches and trainers looking to optimise speed programs. By leveraging this technology, coaches can observe transferability, quantify load, and gain insights into acceleration, velocity, and density metrics. Contextualising data and prioritising key metrics aligned with training goals enable coaches to create effective and targeted training interventions. While GPS technology opens new avenues for analysis, coaches should remember that it is just one piece of the puzzle and should be used in conjunction with other tools and assessments to create a holistic approach to speed development.

Enhancing Your Speed Program with Slow Motion Video Analysis

Slow motion video analysis is a valuable tool that can significantly contribute to the effectiveness of a speed training program. This chapter explores the power of using slow motion video to assess basic speed metrics, remove complexity, and provide actionable insights for coaches and trainers on a budget. By importing videos into software, counting frame rates, and performing simple calculations, coaches can gain valuable information to track progress and refine training interventions.

Identifying Key Performance Indicators (KPIs)

When analysing slow motion video, coaches should consider the KPIs relevant to sprint learning and performance. These may include visual changes in technique, maintenance of maximum velocity, or consistent peak acceleration. By identifying and tracking these leading indicators within the training program, coaches can assess the efficiency and economy of an athlete's sprinting technique, ultimately guiding targeted interventions.

Coaches Belong with Athletes

While data analysis is valuable, coaches should remember their primary role is to be actively engaged with athletes. Coaches must strike a balance between utilising technology and being present on the field, affecting real change and providing effective coaching. Slow motion video analysis should complement the coach's hands-on approach rather than replace it.

REHABILITATION AND THE SPORTS SPEED SYSTEM

Important Note: *This section is not medical advice. Please work closely as possible with a trained medical practitioner when rehabilitating athletes from injury. This is a guide as to how you can integrate the sports speed system with injured athletes.*

Injury rehabilitation is a critical component of athletic training, particularly for those involved in team sports where speed and agility are paramount. Traditional rehabilitation often focuses on basic exercises to restore function, but for athletes aiming to return to high-speed activities like sprinting, a more specific and comprehensive approach is required. The Sport Speed System integrates goal-specific rehabilitation, emphasising the restoration of an athlete's ability to sprint effectively on the field. This approach involves shifting our perspective of how we view rehabilitation and return to speed. We can do this by reducing the range of motion, speed, and force applied to movements during early stages and progressively increasing these variables to ensure a safe and efficient return to full performance. This section is designed to be a guide to inform you on the fundamental principles and processes required to return an athlete to speed. As injuries can be highly specific this would require a whole book on the subject. However with that being said I believe that all coaches should know how to progressively return an athlete back to speed safely and have a system with which to do this.

Blending the Sports Speed System with the Injured Athlete

If you have read up until this point in the book you should be able to see how logical and systematic the sports speed system is. especially when considering the role of return to speed for athletes. When we look to use the sport speed system within an injury rehab process it becomes a very simple model. When you look to integrate the sports speed system you will be focusing primarily on the general speed and the learn to sprint areas of the training system. The table below should create an accurate representation of the key changes that need to be made. This comes from an understanding of the ground reaction forces created during the different general speed activities. The goal throughout any rehabilitation process is to utilise cyclic motion at whatever level we can as soon as we can. These are categorised as "gait availability".

Stage	Gait Availability	Ground Reaction Force	Primary Drill Stack Level	Stability Level	Range of Motion
1	Walk	1.0 - 1.2 x BW	Segment	Stable	Small
	Jog	2.0 - 3.0 x BW	Segment / Movement	Stable Unstable	Medium

Stage	Gait Availability	Ground Reaction Force	Primary Drill Stack Level	Stability Level	Range of Motion
2	Acceleration	2.5 - 3.5 x BW	Movement / Pattern / Skill	Ustable Stable	High
	Change of Direction	3.0 - 4.5 x BW		Unstable Stable	High
	Maximum Velocity Sprinting	4.0 - 5.5 x BW		Unstable	Highest

It is important to acknowledge here that each injury represents a different set of challenges and therefore I do advise an individualised approach. Please consider how you are able to continue or integrate the elements of "speed" training at these phases of restriction. Many rehabilitation processes overly focus their efforts on general strength training and general aerobic conditioning. This is why we see so many recurrences of injury as athletes have not followed S.A.I.D principle appropriately and restored sports speed qualities.

Goal-Specific Rehabilitation

The ultimate objective of rehabilitation within the Sport Speed System is to restore the athlete's ability to sprint, change direction, and perform at their pre-injury level or better. This requires a shift from generic recovery exercises to sport-specific movements that mimic the demands of sprinting.

Key Considerations:

1. **Range of Motion (ROM):** Initially, exercises should be performed within a reduced range of motion to avoid excessive stress on the injured area.
2. **Speed of Movement:** Starting with slow, controlled movements and gradually increasing speed as the athlete's tolerance improves.
3. **Force Applied:** Beginning with low-force activities and progressively increasing the load as the athlete's strength and resilience return.

Return to Running Sequence

A structured return to running sequence ensures that athletes transition smoothly from rehabilitation exercises to full-speed sprints. This sequence should be tailored to the individual, considering the nature of the injury, the athlete's sport, and their specific goals. Below is a simplified version of a return to speed process over a 10-12 week period for a minor injury. As with all injury rehabilitation processes, time doesn't dictate the ability to return to sport or sprinting. There must be defined exit criteria in place, and the athlete needs to build a volume of exposure to the stimulus of each exit criterion before they are ready to progress to the next stage. This increases the likelihood they have made the adaptations needed to support them through the next, more intensive phase. This guide can be condensed and expanded based on the individual you are rehabilitating.

Phase 1: Early Rehabilitation (Weeks 1-3)

— Focus: Reduce pain and inflammation, restore basic movement patterns.
— Activities:

- Range of motion exercises (e.g., passive and active stretching)
- Low-intensity, non-weight-bearing activities - Utilise a pool to work on Marching and patterns, bike for cyclic movements.
- Light strength training focusing on the core and non-injured limbs.

Phase 2: Intermediate Rehabilitation (Weeks 4-6)

- Focus: Begin reintroducing weight-bearing activities, improve muscular strength and endurance.
- Activities:
  - Controlled, weight-bearing exercises (e.g., Yielding, overcoming and full range wall drills, basic strength training, special strength training)
  - Proprioception and balance training (e.g., Low level jumping and skipping, single leg balance)
  - Gradual reintroduction of low-intensity running (e.g., Running drill progressions - walking to jogging).

Phase 3: Advanced Rehabilitation (Weeks 7-9)

- Focus: Increase running intensity, enhance power and speed-specific strength.
- Activities:
  - Dynamic strength exercises (e.g., Resisted sled sprints, long accelerations, plyometrics)
  - Sport-specific drills at moderate intensity (e.g., cone drills, shuttle runs)
  - Incremental increase in running speed and distance (e.g., interval training, extensive and intensive tempo).

Phase 4: Pre-Return to Sport (Weeks 10-12)

- Focus: Full-speed sprinting, agility, and sport-specific conditioning.
- Activities:
  - High-intensity sprint drills (e.g., maximal effort sprints, hill sprints)
  - Complex agility drills mimicking game scenarios (e.g., reaction-based drills, change of direction exercises)
  - Full sport-specific training sessions (e.g., scrimmages, position-specific drills).

Basic Key Performance Indicators for Returning to Speed

When attempting to return an athlete back to their previous level of performance there are many factors to consider as each injury should be treated individually. As each injury is different it is very challenging to highlight one specific way, however below I have listed and outlined the phases of running we can look to rehabilitate our athletes with. To structure and design training please refer to the principles outlined in the general speed section.

Phase	Modality	Goal
Non Weight Bearing	Bike	Maintain Cyclic Activity
Partial Weight Bearing	Cross Trainer	Maintain Cyclic Activity Standing upright
Full Weight Bearing Walk	March Drills / Weighted March Drills/ Wall Drill Variations	Neuromuscular control, aerobic development, strength development
Jog	Running Drills/ Ankle & Shin Dribble Variations	Neuromuscular control, aerobic development, strength development
Stride	Power Skips/ Full Dribble Variations	Utilise specific strength to develop capacity for speed and prepare for increased intensity and ground contact.
Run	Extensive Tempo and Long Accelerations	Build cyclic capabilities and elastic qualities to develop speed and volume tolerance
Accelerate	Intensive Tempo / Resisted Speed Training / Introduce Change of Direction Progressions	Increase mechanical load and joint stress.
Sprint	Circa max speed training / Maximal Acceleration	Increase overall intensity of training and output of the athlete

These are loose velocity and mechanical load categorisations but I feel it's important to have a framework to operate within.

Further Recommendations

The trick to a successful rehabilitation process lies in the continual monitoring and assessment of the injury. As in all training it is important to understand how the body adapts and responds to training. This can be through qualitative and quantitative measurements. This is where it is important to consult with a trained medical practitioner for the best outcomes.

Alongside this ensuring that there is adequate gradual progression will continue to address the athletes specific needs. Sometimes within the injury rehabilitation process we as practitioners can be reluctant to continue to progress training. This is why the sports speed system is incredibly useful within these scenarios. As you have the progressions and intensity gauges laid out for you it is a simple case of ensuring that there has been a reasonable period of training consolidation and then the athlete can progress to the next stimulus in a sequential fashion. If you prioritise that alongside managing the volumes and intensities that we have previously discussed you will be in a great place to create a successful return to speed.

One final point regarding the return to speed process is the understanding of the psychological approach to training. When an athlete is injured they can become incredibly vulnerable and can be highly apprehensive towards running fast and engaging in explosive activity. This is very common. Working within the current confidence level that the athlete possesses and having successful key performance indicators that compound over time will help shortcut the process of overcoming the fear of sprinting again. This is where historical data is incredibly important and also the utilisation of tools such as Speedgate golf and long acceleration modalities for maximum velocity exposure.

By adopting a goal-specific rehabilitation approach and following a structured return to running sequence, athletes can safely and effectively regain their sprinting abilities. This comprehensive method ensures that they not only return to play but also perform at a high level, minimising the risk of re-injury and enhancing overall athletic performance.

Specific Speed

Within this section of the book we are going to be focusing on Specific Speed. Understanding Specific speed requires an understanding of sport specific distances and the specific velocities attained within though. Up until now we have looked at developing the ability to produce speed in the context of physical preparation in absence of sport preparation. Now we are placing our attention as to how we start to bridge the gap between running fast in a straight line and running fast on the field. The goal is to translate general speed into field-specific scenarios. With specific classification in mind our goal is to not imitate the specific movements involved in the games we play but learn to develop speed and capacity of that speed within those distances. Here we will start to look into carrying implements of the sport e.g. ball, stick, hurl or even pads. This will allow us to determine the transfer of general speed to more sport specific speed variations.

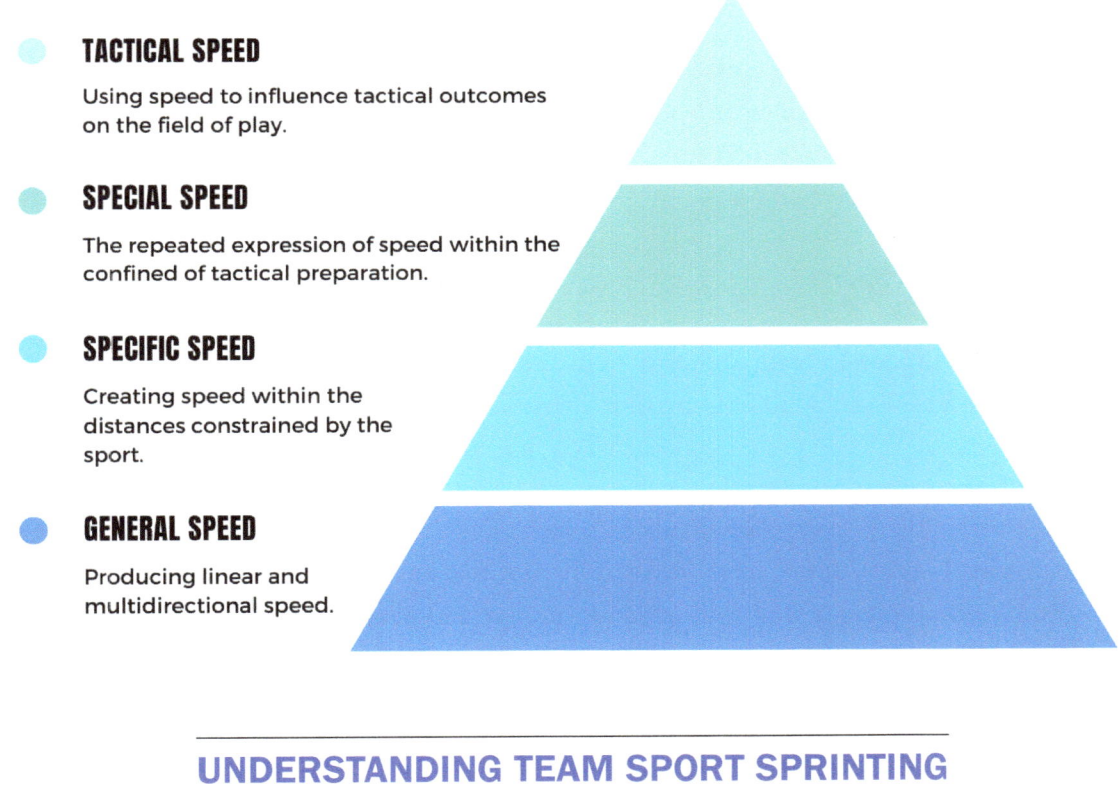

UNDERSTANDING TEAM SPORT SPRINTING

THE PRIMARY GOAL OF SPEED IN TEAM SPORT IS TO BE ABLE TO USE IT

In the realm of team sports, sprinting plays a pivotal role, yet its application within this context often resides in a grey area. This chapter aims to delve into the intricacies of sprinting in team sports, challenging traditional notions and exploring new perspectives. By demonstrating the practical implementation of sprinting techniques in team sports, we can unlock the potential for athletes who may not possess elite sprinting abilities, but still strive to optimise their performance on the field.

Shifting Focus to Application

As we progress further down the specificity continuum, it becomes evident that replicating sport-specific movements directly is not always necessary. Rather, our aim should be to stimulate the developmental pathway that leads to enhanced performance. Recognising the unique characteristics of the athletes we work with, our objective is to qualify and prepare them to achieve their full potential in the most effective manner possible.

Understanding Team Sport Dynamics

Team sports differ from individual track and field events, emphasising the importance of comprehending the specific movements and demands of the game. Gear management, approach play, and tactical awareness all require meticulous attention. To gain a deeper understanding, we must examine team sports from a root cause perspective rather than focusing solely on causation or correlation.

Gear management is a term I refer to with athletes to help them understand how to time their speed when approaching a tactical scenario. Nothing in sport truly happens at maximum speeds unless you are in a foot race. Therefore it is important to teach athletes what their gears feel like. This can be done with the use of zone runs, long accelerations and speed build ups.

The Goal of Speed in Team Sports

The primary objective of speed in team sports is to utilise it effectively on the field. Possessing speed alone, without the ability to harness and apply it in a game situation, renders it futile.

The Significance of Maximum Acceleration

In team sports, maximal output is not solely defined by maximal velocity but also maximal acceleration. The ability to rapidly accelerate plays a vital role in achieving optimal performance. It is crucial to acknowledge that sport-specific skills, such as running, catching, passing, and engaging in contact, further amplify the importance of maximising acceleration capabilities. Thus, the sport itself becomes the essential factor in our equation, as it is the ultimate determinant of an athlete's sprinting effectiveness.

WHEN TO TRANSITION TO SPECIFIC SPEED

The transition to the specific speed phase of the sports speed system is very interchangeable and also dependent upon the phase of the training cycle. As we have touched on within our programming sections of this book, utilising a previously attained level of performance is what unlocks the continued progress and adaptation of training. Therefore, how we utilise specific speed is more important than when we utilise it.

Below I have provided you with a couple of ways you can utilise Specific Speed phases of training into your preparation cycles.

Off Season	Pre-Season	Pre Season 2
General Speed	Specific Speed	Special Speed

In the above example I have shown how your training emphasis will shift between the different classifications of the Sports Speed System throughout the course of a season. In the off-season, like all other qualities we prioritise the development of maximal speed, that will improve all other qualities. Then as we enter pre-season where team sport training increases we will see an increased amount of acceleration work due to the nature of our sports and as coaches we will support that with an increased emphasis on the development of acceleration. Then finally in the later phases of pre-season the focus is solely on specialised speed ensuring that the players can peak into the season effectively.

As we have discussed with our initial rates of adaptation to training stimulus and athlete who finds themselves in the learning to sprint phases of the sport speed system will see a direct transfer to the specific speeds required on the field. they will report that they just feel faster on the pitch. This is the true power and the importance of the learning to sprint phase of the sports speed system. You will find that you can spend a lot more time there than you might initially realise.

As we transition into the development of specific speed It is important to touch on the relationship between maximal output and the operational demands of a task. This is why maximum sprint speed is so important to the development of specific speed. As we know all field based sports are not maximal in nature for the entire game. They are built on athletes running varying percentages of their speed to achieve a desired result. Sometimes they sprint to their max and other times they coast. The Table below demonstrates the difference between 8m/s, 9m/s and 10m/s. You will easily be able to see the large impact that possessing a higher max speed has on the overall performance of a game.

Percentage	8 m/s	9 m/s	10 m/s
95%	7.6	8.55	9.5
90%	7.2	8.1	9
85%	6.8	7.65	8.5
80%	6.4	7.2	8
75%	6	6.75	7.5
70%	5.6	6.3	7
65%	5.2	5.85	6.5
60%	4.8	5.4	6
55%	4.4	4.95	5.5
50%	4	4.5	5

As we progress through this section of the book we will take a closer look at some specific game data from sports to help you develop specific speed.

SPECIFIC SPEED AND MOTOR LEARNING

Within the classification of general speed we heavily focussed on deliberate practice in order to develop the necessary outputs to create speed. We highlighted how becoming stronger in pre-planned movements and exercises will drive a great return on speed in the general context. This is known as a hierarchical approach. Within a team sports environment deliberate practice really serves as a time efficient and effective way to teach the fundamentals of speed to get initial adaptation quickly. As we progress into specific speed and start to bring in certain aspects of the sport the way in which we create speed and movement will change.

I have highlighted the key differences below from general speed to specific speed below.

Type of Speed	General Speed	Specific Speed
Maximum Speed	Focus solely on developing maximum speed and its output.	Implemented with a ball in hand/and or from different starting situations. Assessing the relative difference in speed assessments. E.g. 10m sprint without vs with ball.
Acceleration	Focus solely on developing acceleration and its output.	
Change of Direction	Focus solely on developing change of direction and its output.	
Conditioning	Development of recoverable abilities.	Developing the repeated ability of all criteria of speed.

THE DIRECTION OF TRAINING

As we have looked at in the general element of Speed training we are primarily focused on a modified long to short variation of Speed development. This sits in conjunction with our learning to sprint speed age and the utilisation of long accelerations to develop maximal output of sprint speed. As we progress into the more specific speed classification of movement we change to a short too long approach.

As touched on before, the long to short or the short to Long approach was popularised by the late Charlie Francis in the attempt to categorise volume and intensity of speed training work to ultimately influence track and field sprinters. Inside the sports speed system this has been modified in conjunction to the competitive distance demands of field sports.

THE DATA BEHIND TEAM SPORT SPRINTING

Technology has allowed us to observe the way athletes move on the pitch in great detail. This data allows us to be able to fully understand the training and match demands of athletes. This helps us unlock specific speed and helps us tailor training programs.

Data on match demands is widely available with many studies being conducted. However please do not model your training on those numbers. Use them as a guide. If you don't want to go through the data for your sport you can simply watch a game. This is how you really understand the specific speed demands.

We will now look at how you are able to use velocity data generated from GPS to understand the relative sprint demands of the game of rugby. This data has been modified slightly for the purpose of confidentiality and discretion. However the numbers presented are an accurate representation of the game of rugby union.

Considerations for Maximum Speed as a Loading Tool

The data has been broken down into the major positional groups (front 5, middle 5 and back 5) to demonstrate the general distribution of work. Please bear in mind individual players will play their position differently but from the speed perspective we need to understand how speed is used within the game. All the data presented is based on the relative demands of the athletes playing the game. The GPS classifies movement based upon the percentage of maximum speed. This does not factor in acceleration data. As a sports speed coach this is the only metric you need to be considering.

The below table illustrates some of the general metrics that a game of rugby produces. As you can see the relationship between total distance and distance above 70% of maximum speed is vastly different.

Position Group	Average of Total Distance	Average Max Velocity	Average of % MSS	Average of Metres/Min	Average Distance Above 70%
Back 5	6989.8	9.0	95.9	70.8	402.2
Front 5	4167.0	6.6	84.8	59.5	392.1
Middle 5	4706.3	7.1	82.3	72.1	255.7

This table illustrates the distribution of work covered by percentage of maximum speed bandwidths.

Position Group	Average of 0-20% Distance	Average of 20-60% Distance	Average of 60-70% MSS Distance	Average of 70-80% MSS Distance	Average of 80-90% MSS Distance	Average of 90-95% MSS Distance	Average of 95-100% MSS Distance	Average of >100% MSS Distance
Back 5	3246.1	3137.9	299.2	158.5	94.3	20.3	20.9	10.8
Front 5	1273.4	2442.3	244.9	126.9	66.0	9.3	1.6	1.6
Middle 5	1957.1	2408.3	227.9	90.0	20.6	1.4	0.0	0.0

From this data we are able to determine how little true sprinting activity occurs above 70% in matches. This does not mean we shouldn't focus on it, but it serves as a guide for preparation.

When we consider the number of efforts covered this represents the number of times an athlete enters these brackets. These are cumulative. Therefore when an athlete enters the 100% band they will accumulate an effort in each of the bands. But what is interesting from this data with regards to building specific speed is the 80-90% column.

Position Group	Max. of 0-20% Efforts	Max # of 20-60% Efforts	Max # of 60-70% Efforts	Max # of 70-80% Efforts	Max # of 80-90% Efforts	Max # of 90-95% Efforts	Max # of 95-100% Efforts	Max # of >100% Efforts
Back 5	0.0	212.0	37.0	16.0	10.0	1.0	1.0	2.0
Front 5	0.0	257.0	39.0	22.0	10.0	1.0	1.0	1.0
Middle 5	0.0	254.0	28.0	14.0	4.0	1.0	0.0	0.0

As we continue to break down the date we can dive into the average distance covered by speed zone. This shows us the average distances covered in a single effort in a certain speed zone which give us greater context with regards to preparing athletes for speed.

Position Group	Average of 0-20% Avg Effort Dist	Average of 20-60% Avg Effort Dist	Average of 60-70% Avg Effort Dist	Average of 70-80% Avg Effort Dist	Average of 80-90% Avg Effort Dist	Average of 90-95% Effort Dist	Average 95-100% Avg Effort Dist	Average of >100% Avg Effort Dist
Back 5	0.0	17.0	12.3	13.0	15.6	11.5	9.6	5.2
Front 5	0.0	15.4	12.5	10.0	9.2	6.9	0.8	1.6
Middle 5	0.0	16.7	13.7	12.4	7.3	0.9	0.0	0.0

Here we can determine that the average distance covered in an effort in the 80-90% speed zone is roughly 10-12m across all position groups.

From looking at averages it is also incredibly important to prepare for the maximum distances covered. This table shows us the average maximum distance covered in a single effort in a particular speed zone. Our main concern here are the higher speed zones.

Position Group	Max. of 0-20% Max Effort Dist	Max. of 20-60% Max Effort Dist	Max. of 60-70% Max Effort Dist	Max. of 70-80% Max Effort Dist	Max. of 80-90% Max Effort Dist	Max. of 90-95% Max Effort Dist	Max. of 95-100% Max Effort Dist	Max. of >100% MSS Max Effort Dist
Back 5	0.0	102.4	40.3	32.0	33.2	17.2	20.9	37.6
Front 5	0.0	116.6	54.0	37.7	23.0	20.6	6.5	12.9
Middle 5	0.0	111.8	64.2	45.6	31.8	8.5	0.0	0.0

What you can see is that the players need to be able to tolerate 30+ metres of continuous running above 80% of maximal sprint speed. This is the worst case scenario but they do need to be prepared for this. Training this would look like a 60m effort with a 30m zone dedicated to endure speed. This would take 30m to build up to 8/10 effort and then maintain or increase speed over the second 30m. Performed correctly this can be quite taxing for some platers.

When we combine this data and take an objective view of the numbers we can see some form of training scheme being prepared.

Position Group	Average of 80-90% MSS Distance	Max. of 80-90% Efforts	Average of 80-90% MSS Avg Effort Dist	Max. of 80-90% Max Effort Dist
Back 5	94.3	10.0	15.6	33.2
Front 5	66.0	10.0	9.2	23.0
Middle 5	20.6	4.0	7.3	31.8

Looking at this data we can start to determine how we need to prepare our athletes for the higher percentage speed running that rugby creates. When looking at this data it's important to understand that we are not going to replicate this as a session because there is one important variable that cannot be determined from the data set that we have. The 10 efforts that were between 80 to 90% of maximum speed were covered over the course of an 80-minute game with a 15-minute rest in between. Therefore constructing a training session that consisted of 10 x 10m Fly Sprints would be irresponsible.

This is where we would refer back to our programming considerations and how we build intensity. From the maximum speed data that we can see from the players in the first table, immediately we can see that there is room for improvement to raise the maximum output of these players. What we could advise however is that in an off season preparation training cycle of where we are looking to accumulate maximum speed volumes creating up to six repetitions of 10 to 15 metres up above 80% of maximum speed would help to develop tolerance to speed and also enhance maximum speed.

One thing that is also incredibly important to acknowledge is the maximum effort distance covered which is reported by this data. The mistake that can be made is to try to create situations where the athletes will be sprinting for 30 metres at high percentages. In game, they have not been conducted in a deliberate isolated sprint effort. This could have been chasing down a player or running away from a player to score a try. This is where specificity is so important and a factor that heavily needs to be considered when constructing sprint training workouts to combat the worst case scenarios of field performance. As we understand through our speed ages the degree of mastery which an athlete possesses will determine the distances and intensities that focused speed work needs to be conducted within.

Without trying to emulate this specific data we are able to learn a lot about how we need to prepare our athletes for speed. The challenge within team sports is handling the sheer volume of sprints that are being executed within the game. This is where within specific preparation blocks of speed we need to focus on sprint capacity and distance specific capacity.

Considerations of Acceleration and Decelerations as a loading tool.

When considering the elements of acceleration and deceleration it is important to decide whether your sport is a heavy acceleration and deceleration sport. A simple way to understand this is again to watch the game. Look at each position and watch how the game dictates the way they move initially, and how they move to gain advantages in the game . Even more so, it is important to understand the style of play your athletes use to express themselves within games. In rugby you could have a very jinky winger or a top speed biased athlete both playing in the same position. Therefore discretion is advised when training athletes.

Similarly to the data presented above I have categorised a seasons worth of match data looking at accelerations and deceleration to understand the amount of work each positional group in rugby cover during games.

When we look at the average number of accelerations and decelerations taken place in a game of rugby we can see that a majority of the work is conducted in what would be classified as lower intensity acceleration. This would be essentially standing still and breaking out into a run. What is interesting to see is the number of high intensity accelerations that occur. This would be considered as breaking out into a maximal sprint. These are good indicators as to the preparation demands of rugby.

Position Group	Average Decelerations -2- -3 m/s² Efforts	Average Decelerations -2-0 m/s² Efforts	Average Accelerations 0-2m/s² Efforts	Average Accelerations 2-3m/s² Efforts
Back 5	8	478	450	14
Front 5	2	376	333	4
Middle 5	4	420	387	8

As we progress from seasonal averages it is important to look at the maximum number or efforts covered in these categories. Not too dissimilar to the maximum velocity data, we are seeing somewhere in the region of double the average number of efforts. This gives us again great insight into the development of acceleration and deceleration.

Position Group	Max # of Deceleration Efforts -2- -3 m/s²	Max # of Deceleration Efforts 0- -2 m/s²	Max # of Accelerations 0-2 m/s²	Max # of Accelerations 2 - 3 m/s²
Back 5	17	633	865	25
Front 5	6	674	572	12
Middle 5	17	640	960	21

At this point I do feel it is important to remind you that acceleration and deceleration are general qualities of speed and therefore should be trained in that capacity. The goal of any general speed block of training should be to improve maximum output of those qualities. Then as we transition into the specific blocks of training we then need to incorporate capacities of those qualities and within the working distances of the sport.

VISION, TIMING AND DISTANCE

Understanding and managing speed relative to the sporting action is crucial for athletes in any sport. One of the things that happens so often in evasion is a player making their side step too late because they have not understood their speed and misjudged their distance. Vision, timing, and distance are fundamental components that determine the effectiveness and efficiency of an athlete's movements. The ability to process visual information quickly, time actions precisely, and judge distances accurately can distinguish elite athletes from the rest. These skills are not just innate but can be developed and refined through specific training strategies.

The Science of Vision and Motor Control

Vision is the dominant sense used in sports, providing up to 90% of the information required for performance. The process starts when light enters the eyes and hits the retina, where photoreceptors convert it into neural signals. These signals travel through the optic nerve to the brain's visual cortex for processing. Here, the brain interprets the signals to recognize patterns, depth, and motion.

The visual information is then integrated with the motor system. The brain coordinates with the spinal cord and muscles to execute movements. This process involves several brain areas, including the occipital lobe (visual processing), parietal lobe (spatial awareness), and frontal lobe (motor planning). The cerebellum plays a crucial role in fine-tuning movements and maintaining balance and coordination.

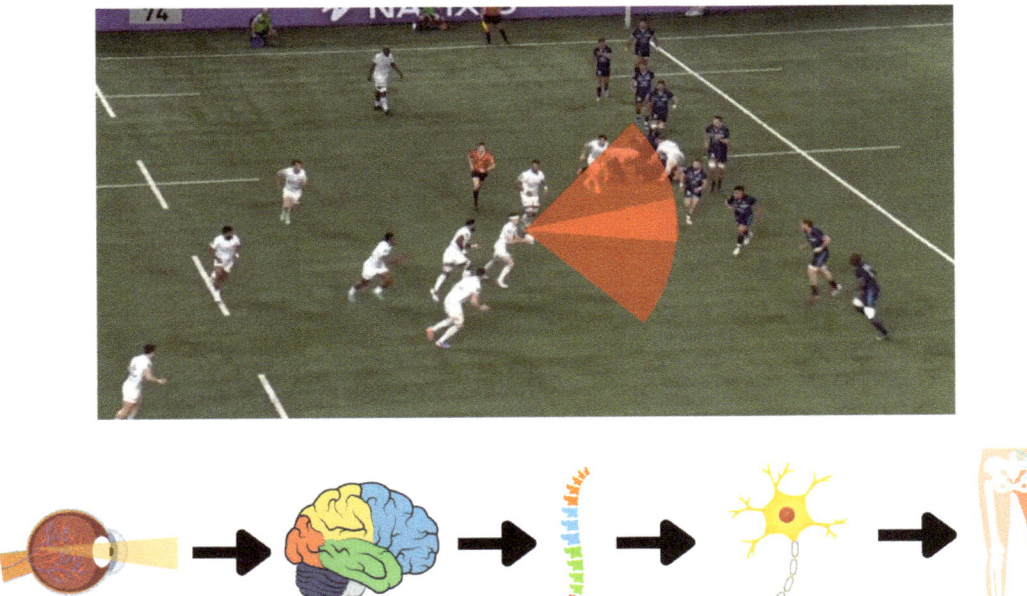

Timing is the synchronisation of movements with external stimuli. It relies heavily on the brain's ability to predict and anticipate events. The cerebellum and basal ganglia are key players in timing, as they help adjust the timing of muscle activations to ensure smooth and coordinated movements. Precise timing enables athletes to react quickly to opponents' actions and environmental changes.

Distance perception is the ability to judge the space between oneself and an object or opponent. It involves binocular vision (both eyes working together) and monocular cues (depth cues from one eye). The brain combines these cues to estimate distances accurately. Proper distance perception allows athletes to position themselves optimally and execute movements with the right amount of force.

Coaching Elements: Developing Vision, Timing, and Distance

This concept might be very new to you reading this book but I hope that you understand the importance of this work. You have the ability to take your athletes to a new level of transfer by understanding how to create specific adaptation. I have included examples of how you can incorporate this type of work into your training.

Visual Training:

Coaches can incorporate drills that enhance an athlete's visual skills. These may include:

- **Tracking Exercises:** Using balls or other objects to improve the ability to follow moving targets. Can be made more complex by doing this in tandem with other athletic drills
- **Peripheral Vision Drills:** Activities that require athletes to be aware of their surroundings, improving spatial awareness.
- **Hand-Eye Coordination Drills:** Catching and throwing exercises to refine the link between vision and motor response.

Timing Drills:

Developing timing involves exercises that challenge an athlete's reaction time and synchronisation abilities:

- **Reactive Drills:** Using visual or auditory cues to prompt quick responses. For example, reacting to a coach's command or a flashing light.
- **Jump and Plyometric Training:** creating challenging ways to help the athlete to time their movement effectively will help train their ability to time effective movements needed for high velocity movement.
- **Sport-Specific Simulations:** Practising game scenarios that require precise timing, such as a football player timing a run to avoid offsides or a rugby player negotiating a 1 vs 1 in a match to score the winning try.

Distance Perception Training:

Improving distance perception involves exercises that enhance depth perception and spatial awareness:

- **Obstacle Courses:** Navigating through obstacles to develop a sense of space and distance.
- **Partner Drills:** Working with teammates to practice judging distances, such as passing drills and deceleration timing.
- **Virtual Reality Training:** Using VR technology to simulate game scenarios and improve spatial awareness.

Integrating Vision, Timing, and Distance into Speed Training

To effectively integrate vision, timing, and distance into speed training, coaches can design drills that combine these elements:

- **Multi-Directional Speed Drills:** Incorporate changes in direction, requiring athletes to use their vision and timing to navigate the drills efficiently.
- **Reaction-Based Sprints:** Athletes react to a visual or auditory cue to start their sprint, enhancing their timing and decision-making under pressure.
- **Cognitive Load Exercises:** Combining physical drills with cognitive tasks, such as solving puzzles or identifying targets while performing speed drills, to simulate game-like situations where athletes must process information quickly.

Neurological Components and Their Impact

The neurological basis for vision, timing, and distance perception lies in the brain's ability to process and integrate sensory information. Neuroplasticity, the brain's capacity to adapt and change, plays a vital role in developing these skills. Regular training can strengthen neural connections, leading to improvements in visual processing speed, reaction time, and spatial awareness.

Practical Application and Examples

Example 1: Football
In football, a player's ability to judge distances and react quickly to opponents' movements is crucial. Coaches can use small-sided games to simulate match conditions, encouraging players to use their vision to scan the field and make quick decisions. Drills that require rapid changes in direction and speed can also enhance their timing and distance perception.

Example 2: Rugby
Rugby players need excellent peripheral vision and timing to execute plays effectively. Coaches can design drills that involve passing and moving while under pressure, forcing players to make quick decisions and react to defenders. Training with varying distances and angles can also improve their depth perception and spatial awareness.

Example 3: American Football
In American football, players must react to the snap of the ball and make split-second decisions based on the movements of their opponents. Coaches can use reaction drills with visual cues, such as a flashing light to start a sprint, to enhance players' timing and reaction speed. Practising route running with defenders can also improve their ability to judge distances and make precise movements.

HOW TO BUILD SPECIFIC SPEED

When we consider the development of creating and building specific speed with our team sports sprinters there are a few things to consider. We are not trying to recreate or mimic the actions that are seen on the field, we are simply trying to develop and improve some of the existing qualities that we have, to prepare the athlete for the field.

At this stage for most team sports it's really important to consider how we are developing aerobic and anaerobic abilities, transfer the previously attained motor qualities and also consider the exercises that we are using. As we work in the specific speed sections it's really important to start creating changes from local exercises into more global exercises. An example of this would be to reduce the amount of time spent on local exercises such as wall drills, and trap bar deadlifts in the gym to emphasise resisted acceleration based work and explosive jumping for gym-based training. The general phases of sprinting have served a purpose to which we then need to apply more specific regimes of work. From an organisation of training standpoint it is important to refer back to the programming for Speed section to understand the way that you would create sequential loading approaches to help improve your athletes performance.

Again I want to remind you just because you move from general speed to specific speed it does not mean that you will never return to this stage. However, for every subsequent performance improvement attained through general speed training, the athlete must learn to express this speed within more specific, special, and tactical situations.

The general premise of developing specific speed is to increase the ability and capacity to accelerate and decrease the distance at which we are able to create top speed. We will then look to add implements such as a ball, pads, or even a hockey stick and start to design training around the addition of those implements. This will help increase the motor learning and control response of the new stimulus. it will also serve as a guide to the coach to understand the deficit that is being created from general to specific speed. I will now take you through some examples of this.

In my most familiar sport of rugby union it can typically be seen that players from a maximal acceleration are able to achieve 90% and above of their top speed between 20 to 30 metres. However through the utilisation of long accelerations and other maximal speed development tools we are able to create significant increases in top speed by utilising greater distances to lengthen out the phases of acceleration. This is where the deficit of general speed to specific speed is created. Therefore the goal when moving from general speed to specific speed phases of training is to not increase maximum speed further it is to improve the ability to reach maximum speed quickly. Increasing the ability to find speed faster makes a significant impact in field sports, due to the number of actions at high speeds. As you can see from the table below, the impact that increases of maximal speed can have on submaximal percentages is very significant.

Max Speed (m/s)	90%	85%	80%
9	8.1	7.7	7.2
9.5	8.6	8.1	7.6
10	9.0	8.5	8.0

Another area of specific speed development is to understand the anaerobic and aerobic qualities of speed training. Contrary to the pursuit of speed in track and field, athletes in field sports must be able to produce speed under fatigued conditions, powered by different energy systems. It is important to develop a high speed reserve which will allow the athletes to continue to reproduce speed continuously throughout again. Speed reserve refers to the difference between an athlete's maximum sprinting speed and their game or competition speed. It is essentially the buffer or surplus speed an athlete possesses beyond the typical speed required during competition. For instance, if an athlete's maximum sprinting speed is 11 metres per second (m/s), and they typically run at 8 m/s during a game, their speed reserve is 3 m/s. This will afford them more opportunity to repeat their speed throughout a game.

There is a crucial difference between developing endurance and capacity. When we consider endurance as coaches our minds will typically navigate towards aerobic training and sub maximal running variations for longer distances. however this is not how we create specific speed. As we have looked at some of the GPS data provided by professional rugby possessing the ability to endure speed and the ability to repeatedly express speed is essential for success. The training of repeat speed is very important at this phase. The goal is to create repeated sprint efforts above 90% for example. In training we would use multiple 30m or 40m sprints. Initially all rest periods would be designed to attain the desired speed and then training would be dedicated to gradually decrease the rest periods to place a greater demand on the athlete to reproduce speed under fatigue. A simple example of this is being able to score a breakaway try in the last minute of the game and needing to sprint 50 metres to do so. To develop this in training we need to construct training sessions that create repeated expressions of speed and acceleration above 90%. An example program is in the appendix.

Special Speed

Within this section we are going to be focussing on what I like to call special speed. As we ascend up the pyramid of classification we start to pull away from isolated training of speed and look to integrate speed into our sport training. This is where we start to determine the transfer of our training. Let me remind you at this point of the book that you will have to start letting go of some of your ideas regarding preparation and start to embrace preparation for sport as it should be.

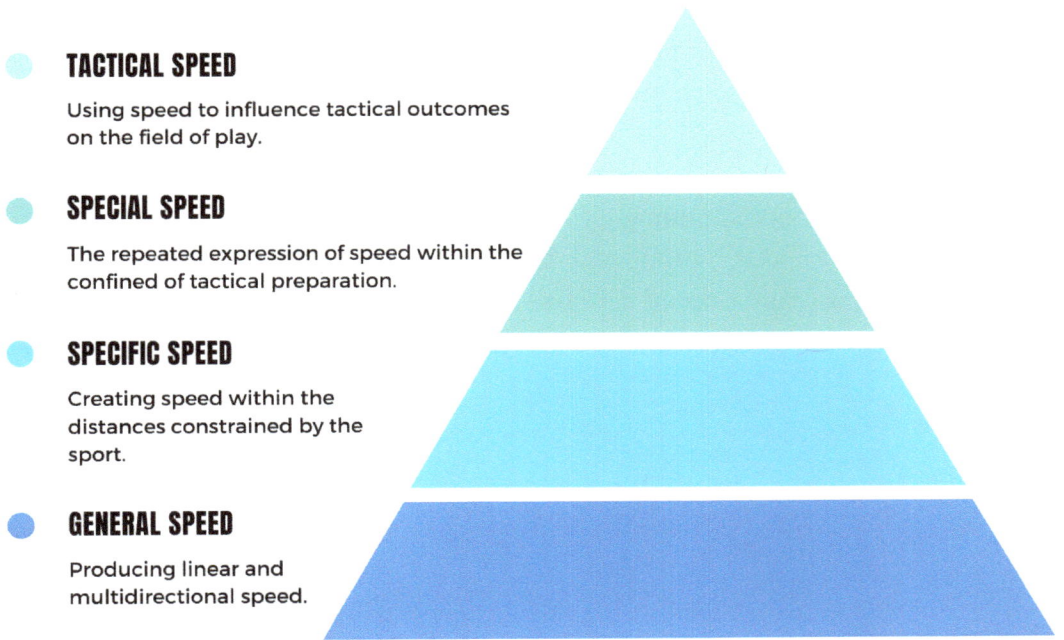

In the role of transfer we are looking to assess the effects of the trained exercises in the non trained exercises. Like we assess the transfer of a broad jump to an acceleration time, here we are assessing the transfer of speed to the exercise of sport itself and continue the process of specialisation. This is where we must redefine the meaning of the term "exercise". Within the context of special speed, sprinting and sprint variations with elements of the sport integrated become the exercise itself. We will expand on this further later in this section.

Specialised speed addresses the nuances of the game, incorporating elements like changes of direction, decelerations, and evasion patterns. It's about being agile and reactive on the field. This is where we start to look at the skill acquisition elements of sporting skills and how speed can help with these. A key element here is where we integrate reactive movement as opposed to planned tasks. Throughout this section we will start to examine different elements of training and coaching that will help you construct drills and exercises for your chosen sport.

INCREASING SPECIALISATION

When increasing the specialisation of training we start to reap the benefits of the previously trained qualities. The role of conjugate sequencing of special strength means can be applied here. Within specialised speed we start to define actions within the chosen sport as special qualities. Adhering to the rules of special strength training we have been increasing the function of the athletes motor abilities to intensify and increase the power output of the sport characteristics. The example below illustrates this process for a winger in football with the objective of running fast down the wing with the ball encountering opposition and either selecting a cross or a shot as the right tactical solution to the situation. This image demonstrates how over time we will introduce exercises that enhance adaptive changes required to perform at a higher level of specificity over the course of a training cycle. When considering this model in the wider context of the sport speed system this would breakdown into the following areas:

- **General Speed:** Linear Speed Training
- **Specific Speed:** Linear Speed Training with ball
- **Special Speed:** Linear / Curve Speed with ball against opponent
- **Tactical Speed:** Linear / Curve Speed with ball against opponent with shot or cross options

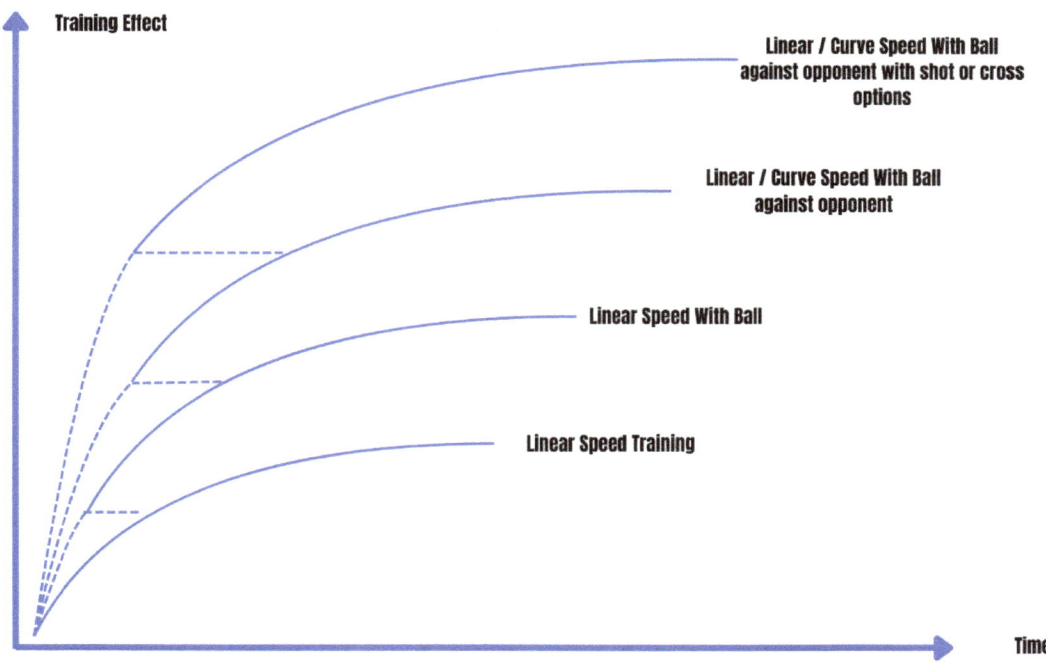

Within the context of specialised speed as coaches we have a huge opportunity to create significant impact with our athletes to create progressive training solutions that directly influence their ability to perform at their sport.

For this to be effective we must take a look at the role of skill acquisition and how it can help us seamlessly integrate the sport specific tasks into our training and take a deeper look at this can be done on a practical level. We will now break down sports to understand how speed and game skills combine, understand space and take a deeper look at skill acquisition to help coach and implement the use of special speed in your sport.

SPEED AND GAME SKILLS

It goes without saying that speed is a critical component in many field sports, playing a significant role in the performance of athletes. It is essential to understand how speed interacts with various game skills and how it can be effectively utilised to enhance overall performance. In this section, we will start to break down the role of speed in the most common field sports, categorising it into basic elements such as speed with the ball, speed without the ball, and evading opponents. This comprehensive approach will provide a clearer understanding of how speed impacts different aspects of field sports and how athletes can develop these skills to excel in their respective sports. As a coach this is where your understanding of the sports you are involved in becomes incredibly important.

Speed with the Ball

Speed with the ball refers to an athlete's ability to move quickly while maintaining control of the ball. This skill is crucial in sports such as soccer, rugby, and field hockey, where handling the ball efficiently while moving at high speeds can create significant advantages.

In most field sports the time you spend in possession of the ball is incredibly limited. In rugby you have 30 players all trying to get the ball over a line and likewise in football you have 22 players trying to put the ball into a net and not their own. Being able to execute skills of the game at high speeds or in speeds that offset defences is incredibly important to success. Let's look at some of the most obvious examples.

1. **Dribbling Speed:** The ability to maintain high velocity while dribbling the ball past opponents.
2. **Passing and Receiving:** Quick movements combined with precise passing and receiving techniques to outmanoeuvre defenders.
3. **Ball Control:** Maintaining control of the ball at high speeds to prevent turnovers and sustain offensive pressure.

These examples are where you as a coach can start to assess the transfer of your athletes speed into the training of the sport. Later in this section we will be outlining this fully for you to implement immediately.

Speed without the Ball

Speed without the ball is equally important as it allows athletes to create space, make effective runs, and support their teammates. This aspect of speed is critical in sports like soccer, American football, and rugby, where off-the-ball movements often dictate the flow of the game. This can be simplified into three main areas when looking at the role of speed without the ball.

1. **Sprinting:** Maximising straight-line speed to beat opponents to critical positions on the field.
2. **Positioning:** Quick movements to get into advantageous positions, both offensively and defensively.
3. **Support Play:** Rapid adjustments to support teammates in possession of the ball. Sometimes a change of pace or direction in support can create space for other players to exploit.

As we progress through this section of the book you will be shown how to utilise skill acquisition theories and techniques in order to structure and embed special speed into your training. But first we need to break down how space and speed interact with one another.

UNDERSTANDING SPACE

In team sports, the effective utilisation of space plays a crucial role in determining the success of team sport sprinters. Understanding how to use space can be categorised into two key aspects: closing space and exploiting space. Whether it's in defence or attack, the ability to manipulate and navigate space strategically can greatly impact the outcome of a game. In this section we will delve into the techniques and considerations for using space as a team sport sprinter.

Closing Space

Closing space typically occurs when an athlete does not have possession of the ball. It primarily revolves around defensive actions aimed at applying pressure on the opposing team. In sports like rugby, football, and others, closing space involves making tackles, intercepting passes, blocking passing lanes, and assuming strategic positions to limit the opponent's options. While closing space is defence-oriented, there are exceptions in games like American football, where offensive players must close space to execute effective pass routes.

Exploiting Space

Exploiting space occurs when an athlete has possession of the ball, mainly in an attacking scenario. This aspect focuses on using space to gain an advantage over opponents. Athletes aim to create line breaks, outpace defenders, and effectively execute sport-specific tasks such as blocking, tackling, heading the ball, or striking it with precision. Exploiting space requires a combination of speed, agility, and tactical awareness to navigate through gaps and capitalise on scoring opportunities.

Maximising Individual Differences

Evaluating an athlete's performance based on their qualification in different areas of the game is essential for effective coaching. Recognising the specific demands of the sport and the role each player fulfils enables coaches to target the necessary skills and techniques. Whether it's enhancing acceleration, improving agility in changing directions, or optimising speed for attacking situations, a thorough understanding of each player's role within the team is crucial in guiding their development.

The ability to utilise space effectively is a key attribute of successful team sport sprinters. By strategically closing space in defence and exploiting space in attack, sprinters can contribute significantly to their team's performance. Observing the actions of athletes on and off the ball provides valuable insights for coaches to identify areas of improvement and tailor their training programs accordingly. By recognising the unique demands of each player's role within the team, coaches can focus on developing the specific skills required to optimise speed and performance. Embracing the art of using space as a team sport sprinter is essential for achieving success on the field.

HIGH FREQUENCY ACTIONS IN TEAM SPORTS TO CREATE SPECIAL SPEED

To truly understand special speed, I have created a table of actions most commonly seen in a range of sports. This table becomes very useful when we start to look at the "Sport involvement Continuum" which enables you as a coach to build specialised speed exercises. As you read through the table please visualise the speed and movement skills that take place prior or during these actions. From here the challenge is to use these actions to create practices and drills that allow you as the coach to blend the role of speed with them.

Skill Action	Football	American Football	Gaelic Football	Rugby
Running	Sprints, long-distance runs	Sprints, agility runs	Sprints, long-distance runs	Sprints, continuous running
Kicking	Passing, shooting, goal kicks	Kickoffs, punts, field goals	Passing, shooting, kickouts	Kicking for touch, conversions, drop goals
Throwing	Throw-ins	Passing, throwing to avoid tacklers	Throw-ins, hand-passes	Passing (lateral, behind)
Catching	Receiving passes	Catching passes, punts, interceptions	Catching passes, high balls	Catching passes, high balls
Tackling	Slide tackles	Tackling ball carriers	Shoulder-to-shoulder tackles	Tackling ball carriers
Dribbling	Ball control, manoeuvres	Ball control after catches	Ball control, manoeuvres	Ball handling, manoeuvres
Blocking	Blocking opponents' paths	Blocking for runners	Blocking for runners	Blocking in rucks/mauls
Dodging	Evading defenders	Evading tackles	Evading tackles	Evading tackles
Strategic Movement	Positioning, formation play	Route running, play execution	Positional play, strategy	Positional play, strategy
Aerial Ability	Heading	Jumping for catches	Jumping for high balls	Jumping for lineouts, high balls
Passing	Short and long passes	Short and long passes	Short and long passes	Short and long passes
Kicking for Distance	Long passes, goal kicks	Kickoffs, punts	Long passes, goal kicks	Kicking for touch, clearance kicks
Ball Handling	Ball control, first touch	Securing the ball after catches	Ball control, handling under pressure	Ball control, secure handling
Contact Skills	Shielding, using body to protect ball	Physical blocking, tackling	Using body for tackles, shielding	Rucks, mauls, scrums
Vision	Scanning field, finding passes	Reading defences, locating receivers	Scanning field, strategic passes	Reading play, identifying gaps

From this table you can see there is an extensive list of qualities that can be enhanced by special speed development. As a coach you are able to directly influence these qualities within the time that you have with the players.

There are some really simple examples that you can immediately develop special speed exercises with. Below I have outlined a simple passing lane drill for rugby union. Here we task the athlete to accelerate maximally at the passing zone and execute a pass within the given space. Each player starts at the same time but with different acceleration distances creating greater speed in the passing lane. This addresses the fundamental attacking skills in rugby. I urge you to build upon this within the context of your own sport.

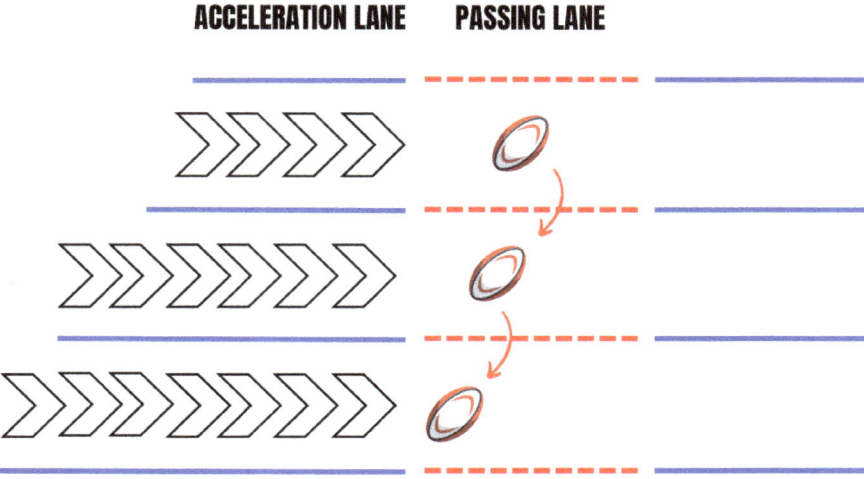

SITUATIONS IN FIELD AND TEAM SPORTS

Progressing from the high frequency actions it is also important to look at some of the tactical situations where these actions fit. As we start to look at how we blend skill acquisition and coaching into the development of specialised speed these scenarios and situations will help you construct your own versions for your sport. I have tried to use typical situations that can apply for a multitude of field sports.

1. 1 v 1 Situations
2. 2 v 1 Situations
3. Overlapping Runs
4. Cover Runs
5. Counter Attacking Runs
6. Runs from Static Positions

By understanding these tactical situations and implementing the corresponding strategies, both attackers and defenders can enhance their effectiveness on the field, contributing to their team's overall performance.

THE SPORT INVOLVEMENT CONTINUUM

Previously in this section we have looked at the process of increasing specialisation, understanding speed and its role in games and the skills we can influence with speed. Now I want to introduce to you the Sports Involvement Continuum. Combining the high frequency actions and the situations of field or team sports we can start taking a deeper view as to how the elements are all pieced together. This is where I like to break down these specialised sporting actions into their component parts or their "ingredients'. The goal of this continuum is to isolate some high frequency actions with typical situations and load them with speed. As a coach I have always wanted to understand how the most successful players go from static to beating two or three players and unlocking a game. I want to be able to analyse this in a way that I can train my athletes to reproduce this every game and not just put it down to luck.

I have broken the continuum down to five specific phases that a majority of these actions go through. In each of these five phases you have an opportunity to coach or set up the environment to let it coach and develop the athlete.. By understanding this continuum, coaches and athletes can optimise their training and enhance their sport-specific skills.

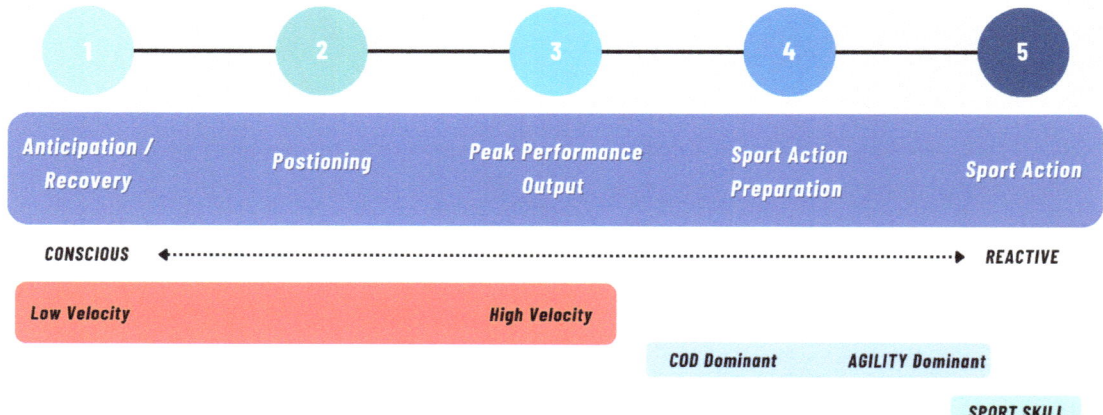

1. Anticipation and Recovery: At the initial stage of the continuum, athletes engage in anticipation and recovery. This phase involves mental and physical preparation, where athletes anticipate the upcoming movements and recover from the previous actions. It sets the foundation for subsequent stages by ensuring athletes are in the right position for optimal performance.

2. Sport Action Preparation: Athletes focus on preparing their bodies for the sport-specific actions they are about to perform. This stage bridges the gap between anticipation and the actual execution of movements.

3. Sport Action: It represents the culmination of preparation, combining physical skills, tactical awareness, and decision-making. During this phase, athletes transition from conscious execution to reactive responses, relying on agility and automatic movements.

4. Velocity and Change of Direction Continuum: Within the Sport Involvement Continuum, there is a progression from low to high velocity movements, accompanied by a continuum of change of direction. In this context velocity is a relative as the change in velocity (acceleration) is always significant in these movements. Athletes gradually increase their speed and agility, mastering the art of change of direction. This continuum is essential for optimising performance in team sport sprinting. This image below illustrated the changes in velocity in these movements.

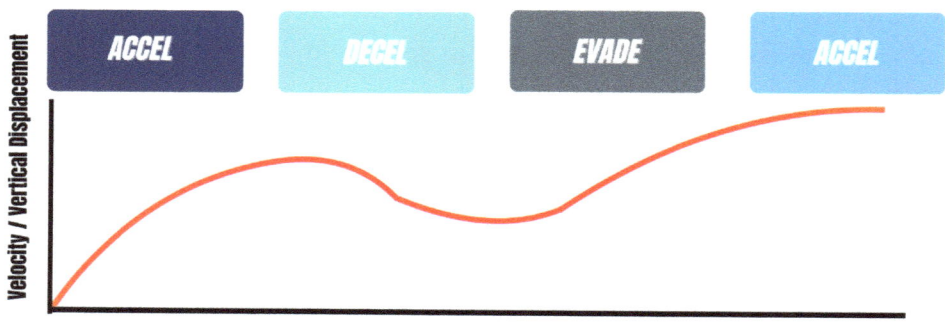

5. Sport Skill: Here, athletes demonstrate exceptional mastery of their sport-specific skills, combining speed, agility, decision-making, and technical prowess. This stage represents the culmination of the sport involvement continuum, showcasing peak performance output.

This five step process can help coaches understand where they can influence coaching to derive positive transfer and adaptation of special speed.

A crucial aspect of special speed is the preservation and utilisation of momentum. In previous chapters we have spoken about gear management and timing. Momentum is a crucial byproduct of this that can be used to execute sporting skills. Athletes aim to control their momentum during deceleration and evasion movements, with the ultimate objective of exiting these manoeuvres at equal or higher speeds than when they entered. Achieving this provides athletes with a strategic advantage, putting them in a favourable position to seize opportunities and take control of the game. At the time of this book, the current England Rugby Fly Half is incredibly good at the conservation of momentum and special speed in rugby. He effectively utilises the goose step to off-set opponents. Visually his legs stop moving but his momentum carries him forward. This off-sets the defender and he sails past them as this "change in leg movement" causes defenders to slow down.

When we look at sporting actions, typically success is driven by creating faster exit speeds than entry speed meaning creating positive acceleration out of evasion. By successfully executing the velocity curve and exiting evasion movements with equal or higher speed, athletes can gain a front foot advantage. This means being proactive, assertive, and in control of the game. It empowers athletes to dictate the pace, respond quickly to changing circumstances, and exploit opportunities to their advantage.

The perception of speed is just as important as high velocity movements. Mastering specialised speed in team sports is understanding the fundamental principle of moving faster than the competition. Athletes must master the velocity curve, understanding the dynamics of acceleration, deceleration, evasion, and re-acceleration. By conserving momentum and exiting evasion movements with equal or higher speed, athletes can gain a front foot advantage, enabling them to dominate their opponents. The primary aim of special speed sprinting is to effectively utilise speed to gain an advantage.

SKILL ACQUISITION AND SPEED IN TEAM SPORTS

Now we draw our attention to the process of skill acquisition of speed in team sports. Here we look to explore and examine the theories of motor learning and how we can create special speed with these. The goal of training is to combine and create training scenarios using these theories to integrate the sporting actions previously discussed.

The Three Stages of Motor Learning

This simple paradigm or motor learning is incredibly powerful. As previously touched on in the use of developing general speed this model has tremendous implication to the development of motor learning and the same rules apply to the development of special speed. Developed by Fits and Posner this model has long stood the test of time in developing skill in sports.

The Cognitive Stage:

The cognitive stage focuses on teaching athletes the basic skills and objectives related to speed. During this stage, athletes rely heavily on coach-led instruction and engage in trial and error. Verbal, visual, and motor cues are utilised to help athletes understand the skills and organise information. Coaches aim to bridge the gap between unconscious incompetence and associative experiences, providing athletes with the necessary foundation to progress further.

The Associative Stage

The associative stage is characterised by the translation of acquired skills into fluid and efficient movements. Athletes may experience difficulties and awkwardness during this phase, accompanied by a series of failures. Proprioceptive motor practice, chunking refinement, and mental rehearsal play crucial roles in developing skill application within specific game environments. Athletes transition from conscious incompetence to conscious competence, refining their technique and understanding the demands of the sport.

The Autonomous Stage

The autonomous stage represents the culmination of effective coaching and skill development. Athletes reach a point where they can execute speed-related actions with minimal cognitive demands. Attentional focus becomes external, enabling athletes to self-correct and make adjustments instinctively. Unconscious competence is achieved, allowing athletes to perform at their highest level. Performance-driven tasks, such as speed gate drills and skill demonstrations, become essential components of this stage.

Stage	Process	Characteristics
Cognitive	Gathering Information	Large Gains, inconsistent performance
Associative	Putting Actions Together	small gains, disjointed performance, conscious effort
Autonomous	Much time and practice	Performance seems unconscious, automatic, smooth

To apply this model to the development of special speed is simple and serves as the first layer of developing special speed. Here is the step by step process to perform this.

1. Identify the sporting task you wish to integrate.
2. Build an isolated scenario for the athlete to cognitively understand and walk through.
3. Generate repetitions of executing this scenario and break down the necessary movement skills involved and key movements. For example accelerating and catching a high ball and immediately stepping away from a hypothetical defender in rugby.
4. Perform complete repetitions of developed scenario and emphasise aggressive explosive movements.

This is a key way to start to integrate the tast demands of the sport with the physical expression of speed.

Implicit and Explicit Learning for Special Speed Development

Implicit and explicit learning approaches are valuable tools in teaching speed. While these methods intersect at times, they should be viewed as separate and employed in a sequential loading pattern. When utilising this approach consider how you can inverse the exposure of implicit and explicit learning in your sessions to maximise transfer of training. Both learning processes play significant roles in how athletes acquire, refine, and perform skills, impacting their overall speed and effectiveness on the field.

Implicit Learning

Implicit learning refers to the unconscious acquisition of knowledge, where athletes learn through experience and practice without direct, detailed instruction. This type of learning is often more durable and less susceptible to performance pressure.

Advantages of Implicit Learning:

1. Automaticity: Skills learned implicitly become automatic, allowing athletes to perform them without conscious thought. This is vital for special speed training, where quick, fluid movements underpin the competitive tasks of sport.

2. Adaptability: Implicit learning often leads to more adaptable skills. Athletes can better adjust their movements to varying conditions, such as changes in opponent behaviour or environmental factors. Here lies the key difference within specialised speed, the movements executed as speed will be shaped by the tactical demands of the game. They will not look like "sprint mechanics" observed in general speed but they will be effective on the field.

3. Reduced Cognitive Load: Since implicit learning relies on unconscious processes, it reduces cognitive load during performance, enabling athletes to focus on strategic aspects of their play. This is where as a coach you can determine how well your integration of specific speed has worked.

Applications in Special Speed Training:

1. Game-like Drills: Using drills that mimic in part real-game scenarios can help athletes implicitly learn how to move quickly and efficiently. To emphasis the development of special speed these games will isolate key elements of performance as opposed just creating full game exposures. For example, the gamification of creating separation in attacking movement can enhance speed without explicit instruction as the task of the game.

2. Repetitive Practice: Repetition engrains skills as discussed. Therefore within the special speed training it is important to repeatedly place your athletes in key sporting scenarios and expose them repeatedly with varying velocities and complexities.

Explicit Learning

Explicit learning involves conscious understanding and application of skills, often through detailed instructions and feedback. This method is highly effective for acquiring new techniques and correcting errors.

Advantages of Explicit Learning:

1. Clarity and Precision: Athletes receive clear instructions and feedback, helping them understand the mechanics of speed and refine the techniques of their sport.

2. Error Correction: Explicit learning allows for immediate identification and correction of errors, leading to more precise skill execution.

3. Knowledge Transfer: Athletes gain a deeper understanding of the principles behind their movements, facilitating the transfer of skills to different contexts.

Applications in Special Speed Training:

1. Technical Drills: Incorporating drills that focus on specific elements of speed, such as stride length combined with a tactical task of the game with detailed feedback helps athletes learn explicitly. An example of this would be catching a ball at pace and then evading an opponent without slowing down in rugby.

2. Video Analysis: Using video analysis to show athletes their form and technique can provide explicit visual feedback, enhancing their understanding of necessary adjustments.

Integrating Implicit and Explicit Learning

For optimal development in speed training, it is beneficial to integrate both implicit and explicit learning strategies. This combined approach ensures that athletes not only understand the mechanics of speed but can also perform them automatically under pressure.

Training Example: This session example could be utilised in rugby union.

Section	Content	Intensity
Warm Up	Perform general speed warm up Integrate foundational skills of the game, passing, catching for reaction and hand eye coordination	Low to Medium
Implicit Game	Non specific game focussing on finding space and passing at speed	Medium
Explicit Coaching	Break out into build up sprints passing and catching at high speed	High
Implicit Game	Rugby scenarios specific game focussing on high speed passing and catching. Points awarded for passing at high speeds that lead to tries scored.	High
Cool Down - Explicit Review	Break out for video review and feedback.	Low

Understanding and applying both implicit and explicit learning methods are crucial for developing special speed and sports-specific actions in athletes. By leveraging the strengths of each approach, coaches can create comprehensive training programs that enhance both the technical and automatic aspects of speed, ultimately leading to improved performance on the field.

The Ecological Approach to Skill Acquisition in Team Sports

The Ecological approach to skill acquisition has gained traction in the realm of sports performance and coaching. This approach emphasises the interaction between the athlete, the environment, and the task at hand, viewing skill acquisition as a dynamic process shaped by these factors. The approach helps coaches create continuity between specific, special and build into tactical speed and builds upon the other approaches to skill aquisition. A big strength of the sports speed system is an embedded thread of sporting application. In the context of team sports, such as soccer, basketball, and rugby, integrating speed, change of direction, and agility becomes paramount for success. The ecological approach to speed training fits perfectly within the definition of special speed. This section will delve into the principles of the ecological approach and how they can be applied to enhance performance in team sports.

Understanding the Ecological Approach

The ecological approach to skill acquisition emphasises the interaction between the individual, the environment, and the task. Rather than isolating specific movements or techniques, this approach acknowledges that skills are developed through dynamic interactions with the surrounding environment. This acts as a great progressions from the previously utilised aspects of motor learning. There are some key differences when using the ecological approach namely being that actions are saped by the intention of the performer as the environment possess meaningful immediate information. In the context of team sports, this means designing training sessions that replicate the complex and unpredictable nature of game situations with an intention to execute at high speed. If applied correctly we can build special and coach special speed as structured in this chapter. Building from structured motor learning to unstructured with the addition of the ecological approach.

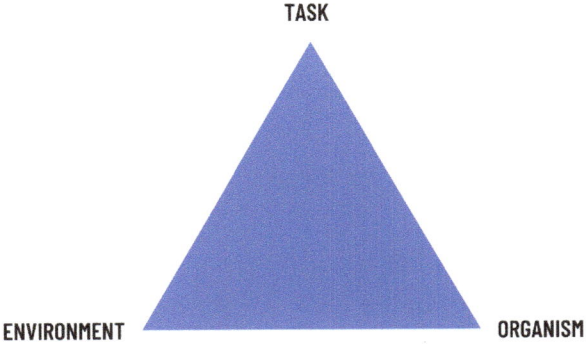

Key Principles of the Ecological Approach:

1. Representative Learning Design: Training drills and exercises should closely mimic the demands of actual game scenarios. By recreating the perceptual cues and decision-making processes encountered during competition, athletes can better transfer their skills from practice to game situations.

2. Constraints-Led Approach: Instead of prescribing specific movements, coaches should manipulate the constraints of the training environment to encourage desired outcomes. This may involve altering the size of playing areas, adjusting equipment, or introducing task-specific rules to challenge athletes and promote adaptive responses.

3. Nonlinear Pedagogy: Recognising that skill acquisition is a nonlinear process, coaches should adopt a variety of training methods and progressions to accommodate individual differences in learning. This may include using games-based approaches, guided discovery, and problem-solving tasks to facilitate skill development.

Key Elements of the Ecological Approach

1. Affordances: Central to the ecological approach is the concept of affordances, which are opportunities for action that the environment offers to an individual. In team sports, the playing field is replete with affordances such as open space, opponents, teammates, and goalposts. Athletes must learn to perceive and exploit these affordances in real time to achieve their objectives.

2. Information-Movement Coupling: The ecological approach emphasises the coupling of perceptual information and motor responses. Athletes attune themselves to relevant information in their environment (e.g., opponent movements, ball trajectory) and use this information to guide their actions (e.g., accelerating, changing direction). Through repeated exposure and practice in varied environments, athletes develop the ability to attune to relevant information and execute appropriate movements.

3. Task Constraints: Task constraints refer to the specific demands and conditions of a given sporting task. These constraints can be related to the physical environment (e.g., field dimensions, weather conditions), the rules of the game, or the tactical situation (e.g., numerical advantage, defensive pressure). By manipulating task constraints in training, coaches can create representative learning environments that mimic the complexity of competition and facilitate skill transfer.

Creating Sports Speed with the Ecological Approach

Here's how the ecological approach can inform the integration of these attributes into training:

1. Perceptual Training: Coaches should prioritise perceptual training that enhances athletes' ability to perceive and anticipate relevant information in their environment. This may involve video analysis, and decision-making drills that replicate game-like scenarios.

2. Task Variability: Training drills should incorporate variability in task constraints to simulate the unpredictable nature of competition. For example, athletes can practise accelerating and changing direction in response to auditory or visual cues, varying the starting position, direction, and intensity of each repetition. Combined with a sport outcome this is a powerful tool for example, score a goal or a try.

3. Representative Design: Training sessions should be designed to closely replicate the perceptual-motor demands of competition. This may involve practising in the same environment (e.g., on the field, court) with the same equipment (e.g., ball, cones) and under similar time constraints. By training under representative conditions, athletes can develop adaptive movement patterns that transfer seamlessly to game situations.

4. Decision-Making Drills: Incorporating decision-making drills into training allows athletes to hone their ability to read and react to situational cues. Coaches can use small-sided games, modified scrimmages, and video simulations to challenge athletes' decision-making skills in real-time, fostering a more intuitive and adaptive style of play.

Some of the best drills and examples of implementing this have come directly from questioning my athletes. Ask them when they feel they need more speed on the field, get them to show you examples and describe the scenario. This is so important in the utilisation of the ecological approach. Whilst we understand the high frequency actions and can progressively apply these theories of motor learning we must include the athletes experience. This will tell you more about how they move and use their speed.

The ecological approach to skill acquisition offers a comprehensive guide for understanding and enhancing performance in team sports. By emphasising the dynamic interaction between athletes, their environment, and the task at hand, coaches can design more effective training programs that develop athletes' perceptual-motor skills, decision-making abilities, and adaptability on the field or court. Through deliberate practice in representative learning environments, athletes can optimise their speed, change of direction, and agility to excel in the complex and unpredictable world of team sports.

Perception-Action Cycle: Enhancing Decision-Making

As we dive deeper into the integration of the sporting task itself it is important to start to unpack the decision making process. Building on fundamental motor learning and intengrating implicit/explicit learning and the ecological approach it is important to start to stress the reactive components of special speed. The role of the perception action cycle within the context of the sports speed system is to try to influence the information gathered by using the ecological approach. Seeing how athletes respond to different environments in isolated sporting scenarios and then instead of aimlessly repeating the same practice intervene with new ways to challenge the athletes to find the right solution. Here we start to examine how the athlete looks at the information provided by the environment.

The ultimate goal of special speed training is to increase the velocity at which successful sporting tasks are executed. The perception-action cycle is a fundamental concept in understanding how athletes interact with their environment and make quick, effective decisions during sports performance. This cycle involves the continuous loop of perceiving sensory information, processing it neurologically, and executing appropriate motor actions. Grasping this cycle's intricacies, particularly the neurological processes involved, is essential for designing effective special speed training programs that integrate movement selections efficiently with tactical tasks of the competitive sport. Coaches guide athletes through this cycle by creating scenarios that prompt athletes to make quick and accurate decisions. By repeatedly practising and refining these actions, athletes develop the ability to execute optimal movements based on their perception of the game situation.

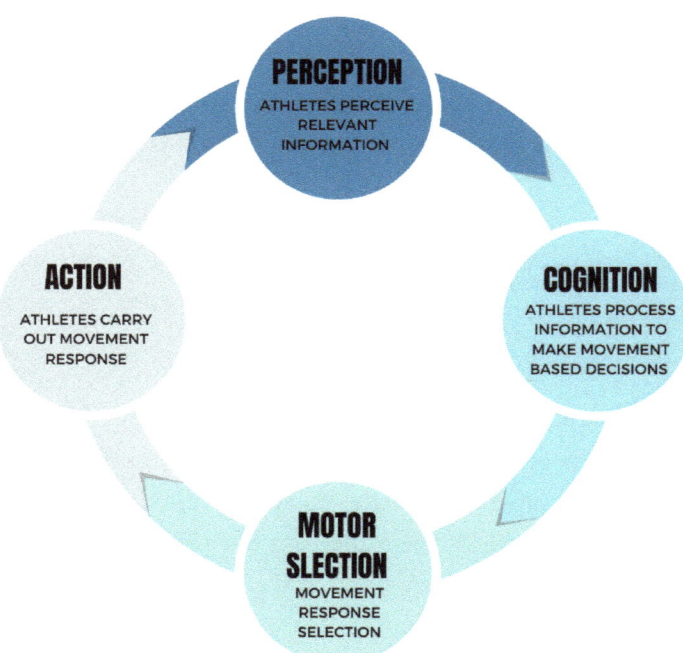

Perception-Action Cycle

The perception-action cycle can be broken down into four main components:

1. **Perception:** Gathering sensory information from the environment.
2. **Cognition:** Processing the sensory information and making decisions based on it.
3. **Motor Selection:** Selecting the most appropriate motor response.
4. **Action:** Executing motor responses based on the decisions made.

Integrating Movement Selections in Special Speed Training

To effectively incorporate the perception-action cycle in special speed training, it's crucial to design exercises that enhance the athlete's ability to perceive, decide, and act quickly. This cycle can be used in conjunction with the ecological approach to help challenge the decision making process in another way. Here are specific strategies and training examples:

1. Enhancing Perception:

- **Reactive Drills:** Use drills that require athletes to react to visual or auditory stimuli, such as reacting to a coach's command or a moving target.
- **Environmental Variability:** Train in different environments and conditions to improve adaptability and sensory processing.

2. Improving Decision-Making:

- **Small-Sided Games:** These create realistic scenarios that require quick decision-making and can be scaled to increase or decrease complexity.

- **Video Analysis and Feedback:** Reviewing game footage and providing feedback helps athletes understand their decision-making processes and make better choices in future situations.

3. Optimising Action:

- **Technical Drills:** Focus on form and technique to ensure that the motor execution of movements is efficient and effective. This is where you can break down the footwork needed to perform the competitive tasks of the sport.
- **Speed and Agility Drills:** Incorporate drills that emphasise quick changes in direction, acceleration, and deceleration, mimicking game situations.

Understanding and leveraging the perception-action cycle is crucial for developing speed and agility in team sports. It serves as the foundation to understand special speed and how we develop it. Integrating the neurological processes involved ensures that training is grounded in science is essential for coaches to help think at a higher level and prepare more strategically. Through the rest of this section we will break down how special speed is developed.

Teaching speed in team sports requires a systematic and comprehensive approach that spans multiple stages of skill acquisition. From establishing fundamentals to translating skills into game situations and ultimately achieving autonomous performance, coaches play a vital role in guiding athletes towards speed mastery. Incorporating implicit and explicit learning, the ecological approach, and the perception-action cycle enhances the learning process and ensures athletes can effectively apply their speed skills in competitive settings.

The Importance of Play in Learning Skills for Sports Speed

At this point we have examined motor learning quite extensively an I hope that you have started to create ideas for sessions and practices to help develop special speed with your athletes. However it is vitally important that we do not neglect play. To encourporate the previously mentioned theories effectively we must use play and unstructured pedagogy. It is important to strive to create an environment that empowers the athletes to express themselves freely. Play is a fundamental aspect of human development and learning, especially in the context of sports. It is through play that individuals acquire and refine their motor skills and cognitive abilities. In sports, play serves as a dynamic and engaging method for learning and perfecting skills, fostering creativity, and enhancing overall performance. When developing special speed, play becomes an important element of training as it helps bridge the gap from physical performance to technical execution.

Benefits of Play in Skill Acquisition

1. Motor Skill Development

- Play provides a natural environment for developing fundamental motor skills such as running, jumping, throwing, and catching. These skills form the building blocks for more complex sports-specific movements.
- Through repetitive play activities, athletes can improve their coordination, balance, agility, and reaction time, which are crucial for success in any sport.

2. Cognitive and Problem-Solving Skills

- Engaging in play encourages athletes to think critically and make quick decisions. Games and playful activities often require strategic thinking, planning, and adaptability.
- Play fosters an environment where athletes learn to solve problems on the fly, improving their ability to anticipate opponents' actions and react appropriately during competition.

3. Creativity and Innovation

- Play allows athletes to experiment with new techniques and strategies without the fear of failure. This experimental approach encourages creativity and innovation, leading to the development of unique playing styles and skills.
- By playing in unstructured environments, athletes can discover novel ways to approach challenges, enhancing their ability to think outside the box during actual games.

4. Confidence Development

- Play is a social activity that promotes teamwork, communication, and cooperation. Athletes learn to work together, build trust, and develop strong interpersonal relationships through playful interactions.
- The emotional benefits of play include stress relief, increased motivation, and a positive attitude toward training and competition. This is sometimes in the confines to "technical training" there can be a lot of emphasis on "getting it right" as opposed to developing a wider skill set. Playful activities can boost an athlete's confidence to extend themselves outside their current movement competencies and strive for positive adaptation.

Integrating Play into Special Speed

The integration of play can serve as a great development tool but also a chance to observe the transfer of training. Consider these options when utilising play in your training.

1. Incorporate Small-Sided Games

- Small-sided games are an excellent way to integrate play into training sessions. These games mimic real-life scenarios in a condensed format, allowing athletes to practise skills in a fun and competitive environment. These provide a great extension from the isolated exposures of the ecological approach.
- Coaches can modify the rules and objectives of these games to focus on specific skills or tactical elements, making them a versatile tool for skill development.

2. Use Playful Drills and Activities

- Coaches should design drills and activities that are playful and engaging. This can include obstacle courses, relay races, or creative challenges that require athletes to use their skills in novel ways.

- By keeping drills varied and fun, coaches can maintain high levels of athlete engagement and enthusiasm, leading to more effective learning.

3. Encourage Free Play

- Allowing time for unstructured free play is crucial. Free play gives athletes the freedom to explore their abilities, try new things, and learn at their own pace.
- Coaches can provide a safe and supportive environment for free play, encouraging athletes to take initiative and be proactive in their skill development.

The importance of play in learning skills in sports cannot be overstated. Play not only enhances motor and cognitive skills but also fosters creativity, and confidence. By integrating playful activities into sports training, coaches can create a more effective and enjoyable learning experience for athletes. Play is an amazing opportunity for us as coaches to step away from the rigid nature of preparation and apply a more Laissez-Faire style to assess transfer and encourage our athletes to push the boundaries of their current movement capabilities.

SKILL - DRILL - PRACTICE - PERFORM

In this chapter we have explored some very complex and high level series of skill acquisition. What I want to arm you with now is a simple four-step, four word framework that will allow you to continually contextualise the work that you are doing in order to understand how this all fits with regards to the bigger picture of creating sports speed. This framework will allow you to understand what practices need to be placed where and how we can build upon skills and drills to create strong practices and Performance. This is more of a linear pedagogy approach however as a strength and conditioning coach looking to understand how we develop practices of games this is a great way to organise your training in order to understand the outcome of your sessions

Skills

The foundation of the preparation progression lies in the development of skills. This stage focuses on honing the cognitive, associative, and autonomous aspects of special speed (e.g. running whilst passing). It emphasises the development of physical literacy, movement competency, and overall physical capacity. Skills serve as the bedrock for subsequent progressions, as they underpin every aspect of team sport sprinting.

Drills

Drills play a pivotal role in introducing new motor learning and cognitive strategies to athletes. These drills extend beyond basic step acceleration and encompass a combination of change of direction and acceleration techniques. By placing athletes in contextual situations, such as one-on-one scenarios or chase simulations, they can recognise and adapt to different shapes and spaces within the game. This stage also simulates sporting tactical strategies, allowing athletes to apply their learning from previous stages in a practical setting.

With rugby wingers this one of my favourite drills. A crossfield kick finishing drill. The goal is to run fast, catch the ball in stride, cleanly beat a defender to score a try. This drill can be manipulated in the following ways.

1. **Kick distance:** The kick distance will alter the flight of the ball influencing the timing of the attacker.
2. **Kick Type:** The type of kick will change the demand on the attack, a flat hard kick will force the attacker to accelerate hard and fast where as a lofted kick we task the attacked to manager their speed. A kick on the ground will change the way the athlete approaches the ball to ensure it is gathered properly and at speed.
3. **Approach distance:** This will dedicate the ability to generate speed and lead to an alteration in how the defender is beaten to score the try.
4. **Approach Angle:** The angle of attack on the ball will influence how the ball is caught/gathered and the following actions to beat the defender, avoid running out of bounds and score the try.
5. **Defender Position:** How the defender is positioned will change the footwork used or even needed by the attacker.

Practice

Practice involves the performance of desired tasks within non-specific play, adhering to the principles of dynamical systems theory. Athletes apply the skills they have developed in the previous stages to the practice of their sport. Whether it's running routes, executing set plays, or engaging in small-sided games, the focus is on observing how athletes accelerate, react, and execute actions within the context of the sport. Coaches assess the ability to find acceleration, maintain speed, and perform specific tasks effectively.

Perform

The ultimate stage of the preparation progression is the performance phase. Here, the emphasis shifts to the outcome of sporting events. Athletes demonstrate their abilities in a competitive setting, driven by the pursuit of success. This stage is characterised by unconscious application, where athletes instinctively utilise the skills and physical capabilities developed throughout the preparation progression. It is at this stage that coaches can observe the impact of the speed program within the overall sport program, highlighting its unconscious influence on performance.

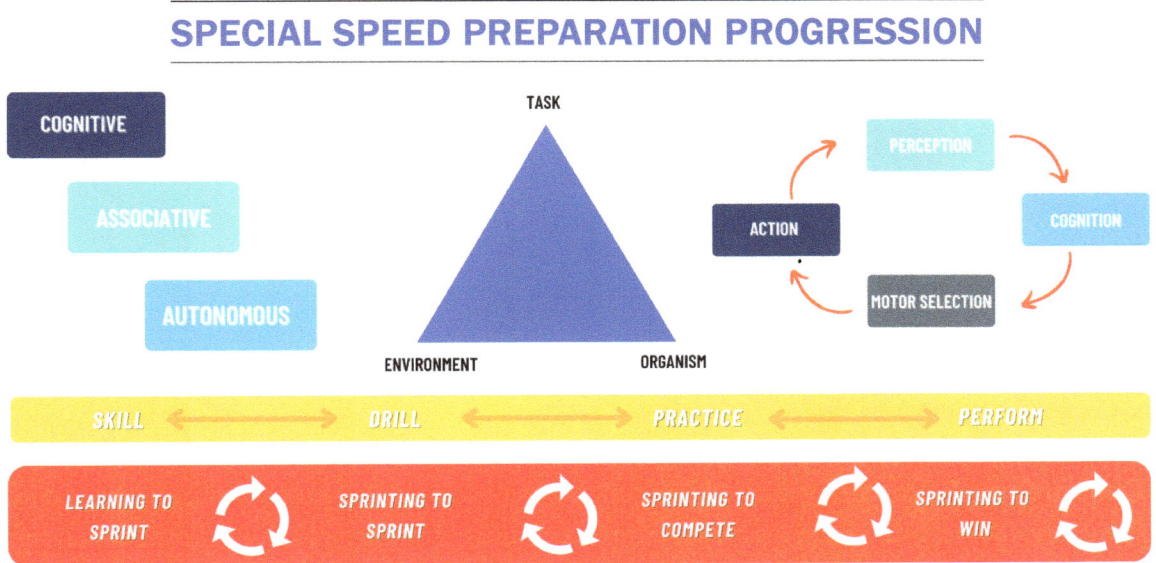

To truly create what we now know as special speed it is important to see how all of the different variables combine to create the coaching pathway. To start making significant progress with your athletes it is important for you to understand how there are many interconnecting variables that create vital links with skill acquisition, and the coaching process itself. When we are developing general speed, we can be fixed and very rigid in our approach to creating an increase in the outputs measured for general speed. As we progress and start to integrate the element of the sports we must surrender the rigid notions of general speed and embrace the more fluid elements of skill acquisition and coaching. The image above demonstrates how as a coach you can understand speed age in conjunction to the creation of the special speed through skill acquisition. We will now break down elements of this to show you how it can be put together.

The team sport sprinting preparation progression provides a structured framework for enhancing speed and performance on the field. By progressing from skill drill practice to drills, practice, and ultimately performance, athletes can maximise their potential. Integrating speed training within the broader sport program ensures that athletes develop the necessary skills, physical capacities, and tactical awareness to excel in their chosen sport. Coaches play a vital role in guiding athletes through each stage, providing feedback, reinforcement, and fine-tuning techniques to optimise performance.

COACHING STYLES AND SPECIAL SPEED

Coaching athletes in various sports requires a blend of science, art, and effective communication. Even more importantly at this phase of the sports speed system, closing the gap between speed and skills through effective coaching is vitally important for the success of special speed. The methodologies used can significantly impact the development, performance, and overall experience of the athletes. This section delves into traditional coaching methodologies, focusing on coaching styles, session structures, and periodisation considerations.

Coaching Styles

There are three main coaching styles all with unique benefits. For the purpose of speed I have broken them down for you in a bullet format.

1. **Authoritative (Command) Style:**

   - **Description:** The coach makes all the decisions, with athletes expected to follow instructions without questioning.
   - **Pros:** Clear expectations, high level of discipline, effective for quick decision-making.
   - **Cons:** Can stifle creativity and reduce athlete autonomy.
   - **Application:** Often used in situations requiring strict adherence to strategy or safety protocols.

2. **Democratic (Cooperative) Style:**

   - **Description:** The coach involves athletes in decision-making, fostering a collaborative environment.
   - **Pros:** Encourages athlete engagement, improves critical thinking, and builds team cohesion.
   - **Cons:** Can be time-consuming and may lead to conflicts if not managed well.
   - **Application:** Effective in team sports where player input can enhance strategies and outcomes, such as soccer or basketball.

3. **Holistic (Laissez-Faire) Style:**

   - **Description:** The coach takes a hands-off approach, allowing athletes to make decisions and learn through experience.
   - **Pros:** Promotes independence, creativity, and self-regulation.
   - **Cons:** Less structure, which can be challenging for less experienced athletes.
   - **Application:** Useful for mature, self-motivated athletes who will do extra training if required.

Session Structures

Effective coaching requires structure or some means of delivering coaching. Here we are going to look at the methods of coaching. As a strength and conditioning coach looking to develop special speed with your athletes this is a great way to integrate speed with technical skills of the sport.

1. **Whole-Part-Whole (WPW) Method:**

   - **Description:** The WPW method involves presenting the entire skill or task first (whole), breaking it down into its constituent parts for focused practice (part), and then re-integrating the parts into the whole skill.
   - **Example:** In football, a coach might first demonstrate the entire dribbling and passing a player sequence (whole), then focus on individual components like high speed dribbling, evasion and ball control (part), and finally have athletes perform the full dribbling sequence again (whole).

- **Benefits:** Helps athletes understand the context and flow of the skill, reinforces learning through repetition, and allows for targeted correction of specific components.

2. **Part-Whole Method:**

    - **Description:** The skill is broken down into its parts from the outset, with each part practised individually before combining them into the whole skill.
    - **Example:** In rugby, wingers catching at high speeds, a coach might focus on the catching with a rotated upper body and square hips, then the speed build up, and finally the build up to catch and continue to build speed.
    - **Benefits:** Allows for detailed focus on each component, suitable for complex skills.

3. **Progressive Part Method:**

    - **Description:** Similar to the part-whole method but with a progressive build-up. Each part is practised and mastered before adding the next part until the entire skill is performed.
    - **Example:** In basketball, teaching a layup might start with footwork, then add the dribble, and finally integrate the shot.
    - **Benefits:** Gradual build-up helps in mastering each part before moving on, reducing cognitive load.

Once you understand these methodologies, you can identify which one to use at different stages and phases of athletic development. These become incredibly valuable when you are short on time and are working with more complex skills.

Integrating Periodisation with Coaching Styles and Session Structures

To create a holistic and effective training program, coaches should integrate periodisation principles with appropriate coaching styles and session structures. This will help drive positive adaptation and allow you as a coach to develop qualities that support the players unique ability to excel at their sport:

Macrocycle Planning:

- **Coaching Style:** Begin with an authoritative approach to establish goals and expectations, gradually incorporating democratic elements as the season progresses.
- **Session Structure:** Use WPW methods to introduce key skills in the preparatory phase, ensuring athletes understand the overall context before breaking down the details.

Mesocycle Focus:

- **Coaching Style:** Employ a cooperative style to involve athletes in setting specific mesocycle goals, such as improving sprint speed or agility.
- **Session Structure:** Utilise the part-whole method during skill acquisition phases and the progressive part method for more complex skills, ensuring a steady build-up of competencies.

Microcycle Execution:

- **Coaching Style:** Adapt coaching styles based on daily objectives—authoritative for high-intensity sessions and holistic for recovery days.
- **Session Structure:** Balance technical drills, conditioning, and recovery within each microcycle to optimise performance and prevent overtraining.

SCHEDULING SPEED TRAINING IN TEAM SPORTS

Speed is a critical component of team sports performance, and incorporating speed training into the training schedule is essential for maximising athletes' capabilities. This section examines the importance of scheduling speed training sessions, particularly in conjunction with other training modalities, to optimise efficiency of movement and enhance overall performance.

Specialisation and Scheduling

Increasing the specialisation of training requires us to revisit some fundamentals of training and preparation. When we are looking to increase the specificity of training it is important to remove the general aspects of training, otherwise there is a significant risk of detraining and negative adaptation.

The following image illustrates the long-term relationship between the development of speed in conjunction with the technical and preparedness of athletes. What this image illustrates is the indirect initial relationship between general speed qualities and sport, but as we progress through and increase the specialisation of speed we will see an increase in preparedness as the athletes are now able to express speed within the context of the sport that they have been technically and tactically preparing for. As coaches we must understand where our current players are on this journey to maximise performance outcome. This can be determined through the specific phase of seasonal preparation.

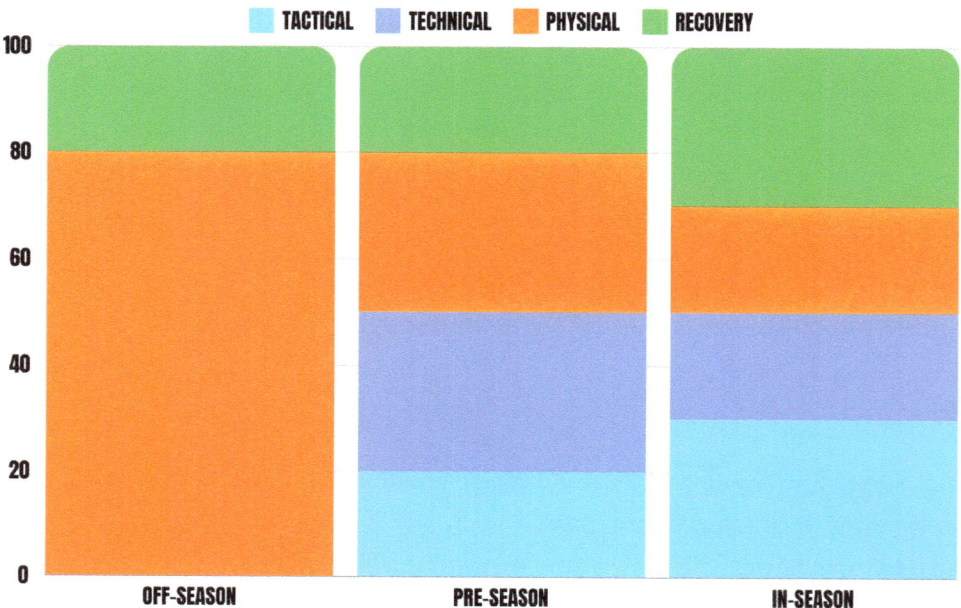

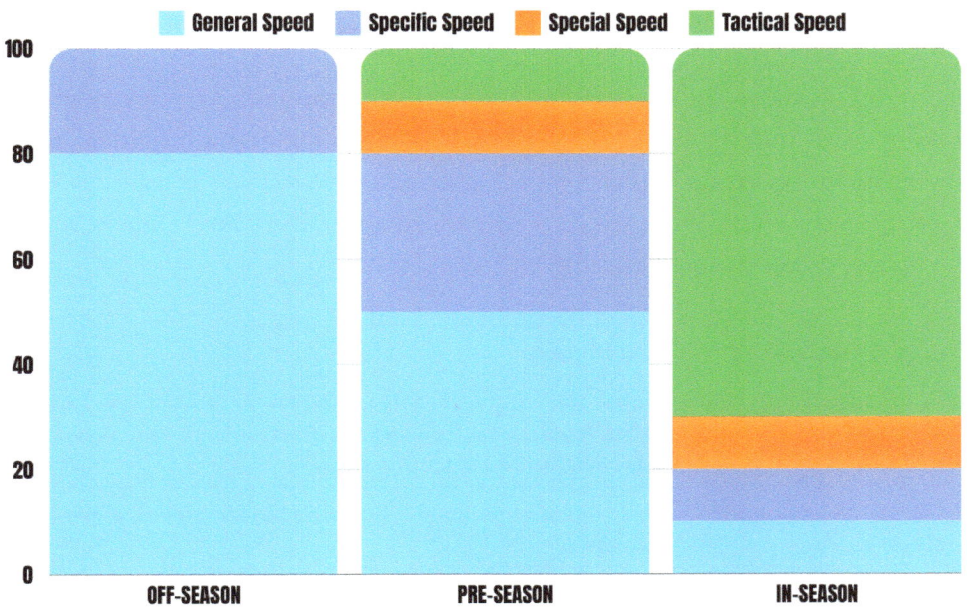

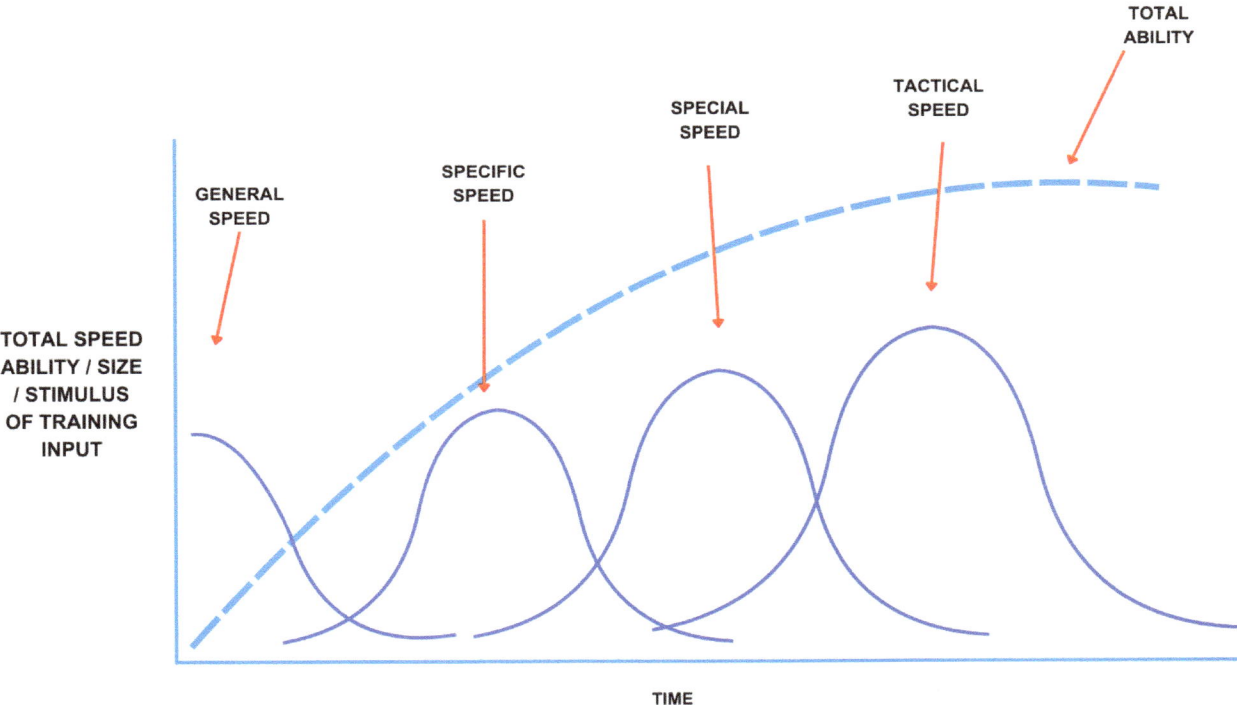

Understanding the Schedule

The preparation period is a crucial time for team sport athletes to prepare physically and mentally for the competition. Coaches and trainers must carefully plan training sessions to cover various aspects of performance, including speed development. Integrating speed-focused sessions into the schedule is a key strategy for enhancing athletes' speed and movement efficiency. But remember it's all speed training but just training different aspects of speed.

Reverse Engineering and Sequential Exposure

To prioritise speed training within limited training time, coaches often adopt a reverse engineered approach. This involves breaking down training components and strategically incorporating them into the schedule. By using the gym environment to expose athletes to ballistics and plyometrics, coaches can create a sequential exposure plan that ultimately leads to improved speed performance. The below table will provide you with an example of how to reverse engineer your training.

Preparation Element	Area of Emphasis	Description
Speed	Short Attack Acceleration	0-5m Acceleration focussing on different angles and potential tasks (finding a gap, making a pass, scoring a goal)
Plyometric	Long Coupling multi planar activity	Fast, explosive jumps and bound variations exploring many angles over short distances.
Ballistic	Resisted Sprint Variation	Heavier loads to support higher force requirements of short acceleration.

Complementing Speed Training with Weights

Combining speed training with weightlifting exercises can be an effective way to enhance power and explosiveness in team sport athletes. It is also very time efficient. By allocating dedicated time slots for speed training sessions combined with weightlifting, coaches can ensure a balanced and comprehensive training program. This combination helps athletes develop the necessary strength and power to execute explosive movements on the field. When we consider the role of weight training in the overall structure of a season there should be a decreasing emphasis on weight training as the season progresses. Especially when we move into the more specific areas of preparation. The image below demonstrates this trend over the course of a season.

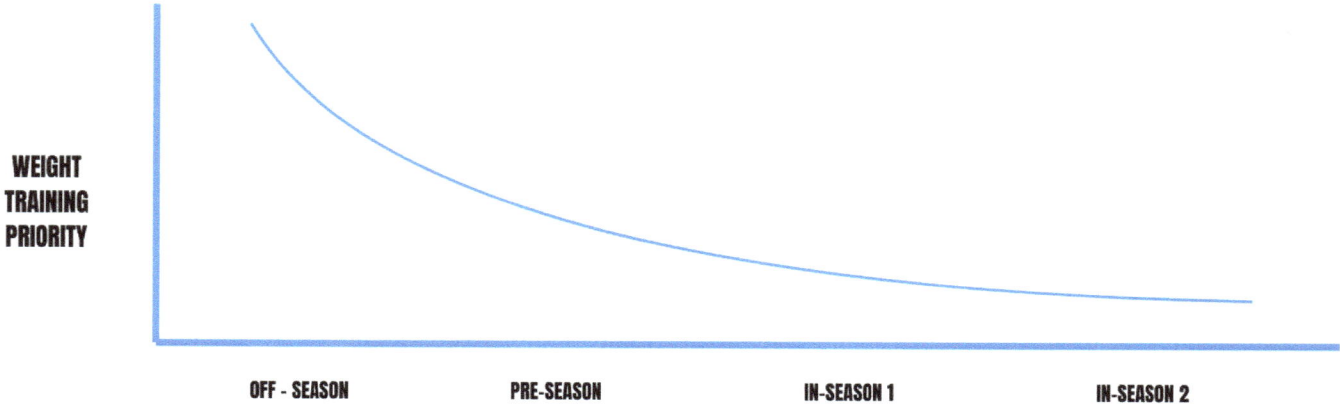

Supporting the Technical Coach and Their Outcomes.

As we have already established the role of specialised speed is to develop and enhance the frequently utilised movements in the Chosen Sport. The goal of an improvement of this speed is to enhance the athletes ability to practise for the game. When we consider what an improvement of Speed can give to a technical or tactical task of a sport it is really important to ensure that the new level of skill has been consolidated. One risk and potential hazard that may occur with the improvement of speed is that the technical execution of the sports specific task may decline. This is where timing and the perception of space becomes really important. In some cases a technical coach may think that their player has actually declined in their sporting ability when they have got faster. This is because the gap between speed and technical skill has not been closed, the athlete has not yet learnt to execute skills and understand space at their new higher speeds.

As a preparation coach it is vitally important not to distance yourself from the technical and tactical outcomes that a coach requires from their players. This will directly influence the way you will start to develop special speed qualities with your athletes. Having a base understanding of the way your tactical coach wants your players to perform will unlock key areas to enhance the use of speed.

When to Train Speed in the Schedule

Effectively placing speed training throughout a program is vital for the development of special speed qualities. When you as the coach arrive at this junction of preparation it is vitally important to focus on how speed influences the specific tasks of the game and how you as the preparation specialist can influence this.

There are a couple of considerations as to when you can schedule special speed. The first is the pre-existing "gym" training time allocated or in the pre-session warm up. If you have built a closer relationship with the technical coach this can bleed into the earlier parts of the technical sessions too.

Manipulating the "Weight Room" for Special Speed

Here I use the term weight room incredibly loosely as I want you to understand and adjust your mindset with regards to the development of physical qualities outside the weight room. In any team sport environment you are typically constrained to a certain amount of time available with the athletes that you have as there is an ongoing battle with training volumes, intensity loads and the freshness of players. If you have understood the sports speed system and its unique methodology correctly this is where we can start to place a tremendous emphasis on special strength training and its capacity for motor learning and the utilisation of resisted exercises that replicate locomotion and variations of Locomotion. I am under no illusion that you may be reading this and not have all the equipment you believe you should, however you can create these environments with simple tools such as resistance bands, sleds, body weight, and medicine balls. In the pursuit of creating special strength exercises that help support the high frequency actions in your chosen Sport we must adhere to the principles of dynamic correspondence and target the specific joint actions within those movements. For specific examples of exercises to use please see the appendix.

Warm up and pre-pitch special speed training

Some of the most successful adaptations that I have seen in my players are utilising the pre-session training time effectively. In most clubs and environments there will be a 15 to 20 minute window prior to the warm-up in which players are able to do their own individual work, or in some cases just mess around. This is an incredibly vital and precious time where you as a coach can influence the work that players are doing. Again it's another opportunity to create a potentiation effect and close a skill acquisition gap in the development of special speed. For this I would like to remind you of the part whole methodology of coaching as an initial start point. We will use this to our advantage to load the athletes appropriately. When you have athletes who are now running fast they have reached a new level of performance, we can use this to our advantage. We will utilise the warm up to create special speed training loads that potentiate the skill elements of the game. At this point warm ups become easier as utilising a holistic approach has enabled us to remove some of the damaging stressors that previous phases of training have produced. For example, if the principles of specialisation have been adhered to, our weight room training will not consist of heavier training loads that create a detraining effect. The athletes will not be carrying any unnecessary fatigue into training. Below is a flow diagram that is recommended when utilising the pre-pitch training.

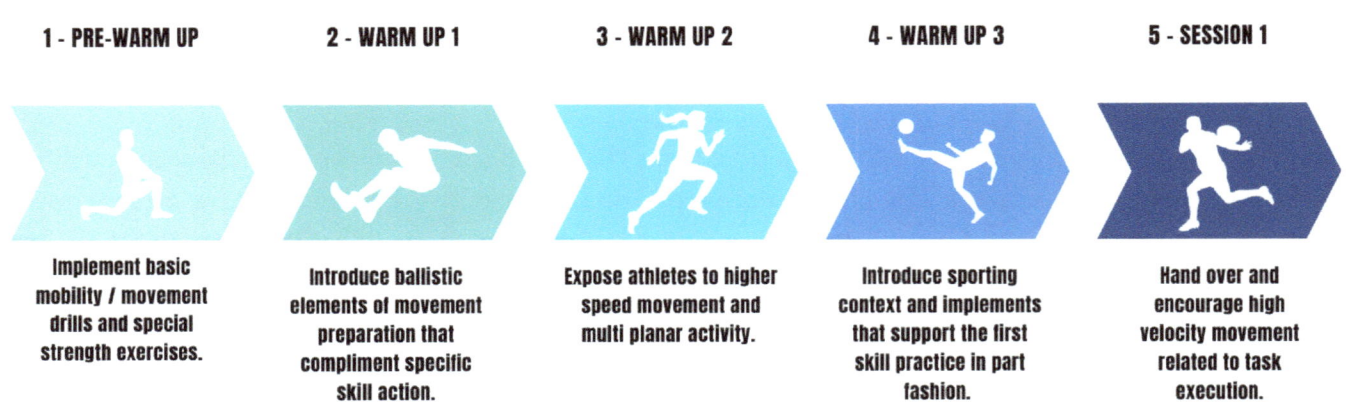

Integrating Speed into Sport

Sometimes this can be quite a daunting area to explore as a strength and conditioning coach or sport preparation coach. This is because sometimes we can feel we are stepping outside the boundaries of our role if we start to make our warm-ups look too much like the sport training. However, this is exactly what we should be doing, our goal is to prepare the athletes to play the sport, and through the context of physical preparation we are able to influence the athletes in a completely different way to the technical or tactical coaches. This understanding really will start to unlock the elements of special speed for you. Some subtle changes will create drastic improvements for your athletes. Remember that your goal is not to improve the technical tasks of the sport, that is the responsibility of the technical coach; however you are responsible for improving the ability to access Speed when required during those tasks. Here we are looking at the high frequency actions in sport and how we can create variations of those in the times that we have through the lens of physical preparation. I will now give you some simple examples that you can take forward with your Sport, but I encourage you to use your imagination and explore all elements of play to help your athletes thrive.

Examples of Speed in Specific Field Sports

As I have only included a couple of sports please use the framework provided.

- Speed with the ball
- Speed without the ball
- Evading Opponents

Football / Soccer:

- **Speed with the Ball:** Dribbling past defenders, quick one-two passes, and breakaway sprints.
- **Speed without the Ball:** Making runs into space, closing down opponents, and tracking back on defence.
- **Evading Opponents:** Using body feints, quick turns, and acceleration to get past defenders.

Rugby:

- **Speed with the Ball:** Breaking through defensive lines, rapid ball exchanges, and counter-attacks.
- **Speed without the Ball:** Supporting the ball carrier, covering defensive positions, and making tackles.
- **Evading Opponents:** Sidesteps, spins, and bursts of speed to evade tacklers.

Basketball:

- **Speed with the Ball:** Fast breaks, dribbling through defences, and quick passes.
- **Speed without the Ball:** Cutting to the basket, defending opponents, and setting screens.
- **Evading Opponents:** Crossovers, hesitation moves, and explosive first steps.

Tactical Speed

Tactical speed is the ability to use speed effectively within the context of your sport. This section is the shortest section in the book but possibly the most important. This is where your work is all on the line. Here we answer the question, was it all worth it?

It's not just about running fast in a straight line but knowing when and how to use your speed to create advantages during play. As coaches and players, understanding the role of speed in specific positions and game scenarios is crucial for improving performance.

Determining Successful Transfer of Speed

As all preparation specialists understand it is really hard to truly determine what worked in our preparation. I would like to share a few thoughts and guidelines for you to not get lost in this question and give yourself reference points to understand the efficacy of your role.

From reading this book you should be able to understand that I have a very biased approach toward sequential systematic training with a holistic perspective. Or to simplify this statement, creating training that actually helps performance on the field and not the numbers in the gym. As a physical preparation specialist there is no way that you are able to truly quantify your effectiveness with regards to team sports. The sport is so varied and unpredictable. Where you can take pride in your work is knowing that you have and continue to prepare the athletes for their sport as best as possible. I truly believe that if you follow the sports speed system as it is intended to you will do this.

If you have followed the system, you will be able to observe the physical adaptations created within your athletes. They will run faster and they will move better but more importantly they will be able to do it more often with a greater awareness of the game. They will become Team Sport Sprinters, prepared to play their sports.

Some sports offer a much more definitive explanation of the transfer of speed whereas others do not. For example in American football a receiver could increase their completion percentage whereas an openside flanker's impact in rugby cannot directly be measured against speed as definitively. I have included a table below to illustrate how you can determine sports improvement.

Sport	Performance Analysis Methods	Key Metrics	Tools and Technology
Soccer	– Video Analysis	– Passing accuracy	– GPS Tracking
	– GPS Tracking	– Dribbling success rate	– Video Analysis Software (e.g., Hudl, Sportscode)
	– Statistical Analysis	– Distance covered	– Heart Rate Monitors
	– Biomechanical Analysis	– Shots on target	– Biomechanical Sensors
	– Tactical Analysis	– Tackles/interceptions	– Wearable Technology
		– Heat maps	– Statistical Software (e.g., Opta, StatsBomb)
American Football	– Film Review	– Completion rate	– GPS Tracking
	– GPS Tracking	– Yards gained	– Video Analysis Software (e.g., Hudl, Coach's Eye)
	– Statistical Analysis	– Tackles	– Biomechanical Sensors
	– Biomechanical Analysis	– Sacks	– Wearable Technology
	– Tactical Analysis	– Turnovers	– Statistical Software (e.g., Pro Football Focus)
Gaelic Football	– Video Analysis	– Passing accuracy	– GPS Tracking
	– GPS Tracking	– Shots on target	– Video Analysis Software (e.g., Dartfish, Hudl)
	– Statistical Analysis	– Tackles	– Heart Rate Monitors
	– Biomechanical Analysis	– Distance covered	– Biomechanical Sensors
	– Tactical Analysis	– Possessions won/lost	– Wearable Technology
Rugby	– Video Analysis	– Tackles	– GPS Tracking
	– GPS Tracking	– Line breaks	– Video Analysis Software (e.g., Hudl, Sportscode)
	– Statistical Analysis	– Rucks/mauls won	– Heart Rate Monitors
	– Biomechanical Analysis	– Passing accuracy	– Biomechanical Sensors
	– Tactical Analysis	– Kicking success rate	– Wearable Technology
Basketball	– Video Analysis	– Shooting percentage	– GPS Tracking
	– GPS Tracking	– Assists	– Video Analysis Software (e.g., Hudl, Synergy Sports)
	– Statistical Analysis	– Rebounds	– Heart Rate Monitors
	– Biomechanical Analysis	– Steals	– Biomechanical Sensors
	– Tactical Analysis	– Turnovers	– Wearable Technology
		– Player efficiency rating (PER)	– Statistical Software (e.g., STATS, Second Spectrum)

The overall take away point from this is understanding that you can only take a player so far from the perspective of physical preparation. We will not look at other ways you can work with coaches and athletes to influence the tactical elements of speed.

Implementing Tactical Speed in Practice

1. Positional unit and Individual Sessions

In your unit or individual sessions, start incorporating elements that challenge athletes to use their speed in realistic scenarios. Begin with basic drills like 1v1s and 2v1s, combining catching and running. The goal is to simulate game situations where speed is crucial.

Focus on:

- Footwork Drills: Emphasise quick foot movements and proper mechanics.
- Change of Direction: Practise cutting and changing direction at game speed.
- Speed and Skill Integration: Combine speed drills with skill-based tasks, such as catching or passing, to mimic in-game demands.

2. Scenario-Based Training

Move on to more complex scenario-based training, focusing on counter attacks and offensive plays. For example, in rugby, set up drills where the fullback must react to a ball hitting the midfield and accelerate quickly to make a play.

Key points include:

- **Reacting Quickly:** Develop the ability to accelerate and change direction swiftly.
- **Decision Making:** Practise making rapid decisions while moving at high speed.
- **Skill Application:** Apply skills learned in previous drills to realistic game situations.

3. Small-Sided Games and Scrimmages

Integrate small-sided games and scrimmages into your training to provide a continuous, game-like environment. These drills should have no breaks in play and be highly dynamic, focusing on:

- **High Pace:** Create drills that require constant movement and quick changes of direction.
- **Real-Time Adjustments:** Encourage athletes to make adjustments on the fly, replicating in-game decision-making.
- **Increased Density:** Increase the frequency and intensity of these drills to condition the brain and body for rapid movements.

Bringing it All Together: Matches

The ultimate test of tactical speed training is match play. The objective is for athletes to integrate all the skills and speed techniques they've practised and use them effectively during games. Focus on:

- **Applying Techniques:** Ensure athletes can execute the correct techniques under pressure.
- **Reading the Game:** Develop the ability to read defensive setups and make strategic plays. Design drills that allow athletes to practise this
- **Execution:** Emphasise executing key movements like cuts, hand-offs, and sprints precisely when needed.

By following this approach to speed development, you can develop athletes who are not only fast but also tactically astute in using their speed to influence game outcomes. Whether you're a coach or an athlete, implementing these strategies will significantly enhance your performance on the field. Remember, the goal is not just to be fast but to be smart and effective with your speed.

Closing Thoughts

Taking on the challenge of writing this book has been a source of immense pride. Building sports speed and team sport sprinters is not a novel or new idea as this has been attempted for many years. This is just my take on it, one that I have found works incredibly well. One thing has separated these ideas from the ones that have been shown to you in this book; understanding team sport preparation as an holistic entity. Combining the principles that we know work in isolation for olympic sports and creating a training system that harnesses them to develop team and field sport athletes. I want to thank you personally and if there is anything I can do to help you in your pursuit, then please contact me directly. This book is merely the start of a really important conversation that will help us advance the preparation of our athletes. Take these ideas and stretch your existing beliefs by applying them and tracking results. Be bold and be brave and remember that the most important metric is the scoreboard.

About the Author

Sam Portland is a renowned Strength and Conditioning Coach and Team Sport Speed Specialist with over a decade of experience in the field of athletic performance. Known for his innovative approach and passion for speed training, Sam has made significant strides in enhancing the capabilities of athletes across various sports, including rugby, football, soccer, and field-based sports.

A former athlete himself, Sam understands the intricacies and demands of high-level competition. His journey from player to coach has equipped him with a unique perspective, allowing him to connect with athletes on a deeper level and tailor training programs that truly resonate with their needs.

Throughout his career, Sam has worked with athletes at all levels, from grassroots to international and professional leagues, including NFL players. His expertise has not only led to remarkable improvements in speed and performance but has also been instrumental in injury prevention and rehabilitation, particularly with hamstring injuries.

Sam's dedication to the field extends beyond coaching. He is a sought-after speaker and educator, regularly sharing his knowledge through workshops, seminars, and online courses and has worked with coaches from international rugby, EPL, NFL and many more. His passion for empowering coaches and athletes to reach their full potential is evident in every aspect of his work.

When he's not on the field or in the gym, Sam enjoys staying active, exploring new training techniques, and spending time with his family. His commitment to continuous learning and innovation keeps him at the forefront of the industry, making him a trusted authority in speed training and athletic performance.

If you would like to learn more how you could work closer with Sam please contact sam@coachsportland.co.uk for more information.

Future Work

When I embarked on this journey I had no idea what it would lead me to. This book has inspired future books and projects that will help dive deeper into specific areas and sports to give you a great applied vision of this work. These are some of the working ideas currently.

- Special Strength Training for Speed Development
- Neurology of Speed Training
- Programming for Speed
- Return to Speed: Rehabilitation of Common Sporting injuries.
- Sports Speed Acceleration Manual
- Sports Speed Maximum Velocity Manual
- Sport Speed Change of Direction and Agility Manual

Recommended Reading

I am a massive proponent of creating a well read view of classical strength and conditioning books and theory. I largely feel that we have lost the art of specificity to modern research. The foundation of our future as a field can be seen in our origins. These are some books that I advise you spend time reading and deliberating over.

- Science and Practice of Sport - Vladimir M. Zatsiorsky
- Super Training - Yuri Verkhoshansky
- Special Strength Training Manual for Coaches - Yuri Verkhoshansky
- Shock Method - Yuri Verkhoshansky
- The Governing Dynamics of Coaching - James Smith
- Applied Speed Training Manual - James Smith
- Transfer of Training - Anatoliy Bondarchuk
- Westside Barbell Book of Methods - Louie Simmons
- Charlie Francis - Key Concepts
- Explosive Running - Dr Michael Yessis
- A Multilevel Approach to the Stufy of Motor Control and Learning - Debris J. Rose
- Anatomy Trains - Thomas Myers
- Secrets of Soviet Sports and Fitness Training - Dr Michael Yessis

Appendix

This appendix has been designed to supplement everything in the book and help you bring your coaching to life even further. I do feel that this section could be quite honestly the most important section of the book. It is hard to combine all of the elements whilst explaining the methodology of the sports speed system, which is why I have packed this appendix with resources, progressions, tables, and many other things for you to go out and start coaching and programming immediately.

My advice for you when working through the appendix is to flip forward and back to the relevant sections as described within the book to gain a deeper understanding on how to utilise them most effectively.

TO ACCESS ALL THE RESOURCES DESCRIBED IN THE APPENDIX SCAN THIS QR CODE.

How to use the Sports Speed System

Throughout the book you might have been asking yourself the question "how do I put this all together?". This is the part of the book that is the most fun for me to write. You may have picked up this book not knowing much about speed training, or you may have a lot of experience but still not sure how the system functions.

Inside this section I am going to break it all down based on the frameworks, key speed ages and give you the exact exercises I use. Even sessions and programs.

The table below will provide you with a summary of how the system blends with the frameworks. The table is a representation of where the coach needs to spend *most* of their coaching time. This is to ensure the optimal transfer of training

Note some of the frameworks are primary frameworks to teach and organise (Learn Load Exercute & Drill Stacking) as opposed to the others that provide physical loading parameters.

THE SPORTS SPEED SYSTEM: COACHES ROADMAP

	LEARNING TO SPRINT	**TRAINING TO SPRINT**	**SPRINTING TO COMPETE**	**SPRINTING TO WIN**
Coaching Objective	Skill: Learn the movement skills of sprinting and train the physical qualities associated with those movements.	Drill: Repeatedly perform those drills to ensure that you are developing motor skill capacity and improving biodynamic and bioenergetic output.	Practice: Develop scenario based sprinting activity. Introduce race and chase pressure. Start to include the ball or tactical constraints.	Perform: The focus here is optimising performance strategy. The merging of speed and sporting action with maximal positive outcome.
How we use speed	Learn the technical points and develop new degrees of freedom.	Develop higher levels of physical capacity and motor learning	The utilisation of maximum velocity as a speed training tool.	Perform as consistently as close to maximal outputs
Coaching Style *Each phase brings an introduction into the new style of coaching*	Deliberate Practice	Deliberate Practice / Dynamical Systems Theory	Deliberate Practice / Dynamical Systems Theory / Perception Action	Deliberate Practice / Dynamical Systems Theory / Perception Action
Drill Stacking	Segment	Movement	Pattern	Skill
Stable to Unstable	Stable - Fixed Segmented & Connected	Stable-Unstable - Unstable -Stable Introduction of hand supported and higher velocity resisted movement.	Unstable -Stable Unstable Resisted Sprinting and Max Effort Sprinting	Unstable Maximum effort and velocity sprinting Overspeed Sprinting
Step By Step	Acceleration: Steps 1-3 / 4-7 Maximum Speed: Build to 50m	Acceleration: Steps 1-15 Maximum Speed: Build to 40m	Acceleration: Steps 1-25 Maximum Speed: Build to 30m	Acceleration: Steps 1-35 Maximum Speed: Build to 30m - Maintain to 50m
Curve Loading	Low and Slow	Gradual	Gradual	Steep
Stage of Conjugate Sequencing	First Level Extensive Variations - submaximal resistance.	Second Level Intensive Variations & Resisted Modalities (Max Effort)	Third Level Circa maximum velocity movements and Maximum velocity sprinting	Fourth Level Overspeed Modalities of training and sprinting.
What data to look at? *based on the assumption of minimal equipment.*	Quantitative: Standing Broad Jump Qualitative: Technical proficiency	Quantitative: Standing Broad Jump / Short Sprint times / Maximum Speed / Force Creation Qualitative: Technical proficiency and technical capacity	Quantitative: Standing Broad Jump / Short Sprint times / Maximum Speed / In depth video analysis / Force Strategy Qualitative: Technical proficiency and technical capacity	Quantitative: Standing Broad Jump / Short Sprint times / Maximum Speed / In depth video analysis / Force Strategy/ Repeatable Volumes Qualitative: Technical proficiency and technical capacity

THE EXERCISES OF THE SPORTS SPEED SYSTEM

Within this section we will be looking at the specific exercises I use within the sports speed system. This is where I will show you the specific exercises of the system and show you how to use them, teach them and progress them.

I do appreciate there is some bandwidth and grey area within these groupings. However this is what I have found to work. As we have discussed the process of exercise selection and classification is the element of team sport speed training that is highly underrated and misunderstood.

It is very important to understand that all of the exercises have specific pathways and progressions. Based on the principle laws of skill acquisition and exercise classification I have found that these exercises ensure specific progression.

How to use the exercises in the Sports Speed System

An exercise is only useful if it is able to solve the problem the athlete faces. Imagine you are a carpenter and you have to carve a beautiful sculpture. Would you use the same chisel for every angle and notch? Probably not. You would assess the wood and the situation knowing if you carve too much…there is no coming back. This principle applies to exercise selection in the sports speed system.

I want to remind you of the three phases of exercise exposure from Chapter 7. This serves as the foundation of exercise progression within the Sports Speed System.

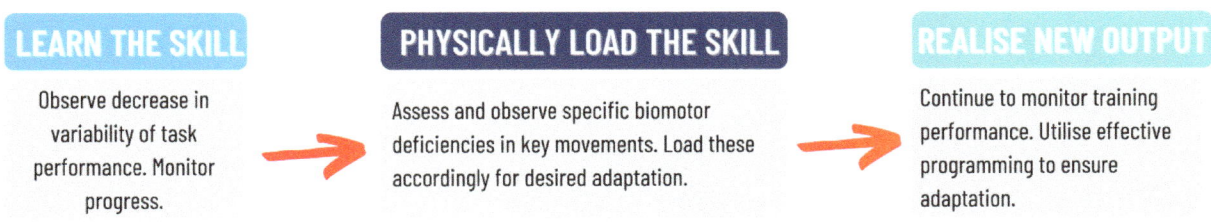

Therefore a simple process to follow when using the program is as such.

Step 1: Identity Speed Age
Step 2: Implement Level 1 exercises to determine adaptation windows in training.
Step 3: Demonstrate skill competency
Step 4: Demonstrate skill capacity
Step 5: Assess transfer.

Once you have determined the effectiveness of the exercise you can then make a decision. If that exercise is providing adaptation by implementation of basic training then do not create more specificity. Continue to utilise the movements you have chosen within your Learn Load Execute frameworks. Feel free to add variation and variety in the movements. For example changing the order you perform your drills can be enough to tax the system slightly.

Sport Speed System Exercise Progressions

Warm Up Drills

Category	Level 1	Level 2	Level 3	Level 4	Level 5	Level 6	Level 7	Level 8
LINEAR	Heel Toe Walk	Ankle Popper	Ankling					
	A March	A Skip	Single Leg A Skip	A Switch	A Switch Double	A Switch Continuous	A Build Up	A Run
	B March	B Skip	Single Leg B Skip	B Switch	B Switch Double	B Switch Continuous	B Build Up	B Run
	Ankle Dribble	Shin Dribble	Knee Dribble					
LATERAL	Lateral A March	Lateral A Skip	Lateral A Switch	Lateral A Run				
	Single Lateral Shuffle	Double Lateral Shuffle	Continuous Lateral Shuffle					
	Single Crossover	Double Crossover	Continuous Crossover					
	Karaoke	Karaoke Rotate						
	Forward Jockey	Backward Jockey						
	Run and Rotate Linear	Run and Rotate Lateral						

WARM UP DRILLS

A Series

Heel Toe Walk

In this exercise, we're focusing on a heel-toe calf raise to teach athletes how to drive forward, maintain a tall posture, and lengthen their steps. Here are some coaching points to consider:

1. Heel-toe Action: Emphasise the rolling action from the heel to the toe as the foot makes contact with the ground. This promotes a smooth and efficient transfer of energy throughout the stride.

2. Posture and Alignment: Encourage athletes to maintain an upright and tall posture throughout the exercise. This helps align the body for optimal force generation and reduces unnecessary movements.

3. Hip Extension: Highlight the importance of driving the hips forward during each step. Emphasise the hip extension motion to generate power and propel the body forward.

4. Step Length and Acceleration: Encourage athletes to focus on lengthening their steps while maintaining a quick cadence. Emphasise the connection between longer strides and increased acceleration.

During the exercise, athletes should aim to drive their foot into the ground and push off forcefully, propelling themselves upward and forward. By practising this movement pattern, athletes develop the ability to generate power and effectively accelerate their movement.

It's important to start with controlled and slower movements initially, gradually building up to more explosive and dynamic actions as athletes become comfortable with the technique. Remember to provide feedback and corrections to ensure proper execution and alignment throughout the exercise.

Ankle Popper

In this drill, called the "popper," we're progressing from the high heel-toe walk and focusing on accessing more range of motion and pushing ourselves into the calf raise. Here are some coaching points for this exercise:

1. Range of Motion: Encourage athletes to push themselves to achieve a greater range of motion in their steps. This helps activate and stretch the muscles involved in the calf raise and enhances overall movement efficiency.

WWW.SAMPORTLAND.COM

2. Vertical Displacement: Emphasise the upward displacement of the centre of mass during each step. Athletes should aim to generate force that propels them off the ground, allowing for a brief moment of suspension in the air.

3. Quick Ground Contact: Reinforce the importance of a quick and explosive ground contact. Athletes should focus on applying force rapidly to generate the upward push and achieve the desired vertical displacement.

4. Coordination and Timing: Help athletes coordinate the movement of their legs and arms in sync with the vertical displacement. The arms should act as counterbalances to the legs, contributing to the overall power and rhythm of the exercise.

By incorporating the "popper" drill into training, athletes learn to generate more explosive power and improve their ability to displace the centre of mass vertically.

Start with controlled and deliberate movements, gradually increasing the intensity and speed as athletes become more proficient. Provide feedback on technique and timing to ensure athletes are executing the drill effectively.

Ankling Vertical Stack

Once athletes have progressed from the "popper" drill, it's time to focus on the "ankling" drill. This drill helps develop ankle strength, mobility, and coordination. Here are some coaching points to keep in mind:

1. Body Position: Emphasise maintaining proper body alignment throughout the drill. Athletes should keep their head, shoulders, and hips in alignment and centred over the balls of their feet. Avoid leaning too far forward or backward, as this can negatively impact the efficiency of the movement.

2. Arm Movement: Teach athletes to coordinate their arm movement with their feet. The arms should mirror the range and rhythm of the foot movements. Emphasise that the role of the arms is to create stability and counter-rotation, helping to maintain proper hip and foot positioning. Discourage excessive arm movement that may interfere with the desired ankle action.

3. Ankle Action: Focus on developing a strong ankle action. Athletes should strive for a full vertical stack position, meaning their ankle, knee, and hip are aligned vertically. Encourage a bouncy and spring-like movement, with an active push-off from the ground and a quick recovery of the foot. Emphasise the importance of actively pulling the foot up off the ground to maximise stride efficiency.

4. Rhythm and Tempo: Encourage athletes to find a smooth and consistent rhythm in their ankling movements. Emphasise maintaining a quick turnover of the feet while preserving the integrity of the ankle action. Strive for a fluid and effortless motion.

5. Progression: Start with slower and controlled movements to ensure athletes grasp the correct technique. As they become more comfortable and proficient, gradually increase the speed and intensity of the drill. Monitor their form and provide feedback to ensure they maintain proper body alignment, arm movement, and ankle action at higher speeds.

The ankling drill is an effective way to optimise the push-off phase of the running stride and promote efficient energy transfer from the ground to propel the body forward. By practising this drill, athletes can develop a bouncy and elastic running style, which can enhance their overall speed and performance.

Remember to provide clear instructions and demonstrations of the desired technique. Give athletes time to practise and provide individual feedback to help them refine their ankling movements. Encourage them to focus on maintaining proper form and gradually increasing their speed as they become more proficient.

A March

Once athletes have progressed from the "ankling" movement, it's time to introduce the "A March" drill. This drill focuses on developing proper thigh drive and coordination with arm movements. Here are some coaching points to consider:

1. Posture and Alignment: Emphasise the importance of maintaining a tall and upright posture throughout the drill. Athletes should keep their head up, shoulders back, and hips square. Discourage excessive hip

hiking, which can disrupt the fluidity of the movement. Encourage athletes to imagine a straight line running through their body from their head to their hips and down their supporting leg.

2. Thigh Drive: Teach athletes to actively engage their hip flexors and hamstrings to lift their thighs in a high marching position. Emphasise the use of the hamstring to pull the thigh upward, rather than relying solely on hip flexor flexion. This helps develop the necessary strength and coordination for maximum velocity sprinting.

3. Arm Movement: Coordinate the arm movements with the thigh drive. Teach athletes to drive their arms forward and backward in sync with the opposite leg. The arms should swing naturally and freely, with a slight bend at the elbows. Encourage athletes to maintain relaxed and rhythmic arm movements that complement the thigh drive.

4. Knee Bend: Instruct athletes to maintain a slight knee bend throughout the A March drill. The knee should be flexed as they lift their thigh, with the foot pulled up towards the shin. This engagement of the hamstrings helps drive the thigh upward and enhances the overall power and efficiency of the movement.

5. Tempo and Rhythm: Encourage athletes to find a comfortable and consistent tempo in their A March. The movement should be controlled and deliberate, allowing them to focus on proper technique. Encourage a smooth transition from one leg to the other, maintaining a balanced and coordinated rhythm.

6. Gradual Progression: Start with slower and controlled A March movements to ensure athletes master the correct technique and coordination between the arms and legs. As they become more proficient, gradually increase the speed and intensity of the drill while maintaining proper form and alignment. Monitor their movements and provide individual feedback to help them refine their A March technique.

The A March drill is an effective way to reinforce proper thigh drive, posture, and coordination with arm movements. By practising this drill, athletes can develop the necessary strength and technique for efficient sprinting and maximise their running speed.

Ensure athletes understand and practise the key coaching points outlined above. Demonstrate the correct technique and provide feedback to help them make necessary adjustments. Encourage athletes to focus on maintaining a tall posture, driving their thighs upward using the hamstrings, coordinating their arm movements, and gradually increasing the tempo as they progress.

A Skip

Moving on from the A March drill, the next progression in the A series is the A Skip. The A Skip drill focuses on developing rhythm, timing, and coordination in a faster-paced fashion. Here are some coaching points to consider:

1. Foot Strike: Emphasise the importance of a proper foot strike during the A Skip drill. Athletes should aim for a mid-foot strike, landing on the balls of their feet. Encourage a quick and snappy action as they lift their knees and extend their legs forward. This will help develop the desired bouncy and energetic movement.

2. Rhythm and Timing: Teach athletes to find the right rhythm and timing between their steps. The A Skip drill involves a skipping motion with alternating legs. Encourage athletes to use a consistent and controlled foot count, such as counting "1-2" for each skip. This will help them maintain a steady pace and coordination.

3. Arm and Hand Movement: Coordinate the arm and hand movements with the leg action. Emphasise a smooth and synchronised motion, with the arms swinging forward and backward in coordination with the leg lift. The arm swing should be natural and relaxed, assisting in propelling the body forward.

4. Knee Drive and Leg Extension: Instruct athletes to focus on driving their knees upward while extending their legs forward. Encourage a quick and snappy action as they lift their knees and extend their legs, maintaining a slight forward lean. This helps develop the desired bouncy and energetic movement.

5. Posture and Alignment: Remind athletes to maintain proper posture and alignment throughout the drill. Encourage a tall and upright position, with the head up, shoulders back, and hips square. Discourage excessive leaning forward or backward, and emphasise the importance of a straight and aligned body position.

6. Gradual Progression: Start with slower and controlled A Skip movements to ensure athletes grasp the proper rhythm, timing, and coordination. As they become more proficient, gradually increase the speed and intensity of the drill while maintaining proper form and alignment. Monitor their movements and provide individual feedback to help them refine their A Skip technique.

The A Skip drill is a valuable tool for developing rhythm, timing, and coordination in a faster-paced manner. By practising this drill, athletes can improve their stride efficiency, enhance their running technique, and develop a more explosive and dynamic stride.

Ensure athletes understand and practise the key coaching points outlined above. Demonstrate the correct technique and provide feedback to help them make necessary adjustments. Encourage athletes to focus on a proper foot strike, maintain a consistent rhythm and timing, coordinate their arm and hand movements, drive their knees upward while extending their legs forward, and gradually increase the speed and intensity as they progress.

A Switch

The final piece in the A series is the A Switch. The A Switch drill focuses on the rapid exchange from one leg to the other, increasing the athlete's ability to switch legs quickly and improving timing. Here are some coaching points to consider:

1. Leg Speed: Emphasise the importance of leg speed in the A Switch drill. Athletes should aim to move their legs rapidly, creating a quick exchange from one leg to the other. Encourage them to generate powerful and explosive leg movements while maintaining control and coordination.

2. Force Application: Highlight that the A Switch drill is a force applicator. As athletes contact the ground with each foot, they should aim to apply force into the ground, propelling themselves upward and forward. Emphasise the need for a quick and snappy action to beat the hips down to the ground.

3. Postural Control: Discuss the importance of postural control during the A Switch drill. Athletes should strive for stability and balance throughout the movement. Encourage them to maintain a tall and upright posture, with their head up, shoulders back, and core engaged. This will help them generate power and maintain efficient movement.

4. Ground Contact: Instruct athletes to focus on their ground contact during the A Switch drill. Emphasise a firm and controlled foot strike, where everything on ground contact should stop, hit, and block. Encourage athletes to imagine that their foot is hitting an immovable object, creating a brief pause before transitioning to the next leg.

5. Coordination and Timing: Highlight the importance of coordination and timing in the A Switch drill. Athletes should aim to synchronise the movements of their legs, arms, and core. Encourage them to maintain a smooth and fluid motion, with the arms swinging in coordination with the leg switch. Focus on developing a rhythm and timing that allows for efficient leg exchange and powerful force application.

6. Progression and Intensity: Begin with slower and controlled A Switch movements to ensure athletes understand the proper technique and timing. As they become more proficient, gradually increase the speed and intensity of the drill while maintaining proper form and control. Monitor their movements and provide individual feedback to help them refine their A Switch technique.

The A Switch drill is valuable for enhancing leg speed, force application, postural control, and coordination. By practising this drill, athletes can improve their ability to rapidly switch legs, generate power, and maintain stability during high-intensity movements.

Ensure athletes understand and practise the key coaching points outlined above. Demonstrate the correct technique and provide feedback to help them make necessary adjustments. Encourage athletes to focus on leg speed, apply force into the ground, maintain postural control, execute firm and controlled ground contact, coordinate their movements, and gradually increase the intensity as they progress.

A Switch Double and Continuous

The last piece of the A Switch series, which encompasses the A series, is the Double Switch with Locomotion. This drill focuses on finding a leg exchange pattern with the addition of a tap in between. Here are some coaching points to consider:

1. Leg Exchange: Emphasise the leg exchange pattern in the Double Switch with Locomotion drill. Athletes should perform a double leg switch followed by a tap in between before executing another double switch. Encourage them to maintain quick and efficient leg exchanges, ensuring proper coordination and timing.

2. Control Momentum: Highlight that this drill allows athletes to control momentum while maintaining stiffness. As they perform the leg switches and taps, they should aim to generate power and maintain

forward propulsion. Emphasise the need to avoid excessive vertical displacement and focus on horizontal movement to maintain momentum.

3. Complexity and Intensity: Discuss how the Double Switch with Locomotion adds complexity and intensity to the movement pattern. By incorporating the double switch and tap, athletes must coordinate their leg movements and maintain rhythm. Encourage them to start with slower tempos and gradually increase speed and intensity as they become more comfortable and proficient.

By incorporating the Double Switch with Locomotion, athletes can progress from lower complexity and velocity to higher complexity and velocity. This progression helps develop technical proficiency, coordination, and the ability to apply force at higher speeds.

Ensure athletes understand and practise the key coaching points outlined above. Demonstrate the correct technique, provide feedback, and encourage athletes to gradually increase the intensity while maintaining proper form.

A Run

Next, we have the A Run, which serves various purposes for dynamic movement and higher velocity demands. Here are coaching points for the A Run:

1. Force Application: Emphasise the need to apply force into the ground during the A Run. Athletes should focus on driving off the ground with each step, using a quick and powerful push-off to generate forward propulsion. Encourage them to maintain a firm and explosive foot strike while minimising ground contact time.

2. Stiffness: Highlight the importance of stiffness in the A Run. Athletes should aim to be springy and responsive, utilising the elastic properties of their muscles and tendons to efficiently transfer energy. Emphasise the need for quick and snappy movements, avoiding excessive sinking or collapsing upon ground contact.

3. Rhythm and Timing: Discuss the significance of rhythm and timing in the A Run. Athletes should strive for a smooth and coordinated motion, with the arms swinging in synchronisation with their leg movements. Encourage them to find a rhythm that allows for efficient and powerful stride execution.

4. Technical Execution: Remind athletes that the A Run is a technical execution drill. While speed is important, prioritise proper technique and form. Encourage athletes to focus on maintaining the key elements learned in the preceding drills, such as leg speed, force application, postural control, and coordination.

5. Progression: Begin with slower A Runs, focusing on mastering the technique and maintaining proper form. Gradually increase the speed and intensity, challenging athletes to execute the drill at higher velocities while still maintaining technical proficiency. Monitor their movements and provide individual feedback to help them refine their A Run technique.

By incorporating the A Run, athletes can progress from lower complexity and velocity to higher complexity and velocity. This progression helps develop technical proficiency, coordination, and the ability to apply force at higher speeds more akin to conventional running.

Ensure athletes understand and practise the key coaching points outlined above. Demonstrate the correct technique, provide feedback, and encourage athletes to gradually increase the intensity while maintaining proper form.

Using Build Ups

Let's take a look at the Build-Ups drill. The purpose of this drill is to gradually increase the frequency, velocity, amplitude of movement, and decrease ground contact times. Here we are gradually building up to a certain speed. It helps athletes access larger ranges of motion and serves as a progression into runs, dribble bleeds, or any other high-speed activities. Here are some coaching points to consider:

1. Progressive Increase: Explain to athletes that the Build-Ups drill is about progressively increasing speed and intensity. Start with a slow and controlled pace, focusing on building a solid foundation of technique and rhythm. Encourage athletes to gradually increase their speed and power as they become more comfortable and proficient with the movement.

2. Hip Height: Emphasise the importance of maintaining a high hip position throughout the drill. Athletes should focus on keeping their hips lifted and aligned with their torso. This helps promote proper posture and allows for efficient force generation and transfer.

3. Bounce and Rhythm: Encourage athletes to maintain a bouncy and rhythmic movement pattern during the Build-Ups. Emphasise the importance of quick ground contact and pushing off explosively with each step. This helps develop reactive strength and improves the ability to generate power rapidly.

4. Gradual Progression: Highlight that the Build-Ups drill serves as a gradual progression into higher-speed activities. It allows athletes to access and build speed in a controlled manner. Encourage them to focus on the specific distance or range they are training for and work on maximising their speed within that distance.

5. Technique Focus: Remind athletes to prioritise proper technique and form during the Build-Ups. This includes maintaining a tall posture, driving the knees up, and pumping the arms in coordination with the leg movements. Provide feedback on their technique and encourage them to make necessary adjustments to optimise their performance.

6. Mental Engagement: Encourage athletes to stay mentally engaged throughout the drill. Remind them to be present and focused on their movement, rhythm, and speed. Encourage them to visualise themselves performing at their desired maximum velocity and use the Build-Ups as a tool to improve their speed development.

7. Recording Progress: Suggest that athletes record their Build-Up sessions to track their progress over time. This allows them to compare their performance, speed, and technique from one session to another. It also serves as a motivational tool and helps them identify areas for improvement.

As athletes progress through the Build-Ups drill, they should aim to increase their speed, power, and efficiency while maintaining proper technique. Encourage them to push their limits and gradually expand their comfort zone in terms of speed and intensity.

Monitor their movements, provide feedback on their technique, and motivate them to continuously challenge themselves. With consistent practice and proper execution of the Build-Ups drill, athletes can enhance their speed capabilities and improve their overall performance.

B Series

B March

The B March drill focuses on maintaining a tall posture and emphasising the movement of the hip and leg. Here are some coaching points to consider:

1. Tall Posture: Emphasise the importance of a tall posture throughout the drill. Athletes should aim to keep their torso upright and their spine aligned. This promotes optimal body positioning and helps with efficient force production and transfer.

2. Hip and Leg Movement: Instruct athletes to actively engage their hip and leg muscles during the B March. As the knee lifts, the hip should open up, allowing the shin to glide forward. Encourage athletes to focus on the feeling of lengthening the leg and extending the hip as they drive forward.

3. Foot Placement: Guide athletes to paw their leg down with control as they bring it back to the ground. Emphasise the importance of proper foot placement, landing on the ball of the foot and then transitioning smoothly to the next step. This helps develop stability and allows for a quick and efficient transition between strides.

4. Hip Over Foot: Explain to athletes that the goal of the B March is to create a strong hip-to-foot connection. Encourage them to actively pull their hip over their foot, driving themselves forward into the space in front of them. This movement pattern helps improve stride length and promotes effective acceleration and deceleration.

5. Rhythm and Tempo: Encourage athletes to find a rhythm and tempo that feels natural and allows for smooth and coordinated movements. Emphasise the importance of maintaining a consistent cadence and avoiding any abrupt or jerky motions. This helps develop fluidity and improves the overall efficiency of the B March.

6. Focus on Muscle Activation: Remind athletes to focus on activating the muscles involved in the B March, particularly the hip flexors, glutes, and hamstrings. Encourage them to engage these muscles throughout the entire movement, ensuring they are actively involved in lifting and extending the leg.

Encourage athletes to practise the B March with intention and focus. By paying attention to proper posture, hip and leg movement, foot placement, and rhythm, they can enhance their running mechanics and develop more efficient and powerful strides.

Provide feedback and corrections as needed, helping athletes fine-tune their technique. As they become more proficient with the B March, they can transfer these skills to their running and other athletic movements.

B Skip

The B Skip drill adds complexity and fluidity to the movement pattern. It involves a skipping motion while emphasising the pawing action of the leg and driving the hip into the space in front. Here are some coaching points to consider:

1. Fluid Skipping Motion: Instruct athletes to perform a skipping motion, alternating between legs. Emphasise the importance of maintaining a smooth and fluid movement throughout the drill. Encourage athletes to find a rhythm and tempo that allows for efficient and coordinated skipping.

2. Pawring Action: Explain to athletes that the B Skip involves actively pawing the leg down as it transitions from the lift phase to the ground contact phase. Encourage them to visualise the leg pawing fluidly, allowing for a controlled contact This helps develop eccentric control and prepares the muscles for the next stride.

3. Hip Drive: Guide athletes to focus on driving their hip forward into the space in front of them. As the leg descends, they should actively pull their hip into extension, maximising the range of motion and creating a powerful driving force. Emphasise the importance of maintaining a tall posture and engaging the hip muscles throughout the movement.

4. Arm Coordination: Highlight the role of the arms in the B Skip drill. Instruct athletes to coordinate their arm movements with the leg action, mirroring the skipping motion. Encourage a 90-degree arm swing, with the arms driving forward and back in sync with the leg movements. Proper arm coordination helps with balance, rhythm, and overall efficiency.

5. Focus on Core Stability: Remind athletes to engage their core muscles throughout the B Skip drill. A stable and engaged core helps maintain proper alignment, allowing for more efficient transfer of force and reducing energy leaks. Encourage athletes to keep their torso upright and avoid excessive rotation or side-to-side movements.

6. Stride Length and Frequency: Discuss the importance of finding the right balance between stride length and stride frequency. Encourage athletes to focus on increasing the length of their strides while maintaining a quick and snappy cadence. This helps develop both power and speed, optimising overall running mechanics.

7. Visualisation and Mental Focus: Encourage athletes to visualise themselves moving effortlessly and efficiently during the B Skip drill. Remind them to stay mentally focused on maintaining proper technique and executing each movement with intention. Visualisation can enhance muscle activation and improve overall performance.

Encourage athletes to practise the B Skip with purpose and precision. By paying attention to fluidity, pouring action, hip drive, arm coordination, core stability, and finding the right balance between stride length and frequency, they can improve their running mechanics and enhance their athletic performance.

Provide feedback and corrections as needed, helping athletes refine their technique. As they become more proficient with the B Skip, they can integrate these skills into their running and other sports-specific movements, ultimately enhancing their overall athletic abilities.

B Switch

The B Switch drill focuses on high velocity of leg movement and emphasises leg lengthening and stiffness to prepare for maximum velocity running. Here are some coaching points to consider:

1. Leg Length and Stiffness: Explain to athletes that the B Switch drill aims to maximise leg length and create higher degrees of stiffness in the muscles. Emphasise the importance of actively lengthening the leg and extending the hip during the movement. This helps develop eccentric control and prepares the muscles for rapid force production.

2. Pawing Action: Instruct athletes to let the leg paw out in a controlled manner during the B Switch drill. As the leg extends and descends, encourage them to focus on catching the hip down and quickly transitioning to the next stride. This pawing action emphasises the rapid exchange of legs and the ability to generate force efficiently.

3. Hamstring Engagement: Highlight the role of the hamstring muscles in the B Switch drill. Explain that the demand on the hamstring increases during this drill, as it needs to actively rip the leg down and contribute to the quick transition. Encourage athletes to engage their hamstrings throughout the movement, emphasising proper muscle activation and control.

4. Rhythm and Timing: Emphasise the importance of rhythm and timing in the B Switch drill. Instruct athletes to find a fast and snappy cadence while maintaining control and coordination. Encourage them to practise the drill at varying speeds, gradually increasing the velocity while maintaining proper technique and form.

5. Core activation and Posture: Remind athletes to maintain core activation and an upright posture throughout the drill. A strong and stable core helps with overall body alignment, ensuring efficient force transfer and reducing energy leaks. Encourage athletes to engage their core muscles and avoid excessive leaning or rotation during the movement.

6. Mental Focus and Intent: Encourage athletes to stay mentally focused and intentional during the B Switch drill. Remind them to visualise the desired movement pattern, emphasising leg lengthening, stiffness, and

quick transitions. Encourage them to execute each repetition with purpose and precision, optimising their training and skill development.

7. Gradual Progression: Remind athletes to gradually progress the intensity and velocity of the B Switch drill. Begin with slower tempos and controlled movements, focusing on technique and proper muscle activation. As athletes become more proficient, they can gradually increase the speed and power of the movement, pushing themselves to higher levels of performance.

Provide feedback and corrections as needed to help athletes refine their technique and maximise the benefits of the B Switch drill. Encourage them to focus on leg length, stiffness, rhythm, timing, core stability, and maintaining a strong mental focus throughout the drill.

B Switch Double

The Double B Switch drill is an advanced progression of the B Switch drill, focusing on attacking the ground and pulling the leg to create more speed and force. It can be performed in a standing position or while moving forward. The drill provides over-speed eccentric lengthening of the hamstring, challenges balance and hip support, and requires a higher level of skill and coordination.

Coaching Points:

1. Attack the Ground: Emphasise a strong and aggressive ground contact, aiming to generate more speed and force with each switch.

2. Pull and Drive: Encourage athletes to actively pull the leg and drive it into the space in front, maximising the range of motion and power.

3. Stagnant or Moving: The Double B Switch can be performed while standing in place or while moving forward. Both variations provide unique challenges and benefits.

4. Over-Speed Eccentric Lengthening: Highlight the eccentric component of the drill, as the leg is rapidly switched and the hamstring undergoes lengthening at high speed. This helps develop eccentric strength and control.

5. Balance and Hip Support: Remind athletes to maintain balance and support their hips throughout the movement. This requires core stability and proper alignment.

6. Progression: Note that the Double B Switch is a higher-level progression, suitable for athletes who have mastered the basic B Switch drill. Ensure athletes have the necessary strength, coordination, and technique before progressing to this exercise.

As athletes perform the Double B Switch drill, provide feedback on their technique and form. Encourage them to focus on attacking the ground, pulling and driving the leg, maintaining balance and hip support, and controlling the speed of the switches. With practice and proper execution, athletes can enhance their speed, power, and overall running mechanics.

B Switch Continuous and Double Tap

The Continuous B Switch and Double Tap drill is designed to challenge athletes by accumulating stress and maintaining proper form, shape, and posture throughout the exercise. The drill involves performing a continuous series of double switches followed by a single tap. As the repetitions progress, the movement becomes increasingly difficult, requiring athletes to focus on technique and control.

Coaching Points:

1. Accumulating Stress: Explain to athletes that the purpose of the drill is to accumulate stress throughout the set. This means that as they perform more repetitions, the movement will become more challenging, requiring greater effort and control.

2. Form, Shape, and Posture: Emphasise the importance of maintaining proper form, shape, and posture throughout the drill. Encourage athletes to stay tall, engage their core, and avoid excessive leaning or twisting.

3. Controlled Double Switches: Instruct athletes to perform consecutive double switches, maintaining a smooth and controlled rhythm. Emphasise the pawing action and the quick transition between legs.

4. Single Tap: After completing the double switches, athletes should execute a single tap, which serves as a reset before starting the next set of double switches. Encourage them to maintain balance and control during the tap.

5. Focus on Technique: Remind athletes to prioritise technique over speed. Encourage them to concentrate on proper execution, even as the movement becomes more challenging.

6. Mental and Physical Endurance: Highlight the mental and physical endurance required for this drill. Encourage athletes to stay focused, persevere through fatigue, and maintain technique and posture until the end of the set.

As athletes perform the Continuous B Switch and Double Tap drill, provide feedback on their form, posture, and execution. Encourage them to challenge themselves while maintaining proper technique and control. This drill can help improve coordination, balance, and endurance, which are essential for overall athletic performance.

B Run

The B Run is the final stage of the movement progression, characterised by increased velocity, complexity, and demand. This drill focuses on kicking the leg out in front and pulling the hip over the feet. It serves as an important preparatory tool for conditioning the hamstrings and hip flexors of athletes.

Coaching Points:

1. Increased Velocity: Emphasise the need to generate greater speed and quickness during the B Run. Encourage athletes to push their limits and increase their stride frequency while maintaining proper form and technique.

2. Leg Kick and Hip Pull: Instruct athletes to kick their leg out in front, creating a powerful and dynamic movement. As the leg extends, they should actively pull their hip over their feet, maximising the range of motion and generating forward propulsion.

3. Posture and Alignment: Remind athletes to maintain good posture and alignment throughout the B Run. Encourage them to stay tall, engage their core, and avoid excessive leaning or hunching forward.

4. Hip Flexor and Hamstring Activation: Highlight the importance of engaging the hip flexors and activating the hamstrings during the B Run. Emphasise the role of these muscles in generating power and driving the movement forward.

5. Smooth Transition and Flow: Encourage athletes to find a smooth and fluid transition between strides, maintaining a rhythmic and flowing motion. Discourage any sudden or jerky movements that may disrupt the flow and efficiency of the B Run.

6. Focus on Conditioning: Explain to athletes that the B Run is not only a speed drill but also a conditioning exercise for the hamstrings and hip flexors. Encourage them to embrace the challenge and push themselves to improve their conditioning and muscular endurance.

As athletes perform the B Run, provide feedback on their technique, posture, and effort level. Encourage them to give their best and strive for continuous improvement in their speed and conditioning. This drill can help athletes develop the necessary strength, power, and endurance to enhance their overall performance in sprinting and other athletic endeavours.

The Use of Single Leg Drills and Variations

Single leg drills, such as single leg B drills, are valuable for challenging technique, turnover frequency, and movement capacity. They are beneficial for rehabilitation, developing movement skills, and enhancing movement tools. By focusing on a single leg, these drills raise the demand placed on that leg and provide an opportunity to improve specific conditioning. The key is to maintain the same technical key performance indicators (KPIs) used in double leg drills while bringing them into a single leg setting. The goal is to create an overload effect by increasing the velocity and frequency of reps and decreasing the time between steps. This helps develop higher levels of specific conditioning and enhances the working tissues.

Coaching Points:

1. Technique Focus: Emphasise the importance of maintaining proper technique during single leg drills. Instruct athletes to pay attention to posture, alignment, and hip drive, similar to double leg drills.

2. Turnover Frequency: Highlight the need to increase turnover frequency during single leg drills. Encourage athletes to move their legs quickly off the ground and generate a faster stride rate.

3. Overload Effect: Explain to athletes that single leg drills provide an opportunity to create overload by performing multiple high-frequency reps and reducing the time between steps. Emphasise the benefits of this overload for specific conditioning and tissue adaptation.

4. Gradual Progression: Start with slower velocities and gradually increase the speed and intensity of single leg drills. Allow athletes to adapt and build the necessary strength and stability before pushing for higher velocities.

5. Focus on Non-Dominant Leg: During single leg drills, use the non-dominant leg as a kickstand or support for stability. This helps improve balance and control while placing greater demands on the working leg.

6. Attention to Timing: Discuss the importance of timing in single leg drills. Explain that by decreasing the time between steps, athletes are challenging their timing capabilities and enhancing their ability to execute quick, precise movements.

7. Monitoring and Feedback: Provide feedback and monitor athletes' technique and effort during single leg drills. Encourage them to focus on maintaining proper form, executing quick leg movements, and maximising their effort in each repetition.

By incorporating single leg drills into training routines, athletes can improve their technique, turnover frequency, and specific conditioning. These drills offer an opportunity to target and develop the working leg while enhancing overall movement skills and capabilities.

Acceleration Progressions - *please refer to the drill stacking model for further understanding.*

Within the acceleration progressions we use a systematic approach to exposing athletes to specific types of muscular contractions to encourage motor learning and physiological adaptation. These are structured in accordance with the drill stacking model.

	Segment		Movement			
Ankle	Yielding Isometric	Overcoming Isometric	Full Range of Motion	Resisted Series	Overspeed	Plyometric
Knee						
Hip Extensors						
Hip Flexors						

Ankle Series

Ankle Series - Yielding Isometrics

The following exercises focus on ankle emphasis yielding isometric drills in bilateral, staggered, and unilateral positions. These drills aim to create tension within the ankle and improve postural awareness. By adopting different positions and holding tension in the ankle, athletes learn to feel and control their body's position in space. The exercises progress from bilateral ankle emphasis to staggered and then to unilateral positions, all while maintaining a good body position and emphasising ankle stability and tension.

Teaching Points :

1. Bilateral Ankle Emphasis Yielding Isometric: Start in the wall drill position and generate tension within the ankle. The goal is to create postural awareness and improve body positioning. Emphasise feeling the front edge of the ball of the foot.

    Coaching Tip: Guide athletes to hold tension through the ankle while maintaining proper body position. Encourage them to focus on creating postural awareness and feeling the stability within the ankle.

2. Staggered Ankle Emphasis Yielding Isometric: Transition from the bilateral position to the staggered position. Take a half step forward with one leg and then a half step forward with the back leg. Maintain tension through both ankles while keeping a good body position.

    Coaching Tip: In the staggered position, emphasise ankle stability and tension in both the front and back foot. Encourage athletes to hold the tension while maintaining proper body alignment.

3. Unilateral Ankle Emphasis Yielding Isometric: From the staggered position, transition to the unilateral position. Adjust the front foot position and hold ankle emphasis. Switch and change to emphasise the ankle in both the front and back foot positions.

   Coaching Tip: Guide athletes to focus on good force application positions and increase intensity. Emphasise ankle stability and tension in both the front and back foot positions during the unilateral drill.

These teaching points highlight the importance of ankle stability and tension in various positions. By incorporating these ankle emphasis yielding isometric drills, athletes can improve their postural awareness, body positioning, and force application. Gradually progressing from bilateral to staggered and then to unilateral positions helps athletes develop stronger ankle stability and control.

Ankle Series - Overcoming Isometrics

The next phase focuses on overcoming isometric variations in ankle-dominant positions. The exercises include bilateral calf raises, overcoming ankle isometric in staggered positions, and unilateral overcoming ankle isometric. These exercises aim to build tension and strength in the ankles while maintaining proper body position and emphasising ankle dominance. The variations in positioning allow for different emphasis on the gastrocnemius and soleus muscles.

Teaching Points:

1. Bilateral Calf Raises: Begin in a slightly flexed position with emphasis on the ankles. Perform calf raises, focusing on pushing against the ground to drive the ankles up. The goal is to maintain body position without rising up.

   Coaching Tip: Guide athletes to actively push themselves back into the ground while generating tension through the ankles during the calf raises. Emphasise ankle dominance and stability.

2. Overcoming Ankle Isometric in Staggered Position: Transition from bilateral to the staggered position. Perform the half step forward and half step back motion while maintaining tension and pushing against the ground in the ankle-dominant position. Ensure that you alternate feet so establish loading in both positions.

   Coaching Tip: Encourage athletes to focus on ankle dominance and create tension by actively pushing against the ground. Emphasise the distinction between gastrocnemius dominance in the back leg and soleus dominance in the front leg.

3. **Unilateral Overcoming Ankle Isometric:** Move into the unilateral overcoming ankle isometric position. Maintain a comfortable position and find the staggered stance. Lift and push while maintaining tension in the ankle. There should be no movement, but plenty of tension.

   Coaching Tip: Guide athletes to focus on generating tension and strength through the ankle while maintaining proper body position. Emphasise blending both gastrocnemius and soleus dominance and address any imbalances using appropriate corrective measures within your coaching system.

These teaching points highlight the importance of building tension and strength in ankle-dominant positions through overcoming isometric variations. By incorporating these exercises, athletes can improve ankle stability, dominance, and overall ankle strength. Proper technique and position should be maintained throughout each exercise, focusing on generating tension and building strength in the ankles.

Ankle Series - Full Range

In the full range series, the focus shifts to taking the ankles through full ranges of motion in various positions. Starting with bilateral, the goal is to observe ankle dorsiflexion and plantarflexion while applying force in the desired direction of movement. The use of elbow bending can assist in achieving the desired ankle motion. In the staggered position, emphasis is placed on driving the ankles towards the floor, with the front foot emphasising the soleus and the back foot emphasising the gastrocnemius. Lastly, the unilateral position exponentially increases the load on the ankles, incorporating full-length and soleus-dominant staggered positions.

Teaching Points (Teaching Manual Style):

1. Bilateral Full Range: Begin in the familiar bilateral position. Focus on ankle dorsiflexion and plantarflexion, ensuring the ankles move in the desired direction while applying force. Pay attention to the proper use of elbow bending to assist ankle motion.

    Coaching Tip: Guide athletes to perform ankle movements with control and precision. Emphasise the direction of movement and the application of force in the desired region.

2. Staggered Full Range: Transition to the staggered position, maintaining the emphasis on ankle dominance. Drive the ankles towards the floor, focusing on peak contractions in the soleus for the front foot and the gastrocnemius for the back foot.

    Coaching Tip: Encourage athletes to achieve full ankle range of motion while maintaining tension and emphasising the specific muscles for each foot. Ensure proper technique and execution of movements.

3. Unilateral Full Range: Move into the unilateral position, which exponentially increases the load on the ankles. Incorporate both full-length and soleus-dominant stagger positions, challenging ankle strength and control.

   Coaching Tip: Highlight the increased difficulty and load in the unilateral full range position. Guide athletes to perform ankle movements with proper form, focusing on control, tension, and maintaining balance throughout.

These teaching points highlight the importance of taking the ankles through full ranges of motion in different positions. By incorporating the full range series, athletes can improve ankle mobility, strength, and control. Emphasise proper technique, the direction of ankle motion, and the specific muscle groups involved. Gradually progressing through bilateral, staggered, and unilateral positions challenges athletes' ankle capabilities and prepares them for more advanced movements.

Ankle Series - Resisted Full Range Movement

The next phase introduces the resisted variations of ankle-dominant movements. These exercises focus on anchoring the resistance in the appropriate direction of force application to ensure specificity. The easiest method, especially for individual training, is to use a backpack as a resistance tool. By anchoring the bands appropriately, athletes can perform ankle movements in different positions while experiencing resistance. The exercises include bilateral, staggered, and unilateral variations, challenging ankle strength and providing specific overload. Here we are applying an external resistance to the full range of motion movements previously described.

The simple but effective setup as pictured demonstrates the lack of specific equipment needed and the scalable nature of this exercise.

Teaching Points:

1. Resisted Bilateral Ankle Dominant: Anchor the resistance, such as a band, in the appropriate direction (low to high). Ensure specificity by aligning the resistance with the direction of force application. Stand close to the wall and perform ankle movements through the full range of motion, experiencing resistance and loading the calves.

    Coaching Tip: Guide athletes to focus on maintaining proper form and technique while performing ankle movements with resistance. Emphasise the specificity of force application and the challenge provided by the resistance.

2. Resisted Staggered Ankle Dominant: Adjust the resistance tool to accommodate the staggered stance. Negotiate any obstacles, such as dumbbells, and perform ankle movements in both legs simultaneously. This creates a resisted overload throughout the full range of motion in the ankle-dominant position.

Coaching Tip: Encourage athletes to maintain stability and control while performing ankle movements in the staggered stance. Emphasise the specific muscles targeted in each leg (gastrocnemius for the leg behind and soleus for the leg in front).

3. Resisted Unilateral Ankle Dominant: Modify the resistance tool for the unilateral position. The leg behind, positioned further back, emphasises the gastrocnemius, while the leg in front emphasises the soleus. Perform ankle movements with the appropriate resistance, focusing on quality load and specific muscle activation.

   Coaching Tip: Guide athletes to maintain proper form and balance while performing ankle movements with the resistance in the unilateral position. Emphasise the specific muscle activation and the challenge provided by the resistance.

These teaching points emphasise the importance of anchoring the resistance appropriately for resisted ankle-dominant movements. By incorporating the resistance tool, athletes can experience specific overload and challenge their ankle strength. Encourage athletes to focus on maintaining proper form, technique, and muscle activation throughout each exercise. Gradually progressing from bilateral to staggered and then to unilateral variations provides athletes with a comprehensive and specific ankle training experience.

Ankle Series - Overspeed

In the overspeed variations, the focus shifts to eccentric rate of force development, motor unit recruitment, and increasing velocities. These exercises emphasise the eccentric phase of ankle movement and can be used with resistance bands or as bodyweight exercises. It is recommended to initially perform them as bodyweight exercises in conjunction with a plyometric jump program. The overspeed variations are ankle-dominant and aim to push into the floor and quickly stop the movement. Again all positions remain as pictured previously.

Teaching Points :

1. Bodyweight Overspeed Variation: Start in a bilateral position and focus on the eccentric phase of ankle movement. Drop the calf quickly and stop the movement abruptly. Emphasise pushing into the floor and engaging the calf muscles.

   Coaching Tip: Guide athletes to exert maximum effort in pushing into the floor and quickly stopping the movement. Ensure that no other body segment changes position, maintaining focus on ankle dominance.

2. Staggered Overspeed Variation: Transition to the staggered position, taking into account any obstacles such as dumbbells. Drop and catch the calf quickly and stop the movement abruptly. Maintain ankle dominance and focus on the eccentric phase of ankle movement.

Coaching Tip: Encourage athletes to perform the overspeed variation with intensity and precision. Emphasise the importance of no segment of the body changing its position, keeping the focus solely on ankle dominance.

3. Unilateral Overspeed Variation: Move into the unilateral position, considering the appropriate foot positioning for gastrocnemius and soleus dominance. Drop and stop the calf quickly and abruptly, maintaining ankle dominance throughout the movement.

    Coaching Tip: Guide athletes to focus on exerting maximum effort and performing the overspeed variation with control and precision. Emphasise the eccentric phase of ankle movement and the importance of stopping the movement abruptly.

After a period of time, athletes can incorporate band overload in conjunction with the overspeed variations to further challenge the ankle muscles and enhance training effectiveness.

These teaching points highlight the eccentric phase of ankle movement in overspeed variations. By incorporating these exercises, athletes can improve eccentric rate of force development, motor unit recruitment, and movement velocities. Emphasise proper form, intensity, and control throughout each exercise. Gradually progressing from bodyweight variations to band overload provides athletes with a comprehensive ankle training experience.

Ankle Series - "Plyometric" Series

In the final piece of the puzzle, angular displaced positions or wall drill positions are used to create plyometric variations. These exercises focus on creating specific stiffness and reactive strength qualities within the ankle and foot complex. The goal is to develop vertical and horizontal displacement qualities that cannot be replicated through traditional jump means. The exercises include bilateral, staggered, and unilateral variations, emphasising ankle stiffness and reactivity.

Wall pogo

Teaching Points (Teaching Manual Style):

1. Bilateral Angular Displaced Position: Start in a bilateral position, focusing on ankle stiffness and reactivity. Perform the wall pogo exercise, maintaining stability and avoiding changes in hip and knee angles. Emphasise the bouncing motion at the ankle while keeping other body segments steady.

    Coaching Tip: Guide athletes to maintain ankle stiffness and reactivity throughout the wall pogo exercise. Encourage a steady bounce motion at the ankles while avoiding excessive movement in other body segments.

2. Staggered Angular Displaced Position: Transition to the staggered position, using the same principles of ankle stiffness and reactivity. Utilise an elbow bend to push against the wall and create stiffness. Perform the wall pogo exercise, maintaining stability and stiffness in the ankles.

   Coaching Tip: Encourage athletes to use the elbow bend to their advantage, allowing them to push against the wall and maintain ankle stiffness. Emphasise the importance of stability and controlled bouncing in the staggered position.

3. Unilateral Angular Displaced Position: Move into the unilateral position, which provides a challenging exercise for ankle development. Perform the wall pogo exercise, focusing on ankle stiffness, reactivity, and controlled bouncing. This exercise is intense and demanding on the ankles.

   Coaching Tip: Guide athletes to maintain ankle stiffness and reactivity in the unilateral position. Emphasise controlled bouncing and stability while avoiding excessive movement in other body segments.

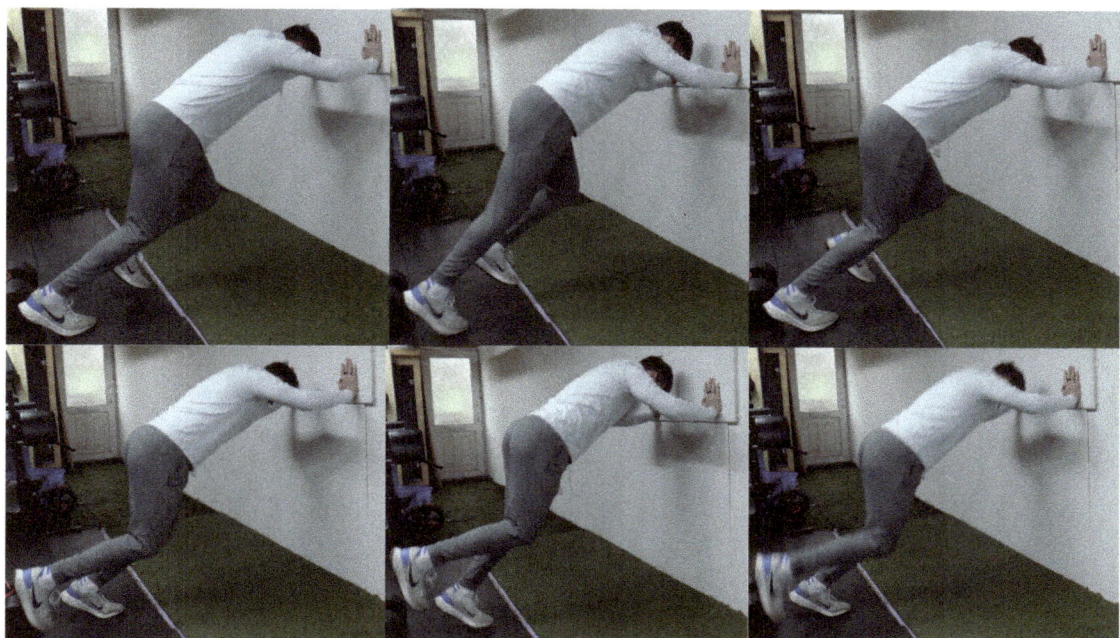

These teaching points highlight the importance of ankle stiffness and reactivity in inclined positions. The wall drill exercises help develop specific qualities needed for ankle performance. Encourage athletes to focus on maintaining stability, controlled bouncing, and ankle reactivity throughout each exercise. These exercises provide a challenging workout that targets the ankle complex and enhances its reactive capabilities.

Note: Ensure that athletes perform these exercises within their capabilities and avoid overexertion. Gradually progress the intensity and duration as athletes develop strength and stability in the ankle complex.

Knee Series

Knee Series - Yielding Isometric

In the yielding knee dominant activity, the focus is on optimising knee flexion and loading the knee in the correct area. This is especially important for athletes who struggle with creating optimal knee flexion and experience knee pain. By emphasising the knee segment, athletes can improve knee function and reduce discomfort. The exercises build on the calf and ankle variations, with specific tweaks to target the knee.

Teaching Points:

1. Bilateral Yielding Knee Dominant: Start in a bilateral position, similar to the calf and ankle variations. However, now focus on creating a deeper knee angle while maintaining stability in the calf and hip. Increase knee flexion without changing the ankle or hip positions.

   Coaching Tip: Guide athletes to achieve optimal knee flexion by emphasising a deeper knee angle while keeping the ankle and hip stable. Emphasise loading the VMO (vastus medialis obliquus) and the distal quad muscles.

2. Staggered Yielding Knee Dominant: Transition to the staggered position, maintaining the changes in knee angle and loading. In this position, the knee flexion is deeper, and there is increased tension through the knees. To intensify the load, dip the hips slightly while maintaining stability.

   Coaching Tip: Encourage athletes to maintain a stable ankle and hip position while focusing on the increased knee flexion and tension. Emphasise loading the VMO and distal quad muscles in the staggered position.

3. Single-Leg Yielding Knee Dominant: Progress to the single-leg variations, both in the front stagger and back stagger positions. As the knee angle becomes more pronounced, athletes may experience shaking due to increased tension and demand on the knee muscles.

Coaching Tip: Guide athletes to maintain balance and stability while performing the single-leg variations. Emphasise the deep knee flexion and the load placed on the VMO and distal quad muscles. Encourage rotation between the front stagger and back stagger positions to work both sides of the knee.

These teaching points highlight the importance of optimising knee flexion and loading in the yielding knee dominant activity. By emphasising the knee segment and making slight adjustments to the calf and ankle variations, athletes can improve knee function and reduce discomfort. Emphasise proper form, stability, and control throughout each exercise. Gradually progress the depth of knee flexion as athletes develop strength and stability in the knee complex.

Knee Series - Overcoming Isometrics

In overcoming, knee-dominant, activity the focus is on creating sensations of overcoming resistance in the knee joint. This involves pushing through the knees while maintaining optimal knee and ankle positions. The exercises target the knee joint specifically and emphasise opening up the knee joint with maximal effort. The positions include bilateral, single-leg, and backside staggered variations.

Teaching Points:

1. Bilateral Overcoming Knee Dominant: Start in a bilateral position with more knee bend, ensuring that the ankles remain stable and do not move. The goal is to push through the knees and generate maximum tension in the knee joint. Focus on opening up the knee joint with forceful effort.

   Coaching Tip: Encourage athletes to push through the knees while maintaining stability in the ankles. Emphasise creating sensations of overcoming resistance in the knee joint by generating maximal tension. Instruct athletes to drop their hips into lower knee-dominant positions to intensify the knee joint loading.

2. Staggered Overcoming Knee Dominant: Progress to the staggered-leg variation, maintaining the focus on opening up the knee joint. With one leg at a time, athletes should push through the knee, creating a sensation of overcoming resistance and generating tension in the knee joint.

   Coaching Tip: Guide athletes to maintain balance and stability while focusing on pushing through the knee joint. Emphasise the effort to open up the knee joint and generate maximal tension. Encourage proper form and control throughout the exercise.

3. Unilateral Knee Emphasis Overcoming: Move to the unilateral variation, which places the emphasis on end-range knee extension loading. Similar to the previous variations, athletes should push through the knee joint, aiming to open it up with maximal effort.

   Coaching Tip: Instruct athletes to adopt the backside staggered position and Emphasise pushing through the knee joint. Encourage athletes to focus on end-range knee extension loading, feeling the tension in the knee joint. Use time brackets that support the desired adaptation and provide sufficient challenge.

Rehabilitation and the Sports Speed System

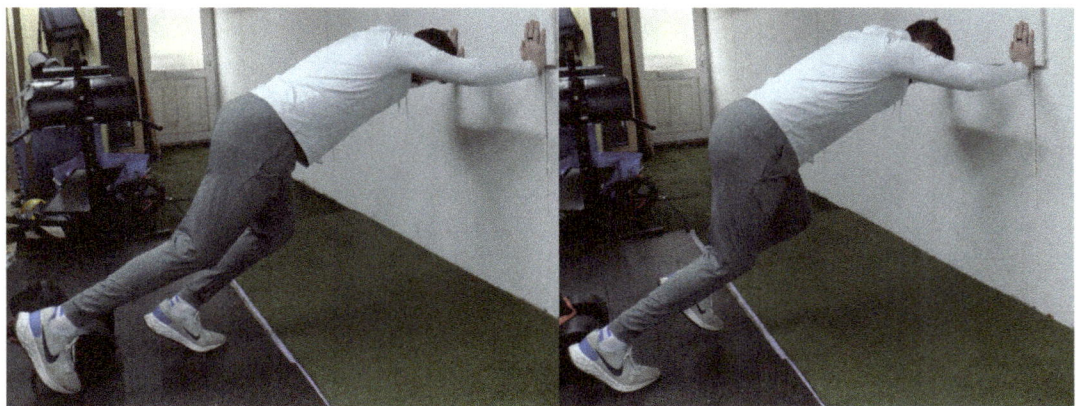

These teaching points highlight the importance of generating sensations of overcoming resistance in the knee joint through the overcoming knee dominant activity. Emphasise the push through the knees and the effort to extend the knee joint with maximal tension. Encourage athletes to maintain stability and control in each position while focusing on the knee joint. Gradually progress the intensity and duration of the exercises to support adaptation and improve knee function.

Knee Series - Full Range of Motion

The full range of motion variations for knee-dominant movement aims to combine different positions and ranges of motion while emphasising knee-dominant action. These exercises help develop knee strength, mobility, and stability. Coaches should use their intuition to observe and adjust the exercises according to their athletes' needs.

1. Bilateral Full Range: Start in a bilateral position and focus on deepening the knee flexion range. Move through deep squats while maintaining proper form and control. Open up through knee extension to complete the full range of motion.

    Coaching Tip: Encourage athletes to go deep into the squat position while maintaining stability and control. Emphasise the full range of motion from deep flexion to full knee extension.

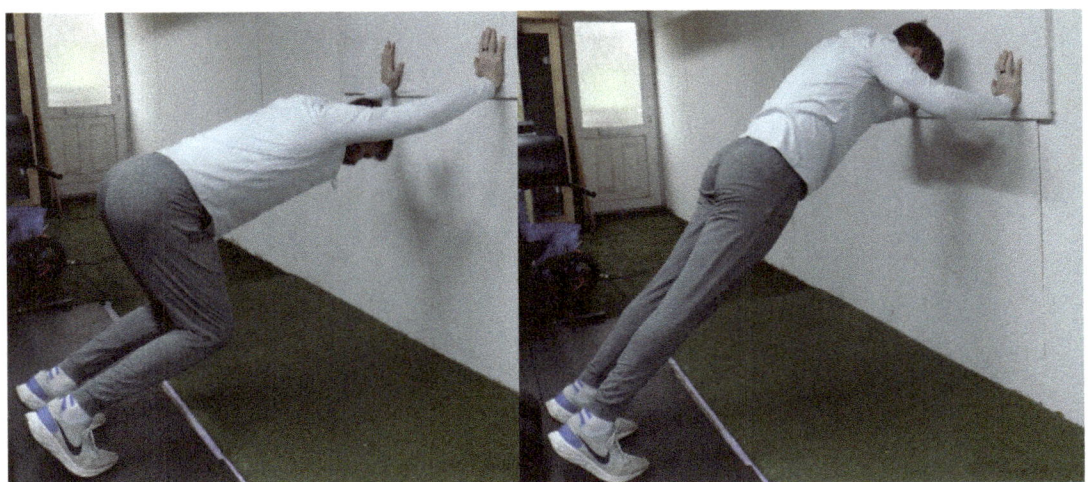

2. Staggered Full Range: Progress to the staggered position, where athletes can further deepen their knee range of motion. Lower the hips closer to the ground and push through the knees to activate the knee-dominant action. Alternate between legs, ensuring proper form and control throughout.

   Coaching Tip: Guide athletes to deepen and compress their positions by getting lower to the ground. Emphasise the direction of force through the knees while maintaining stability. Encourage smooth transitions and control during the exercise.

3. Unilateral Full Range: The unilateral variation challenges knee health and stability by placing a greater load on a single leg. Start with the typical single-leg position and then work on achieving a deeper knee flexion range. Focus on maintaining proper form and control while pushing through the knee.

   Coaching Tip: Help athletes find their balance and stability in the single-leg position. Encourage deeper knee flexion and Emphasise the outer range of the knee movement. Highlight the knee health benefits of these exercises, particularly for athletes with knee pain.

These full range of motion variations for knee-dominant movement provide opportunities to develop knee strength, mobility, and stability. Encourage athletes to explore the full range of motion, from deep flexion to full extension, while maintaining proper form and control. Adjust the exercises based on individual needs and goals.

Knee Series - Resisted

The resisted knee variations focus on developing specific strength and power qualities for acceleration. These exercises provide a simple setup using resistance bands, making them accessible even without a gym. They target the knee joint and the quad muscles. Here we are applying an external resistance to the full range of motion movements previously described.

1. Bilateral Resisted Knees: Attach a resistance band around the knees or use red bands as an alternative. Start with a deep knee angle and sink into the squat position. Push out against the resistance, emphasising the quad muscles. Sink and push for a challenging quad-dominant movement.

   Coaching Tip: Encourage athletes to sink deeper into the squat position to increase the loading on the quads. Emphasise the pushing action against the resistance bands.

2. Staggered Resisted Knees: Maintain the resistance band setup. Assume a staggered stance and drop into a deeper knee angle. Push out against the resistance, focusing on the quad-dominant action. Alternate between legs to work both sides.

   Coaching Tip: Guide athletes to drop deeper into the staggered position, feeling the increased quad activation. Emphasise the sinking and pushing motions to generate force against the resistance bands.

3. Unilateral Resisted Knees: Use the resistance band setup for a single leg. Drop into a deep knee angle and push against the resistance. This exercise places a greater load on a single leg, challenging strength and stability.

Coaching Tip: Assist athletes in finding their balance and stability in the single-leg position. Encourage them to push against the resistance band, targeting the quad muscles. Emphasise control and proper form throughout the movement.

These resisted knee variations offer a challenging and effective way to develop quad strength and power for acceleration. The simplicity of the setup makes them accessible for athletes with limited gym access. Adjust the resistance bands according to individual strength levels and gradually increase the load over time.

Knee Series - Overspeed

The overspeed variations for knee-dominant movements are challenging and specific, targeting the knee and hip flexors. These exercises involve a unique body position that alters the force curve and requires precise control. The overspeed variations are knee dominant and aim to rapidly decrease the knee angles and achieve abrupt stops at the desired eagles as pictured. Again all positions remain as pictured previously.

1. Bilateral Overspeed Knees: Begin in a compressed position with elbows on the knees. Drop into a deep squat with a focus on knee flexion and hip flexor engagement. Sink into the squat while maintaining control and stability.

   Coaching Tip: Emphasise the compression and sinking motion, ensuring athletes maintain proper form and control throughout the movement.

2. Staggered Overspeed Knees: Assume a tall position and drop into a staggered stance. Focus on dropping and sinking into a deep knee angle while keeping the hip flexors engaged. Alternate between legs to work both sides.

   Coaching Tip: Guide athletes to drop deeper into the staggered position, maintaining control and stability. Emphasise the importance of hip flexor activation in this exercise.

3. Unilateral Overspeed Knees: Perform the exercise unilaterally, focusing on a single leg. Drop into a deep knee angle, emphasising knee flexion and hip flexor engagement. Control the movement and maintain stability throughout.

   Coaching Tip: Assist athletes in finding their balance and stability in the single-leg position. Encourage them to drop and sink deeper, maintaining control and engaging the hip flexors.

These overspeed variations are challenging due to the altered force curve and specific demands placed on the knee and hip flexors. They require athletes to control their movement while generating force in a compressed position. Proper form, control, and stability are crucial for these exercises. Gradually increase the intensity and speed of the movements over time to further enhance knee-dominant strength and power for acceleration.

Knee Series - "Plyometric"

The plyometric variations for knee-dominant activity focus on developing specific strength and power around the knee joint. These exercises are challenging and aim to reduce contact times while generating explosive force.

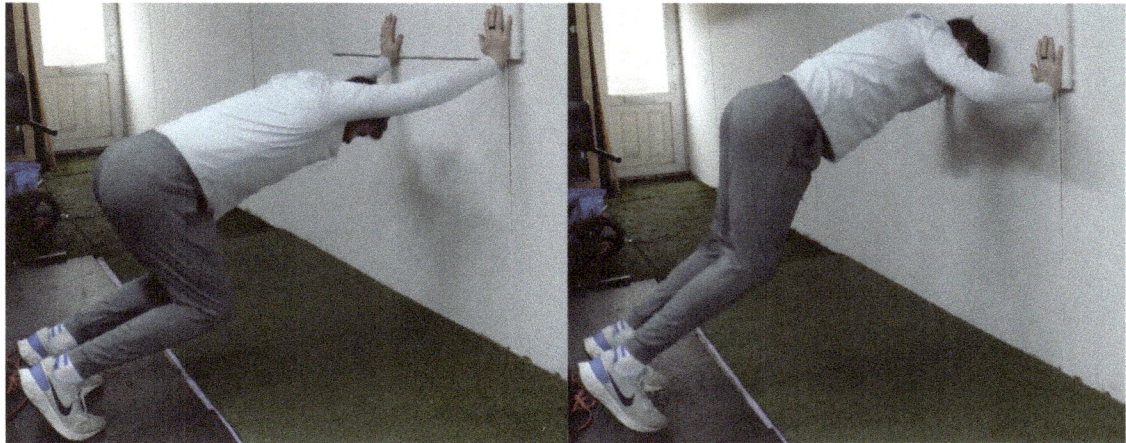

1. Bilateral Plyometric Knees: Start in a deep knee flexion position and focus on pushing yourself back into the ground, emphasising knee flexion. The goal is to generate force quickly and explosively, reducing contact times.

   Coaching Tip: Emphasise the explosive push-off and the quick transition from the deep knee flexion position. Encourage athletes to generate maximum power while maintaining control and stability.

2. Staggered Plyometric Knees: Perform the exercise in a staggered stance, pushing off explosively and driving the knee angles. Focus on reducing contact times and generating power in each repetition.

   Coaching Tip: Guide athletes to push off forcefully from the staggered position, emphasising the explosive movement and quick transitions. Ensure proper knee flexion and stability throughout the exercise.

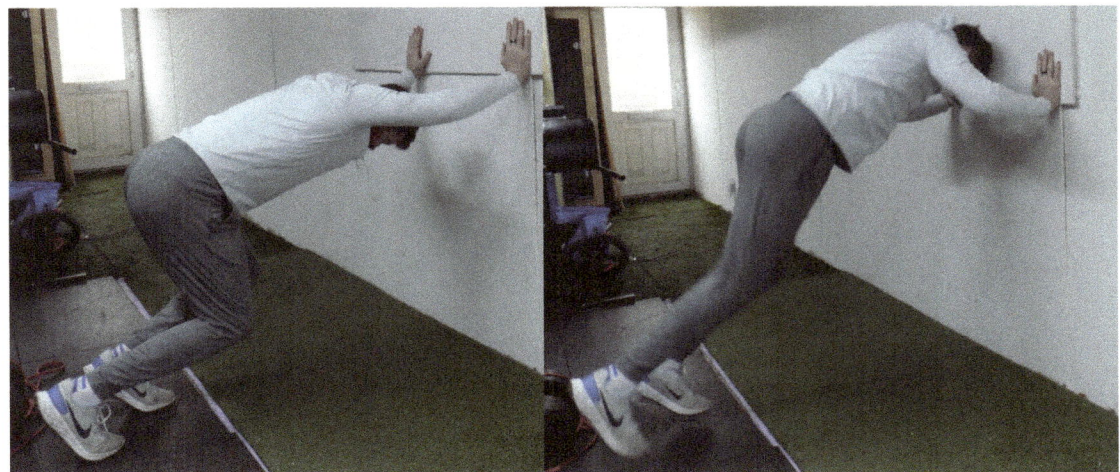

3. Unilateral Plyometric Knees: Perform the exercise unilaterally, focusing on a single leg. Generate explosive force by pushing off the ground and driving the knee angle. Aim for minimal contact times and maximum power output.

   Coaching Tip: Assist athletes in maintaining balance and stability during the single-leg plyometric movements. Encourage them to generate explosive power from the knee dominant position while ensuring proper form and control.

These plyometric variations are intense and focus on generating explosive force from knee-dominant positions. The goal is to reduce contact times and increase power output. Proper form, control, and stability are crucial for performing these exercises safely and effectively. Start with lower intensity and gradually increase the speed and power as athletes become more proficient. Use these variations sparingly, incorporating them strategically into training programs to enhance knee-dominant strength and power for acceleration.

Hip Series

Hip Series - Yielding Isometrics

The yielding hip sequence focuses on activating and strengthening the hip muscles, particularly the glutes. These exercises Emphasise different angles and hip hinge positions to target the hip muscles effectively.

1. Bilateral Hip Hinge: Begin with a bilateral stance, bringing the feet closer together to create a greater hip hinge angle. Focus on tucking the pelvis, engaging the glutes, and holding the position to activate the hip muscles.

   Coaching Tip: Encourage athletes to maintain proper form and alignment throughout the exercise, emphasising the activation of the glutes. Ensure they understand the hip hinge movement and feel the tension in their hip muscles.

2. Staggered Hip Hinge: Transition into a staggered stance, maintaining the hip hinge position. Sink into the stance, focusing on hinging the hip out and feeling the activation in the glutes. This exercise targets the hip muscles from a different angle.

   Coaching Tip: Guide athletes to maintain stability and control in the staggered position while hinging at the hips. Emphasise the activation of the glutes and the feeling of tension in the hip muscles.

3. Single-Leg Hip Hinge: Progress to a single-leg stance, alternating between legs in a staggered position. Focus on hinging the hip out, engaging the glutes, and holding the position. This exercise challenges stability and further activates the hip muscles.

   Coaching Tip: Assist athletes in maintaining balance and control during the single-leg stance. Encourage them to focus on the hip hinge movement, feeling the glutes working and maintaining stability throughout.

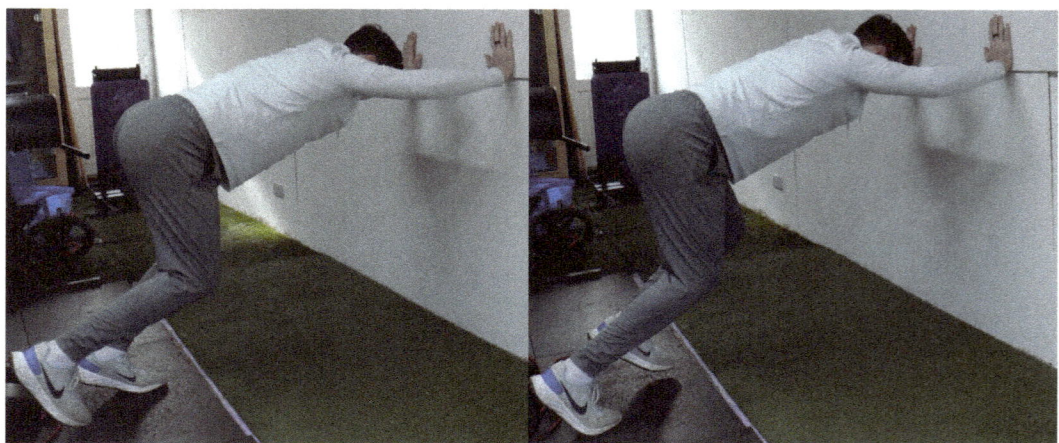

By emphasising different angles and positions in the yielding hip sequence, athletes can effectively activate and strengthen their hip muscles, specifically the glutes. These exercises target the hip hinge movement, promoting stability, strength, and activation of the hip muscles. Ensure athletes maintain proper form and gradually increase the intensity as they become more comfortable and proficient with the exercises.

Hip Series - Overcoming Isometrics

Exercise Summary: The overcoming isometric series for hip emphasis focuses on activating and strengthening the hip muscles, particularly the glutes, through isometric contractions. These exercises involve driving the hips into the wall while maintaining a locked torso and a hinged hip position.

1. Bilateral Hip Drive: Assume the wall drill position with an Emphasised hip hinge. Tuck the pelvis to engage the glutes and maintain a locked torso. Drive the hips into the wall, creating tension and activation in the hip muscles.

   Coaching Tip: Emphasise the importance of maintaining proper form and activating the glutes during the hip drive. Encourage athletes to generate as much tension as possible while driving their hips into the wall.

2. Staggered Hip Drive: Transition to a staggered stance while maintaining the hinged hip position. Again, drive the hips into the wall, focusing on maintaining the activation and tension in the hip muscles.

   Coaching Tip: Guide athletes to find the proper hinge position in the staggered stance and push their hips into the wall. Ensure they feel the activation in the hip muscles, especially the glutes, while maintaining stability.

3. Single-Leg Hip Drive: Progress to a single-leg stance, alternating between legs in a staggered position. Drive the hips into the wall, maintaining the hinged hip position and activating the glutes on each leg.

   Coaching Tip: Assist athletes in finding balance and stability during the single-leg stance. Encourage them to focus on driving their hips into the wall and maintaining tension in the hip muscles, particularly the glutes.

The overcoming isometric series for hip emphasis helps develop specific strength and muscle activation in the hip muscles. By driving the hips into the wall and maintaining the hinged hip position, athletes can effectively target and strengthen their hip muscles, particularly the glutes. Emphasise proper form, tension generation, and muscle activation throughout the exercises.

Hip Series - Full Range of Motion

Exercise Summary: The full range of movement exercises for hip emphasis aim to take the hip through its complete range of motion while focusing on specific muscle actions. These exercises involve driving the hips forward and backward while maintaining a hinged hip position and activating the targeted hip muscles.

1. Bilateral Hip Extension: Start in a bilateral position with a hinged hip, emphasising hip extension. Maintain a stable torso and avoid excessive movement at the knee and ankle joints. Drive the hips forward, extending them as much as possible, and then pull them back, maintaining tension in the hip muscles.

   Coaching Tip: Encourage athletes to focus on driving their hips forward and backward, feeling the activation and stretch in the hip muscles throughout the movement. Emphasise the maintenance of proper form and tension in the hip muscles.

2. Staggered Hip Extension: Transition to a staggered stance while maintaining the hinged hip position. Repeat the hip extension movement, driving the hips forward and backward, and maintaining activation and tension in the hip muscles.

   Coaching Tip: Guide athletes to find stability in the staggered stance and drive their hips forward and backward. Help them understand the importance of rolling their body weight forward and dropping the shin to engage the hip muscles effectively.

3. Single-Leg Hip Extension: Progress to a single-leg stance, alternating between legs. Drive the hip of the working leg forward and backward, maintaining the hinged hip position and activating the hip muscles on each leg.

    Coaching Tip: Assist athletes in finding balance and stability during the single-leg stance. Encourage them to drive their hips forward and backward, engaging the hip muscles and maintaining tension throughout the movement.

The full range of movement exercises for hip emphasis allows athletes to explore and strengthen their hip muscles through the complete range of motion. By driving the hips forward and backward while maintaining a hinged hip position, athletes can activate and strengthen the targeted hip muscles effectively. Emphasise proper form, tension generation, and muscle activation during the exercises.

Hip Series - Resisted Series

The resisted variations of hip extension aim to develop specific strength in the hip extensor muscles. These exercises utilise resistance bands placed around the waist to provide horizontal loading and create resistance during the hip extension movement. Ideally you would either anchor resistance directly to a rack or wall behind the athlete. Or in groups you can use an athlete to hold the band. Here we are applying an external resistance to the full range of motion movements previously described.

1. Bilateral Hip Extension: Place the resistance bands around the waist and assume a hinged hip position with a tucked pelvis. Drive the hips forward, extending them as much as possible, while maintaining tension in the hip extensor muscles. Emphasise the specific strength of hip extensors and the displacement of the centre of mass.

   Coaching Tip: Remind athletes to focus on driving their hips forward and extending them while maintaining proper form and tension in the hip extensor muscles. Emphasise the unique appearance of the movement due to the specific strength development.

2. Staggered Hip Extension: Transition to a staggered stance and maintain the hinged hip position. Drive the hips forward, extending them and creating tension in the hip extensors. Perform the movement with emphasis on end-range hip extension and push off both feet.

   Coaching Tip: Guide athletes to find stability in the staggered stance and drive their hips forward to engage the hip extensors. Encourage them to push through both feet to generate force during hip extension.

3. Single-Leg Hip Extension: Adjust the bands as needed and perform the hip extension exercise on a single leg. Drive the hip of the working leg forward, extending it while maintaining tension in the hip extensors. Focus on end-range hip extension to maximise the effectiveness of the exercise.

   Coaching Tip: Help athletes find balance and stability during the single-leg stance. Instruct them to drive their hips forward and extend the working leg while maintaining tension in the hip extensors. Emphasise the importance of maintaining proper form and muscle activation throughout the movement.

The resisted variations of hip extension provide an effective way to develop specific strength in the hip extensor muscles. By using resistance bands around the waist, athletes can create horizontal loading and resistance during hip extension movements. Emphasise proper form, tension generation, and targeted muscle activation during the exercises.

Hip Series - Over speed

Exercise Summary: The drop or overspeed variations for hip flexion aim to create forceful and aggressive movements into hip flexion, which ultimately supports hip extension. These exercises involve forcefully pushing the hips back into flexion and then driving them forward.

1. Bilateral Hip Flexion: Begin in an extended position, ensuring that the hamstrings and other muscles are relaxed. Lock the hips into position and thrust them back forcefully, emphasising hip flexion. The knee angle should remain relatively stable during the movement.

   Coaching Tip: Encourage athletes to find the proper position and forcefully push their hips back into flexion. Emphasise that the movement should primarily occur at the hips, rather than the knees or ankles.

2. Staggered Hip Flexion: Transition to a staggered stance, getting slightly lower to the ground. Again, drop the hips back and drive them forward forcefully, focusing on hip flexion. Maintain stability in the staggered stance and avoid excessive changes in knee angle.

   Coaching Tip: Guide athletes to find balance in the staggered position and Emphasise forceful hip flexion. Remind them to maintain stability in the stance and generate power from the hips.

3. Single-Leg Hip Flexion: Perform the hip flexion exercise on a single leg. Extend the non-working leg and drop the hips back, forcefully driving them forward into flexion. Maintain stability and control throughout the movement.

   Coaching Tip: Assist athletes in finding stability during the single-leg stance. Encourage them to generate power from the working hip and drive it forcefully into flexion. Emphasise the importance of maintaining balance and control during the exercise.

The drop or overspeed variations for hip flexion provide an opportunity to explore forceful movements into hip flexion, which supports hip extension. By focusing on aggressive hip flexion and maintaining stability in various stances, athletes can develop strength and power in the hip muscles. Emphasise proper form, stability, and the transfer of force from the hips during these exercises.

Hip Series - Plyometric

Exercise Summary: The plyometric variations for hip extension focus on explosive movements that involve the body leaving the ground. These exercises increase the rate of loading and require rapid absorption and dissipation of force through the body.

1. Bilateral Hip Extension: Begin in an extended position and Emphasise hip extension to generate a powerful pop off the ground. As you land, focus on rapidly increasing system stiffness and absorbing the force before pushing back into hip extension.

Coaching Tip: Encourage athletes to explosively extend their hips and generate upward force. Emphasise the need to quickly absorb and redirect the force upon landing.

2. Staggered Hip Extension: Perform the same explosive hip extension movement, but from a staggered stance. Drive the hips into extension and generate a powerful pop off the ground. As you land, focus on absorbing and redirecting the force, maintaining stability in the staggered position.

Coaching Tip: Guide athletes to generate explosive force from the hips and coordinate the movement with the staggered stance. Emphasise the importance of stability and control during the landing and transition back into hip extension.

3. Single-Leg Hip Extension: Challenge yourself with the single-leg variant of the plyometric hip extension. Focus on effectively transitioning into and out of hip extension, emphasising explosive extension without the leg leaving the ground too much. Maintain stability and control throughout the movement.

Coaching Tip: Assist athletes in finding balance and stability during the single-leg movement. Encourage them to generate power from the working hip and focus on the quality of the hip extension rather than the height of the leg lift.

The plyometric variations for hip extension aim to develop explosive power and force absorption capabilities in the hip muscles. These exercises involve explosive movements that require rapid force generation and control upon landing. Emphasise proper form, explosiveness, and stability during the movements to maximise their effectiveness.

Hip Flexion Series

Summary: The hip flexion action in sprinting is often overlooked and undertrained. However, it plays a crucial role in acceleration and early steps. To develop hip flexor strength, the wall drill can be used with the assistance of a resistance band. By lassoing the band around the thigh, the force against the lever grows, emphasising loading from the thigh instead of the foot. The drill includes yielding positions, activation from short and overcoming positions, full range of motion movement, and over-speed variations. These specialised exercises target the hip flexors and improve length tension relationships.

Teaching and Coaching Points:

1. Yielding Position:
   - Instruct athletes to assume a yielding position with optimal hip flexor length for acceleration, achieving a 90-degree thigh-torso angle in early steps.
   - Emphasise maintaining this position to create the desired muscular tension and alignment.

2. Activation from Short Position:
   - Teach athletes to activate the hip flexors from a short position, such as in a staggered stance, by driving the thigh forward and upward.
   - Encourage proper lumbar pelvic alignment and avoid excessive movement or breaking in the pelvis.

3. Resistance Band Placement:
   - Explain the importance of lassoing the resistance band around the thigh instead of the foot to emphasise hip loading from the thigh.
   - Ensure the band is securely anchored, either by hooking it under heavy dumbbells or having a partner assist.

4. Full Range of Motion Movement:
   - Guide athletes through a full range of motion movement, starting with a half step in a staggered position.
   - Emphasise maintaining a neutral pelvis and avoiding excessive backward movement of the thigh, focusing on hip extension through hip flexion.

5. Over-Speed Variations:
   – Over-speed variations can be performed by removing the resistance band initially.
   – Instruct athletes to forcefully drive the thigh backward using the glutes, rapidly extending the hip flexor and emphasising speed of movement.

6. Shock Variations (Optional):
   – Mention the possibility of incorporating plyometric variations, such as allowing the band to bounce back and hit the thigh, for further muscle fibre activation.
   – Note that plyometric variations can be explored in more advanced training stages.

7. Individualisation and Progression:
   – Remind athletes and coaches to adjust the resistance band tension and exercise intensity based on individual abilities and training goals.
   – Encourage gradual progression and proper form to ensure effective and safe hip flexor development.

Lumbar Pelvic considerations

Lightening Method

The lightening method is a training technique that uses a resistance band anchored to a rack to challenge pelvic stabilisation and core control. By pulling the athlete down, the band creates tension that requires the athlete to work hard to maintain stability. This method can be beneficial for groin rehab, hernia rehab, back rehab, and training deconditioned athletes. It activates the abdominal muscles and engages the entire kinetic chain. When using this method, it's important to focus on proper setup, body position, pelvic stabilisation, and individualisation of intensity and progression.

Teaching and Coaching Points:

1. Setup and Band Placement:
   – Attach the resistance band to the furthest attachment point on the rack and step over it.
   – Position the band on the small of the back, over the pelvis bone (iliac crest).

2. Proper Body Position:
   – Emphasise hip hinge and neutral spine alignment.
   – Engage the core muscles to maintain stability and resist the band's pull.

3. Stabilising Pelvic Rotation:
   – Highlight the significance of stabilising the pelvis to prevent excessive anterior-posterior pelvic rotation during the movement.
   – Cue the athlete to engage the trunk muscles and maintain a controlled pelvic position.

4. Application in Rehabilitation:
   – Explain the potential benefits of the band pull method for groin, hernia, and back rehabilitation.
   – Note how it helps develop core strength and stability, particularly in individuals with varied conditioning levels.

5. Engagement of Abdominal Muscles and Kinetic Chain:
   – Emphasise the activation of the abdominal muscles throughout the movement.
   – Discuss how the band pull method recruits and engages the entire kinetic chain.

6. Programming Considerations:
   - Recommend using the band pull method sparingly and incorporating it into conditioning workouts or as an adjunct to core training.
   - Highlight its versatility and adaptability for different training contexts, including rehabilitation and deconditioned athletes.

7. individualisation and Progression:
   - Encourage athletes and coaches to adjust the band tension according to individual capabilities and goals.
   - Emphasise the importance of gradual progression, proper form, and technique to ensure safe and effective training outcomes.

Lumbar Pelvic considerations - Accommodating Resistance

The band pull method is a valuable training tool that challenges athletes to stabilise their hips and core through movement. It involves using a resistance band attached to a rack and placing it on the small of the back. The band pulls the athlete down, creating an increased demand for pelvic stabilisation and trunk control. This method can be useful for various purposes, including groin rehab, hernia rehab, back rehab, and training deconditioned athletes. It serves as a substitute for core training and effectively engages the abdominal muscles and the entire kinetic chain.

Teaching and Coaching Points:

1. Setup and Band Placement:
   - Instruct athletes to hook the resistance band onto the furthest attachment point of the rack and step over it.
   - Guide them to position the band on the small of their back, over the pelvis bone (iliac crest).

2. Proper Body Position:
   - Emphasise bending over from the hips, maintaining a neutral spine, and engaging the core.
   - Encourage athletes to find a comfortable and stable position while feeling the band's tension pulling them down.

3. Stabilising Pelvic Rotation:
   - Highlight the importance of pelvic stabilisation, particularly in preventing excessive anterior-posterior pelvic rotation during the movement.
   - Explain how this method increases the demand on the trunk muscles to stabilise the pelvis effectively.

4. Application in Rehabilitation:
   - Discuss the potential benefits of using the band pull method in groin rehab, hernia rehab, and back rehab.
   - Note that it can assist in developing core strength and stability in individuals with various conditioning levels.

5. Engagement of Abdominal Muscles and Kinetic Chain:
   - Remind athletes that this method effectively targets the abdominal muscles and activates the entire kinetic chain.
   - Encourage them to focus on engaging the core and maintaining stability throughout the movement.

6. Programming Considerations:
   - Mention that the band pull method should be used sparingly and with proper programming.
   - Suggest incorporating it into conditioning workouts or as an adjunct to core training.
   - Highlight its versatility in different training contexts, including rehabilitation and conditioning for deconditioned athletes.

7. Individualisation and Progression:
   - Remind athletes and coaches to adjust the band tension and exercise intensity based on individual needs and capabilities.
   - Encourage gradual progression and proper form to ensure safe and effective training outcomes.

Using Wall Drills to Develop the Acceleration Pattern

Pushing from Bilateral Positions

Within the Sports Speed System we use wall drills with a lot of purpose. We use them in accordance with the development of the initial steps of acceleration. The focus is on learning how to piece together different movements and positions to create an effective run.

Teaching Points:

1. Front-side positions: Start in a bilateral position, which is a comfortable stance with feet shoulder-width apart. Lower into a squat position with triple flexion of the ankle, knee, and hip. From here, push into extension, emphasising the pattern of movement that is familiar to us.

Coaching Tip: Encourage athletes to practise and become familiar with the front-side positions, ensuring they can smoothly transition from the bilateral stance to the squat and extension movements.

2. Pushing into the front-side position: Once athletes are comfortable with the bilateral position, teach them to push from the double-leg stance into the front-side position. This involves shifting weight and pushing off one leg while bringing the other leg forward.

   Coaching Tip: Focus on developing the ability to generate power and push off forcefully when transitioning from the double-leg stance to the front-side position. Emphasise maintaining stability and balance throughout the movement.

3. Adopting the staggered position: Progressing from the front-side position, introduce the staggered position where one foot is slightly ahead of the other. From this position, practice pushing off forcefully into the front-side position again.

   Coaching Tip: Help athletes understand the importance of the two-point stance and how it contributes to stability and power generation. Emphasise the need to maintain proper alignment and balance in the staggered position for effective acceleration.

Overall, the teaching points focus on mastering the front-side positions, transitioning from double-leg stance to front-side position, and adopting the staggered position for improved acceleration. It's crucial to emphasise power generation, stability, and balance throughout the exercise.

Mastering the Unilateral Positions

Once athletes have mastered the transition from two legs to front-side positions (bilateral and staggered), the focus shifts to developing unilateral strength and power. This exercise places a higher emphasis on forcefully pushing through the front leg. By adopting a staggered position and leaving the back foot out, athletes are encouraged to generate a powerful push-off. Coaches should pay attention to proper hip extension, avoiding thigh rise or overextension, and emphasising a controlled stop.

Teaching Points:

1. Unilateral emphasis: After athletes have become proficient in transitioning from bilateral to front-side positions, it's time to introduce unilateral emphasis. This stage emphasises the ability to generate force and push strongly through the front leg.

    Coaching Tip: Explain to athletes that this exercise will require a higher level of emphasis on pushing forcefully through the front leg while maintaining balance and stability.

2. Staggered position with back foot off: Begin by adopting the staggered position with one foot slightly ahead of the other. In this exercise, the back foot is intentionally left out, creating an opportunity for a more pronounced push-off.

    Coaching Tip: Encourage athletes to focus on pushing off forcefully from the ground using the front leg. Emphasise the need for a proper depth change and extension for optimal results.

3. Proper hip extension and controlled stop: As a coach, pay attention to the near-side hip and its extension. The hip should smoothly move through flexion and achieve full extension as the athlete propels forward. Avoid any rise in the front thigh or overextension of the hip.

    Coaching Tip: Guide athletes to push and then come to a controlled stop. It is essential to maintain proper technique and positioning throughout the exercise, emphasising the unilateral emphasis and the ability to generate power.

These teaching points aim to develop unilateral strength and power by focusing on forcefully pushing through the front leg. Emphasise proper hip extension, avoiding thigh rise or overextension, and achieving a controlled stop. By mastering these elements, athletes can enhance their ability to generate force and power in a unilateral context.

Building Unilateral to Exchange

Exercise Summary: As we progress into movement, it becomes essential to focus on leg exchange and leg pattern exchange. These exercises possess a high level of skill transfer and dynamic correspondence, but they are specialised preparatory exercises. It's crucial to spend enough time working through these exercises to ensure proper development. When performing exchanges, it's important to understand that the body should stop moving upon ground contact. There should be stiffness, and the thigh should be in the same position as when the leg exchanges without excessive momentum carryover. The exercises are organised in levels and layers, with initial sessions starting from bilateral movements and gradually progressing to unilateral movements. This progression nurtures athletes and allows for skill acquisition. The exercise progression includes bilateral exchanges, adopting the staggered position, and finally moving into unilateral movements that emphasise a higher degree of ground reaction force and impulse.

Teaching Points

1. Leg exchanges and stiffness upon ground contact: When performing leg exchanges, it's crucial to emphasise that upon ground contact, the body needs to stop moving, exhibiting stiffness. The thigh should remain in the same position during the leg exchange without excessive momentum carryover.

   Coaching Tip: Coach athletes to focus on generating power and achieving a rapid scissoring motion of the legs during exchanges. Emphasise the importance of stiffness and stopping the body's movement upon ground contact.

2. Progression from bilateral to unilateral movements: Begin with bilateral exchanges, where athletes push off from a bilateral stance and exchange their legs. Gradually progress to adopting the staggered position and practising exchanges from this stance. Finally, move into unilateral movements that place a higher emphasis on the front leg for increased ground reaction force and impulse.

   Coaching Tip: Start with lower-level athletes, introducing them to sprinting and bilateral movements. Use load and execute principles, gradually adding complexity and load. Progress to staggered positions and unilateral movements, constantly nurturing and developing athletes' skills.

These teaching points aim to highlight the importance of leg exchanges and stiffness upon ground contact. They also emphasise the progression from bilateral to unilateral movements, focusing on developing power, scissoring motion, and ground reaction force. By following the recommended progression, coaches can effectively nurture athletes' skills and piece together the various elements of leg pattern exchanges.

Finding the Second Exchange

As we continue building the first three steps of acceleration with these drills, the focus now shifts to the second exchange. The goal is to understand the overall picture, which revolves around creating forward momentum while maintaining stability. The learn-load-execute principle and the stable-to-unstable framework play important roles in this process. With exchanges, the emphasis is not on forward movement, but rather on consistency, sharpness, and repeatability of the movement. The desired outcome is a sharp scissor-like movement pattern. The exercises progress similarly for bilateral, staggered, and unilateral positions, with a focus on sharp changes and aggressive movements.

Teaching Points:

1. Understanding the goal and creating sharp exchanges: Emphasise the importance of creating forward momentum while maintaining stability. With exchanges, the primary focus is on consistency, sharpness, and replicability of the movement. Athletes should aim for sharp and distinct changes between positions.

Coaching Tip: Guide athletes to perform exchanges with precision and intensity, ensuring that nothing is moving except for the legs during the scissor-like movement. Encourage them to emphasise the pop and sharpness of the exchanges.

2. Progression through variations: The exercises progress similarly for bilateral, staggered, and unilateral positions. Start with bilateral exchanges, then transition to staggered positions, and finally move into unilateral movements.

Coaching Tip: In each variation, emphasise big, aggressive movements and high volume. Athletes should aim for intensity and focus on intensifying the movement while maintaining proper technique and positioning.

By following these teaching points, athletes can develop the desired sharpness, consistency, and replicability in their exchanges. Emphasising the scissor-like movement pattern and progressing through variations will help athletes build their acceleration capabilities effectively.

Developing Wall Rhythm

As we progress from the initial steps of the pattern, developing rhythm becomes crucial. The Wall Rhythm Drill is an effective tool for achieving this. The drill focuses on building consistency, sharpness, and fluidity in movement, as sprinting relies on rhythm, timing, and coordination combined with force to create speed. By incorporating the Rhythm Drill, coaches can introduce variation and help athletes develop a consistent and rhythmic pattern within the coaching system. The drill emphasises maintaining a consistent step pattern, sharp ground contact, and minimal variation in leg movement.

Teaching Points:

1. Importance of rhythm: Emphasise that sprinting relies heavily on rhythm, timing, and coordination, which, when combined with force, leads to speed. Developing a consistent and rhythmic pattern is essential in building acceleration capabilities.

    Coaching Tip: Highlight the significance of rhythm in stable-to-unstable conditions and the step-by-step principle. Explain that while the rhythm remains consistent, the timing increases, resulting in faster movements.

2. Wall Rhythm Drill: Introduce the Wall Rhythm Drill as a valuable tool for developing consistency and sharpness in movement. Emphasise that the goal is not to perform the drill as fast as possible, but to maintain consistent steps and demonstrate sharp ground contact.

    Coaching Tip: Encourage athletes to focus on consistency in their step pattern, maintaining sharpness and fluidity in their movement. Listen for the rhythmic sound of steps and observe minimal variation in leg movement.

By incorporating the Wall Rhythm Drill, coaches can help athletes develop and refine their rhythm, leading to improved timing, coordination, and overall sprinting performance. The drill serves as a valuable tool within the coaching system, facilitating variation and consistent progress in acceleration training.

Introducing External Load

I encourage you to not use external load within these movements too soon. The reason being is that the athlete will need time to develop the key movements. They are layered in a specific approach in order to maximise the transfer of velocity and skill. This is in keeping with dynamic correspondence. After the athletes have demonstrated good skill competency feel free to include light band resistance.

Introducing Pattern Movements in the Sports Speed System

The pattern movement criteria becomes really useful when an athlete has demonstrated they have established skill and physical capacity in the segment and pattern based conditions. This unlocks the ability to explore projection and low to high horizontal orientation. An essential quality for acceleration.

Kneeling Wall Shoot

The kneeling wall shoots progression is a highly effective exercise for developing explosive power and force production. It involves starting in a kneeling position with the goal of generating force and propelling the body forward off the wall. The exercise focuses on progressing from stable to unstable to stable conditions, challenging the body to adapt and improve its ability to generate and control force. Key coaching points include proper setup and alignment, initiating the movement by leaning forward, unravelling the body to extend the pushing leg, gradual progression in speed and intensity, generating force through aggressive thigh punching, maintaining balance and stability during leg exchanges, and emphasising regular practice and repetition for skill refinement. The kneeling wall shoots can greatly enhance an athlete's power and performance capabilities.

1. Kneeling Setup:
   – Coach athletes to align the ball of their foot with the inside of their knee. This ensures proper positioning and stability during the exercise.
   – Emphasise the importance of maintaining an upright posture with shoulders down and core engaged.
   – Instruct athletes to find a comfortable and balanced position before initiating the movement.

2. Leaning Forward:
   – Encourage athletes to initiate the movement by leaning forward from the hips, while maintaining a strong and stable torso.
   – Remind them to keep their shoulders relaxed and avoid any excessive tension or rounding of the back.
   – Emphasise the need to maintain proper body alignment, with the head in line with the spine.

3. Unravelling the Body:
   – Guide athletes to allow their body to naturally unravel and extend as they push off the wall.
   – Cue them to extend the pushing leg fully, driving through the heel and engaging the glutes.
   – Remind athletes to keep their shin in line with the foot, avoiding excessive dorsiflexion or dropping of the knee.

4. Gradual Progression:
   - Start with slower and controlled movements, focusing on technique and body positioning.
   - Gradually increase the speed of the movement as athletes become more comfortable and confident.
   - Encourage athletes to find the right balance between speed and control, ensuring they can recover the leg before making contact with the wall.

5. Generating Force:
   - Coach athletes to generate force by punching the thigh aggressively during the movement.
   - Emphasise the importance of a powerful and explosive push-off from the wall.
   - Cue athletes to drive their hips forward and engage the glutes to maximise force production.

6. Controlled Exchanges:
   - Instruct athletes to maintain balance and stability during the exchange from one leg to the other.
   - Encourage them to focus on smooth and controlled movements, avoiding any sudden shifts or instability.
   - Remind athletes to maintain proper alignment and posture throughout the exchange, especially in the core and upper body.

7. Practice and Repetition:
   - Stress the importance of regular practice and repetition to improve proficiency in the kneeling wall shoots.
   - Encourage athletes to focus on refining their technique and progressively challenging themselves with increased speed and power.
   - Provide feedback and corrections as needed to help athletes develop proper form and maximise their training outcomes.

Remember to tailor the coaching points to the specific needs and abilities of the athletes and provide individualised feedback to support their progress.

Kneeling Wall Shoot Double

In this exercise, we continue to progress the kneeling wall shoots by focusing on increasing the number of steps taken on the ground before pushing off the wall. The goal is to achieve two steps on the ground in a crouched position before generating the force to propel forward. This is important for building momentum and creating a powerful push-off. As athletes become more proficient, resisted modalities can be introduced to slow down the movement and further enhance force development. The exercise involves a quick and explosive leg exchange, pushing off the wall, and finishing with speed and power. The extended variations demonstrate the potential for increased ground coverage and emphasise the need for controlled force application. Coaches should understand how to adjust the starting positions and implement resistance to suit the athlete's developmental stage and training goals.

Teaching and Coaching Points:

1. Starting Position and Leg Exchange:
   – Emphasise the importance of the correct starting position with the ball of the foot in line with the inside of the knee.
   – Ensure athletes understand the purpose of the leg exchange, which involves quickly transitioning from one leg to the other.
   – Encourage athletes to maintain stability and balance throughout the leg exchange.

2. Pushing Off the Wall:
   – Teach athletes to generate explosive force by pushing off the wall with power and speed.
   – Emphasise the need for a quick and aggressive push, utilising the leg that exchanged to attack and come through into the open space.
   – Remind athletes to maintain a low and crouched position during the push to optimise force generation.

3. Ground Contact and Momentum:
   – Explain the importance of achieving two steps on the ground before executing the push-off.
   – Emphasise the need for quick foot contact and an efficient transfer of force from the ground to propel forward.
   – Teach athletes to focus on building momentum by utilising the leg exchange and powerful push to generate speed and drive.

4. Resisted Variations:
   - Introduce resistance to slow down the movement and enhance force development.
   - Explain that resisted variations are more advanced and can help athletes develop greater force application.
   - Instruct athletes to adapt their technique to overcome the resistance while maintaining explosiveness and power in their movements.

Note: It's important to provide individualised feedback and corrections to athletes based on their specific needs and performance during the exercise.

Specific and Specialised Exercises for Developing Acceleration

As we progress through the stages of exercises used within the Sports Speed System, we are able to start to use more resisted variations of acceleration related movement. These have been structured in the order they are used within programming.

Kneeling Medicine Ball Wall Series

The exercise focuses on developing explosive hip extension through the use of a ball and wall. It aims to address the common issue of athletes accelerating with their feet instead of their hips or shoulders. By explosively driving the hips forward, the ball is propelled horizontally rather than vertically. The exercise starts with a bilateral movement, progressing to a step and driving variation. It emphasises finishing with the head over the ball and encourages upward rotation of the shoulders. The exercise can be performed with a lightweight metal ball and a wall. It can also be modified by incorporating a band for resistance, although this may reduce the emphasis on skill and velocity development.

Teaching and Coaching Points:

1. Understanding Center of Mass:
   - Explain to athletes that the ball represents the centre of mass.
   - Emphasise that the goal is to explode the hips forward, propelling the ball horizontally rather than vertically.

2. Hip Extension and Momentum:
   - Teach athletes to drive their hips through and finish with the ball hitting the wall.
   - Emphasise that the power comes from hip extension and momentum rather than the force of impact on the ball.

3. Head and Shoulder Position:
   - Instruct athletes to finish with their head over the ball, pushing themselves in the desired direction.
   - Encourage upward rotation of the shoulders to achieve proper alignment and movement.

4. Bilateral Hip Drive:

- Begin with a bilateral movement, focusing on explosively popping the hips forward and propelling the ball.
- Encourage athletes to generate power from the hips and achieve a strong forward motion.

5. Step and Drive Variation:

- Progress to a step and drive variation, where athletes sit back and then explosively drive the hips forward into a step.
- Emphasise the importance of getting the hips into the desired space and allowing the thigh to come through for ball contact.

6. Skill Development vs. Resistance:
   - Discuss the balance between skill development and resistance training.
   - Explain that while using a band for resistance can be beneficial for strength development, it may detract from skill and velocity aspects.

7. Speed and Specific Conditioning:
   - Emphasise that athletes who struggle with hip extension need specific conditioning and strengthening, followed by teaching them to speed up.
   - Note that heavy resistance may not be necessary, and the focus should be on developing explosive hip extension.

8. Encouragement of Hip Extension:
   - Motivate athletes to actively and forcefully extend their hips during the exercise.
   - Encourage them to pop through and finish with a strong hip extension for optimal results.

Kneeling Medicine Ball Release

This exercise focuses on building explosive hip extension and developing acceleration and speed. It bridges the gap between gym training and on-field application. By incorporating kneeling positions and using loaded or assisted variants, athletes learn to pop their hips through and attack space with power and speed. The exercise Emphasises ballistic muscle contractions and localised effort by decreasing rotational arm involvement. It offers a step-by-step progression, starting from simple explosive hip extension, adding a step, and eventually integrating it into a full step sequence. Athletes can perform the exercise facing each other for added challenge and variation.

Teaching and Coaching Points:

1. Importance of Explosive Hip Extension:
   - Highlight the significance of explosive hip extension for building acceleration and speed.
   - Explain how the exercise targets the specific muscle contractions required for optimal performance.

2. Kneeling Position:
   - Emphasise the benefits of starting from a kneeling position to isolate and load the hip extension movement.
   - Encourage athletes to focus on driving their hips through and attacking the space with force.

3. Variations for Overload or Assistance:
   – Introduce loaded or assisted variants to provide additional resistance or assistance.
   – Explain that these variations can help develop strength and power in the hip extension movement.

4. Localization of Effort:
   – Discuss the advantage of reducing the rotational arm involvement to localise the effort and target specific muscle groups.
   – Compare this approach to other exercises like granny toss or broad jumps.

5. Step-by-Step Progression:

   – Guide athletes through a step-by-step increase in intensity and difficulty.
   – Start with simple explosive hip extension, then add a step while maintaining the explosive movement.
   – Gradually build up to incorporating the exercise into a full step sequence.

6. Ballistic Contractions:
   – Highlight the importance of generating power and speed in the movement.
   – Encourage athletes to push themselves and perform the exercise with maximum effort.

7. Integration into Step Sequence:
   – Demonstrate how the exercise can be integrated into a full step sequence.
   – Explain the significance of transferring the explosive hip extension into practical on-field movements.

8. Partner Variation:
   – Suggest performing the exercise facing a partner for added challenge and variation.
   – This can create a competitive and engaging training environment.

9. Safety Precautions:
   – Remind athletes to be mindful of their surroundings and not to throw the ball outside of designated areas or at high velocities that could cause injury.

Kneeling Medicine Ball Step Up

In this exercise, the focus is on building step sequences and generating power and momentum using a medicine ball. A box or bench is used initially to create deceleration, as the work is primarily done off the ground. The exercise progresses from a single-leg loaded hip position to developing explosive strength for higher sprinting speeds.

Teaching and Coaching Points:

1. Importance of Starting Position:
   - Explain that starting from a compressed, loaded position with the ball in front of the body is specific to velocity and teaches explosive strength and acceleration.

2. Hip Pop and Step:
   - Instruct athletes to initiate the movement by popping the hips and stepping forward.
   - Emphasise the importance of generating power from the hips and driving through the step.

3. Punching the Ball Out:
   - Explain that punching the ball out in front of the body represents the centre of mass and the direction of force.
   - Highlight that this action helps generate momentum and speed in the desired direction.

4. Maintaining Proper Ball Position:
   - Remind athletes to keep the ball down in the early phase of the movement and ensure it travels with their hips.
   - Avoid over-rotation, as it can slow down the movement instead of accelerating it.

5. Generating Power and Momentum:
   - Emphasise the goal of creating significant power and momentum during the exercise.
   - Encourage athletes to focus on explosive hip drive and maintaining speed throughout the step sequence.

6. Progression and Step Sequences:
   - Explain that the exercise is designed to build step sequences, allowing athletes to develop higher sprinting speeds.
   - Encourage athletes to progress from the initial box or bench setup to performing the exercise without it, focusing on explosive power and smooth transitions between steps.

7. Importance of Proper Technique:
   - Emphasise the need for proper technique and form throughout the movement.
   - Instruct athletes to maintain good posture, engage the core, and drive with maximum effort.

8. Safety Precautions:
   - Remind athletes to be aware of their surroundings and perform the exercise in a safe and controlled manner.
   - Start with appropriate box or bench heights to ensure stability and reduce the risk of injury.

9. individualisation and Progression:
   - Remind coaches and athletes to adjust the difficulty and intensity of the exercise based on individual capabilities and training goals.
   - Encourage gradual progression and proper form to maximise the benefits of the exercise.

Implementation Of Prowlers

Progression in the exercises involves varying the start and hip heights and gradually increasing stride length, reducing ground contact time, and increasing momentum. Starting with an anterior load helps athletes focus on pushing forward and displacing their hips effectively. Key performance indicators (KPIs) include seeing a gradual increase in stride length, decreasing ground contact time, and observing the sled falling away from the athlete as a sign of speed improvement. Progressions can involve loading with posterior anchors like sleds and bands, but caution should be exercised to avoid excessive loads and rapid progression, as bands provide kinetic force and can increase tendon loading, potentially leading to injury.

Teaching and Coaching Points:

1. Importance of Mindset:
   - Explain the advantage of starting with an anterior load, as it helps athletes push forward and overcome external objects, creating a psychological advantage.

2. Gradual Increase in Stride Length and Momentum:
   - Emphasise the goal of gradually increasing stride length while reducing ground contact time and generating greater momentum.
   - Highlight that the sled should fall away from the athlete as an indication of speed improvement.

3. Loading with Posterior Anchors:
   - Discuss the use of sleds, bands, or other posterior anchors for added resistance and conditioning.
   - Remind coaches to consider the energy and kinetic force of bands and avoid excessively heavy loads to prevent excessive pulling and increased tendon demand.

4. Caution in Progression:
   - Stress the importance of gradual progression and avoiding rapid increases in speed or load.
   - Warn against spiking athletes too quickly or asking them to move too fast, as it can lead to potential injury and hinder their progress.

5. individualisation and Monitoring:
   - Remind coaches to tailor the progression and resistance levels based on individual athlete capabilities and goals.
   - Encourage monitoring and observation of KPIs to track improvements in stride length, ground contact time, and momentum.

6. Proper Technique and Form:
   - Reinforce the need for athletes to maintain proper technique and form throughout the progressions.
   - Emphasise the importance of maintaining good posture, engaging the core, and maximising effort and power in each step.

7. Injury Prevention and Recovery:
   - Discuss the importance of incorporating adequate rest and recovery periods into training to minimise the risk of injury and promote overall athlete well-being.
   - Encourage athletes to listen to their bodies and communicate any discomfort or pain to coaches and trainers.

Prowler Kneeling Push

The progression moves into resisted means, specifically using the prowler, to develop acceleration and maximal force production. The stable-to-unstable continuum is followed, gradually reducing stability to increase velocity while maintaining technical capacity. The focus is on isolating specific movements and maximising the window of opportunity for force production. The first progression involves starting from a kneeling half split position and transitioning into a shoot position while pushing the prowler forward. This challenges the body to react and maintain stability in an unstable environment.

Teaching and Coaching Points:

1. Understanding the Purpose:
   - Explain the purpose of using resisted means, particularly the prowler, to develop acceleration and maximise force production.
   - Emphasise the importance of gradually reducing stability to increase velocity while maintaining technical capacity.

2. Kneeling Half Split to Shoot Position:
   - Instruct athletes to start in a kneeling half split position, with one knee on the ground and the other foot forward.
   - Teach them to transition into a shoot position, where the rear knee is lifted off the ground and the body is leaning forward.
   - Emphasise the importance of staying connected, maintaining a strong core, and keeping the centre of mass oriented forward.

3. Pushing the Prowler:
   - Demonstrate how to push the prowler forward while maintaining stability and proper body alignment.
   - Encourage athletes to focus on generating force through the hips and maintaining a powerful pushing action.
   - Remind them to react and adapt to the prowler's movement, as it creates an unstable environment.

4. Gradual Progression:
   - Discuss the importance of gradual progression, starting with lighter resistance or fewer repetitions, and gradually increasing the challenge.
   - Encourage athletes to listen to their bodies and progress at a pace that allows for proper technique and control.

5. Maintaining Technique and Stability:
   - Remind athletes to maintain proper technique and body alignment throughout the movement.
   - Emphasise the importance of a strong core, engaged glutes, and a stable lower body to generate power and maintain stability.

6. Monitoring and Adjusting Resistance:
   - Advise coaches to monitor athletes' performance and adjust the resistance level accordingly.
   - Ensure that the resistance is challenging but allows for proper execution of the movement.

7. Safety Considerations:
   - Highlight the importance of proper warm-up and conditioning to prepare the body for the demands of resisted means.
   - Encourage athletes to communicate any discomfort or pain during the exercise and ensure they have proper supervision and guidance.

Rehabilitation and the Sports Speed System

Prowler Wall Shoot

In step two of the Prowler series, the focus is on developing stability and timing before overcoming resistance. The hands-off variation is introduced, where athletes start with their hands slightly further away from the Prowler. This creates instability and teaches athletes to shift their weight forward. The goal is to time the movement so that the shin drops and makes contact with the Prowler just before applying force. The emphasis is on maintaining a consistent and seamless movement.

Teaching and Coaching Points:

1. Understanding the Purpose:
   - Explain the purpose of step two in the Prowler series, which is to develop stability and timing before overcoming resistance.
   - Emphasise the importance of finding the optimal position and timing for effective force application.

2. Hands-Off Variation:
   - Instruct athletes to position their hands slightly further away from the Prowler compared to the hands-on variation.
   - Explain that this creates instability and challenges athletes to shift their weight forward.

3. Timing the Shin Drop:
   - Emphasise the importance of timing the movement so that the shin drops and makes contact with the Prowler just before applying force.
   - Demonstrate the seamless movement where the shoulders are forward, hands are on, and then the push occurs.

4. Consistency and Seamlessness:
   – Encourage athletes to aim for a consistent and seamless movement throughout the repetition.
   – Remind them to avoid initiating the movement before making contact with the Prowler, as it disrupts force application.

5. Maintaining Proper Body Position:
   – Remind athletes to maintain proper body position throughout the movement.
   – Emphasise the importance of a forward lean, engaged core, and an active shin drop to optimise force transfer.

6. Monitoring and Adjusting Technique:
   – Advise coaches to monitor athletes' technique and provide feedback to ensure proper positioning and timing.
   – Encourage athletes to make adjustments and refine their technique to achieve optimal results.

7. Gradual Progression:
   – Discuss the importance of gradual progression, starting with lighter resistance or fewer repetitions, and gradually increasing the challenge.
   – Remind athletes to focus on mastering the technique and timing before adding more resistance or intensity.

8. Safety Considerations:
   – Highlight the importance of proper warm-up and conditioning to prepare the body for the demands of the Prowler series.
   – Encourage athletes to communicate any discomfort or pain during the exercise and ensure they have proper supervision and guidance.

Prowler One Step Exchange

Summary: In step three of the Prowler series, the focus is on accessing the whole or close-to-whole parts of the acceleration movement specific to team sports. The progression moves from steps zero to three (focused on the first three steps of acceleration) to steps four to seven (targeting a 10-metre acceleration). The goal is to push, hit, and find step two while focusing on forward hip movement, toe-off, projection of the centre of mass, leg turnover, and solid ground contact. The emphasis is on creating a seamless movement and transferring the skills and adaptations learned from previous exercises.

Teaching and Coaching Points:

1. Understanding the Purpose:
   – Explain the purpose of step three in the Prowler series, which focuses on accessing the whole or close-to-whole parts of the acceleration movement specific to team sports.
   – Emphasise the opportunity to transfer the skills and adaptations learned from previous exercises.

2. Progression from Steps Zero to Three:
   – Discuss the progression from steps zero to three, which focused on the first three steps of acceleration.
   – Highlight the importance of building a foundation and mastering the key components before moving on to steps four to seven.

3. Forward Hip Movement and Toe-Off:
   – Emphasise the importance of driving the hips forward and achieving a powerful toe-off for effective acceleration.
   – Instruct athletes to focus on projecting their centre of mass forward and generating force through the back leg.

4. Leg Exchange and Ground Contact:
   – Explain the concept of leg turnover and solid ground contact for efficient acceleration.
   – Encourage athletes to aim for a seamless movement, with smooth transitions between the legs and a strong ground contact.

5. Focus on Technique and Coordination:
   - Remind athletes to maintain proper technique, body alignment, and coordination throughout the movement.
   - Provide feedback and cues to help athletes optimise their hip movement, toe-off, leg turnover, and ground contact.

6. Gradual Progression and Mastery:
   - Discuss the importance of gradual progression, starting with lighter resistance or fewer repetitions, and gradually increasing the challenge.
   - Encourage athletes to focus on mastery of each step before moving on to the next.

7. Monitoring and Adjusting Resistance:
   - Advise coaches to monitor athletes' performance and adjust the resistance level accordingly.
   - Ensure that the resistance is challenging but allows for proper execution of the movement.

8. Safety Considerations:
   - Highlight the importance of proper warm-up and conditioning to prepare the body for the demands of the Prowler series.
   - Encourage athletes to communicate any discomfort or pain during the exercise and ensure they have proper supervision and guidance.

Ballistic Prowler Push

In the resisted one to ten step motion, the focus is on accelerating from higher positions and creating momentum. The progression involves pushing and driving with maximum effort to generate explosive capabilities for early steps in acceleration, which are crucial in team sports. The goal is to perform multiple high ballistic efforts in continuous steps, teaching athletes to maintain explosive power and speed throughout the acceleration phase.

Teaching and Coaching Points:

1. Purpose of Resisted One to Ten Step Motion:
   - Explain the purpose of the resisted one to ten step motion, which is to develop explosive capabilities for early steps in acceleration.
   - Emphasise the importance of creating momentum and generating maximum effort.

2. Pushing and Driving with Maximum Effort:
   - Instruct athletes to push and drive with maximum effort during each step.
   - Encourage them to focus on generating explosive power and speed.

3. Creating Continuous Steps:
   - Explain the progression of performing continuous steps rather than isolated movements.
   - Emphasise the importance of maintaining explosive capabilities throughout the acceleration phase.

4. Ballistic Efforts and Early Steps:
   - Highlight the significance of early steps in acceleration, as they are crucial in team sports.
   - Encourage athletes to give their highest ballistic efforts during these early steps.

5. Technique and Power Transfer:
   - Remind athletes to maintain proper technique and body alignment during each step.
   - Explain the importance of effectively transferring power from one step to the next.

6. Monitoring and Adjusting Resistance:
   - Advise coaches to monitor athletes' performance and adjust the resistance level accordingly.
   - Ensure that the resistance is challenging enough to stimulate explosive capabilities, but not so heavy that it compromises technique.

7. Gradual Progression and Mastery:
   - Discuss the importance of gradual progression, starting with fewer steps or lighter resistance, and gradually increasing the challenge.
   - Encourage athletes to focus on mastering each step before progressing to the next.

8. Safety Considerations:
   - Highlight the importance of proper warm-up and conditioning to prepare the body for the demands of the resisted one to ten step motion.
   - Encourage athletes to communicate any discomfort or pain during the exercise and ensure they have proper supervision and guidance.

Prowler March

In the marching progressions with resisted anchor, the focus is on accessing the early stages of locomotion and developing dynamic flexibility. The goal is to continuously put the weight forward and maintain a forward momentum while marching. By pushing and driving with the sled in constant motion, athletes can work on creating horizontal and vertical displacement and accessing strength at length. The emphasis is on maintaining proper technique and encouraging weight forward throughout the movement.

Teaching and Coaching Points:

1. Purpose of Resisted Marching Progressions:
   – Explain the purpose of resisted marching progressions, which is to develop early stages of locomotion and dynamic flexibility.
   – Emphasise the importance of continuously putting the weight forward and maintaining forward momentum.

2. Technique and Weight Forward:
   – Instruct athletes to maintain proper technique throughout the movement.
   – Emphasise the importance of putting the weight forward and avoiding the tendency to attack the legs back.

3. Focus on One Foot in Front of the Other:
   – Encourage athletes to focus on putting one foot in front of the other in a continuous marching motion.
   – Remind them to maintain forward momentum and avoid negative steps.

4. Big Ranges of Motion:
   – In the early stages, encourage athletes to work through big ranges of motion to develop dynamic flexibility.
   – Emphasise the importance of accessing strength at length.

5. Continuous Sled Movement:
   – Ensure that the sled is continuously moving throughout the marching progressions.
   – Remind athletes to push and drive with the sled, maintaining a constant and consistent motion.

6. Monitoring Technique and Momentum:
   – Advise coaches to monitor athletes' technique and momentum during the resisted marching progressions.
   – Provide feedback on maintaining proper weight distribution and forward momentum.

7. Gradual Progression and Load Adjustments:
   – Discuss the importance of gradual progression, starting with lighter resistance or fewer repetitions, and gradually increasing the challenge.
   – Advise coaches to adjust the load on the sled to maintain proper technique and control.

8. Safety Considerations:
   – Highlight the importance of proper warm-up and conditioning to prepare the body for the demands of the resisted marching progressions.
   – Encourage athletes to communicate any discomfort or pain during the exercise and ensure they have proper supervision and guidance.

Prowler Bound

The next progression involves using a resisted bound to work on sequencing and timing in sprinting and acceleration. The goal is to develop explosive ballistics and create a gradual change in velocity. Key performance indicators include a stiff ankle, continuous forward hip movement, and driving the legs from behind. The sled should be continuously moving, and athletes should aim to gradually increase the distance between themselves and the sled. This will help decrease ground contact times, increase flight times, and alter the impulse on the ground.

Teaching and Coaching Points:

1. Purpose of Resisted Bound Progression:
   – Explain the purpose of using a resisted bound to work on sequencing and timing in sprinting and acceleration.
   – Emphasise the importance of developing explosive ballistics and gradually changing velocity.

2. Technique and Key Performance Indicators:
   – Instruct athletes to maintain a stiff ankle throughout the movement.
   – Focus on continuous forward hip movement and driving the legs from behind.
   – Remind athletes to pay attention to the key performance indicators of the movement.

3. Pushing and Bounding:
   – Encourage athletes to push and bound continuously, maintaining a consistent and rhythmic motion.
   – Emphasise the importance of a gradual increase in distance between the athlete and the sled.

4. Decreasing Ground Contact Time and Increasing Flight Time:
   – Highlight the goal of decreasing ground contact times and increasing flight times.
   – Explain how this can be achieved by bounding with the sled and gradually increasing the distance from it.

5. Monitoring Velocity and Technique:
   – Advise coaches to monitor athletes' velocity and technique throughout the resisted bound progression.
   – Provide feedback on maintaining a consistent velocity and proper technique.

6. Load Selection:
   – Discuss load selection based on the athletes' capabilities and progression.
   – Consider starting with a moderate to light resistance and adjust accordingly.

7. Gradual Progression:
   – Discuss the importance of gradual progression, starting with fewer repetitions or shorter distances, and gradually increasing the challenge.
   – Advise coaches to monitor athletes' response to the progression and adjust accordingly.

8. Safety Considerations:
   – Highlight the importance of proper warm-up and conditioning to prepare the body for the demands of the resisted bound progression.
   – Encourage athletes to communicate any discomfort or pain during the exercise and ensure they have proper supervision and guidance.

Prowler Prance

The next progression involves a resisted prance, also known as the Prowler prance. This drill focuses on combining stiffness, fast rhythms, impulse manipulation, and system stiffness. The goal is to develop the ability to utilise stored energy for continuous acceleration. Unlike the bound, the emphasis in the prance is on being effective and stiff on the ground rather than maximising forward distance. The drill requires a high cadence of leg action and Emphasises ankle stiffness at ground contact while managing the relationship between ground contact time and hip translation.

Teaching and Coaching Points:

1. Purpose of Resisted Prance:
   - Explain the purpose of the resisted prance in developing stiffness, fast rhythms, and impulse manipulation.
   - Emphasise the importance of system stiffness and utilising stored energy for continuous acceleration.

2. Technique and Key Performance Indicators:
   - Instruct athletes to maintain a high cadence of leg action during the prance.
   - Focus on being effective and stiff on the ground, emphasising ankle stiffness at ground contact.
   - Highlight the key performance indicators of continuous movement and a sled that never stops moving.

3. Emphasising Ankle Stiffness and Hip Translation:
   - Discuss the importance of ankle stiffness at ground contact and managing the relationship between ground contact time and hip translation.
   - Explain how these factors contribute to efficient acceleration and continuous forward momentum.

4. Rhythmic Leg Action:
   - Encourage athletes to maintain a rhythmic leg action throughout the prance.
   - Emphasise the need for a quick turnover and efficient foot placement to maximise the benefits of the drill.

5. Monitoring Ground Contact Time:
   - Advise coaches to monitor athletes' ground contact time during the prance.
   - Provide feedback on reducing ground contact time while maintaining proper technique and stiffness.

6. Gradual Progression:
   - Discuss the importance of gradual progression, starting with shorter distances or fewer repetitions, and gradually increasing the challenge.
   - Advise coaches to monitor athletes' response to the progression and adjust accordingly.

7. Safety Considerations:
   - Highlight the importance of proper warm-up and conditioning to prepare the body for the demands of the resisted prance.
   - Encourage athletes to communicate any discomfort or pain during the exercise and ensure they have proper supervision and guidance.

Implementation of Resisted Drags

In the absence of a prowler, the same progressions can be done using another person as a resistance or support. The goal is to systematically unload stability and encourage technical changes while maintaining the direction of movement. With hands off, the focus shifts to counter rotation and maintain stability without over or under rotating. If an athlete pops straight up during the exercise, it indicates the need for regression to reinforce and teach proper positions in a closed environment. The walk and march variations involve mimicking the arm movements with the legs and emphasising larger ranges of motion to access and change the degrees of freedom. With heavy resistance, it's important to observe athletes' ability to push their hips forward and apply force against the resistance.

Resisted March

Teaching and Coaching Points:

1. Using Another Human as Resistance:
   – Explain that if a prowler is not available, another person can be used as resistance or support for the progressions.
   – Emphasise the importance of maintaining stability and following the same systematic progressions.

2. Counter Rotation and Stability:
   – Instruct athletes to focus on counter rotation while keeping the hips in the desired position.
   – Encourage them to avoid over or under rotating and maintain stability throughout the movement.

3. Monitoring Vertical Movement:
   – Alert coaches to observe athletes for excessive vertical movement during the exercise.
   – If an athlete pops straight up, it indicates the need for regression and reinforcing proper positions in a closed environment.

4. Mimicking Arm Movements:
   – Explain the importance of synchronising the arm movements with the legs during the walk and march variations.
   – Emphasise larger ranges of motion to access and change the degrees of freedom.

5. Observing Force Application:
   – Advise coaches to watch for the ability of athletes to push their hips forward and apply force against the resistance.
   – Highlight that seeing the foot hit the ground and the hip pushing forward indicates successful force application.

6. Gradual Progression:
    - Discuss the importance of gradual progression, starting with lighter resistance or shorter distances, and gradually increasing the challenge.
    - Remind coaches to monitor athletes' response to the progression and adjust accordingly.

7. Safety Considerations:
    - Highlight the importance of proper warm-up and conditioning to prepare the body for the demands of the exercise.
    - Encourage athletes to communicate any discomfort or pain during the exercise and ensure they have proper supervision and guidance.

Resisted Bound

The resisted bound is a speed training exercise that focuses on developing explosive power and improving the sequencing and timing of sprinting and acceleration. By combining resistance and bounding movements, athletes can enhance their ability to utilise stored energy and maintain acceleration over longer distances. The exercise Emphasises ankle stiffness, ground contact time reduction, and effective hip translation. It is important to maintain a consistent rhythm and continuously push the sled to create momentum and increase impulse on the ground.

Coaching Points for Resisted Bound:

1. Purpose of Resisted Bound:
    - Explain that the resisted bound aims to improve explosive power, sequencing, and timing in sprinting and acceleration.
    - Emphasise the importance of utilising stored energy and maintaining acceleration over longer distances.

2. Establish Proper Resistance Level:
    - Select an appropriate resistance level that allows athletes to perform explosive movements without compromising technique.
    - Ensure that the resistance provides enough challenge to develop power but does not hinder proper execution.

3. Focus on Ankle Stiffness:
   – Instruct athletes to maintain a stiff ankle during ground contact to generate maximum power and energy transfer.
   – Emphasise the importance of driving off the ground with force and maintaining a quick rebound.

4. Reduce Ground Contact Time:
   – Encourage athletes to focus on minimising ground contact time during each bound.
   – Emphasise the need for quick and explosive movements to effectively utilise stored energy.

5. Maintain a Consistent Rhythm:
   – Guide athletes to maintain a steady and consistent rhythm throughout the exercise.
   – Encourage them to avoid any abrupt changes in pace or rhythm that may disrupt the flow of the exercise.

6. Push the Sled Continuously:
   – Remind athletes to continuously push the sled forward throughout the exercise.
   – Emphasise that the sled should never come to a stop, as the goal is to create momentum and increase impulse on the ground.

7. Monitor Technique and Adjust Resistance:
   – Regularly assess athletes' technique during the resisted bound and provide feedback for improvement.
   – Adjust the resistance level if necessary to ensure athletes can maintain proper form and execution.

8. Gradual Progression:
   – Start with lighter resistance and fewer repetitions, focusing on mastering proper technique and explosiveness.
   – Gradually increase the challenge by adding more resistance or extending the distance of the bounds as athletes progress.

9. Safety Considerations:
   – Prioritise proper warm-up and conditioning to prepare the body for the demands of the exercise.
   – Ensure athletes have proper supervision and guidance to prevent injuries and address any discomfort or pain that may arise.

Resisted Prance

The prance variations in speed training focus on developing velocity and improving force distribution and conversion. It is important to maintain the same relative load throughout the different prance exercises to assess the athlete's effectiveness in force distribution. Counter rotation and holding proper form are key technical aspects to focus on. Athletes should aim to hold shape and avoid overextension, which may occur with lighter resistance. Slowing down the movement and cueing the hip forward and feet off the ground aid in creating an effective transfer of force.

Coaching Points for Prance Variations:

1. Purpose of Prance Variations:
   – Explain that prance variations aim to develop velocity and improve force distribution and conversion.
   – Emphasise the importance of maintaining proper form and holding shape throughout the exercises.

2. Maintain Relative Load:
   – Keep the resistance load relatively constant across the different prance variations to assess force distribution and improvement.
   – Use the resistance as a guide for progress and adaptation.

3. Focus on Counter Rotation:
   – Instruct athletes to engage in counter rotation by twisting the upper body in the opposite direction of the lower body during the prance movements.
   – Emphasise the importance of controlled and coordinated rotation to enhance force production and efficiency.

4. Avoid Overextension:
   – Encourage athletes to avoid overextending or excessively pushing out in the prance movements, particularly when the resistance is lighter.
   – Emphasise the need to maintain proper form and control throughout the exercise.

5. Slowing Down the Movement:
   – Guide athletes to perform the prance exercises at a controlled and deliberate pace.
   – Remind them to focus on the transfer of force by slowing down and cueing the hip forward and feet off the ground.

6. Assessing Form and Shape:
   – Regularly monitor athletes' form and shape during the prance variations.
   – Provide feedback and cues to help athletes maintain proper alignment and technique.

7. Gradual Progression:
   - Start with lighter resistance and fewer repetitions to allow athletes to focus on technique and control.
   - Gradually increase the resistance or duration of the prance exercises as athletes demonstrate proficiency and improvement.

8. Monitor Fatigue and Recovery:
   - Pay attention to athletes' fatigue levels and ensure adequate rest and recovery between sets and sessions.
   - Adjust the training volume and intensity as needed to prevent overexertion and maintain optimal performance.

9. Safety Considerations:
   - Emphasise the importance of proper warm-up and preparation before performing prance variations.
   - Ensure athletes have proper supervision and guidance to prevent injuries and address any discomfort or pain.

Bound Variations to Improve Acceleration

Bound variations, including the floaty bound and speed bound, offer distinct benefits in training. The floaty bound focuses on rhythm, timing, coordination, and force properties within the developmental cycle. It emphasises the ability to maintain contact with the ground while moving forward. On the other hand, the speed bound emphasises stiffness and frequency. The goal is to hit the ground with maximum speed and force, propelling the athlete forward.

Let's dive deeper into the differences between speed bounds and floaty bounds and explore how they can be demonstrated in training:

1. Speed Bounds:

Speed bounds are characterised by quick and reactive movements, focusing on maximum ground contact force and forward propulsion. Here are some coaching points to emphasise during speed bound training:

- Quick Ground Contact: Emphasise the importance of minimal ground contact time. Encourage athletes to focus on pushing off the ground rapidly and forcefully, generating explosive power.

- Horizontal Projection: Emphasise forward momentum and the extension of the hip and knee joints to propel the body forward. Athletes should drive their legs forcefully into the ground, utilising the stretch-shortening cycle to maximise energy transfer.
- Stiffness and Rebound: Highlight the need for stiffness in the lower limbs during speed bounds. The ankles, knees, and hips should act like springs, absorbing and quickly releasing energy to maintain a rapid cadence.
- Arm Action: Emphasise the synchronisation of arm movements with leg actions. Encourage athletes to maintain an aggressive and powerful arm swing, driving the elbows back and forth to complement the lower limb actions.

To demonstrate the speed bound, athletes can perform a series of bounding exercises with a focus on maximising speed, power, and forward projection. The emphasis should be on explosive, rapid movements with minimal ground contact time.

2. Floaty Bounds:

Floaty bounds are characterised by a longer duration of ground contact, focusing on rhythm, timing, and coordination. Here are some coaching points to consider during floaty bound training:

- Controlled and Smooth Movements: Encourage athletes to maintain a controlled and smooth rhythm during the floaty bounds. The goal is to Emphasise the sensation of "floating" or remaining connected to the ground for a slightly longer duration compared to speed bounds.
- Hip Extension and Thigh Angle: Highlight the importance of hip extension and maintaining an optimal thigh angle during the floaty bounds. Athletes should focus on driving the knee forward and upward while maintaining a tall posture and elongated stride.
- Absorbing and Loading: Emphasise the ability to absorb and load energy during the landing phase of each bound. Athletes should focus on bending their knees and hips slightly upon landing to efficiently store and release energy for the subsequent bound.
- Rhythm and Timing: Encourage athletes to find a comfortable rhythm and timing between bounds. It should feel controlled and rhythmic, allowing for smooth transitions from one bound to the next.

To demonstrate the floaty bounds, athletes can perform a series of bounding exercises with a focus on maintaining a longer ground contact time, fluid movements, and an emphasis on rhythm and coordination.

By incorporating both speed bounds and floaty bounds into training sessions, athletes can develop a well-rounded skill set that encompasses explosive power, speed, coordination, and rhythm. Remember to gradually progress the intensity and volume of these exercises while providing individualised adjustments based on athletes' capabilities and training goals.

Utilising Different Start Heights as a means of Special Strength

Different height starts in the coaching program offer variability and variety, increasing the amount of force and time spent on the ground in early steps. These height starts also play a role in the force-velocity relationship. In the early stages of an athlete's journey, focusing on positions that allow them to discover and learn proper techniques is essential. As they progress, they can be tested in positions that require higher force and speed. Various height starts can aid in developing acceleration, explosiveness, and specific skills required on the field. Here's a breakdown of the different height starts:

1. Face-Down Start: Lay on the ground face down and pop up, bringing the foot through and driving to overcome mass. This position challenges athletes to exert force quickly from a static position.

2. Double Kneel Start: Start in a double kneel position and explode forward, emphasising early acceleration and hip drive.

3. Half Kneel Start: In a half kneel position, push forward to increase backside mechanics and force production.

4. Floating Shin Start: With a floating shin, maintain a low position while allowing the leg to move faster, enabling quicker movement.

5. Crouch Start: From a crouch position, launch and explode in various angles, emphasising quad dominance and force generation.

6. Quarter Squat Start: Positioned between a crouch and two-point stance, emphasise quick force production and the transition to standing.

7. High Two-Point Stance Start: From a high two-point stance, launch forward with long levers, simulating movements commonly seen on the field.

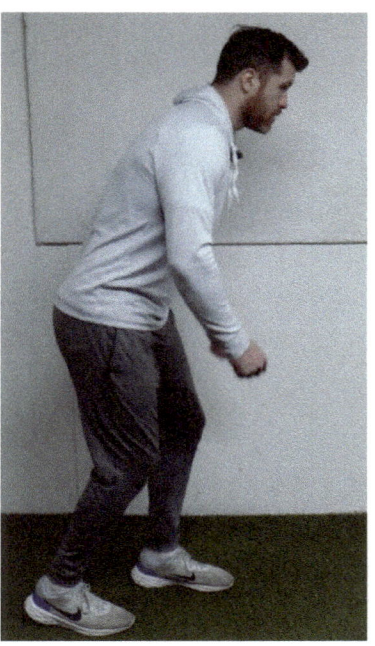

Coaching Points:

1. Emphasise Technique: Focus on proper technique in each height start position, ensuring athletes maintain the correct posture and alignment throughout.

2. Gradual Progression: Progress through the height start positions as athletes become more proficient, gradually introducing higher force and speed demands.

3. Specific Skill Development: Use different height starts to target specific skills required for their sport, replicating movements and positions they encounter on the field.

4. Individualised Approach: Tailor the selection of height starts based on individual athletes' body mass, limb length, and athletic capabilities, allowing them to explore positions that challenge them uniquely.

5. Strategic Use: Implement different height starts strategically in training sessions to focus on different aspects of acceleration and force production.

6. Time Under Tension: Utilising lower height starts to allow more time under tension and learning of positions, building a solid foundation for subsequent progressions.

By incorporating various height starts into the training program, coaches can effectively develop acceleration, explosiveness, and sport-specific skills in their athletes while ensuring a proper and progressive training approach.

Maximum Velocity Exercises within the Sports Speed System

To achieve maximum speed, a structured approach that includes special strength training and specific progressions is essential. Whether you are an athlete or a coach, this comprehensive guide will offer valuable insights and practical examples to help you excel in your quest for speed.

1. Understanding the Force-Velocity Curve:

To lay a solid foundation for speed development, it is crucial to grasp the concept of the force-velocity curve. This curve illustrates the relationship between force production and movement velocity. By understanding the force-velocity profile, athletes and coaches can identify the optimal zones for speed training. For example, sprinters often work on explosive starts to generate maximal force and velocity simultaneously.

Long Accelerations

Long accelerations play a vital role in speed development. This training method involves gradually increasing speed and loading on the working tendons. Athletes can implement long accelerations through progressive runs. For instance, a track athlete might start with a 30-metre sprint, gradually increasing the distance over time to 60 metres, 80 metres, and so on. This progression builds strength, power, and elasticity in the muscles and tendons required for maximum speed.

Bouncy Runs

Incorporating bouncy runs can further enhance speed development. Bouncy runs focus on maximising deformation at the hip joint, promoting bounce and stimulating the stretch-shortening cycle. Athletes can practise bouncy runs by emphasising a powerful knee drive and quick leg turnover.

Here are some important considerations when including bounce runs in your training program.

1. Specificity and Range of Motion:
   - Teach athletes the importance of specificity in training for speed development.
   - Explain how understanding the range of motion and amplitude of movement is crucial.
   - Emphasise that different drills and exercises can be used to target specific angles and ranges.

2. Developmental Physical Capacities:
   - Highlight the significance of proper physical development for athletes to effectively utilise higher velocity movements.
   - Explain that athletes should have the necessary strength, stability, and mobility to perform speed-focused exercises.

3. Bounce Runs:
   - Demonstrate and explain the concept of bounce runs, which involve spending more time on the ground to absorb and redistribute force.
   - Teach athletes the proper technique for ankle bounce runs, knee bounce runs, and high-angle knee bounce runs.
   - Emphasise the importance of maintaining appropriate knee bend and stiffness throughout the movements.

4. Complexity and Intensity:
   - Discuss how increasing the range of motion and velocity adds complexity and intensity to the exercises.
   - Help athletes understand that as they progress in their training, they can challenge themselves by expanding the range of motion and increasing the speed of execution.

5. Full Bounce Runs:
   - Explain the concept of full bounce runs, which start with a jump to overload the stretch-shortening cycle.
   - Teach athletes the proper technique for transitioning smoothly from the jump into the bounce phase.
   - Emphasise the importance of maintaining proper mechanics and form throughout the exercise.

6. Programming Considerations:
   - Teach athletes the importance of programming and determining the appropriate speed at which to perform these exercises.
   - Explain that speed improvement may not always require executing the exercises at maximum speed.
   - Emphasise the need to align the programming with the specific speed development goals and training phase.

7. Observation and Analysis:
   - Encourage coaches to observe athletes closely during these exercises.
   - Teach them how to analyse and assess an athlete's movement patterns, range of motion, and rate of force development.
   - Emphasise the importance of providing individualised feedback and making adjustments based on the observed performance.

By incorporating these coaching and teaching points, coaches and trainers can effectively guide athletes through the process of improving their speed development, ensuring proper technique, and maximising the benefits of the exercises.

Springy Runs

Springy runs are a type of exercise used to improve speed and enhance athletic performance. These runs involve variations of bounce runs and spring runs, which target specific joints such as the ankle, shin, and knee. The purpose of springy runs is to develop motor control, groove neural pathways, and increase power and speed through efficient movement patterns. By incorporating these exercises, athletes can learn to generate force quickly and improve their ability to move their legs at higher rates. Springy runs are beneficial for enhancing speed and overall athletic performance.

Here are some important considerations when including bounce runs in your training program.

1. Spring Variations:
   – Explain the concept of spring variations, which limit deformation at the joint angles compared to bounce variations.
   – Emphasise that the focus in spring variations is manipulating the time side of impulse rather than the force side.
   – Teach athletes to execute spring variations targeting the ankle, shin, and knee joints.

2. Neural Pathways and Motor Control:
   – Highlight the importance of grooving neural pathways through these progressions.
   – Explain that motor control is a key aspect, and athletes need to learn to move their legs at higher rates even at slower velocities.
   – Emphasise that developing motor control in slower movements will enhance speed performance in the future.

3. Ankle Spring:
   – Demonstrate and teach athletes the technique for the ankle spring, focusing on quick ground contact and maintaining an upright posture.
   – Explain how this exercise targets the ankle joint and helps develop the ability to generate power rapidly.

4. Shin Spring:
   – Teach athletes how to perform the shin spring, emphasising quick ground contact and an explosive push-off.
   – Explain that the shin spring targets the shin muscles and helps develop the ability to generate force and speed.

5. Knee Spring:
   – Demonstrate and explain the technique for the knee spring, emphasising fast movement through the knee joint.
   – Teach athletes to be deliberate and intentional in their knee spring, focusing on generating power and speed.

6. Progressions and Programming:
   – Discuss the use of progressions in incorporating these exercises into training.
   – Explain that the exercises can be used in different stages, such as low, medium, and high intensity.
   – Encourage coaches to incorporate the exercises strategically based on individual needs and training goals.

7. Jump Spring:
   – Teach athletes the technique for the jump spring, which involves overloading and shocking the stretch reflex in the body.
   – Explain that the jump spring helps build stored energy within the tendons, which contributes to speed development.
   – Emphasise the need for athletes to use their distance effectively and to focus on technique and explosiveness.

By providing coaching and teaching points for these spring variations, coaches and trainers can help athletes understand the purpose and execution of each exercise. This will enable athletes to develop proper motor control, improve their ability to generate power and speed, and effectively incorporate these exercises into their training programs.

Spaced Runs

Spaced runs, also known as Wicket runs, introduce constraints that aid in speed development. By manipulating the distance between cones or markers, athletes can challenge themselves to maintain stride length while increasing velocity. For example, a soccer player might set up cones at progressively wider distances and sprint through them, maintaining proper form and stride length. This type of training optimises acceleration and stride mechanics, leading to improved speed performance on the field.

Sprint Float Sprint

The Sprint Float Sprint method helps athletes maintain speed over a specific distance. It involves accelerating to top speed, maintaining that speed for a set duration, briefly reducing effort while maintaining proper mechanics (the float phase), and then accelerating again. A track athlete training for the 200-metre dash might implement the Sprint Float Sprint method by running 50 metres at maximum speed, floating for 20 metres while maintaining good form, and then accelerating for the final 50 metres. This method enhances an athlete's ability to sustain maximum velocity and trains the body to recover quickly between high-intensity efforts.

Scissor Runs and Progressions

Scissor runs, also referred to as prime time runs, are dynamic exercises that offer a range of benefits, including enhanced strength, length, speed, and power. These runs specifically target the posterior chain and Emphasise the development of extensor mechanisms. By incorporating scissor runs into training, athletes can improve their performance in explosive movements while maintaining a lengthened position.

When performing scissor runs, it is crucial to focus on the thigh angle, as this is a key element of the exercise. By emphasising the thigh angle, athletes can effectively load and activate the extensor muscles, promoting greater posterior chain engagement. This leads to increased stiffness and eccentric load throughout the movement, which contributes to enhanced strength and power production.

Coaching Points:

1. Horizontal Emphasis: During scissor runs, it is important to minimise vertical displacement and concentrate on horizontal movement. This horizontal emphasis allows for explosive ballistic action from the hip extensors, promoting power development.

2. Gradual Build-up: It is recommended to start with a gradual build-up when incorporating scissor runs into a training program. This approach helps generate momentum and ensures that athletes have enough forward propulsion to execute the movement effectively. Beginning with smaller amplitudes and gradually increasing leg opening allows for a smooth transition into full scissor runs.

3. Programming Considerations: Similar to a gym program, scissor runs can be programmed to address different training objectives. Starting with exercises that focus on maximum force development and progressing to drills that target speed and power is an effective strategy. This progression helps athletes develop a well-rounded skill set and maximise their performance potential.

4. **Fast Limb Movement:** Encourage athletes to perform scissor runs with fast limb action. This not only enhances the reactivity and explosiveness of the movement but also helps simulate the demands of sprinting at maximum velocity. Striving for fast limb movement while covering substantial ground is a key objective of scissor runs.

5. **Mid-Range Thigh Movement:** Aim to achieve a mid-range thigh movement during scissor runs. By working within this range, athletes can generate the desired aggressive movement and effectively train for various acceleration phases. The emphasis on fast, powerful limb movement within the optimal thigh range will contribute to improved speed and power development.

In summary, scissor runs are a valuable addition to training programs as they promote strength, length, speed, and power. By focusing on the thigh angle, minimising vertical displacement, gradually building up momentum, and emphasising fast limb movement within the optimal range, athletes can optimise their performance and develop the skills necessary for explosive movements and maximum velocity sprinting.

Developing maximum speed requires a systematic and progressive approach that incorporates special strength training and targeted progressions. By understanding the force-velocity curve, implementing long accelerations, incorporating bouncy and springy runs, utilising spaced runs, and implementing the Sprint Float Sprint method, athletes and coaches can optimise speed development. By applying these principles with creative adaptations to specific sports, and by monitoring progress and adjusting training protocols, athletes can continually improve their maximum velocity. With this comprehensive roadmap, you can unlock your full speed potential and excel in your chosen sport.

Applying Special Strength Training to Various Sports

The principles and progressions discussed in this guide can be adapted to different sports and training environments. Coaches and athletes can apply these concepts creatively to tailor speed development programs. For instance, a football player might incorporate long accelerations and bouncy runs in their training routine to improve their burst speed off the line of scrimmage. Similarly, a tennis player might utilise spaced runs and the Sprint Float Sprint method to enhance their court coverage and quickness.

Monitoring and Progressing Speed Development

Monitoring an athlete's progress is essential to ensure continual improvement in speed. Coaches can utilise various metrics such as step counts, ground contact times, and visual analysis to track performance. As progress is made, training protocols can be adjusted gradually. This includes increasing distances, reducing recovery times, and intensifying the workouts. By progressively challenging the body, athletes can push their boundaries and reach new levels of speed.

Step Loading Table for 0-15 Step Acceleration

Use this table to guide your programming to balance loading an technical steps when building acceleration.

Approx Distance	Loading Steps	Technical Steps
5m	1	2
	2	1
	3	4
10m	4	3
	5	2
	6	1
15m	7	8
	8	7
	9	6
20m	10	5
	11	4
	12	3
25m	13	2
	14	1
	15	0

Speed Gate Setup Considerations

Speed Timing Set Up Considerations

- Ensure that your athlete has a 50cm run in distance prior to the laser beam. This standardised the procedure and ensures accuracy.

- Ensure that the start laser is no higher than the knee of the athletes. This will avoid the lead hand breaking the beam and strating the timer prematurely.

Technique Analysis Videos - Scan QR CODES

- How to set up the 2 point stance
- Acceleration
- Change of Direction
- Maximum Velocity

Sports Speed Programs

Now that you have a real grasp on a majority of the exercises in the system I am going to show you a real life programming solution. The exact training programs that I use. The challenge with true speed development in team sport is balancing the need for acquiring motor potential over physical output. Therefore running a bias towards skill development is your priority as this lays the foundation for superior speed improvements. See me talk through these by scanning the QR Code at the beginning of the appendix.

Within this section we will cover:

- Speed Training Macro Cycle
- Speed Training Meso Cycle
- Speed Training Micro Cycle
- The Sports Speed Signature Warm Up
- Sports Speed "15 Minute" Speed Session for pre-training
- Sports Speed Foundations Program - Speed / Gym / Conditioning
- Speed Faults Solutions Sheets
- Speed Gate Golf Timing Zones

Sports Speed Training Cycles

Within these cycles I have demonstrated the key aims and objectives of the training cycles. I have specifically focussed on the off-season and preseason cycles. This being as a coach it is the best time you can implement deliberate practice to build Sports Speed. If you have read carefully and understood the book so far you will be well equipped to tackle in-season training.

Sports Speed Macro Cycle

	OFF SEASON 1	OFF SEASON 2	PRE SEASON 1	PRE SEASON 2	IN SEASON 1	IN SEASON 2
AIM	Recover the body post season	Accumulate specific speed training volume.	Unload the body to tolerate increased running demands of team specific training.	Start to peak physical qualities obtained to maximise freshness and explore new speed in pre-season fixtures.	Introducing a new training cycle and focus. Continue to use streams of athletic development using metrics to drive training.	Ensure optimal recovery repeatability. Continue to be fast when it matters.
GOAL	Introduce specific technical training	Introduce velocity to the body as a stimulus and develop new levels of speed.	Maintain working speed maximum and demonstrate the ability to continue to express speed in training.	Expose athletes to peak acceleration loads and peak velocity loads. Achieve PB's.	Continue to train submaximally focussing on specific technical and physical markers.	Stay fit, healthy and fresh. Reduce "noise" based training to optimise performance.

Sports Speed MesoCycle - Off Season Example

This example is typical of sports such as rugby union. It would be generous to assume an 8 week off-season in some professional cases. If the situation only required a 4-6 week off-season then the general phases would only be required.

Month	May				June			
Week	1	2	3	4	1	2	3	4
Goal	General Preparation 1		General Preparation 2		Specific Preparation 1		Specific Preparation 2	
Primary Objective	Get "Speed Ready". Build adaptive reserves to intensify in the next training block		Increase the density of training specific qualities. Remove general weight training.		Be FAST! Hit fast speed, be explosive and deliberate.		Increase in session density of higher % speed training.	
Secondary Objective	Refresh the body via aerobic training.		Start to develop a data set of comparable information.		Recover from more intense and specific sessions.		Reduce total volume to taper.	
Total Sessions	3	4	5	4	4	3	3	3

Sports Speed MesoCycle - Pre- Season Example

Month	July				August			
Week	1	2	3	4	1	2	3	4
Goal	Specific Preparation 3		Specific Preparation 4		Taper	Pre-Season Fixtures		
Primary Objective	Adapt to team training schedule and increased running volume		Implement "Team Sport" Sprinting		Realise new abilities	Adjust to game load and reaction to competition.		
Secondary Objective	Maintain ability to reach fast running speed via "top ups" or speed training		Continue to improve Specialised developmental exercise performance		Reduce overall stress	Stay Healthy.		
Total Sessions	3	3	3	3	3	2	2	2

Microcycle Organisation

I have highlighted these examples as to the specific population they would fit with. I urge caution when applying these models. Pay attention to the recommended session volumes as indicated in the tables.

Full Time Athlete - Off-Season General Preparation 1 - Good Training History

Day	1	2	3	4	5	6	7
Training Intensity	Low	High	OFF	Low	High	Low	OFF
Session Type	Movement Skills Upper Body Weights	Maximum Velocity Lower Body Weights		Movement Skills Upper Body Weights	Acceleration Lower Body Weights	Movement Skills Upper Body Weights	
Session Duration	<90 Mins	< 90 Mins		<90 Mins	< 90 Mins	<60 Mins	

Note:

Context here is imperative. Alternating intensity days is a great way to ensure we undulate the training. This allows for windows of recovery.

Notice in this there are only two "High" days of training. This is due to the specific time of year and goal of the phase.

Movement Skills constitutes submaximal technical running for aerobic training and technical learning drills performed for an aerobic training effect.

Full Time Athlete - Off-Season Specific Preparation - Good Training History

Day	1	2	3	4	5	6	7
Training Intensity	High	Low	OFF	High	Low	High	OFF
Session Type	Maximum Velocity Lower Body Weights	Movement Skills Upper Body Weights		Acceleration Lower Body Weights	Movement Skills Upper Body Weights	Change of Direction Lower Body Weights	
Session Duration	<90 Mins	< 90 Mins		<90 Mins	< 75 Mins	<75 Mins	

Note:

Context here is imperative. Alternating intensity days is a great way to ensure we undulate the training. This allows for windows of recovery.

Notice in this there are only two "High" days of training. This is due to the specific time of year and goal of the phase.

Movement Skills constitutes submaximal technical running for aerobic training and technical learning drills performed for an aerobic training effect.

Part Time Athlete - Moderate Training History

One key adjustment to make when working with part time athletes (those who work alongside training) is to spread the training prescription over 14 days instead of 7. This allows a greater quality of training to be completed. As the cost of training is less the athletes do improve at a higher rate when compared to a greater density of workouts. As a caveat to this. Certain athletes in full time training situations do respond well to this type of load. Usually this happens with the players who can produce the highest output.

Day	1	2	3	4	5	6	7
Training Intensity	Low	OFF	High	OFF	Low	High	OFF
Session Type	Movement Skills		Max Speed		Upper Body	Acceleration	
Session Duration	<45Mins		<60mins		<30mins	<60mins	
Day	8	8	10	11	12	13	14
Training Intensity	OFF	Low	OFF	High	OFF	Low	OFF
Session Type		Upper Body		Max Speed		Movement Skills	
Session Duration		<30mins		<60mins		<45Mins	

The Sports Speed Signature Warm Ups

The warm up is a vital tool for a speed coach. It can tell you so much about the athlete you are working with. It can also educate the athlete and learn "how they feel" with respect to training. Too much variation in warm ups will fail to serve your athlete for their intended purpose. Prepare the athlete for training. The Sports Speed Signature Warm Ups are a staple in the system.

Linear Speed Base Warm Up

Section	Number	Exercise	Purpose
Dynamic Mobility	1	Inchworm	Open up the posterior chain
	2	Squat to Stand	Prepare the hips for deep ranges
	3	Inverted Hamstring Stretch	Lengthen the hamstring in full hip flexion
	4	Lying Thoracic Rotation	Mobilise torso rotation to enable fluid upper body motion.
	5	Spiderman Reach	Create deep range hip extension/flexion combined with upper body rotation.
	6	Long Adductor Rock	Lengthen the long adductor
	7	Lying Scorpions	Open the anterior oblique sling of the body.
Activation	1	Plank	Create full body tension in the sagittal plane.
	2	Supine Plank	Create full body tension in frontal plane
	3	Lying Hip Flexor Isometric	Increase motor unit activation of the hip flexors

Section	Number	Exercise	Purpose
Dynamic Flexibility	1	Russian Walk	Increase hamstring length with full hip flexion and posture reinforcement.
	2	Backward RDL	Activate proprioception of the posterior chain.
	3	Toy Soldier	Rapidly increase hamstring length.
	4	Walking Sprinter Lunge	Start to increase eccentric loading in a deep range position.
Speed Drills	1	Ankling	Ankle conditioning and stiffness.
	2	A Skip	Timing and foot striking.
	3	B Skip	Rapid Hamstring Lengthening
	4	High Knees	Postural reinforcement and torso orientation.
	5	Butt Kicks	Distal hamstring conditioning.
	6	Egg Cracker	Hip Flexor and Knee Flexor Activation
	7	A Switch	Prime high speed leg movement.
	8	Single Leg A	Ingraining the leg cycle pattern.
	9	Scissor Run	Higher speed hamstring activation.
	10	Build Up	Gradual exposure to higher speed running.
Specific Drills	1		This is where you would implement some of the specific "Learning" Based Drills for the training day.
	2		
	3		
	4		

Change of Direction Speed Base Warm Up

Section	Number	Exercise	Purpose
Dynamic Mobility	1	Inchworm	Open up the posterior chain
	2	Squat to Stand	Prepare the hips for deep ranges
	3	Inverted Hamstring Stretch	Lengthen the hamstring in full hip flexion
	4	Lying Thoracic Rotation	Mobilise torso rotation to enable fluid upper body motion.
	5	Spiderman Reach	Create deep range hip extension/flexion combined with upper body rotation.
	6	Long Adductor Rock	Lengthen the long adductor
	7	Lying Scorpions	Open the anterior oblique sling of the body.
Activation	1	Side Plank	Create full body tension in the sagittal plane.
	2	Supine Plank	Create full body tension in the frontal plane.
	3	Lying Hip Flexor Isometric	Increase motor unit activation of the hip flexors.

Section	Number	Exercise	Purpose
Dynamic Flexibility	1	Russian Walk	Increase hamstring length with full hip flexion and posture reinforcement.
	2	Backward RDL	Activate proprioception of the posterior chain.
	3	Toy Soldier	Rapidly increase hamstring length.
	4	Lateral Lunge	Start to increase eccentric loading in a deep range position.
Speed Drills	1	Ankling	Ankle conditioning and stiffness.
	2	A Skip	Timing and foot striking.
	3	B Skip	Rapid Hamstring Lengthening.
	4	Lateral A Skip	Lateral Striking with Timing.
	5	Lateral B Skip	Rapid Hamstring Lengthening.
	6	Karaoke Run	Hip rotation and activation.
	7	Lateral Shuffle	Abductor and Adductor Activation.
	8	Relaxed Zig Zags	Increasing impact forces in the frontal plane.
	9	Lateral Run	Increasing velocity to the hip and groin in the frontal plane.
	10	Slalom Runs	Gradual build up to higher speeds whilst changing direction.
Specific Drills	1		This is where you would implement some of the specific "Learning" Based Drills for the training day.
	2		
	3		
	4		

Sports Speed "15 Minute" Speed Session for pre-training

In my experience most coaches and athletes get "15 Minutes" before training to work on their speed. Or it is bled into a longer warm up. Having a structure and framework for this is essential. As a sports speed coach it's imperative to create speed in your athletes with the little time you have.

If you have been with the team for an extended period of time you can teach them the Signature warm and encourage them to get through this prior to training. There is always a little bit of dead time prior to training. It is important to note that good warm ups help develop physical qualities with your athletes. If they can get a version of this warm up completed before you coach them, you have maximised their opportunity to develop. The below template demonstrates how effective you can be in 15 Minutes. But you need to ensure that you are fluent in the frameworks of Sports Speed to maximise your return.

Section	Time Allocation	Total Exercises	Instruction
Warm Up	7 Mins	N/A	Condensed Version of the Signature Warm up Covering all areas.
Learn 1	3 Mins	1	Segment Based Movement
Learn 2		1	Pattern Based Movement
Load	3 Mins	1	Utilisation of External Load
Execute 1	2 Mins	1	Exploration Repetition
Execute 2		1	Confirmation Repetitions
Totals	15	5	

Sports Speed Foundations Program - Speed / Gym / Conditioning

Within this section I will be demonstrating to you a phase of training. I will be including the entirety of the contents covered within the program. Here you will be able to see how all elements of the training blend together. This program will consist of four training days per week and was used with a professional rugby player in his off-season. This athlete is in the later phases of "Learn to Sprint".

Here is the organisation of training. The Sports Speed Signature Warm Ups were used throughout.

Day	1	2	3	4	5	6	7
Training Intensity	Low	High	OFF	Low	High	OFF	OFF
Session Type	Upper Body and Extensive Technical Running	Maximum Velocity Lower Body Weights	YOGA RECOVERY	Upper Body and Extensive Technical Running	Acceleration / Change of Direction Lower Body Weights	YOGA RECOVERY	
Session Duration	<60 Mins	< 90 Mins		<60 Mins	< 90 Mins		

Session One: Upper Body and Extensive Technical Running

Section	No.	Exercise	Week 1 Sets	Week 1 Reps	Week 1 Rest	Week 1 Int.	Week 2 Sets	Week 2 Reps	Week 2 Rest	Week 2 Int.	Week 3 Sets	Week 3 Reps	Week 3 Rest	Week 3 Int.	Week 4 Sets	Week 4 Reps	Week 4 Rest	Week 4 Int.
TECHNICAL RUNNING	1a	Technical Running (100m per run)	2	8x100m	Rolling 80s set. 120s Between Sets	5/10	2	8x100m	Rolling 80s set. 120s Between Sets	6/10	2	8x100m	Rolling 80s set. 120s Between Sets	7/10	2	5x100m	Rolling 80s set. 120s Between Sets	5/10
ROTATOR CUFF HEALTH	1a	Scapular Depressions	2	15	30s	3/10	2	15	30s	3/10	2	15	30s	3/10	2	15	30s	3/10
	1b	Prone Reverse Fly																
	1c	Banded External Rotations																
BALLISTICS *(Completed as a continuous circuit)*	1a	Kneeling Overhead Medicine Ball Throw	2	5	90s	4/10	2	8	90s	5/10	2	10	90s	6/10	2	5	90s	4/10
	1b	Kneeling Side Throw																
	1c	Tall Kneeling Medicine Ball Slam																
	1d	Tall Kneeling Medicine Ball Chest Pass																
STRENGTH ONE	1a	Bench Press	3	12	60s	5/10	3	10	60s	6/10	3	12	60s	7/10	3	5	60s	5/10
	1b	Weighted Chin Up																
STRENGTH TWO	1a	Incline Bench Press	3	8	60s	5/10	3	8	60s	6/10	3	8	60s	7/10	3	8	60s	5/10
	1b	Single Arm Dumbbell Row																
	1c	Ab Wheel RollOut																
STRENGTH THREE	1a	Dumbbell Bicep Curl	3	15	60s	5/10	3	12	60s	6/10	3	10	60s	7/10	3	5	60s	5/10
	1b	Dumbbell Tricep Extension																

Session Two: Maximum Velocity and Lower Body Weights

Section	No.	Exercise	Week 1 Sets	Week 1 Reps	Week 1 Rest	Week 1 Intensity	Week 2 Sets	Week 2 Reps	Week 2 Rest	Week 2 Intensity	Week 3 Sets	Week 3 Reps	Week 3 Rest	Week 3 Intensity	Week 4 Sets	Week 4 Reps	Week 4 Rest	Week 4 Intensity
MAX SPEED LOADING	1a	Long Accelerations (40-50m)	2	2	Full Rest	7/10	2	2	Full Rest	7/10	2	2	Full Rest	7/10	2	2	Full Rest	7/10
Special Strength / Learn	1a	Ankling Yielding Series	2	20s	30s	3/10	2	20s	30s	3/10	2	20s	30s	3/10	2	20s	30s	3/10
	1b	Knee Yielding Series																
	1c	Hip Yielding Series																
Specific Strength / Load	1a	Kneeling Wall Shoot	2	10	60s	6/10	2	8	60s	7/10	2	6	60s	8/10	2	5	60s	5/10
Specific Strength / Execute	1a	3 Step Push		2				2				2				2		
	1b	Resisted March	2	30m	120s		2	30m	120s		2	30m	120s		2	30m	120s	
PLYOMETRIC AND JUMP TRAINING	1a	Extensive Pogo Jumps	2	15	90s	5/10	2	15	75s	6/10	2	12	60s	7/10	2	10	120s	5/10
	1b	Extensive CMJ																
		Extensive Linear Hop																
STRENGTH TRAINING	1	Trap Bar DeadLift	2	5	120s	5/10	2	5	120s	5/10	2	5	120s	5/10	1	5	120s	5/10
	2	Isometric Glute Ham Raise	2	30s	90s	BW	2	30s	90s	BW	2	30s	90s	BW	1	30s	90s	BW
	3	Hand Supported Skater Squat	2	15	60s	BW	2	15	60s	BW	2	15	60s	BW	1	15	60s	BW
	4	Barbell Calf Raise	2	8		8/10	2	8		8/10	2	8		8/10	1	8		8/10
	5	Weighted Sit Up	2	15		6/10	2	15		6/10	2	15		6/10	1	15		6/10

Session Three: Change of Direction and Lower Body Strength

Section	No.	Exercise	Week 1				Week 2				Week 3				Week 4			
			Sets	Reps	Rest	Intensity	Sets	Reps	Rest	Intensity	Sets	Reps	Rest	Intensity	Sets	Reps	Rest	Intensity
Special Strength / Learn	1a	Ankling Yielding Series	2	15	30s	3/10	2	15	30s	3/10	2	15	30s	3/10	2	15	30s	3/10
	1b	Knee Yielding Series																
	1c	Hip Yielding Series																
	2a	Crossover Wall Hold		30s				30s				30s				30s		
	2b	Open Step Wall Hold																
Specific Strength / Load	1a	Lateral Wall Shoot	2	10	60s	6/10	2	8	60s	7/10	2	6	60s	8/10	2	5	60s	5/10
Specific Strength / Execute	1a	3 Step Crossover Push		2				2				2				2		
	1b	Resisted Crossover March	2	30m	120s		2	30m	120s		2	30m	120s		2	30m	120s	
PLYOMETRIC AND JUMP TRAINING	1a	Extensive Pogo Jumps	2	15	90s	5/10	2	15	75s	6/10	2	12	60s	7/10	2	10	120s	5/10
	1b	Extensive Zig Zag Jump																
		Extensive Lateral Hop																
STRENGTH TRAINING	1	Trap Bar DeadLift	2	5	120s	5/10	2	5	120s	5/10	2	5	120s	5/10	1	5	120s	5/10
	2	Isometric Glute Ham Raise Bent Knee	2	30s	90s	BW	2	30s	90s	BW	2	30s	90s	BW	1	30s	90s	BW
	3	Barbell Lateral Squat	2	15	60s	BW	2	15	60s	BW	2	15	60s	BW	1	15	60s	BW
	4	Seated Calf Raise	2	8		8/10	2	8		8/10	2	8		8/10	1	8		8/10
	5	Tall Kneeling Pallof Rotation	2	15		6/10	2	15		6/10	2	15		6/10	1	15		6/10

Session Four: Upper Body and Extensive Technical Running

Section	No.	Exercise	Week 1 Sets	Week 1 Reps	Week 1 Rest	Week 1 Intensity	Week 2 Sets	Week 2 Reps	Week 2 Rest	Week 2 Intensity	Week 3 Sets	Week 3 Reps	Week 3 Rest	Week 3 Intensity	Week 4 Sets	Week 4 Reps	Week 4 Rest	Week 4 Intensity
TECHNICAL RUNNING	1a	Technical Running (100m per run)	2	8x100m	Rolling 80s in set. 120s Between Sets	5/10	2	8x100m	Rolling 80s in set. 120s Between Sets	6/10	2	8x100m	Rolling 80s in set. 120s Between Sets	7/10	2	5x100m	Rolling 80s in set. 120s Between Sets	5/10
ROTATOR CUFF HEALTH	1a	Scapular Depressions	2	15	30s	3/10	2	15	30s	3/10	2	15	30s	3/10	2	15	30s	3/10
	1b	Prone Reverse Fly																
	1c	Banded External Rotations																
BALLISTICS (Completed as a continuous circuit)	1a	Kneeling Overhead Medicine Ball Throw	2	5	90s	4/10	2	8	90s	5/10	2	10	90s	6/10	2	5	90s	4/10
	1b	Kneeling Side Throw																
	1c	Tall Kneeling Medicine Ball Slam																
	1d	Tall Kneeling Medicine Ball Chest Pass																
STRENGTH ONE	1a	Barbell Shoulder Press	3	12	60s	5/10	3	10	60s	6/10	3	12	60s	7/10	3	5	60s	5/10
	1b	Pendlay Row																
STRENGTH TWO	1a	Weighted Push Up	3	8	60s	5/10	3	8	60s	6/10	3	8	60s	7/10	3	8	60s	5/10
	1b	Chin Up																
	1c	Russian Twist																
STRENGTH THREE	1a	Lateral Raise	3	15	60s	5/10	3	12	60s	6/10	3	10	60s	7/10	3	5	60s	5/10
	1b	Front Raise																
	1c	Upper Back Row																
	1d	Barbell Shrug																

Speed Faults Solutions

The tables below outline the exact process you can take yourself or athletes through to fix the most common errors seen in speed training.

Initial Acceleration

	PROBLEM	FIX		
	ACCELERATION	LEARN	LOAD	EXECUTE
Start	Lack of Tension	Stable Bilateral Wall Projection	Banded Load and Smash - Bilateral - Unilateral	Heavy Prowler Pulley March
STEP 1		LEARN	LOAD	EXECUTE
1	Poor Initial rate of projection	Stable Bilateral Wall Projection	Banded Load and Smash - Bilateral - Unilateral	1 Step Push
2	Casting Shin	Wall Smash and Retract	Band Stomp	Incline/Light resisted Drive
3	Foot contact in front of COM	Wall Smash and Retract	Powler 2 Step Push	Prowler Resisted Kneeling Drive
STEP 2		LEARN	LOAD	EXECUTE
1	Not Enough Leg Separation	Stable Leg Exchange	Kneeling Load and Smash	Kneeling 1 Step Push
2	Frontside Thigh too high	Stable Leg Exchange Variation	Leg Banded Stable Leg Exchange	Prowler Kneeling 1 Step Push
3	Late Retraction	Stable Leg Exchange Variation	Kneeling 2 step Load and Smash	Resisted Kneeling Acceleration
STEP 3		LEARN	LOAD	EXECUTE
1	Early Torso Rise	Load and Smash	Kneeling Load and Smash	Prowler Kneeling 3-5 Step Push
2	Leg Too Cyclic	Banded (Foot) Load and Smash	Prowler Pulley Leg Exchange	Kneeling 3-5 Step Drive
3	Lack of Vertical Displacement	Resisted Kneeling Drive		Kneeling 10 Drive
	TRANSITIONAL ELEMENTS			
	PROBLEM	FIX		
	TRANSITION	LEARN	LOAD	EXECUTE
1	Lack of Rise	Dribble Bleeds	Accel Spacing / Med Strength Resisted Runs	Technical Accelerations
2	Excessive "Forward" Lean	3-5 Step Push	Chest Harness / Arm Placements	Technical Accelerations
3	Excessive Backside Mechanics	Dribble Bleeds	Accel Spacing / Med Strength Resisted Runs	Acceleration "cone" Runs

Speed Gate Golf Timing Zones for Training Intensities

When implementing Speed Gate Golf use these timing guides to adjust intensity of the work completed.

TEST	Time	95%	90%	85%	80%	75%	70%	65%	60%	55%	50%
5M	0.8	0.8	0.7	0.7	0.6	0.6	0.6	0.5	0.5	0.4	0.4
	0.85	0.8	0.8	0.7	0.7	0.6	0.6	0.6	0.5	0.5	0.4
	0.9	0.9	0.8	0.8	0.7	0.7	0.6	0.6	0.5	0.5	0.5
	0.95	0.9	0.9	0.8	0.8	0.7	0.7	0.6	0.6	0.5	0.5
	1	1	0.9	0.9	0.8	0.8	0.7	0.7	0.6	0.6	0.5
	1.05	1	0.9	0.9	0.8	0.8	0.7	0.7	0.6	0.6	0.5
	1.1	1	1	0.9	0.9	0.8	0.8	0.7	0.7	0.6	0.6
	1.15	1.1	1	1	0.9	0.9	0.8	0.7	0.7	0.6	0.6
	1.2	1.1	1.1	1	1	0.9	0.8	0.8	0.7	0.7	0.6
	1.25	1.2	1.1	1.1	1	0.9	0.9	0.8	0.8	0.7	0.6
	1.3	1.2	1.2	1.1	1	1	0.9	0.8	0.8	0.7	0.7
	1.35	1.3	1.2	1.1	1.1	1	0.9	0.9	0.8	0.7	0.7
	1.4	1.3	1.3	1.2	1.1	1.1	1	0.9	0.8	0.8	0.7
	1.45	1.4	1.3	1.2	1.2	1.1	1	0.9	0.9	0.8	0.7
	1.5	1.4	1.4	1.3	1.2	1.1	1.1	1	0.9	0.8	0.8
10M	1.55	1.5	1.4	1.3	1.2	1.2	1.1	1	0.9	0.9	0.8
	1.6	1.5	1.4	1.4	1.3	1.2	1.1	1	1	0.9	0.8
	1.65	1.6	1.5	1.4	1.3	1.2	1.2	1.1	1	0.9	0.8
	1.7	1.6	1.5	1.4	1.4	1.3	1.2	1.1	1	0.9	0.9
	1.75	1.7	1.6	1.5	1.4	1.3	1.2	1.1	1.1	1	0.9
	1.8	1.7	1.6	1.5	1.4	1.4	1.3	1.2	1.1	1	0.9
	1.85	1.8	1.7	1.6	1.5	1.4	1.3	1.2	1.1	1	0.9
	1.9	1.8	1.7	1.6	1.5	1.4	1.3	1.2	1.1	1	1
	1.95	1.9	1.8	1.7	1.6	1.5	1.4	1.3	1.2	1.1	1
	2	1.9	1.8	1.7	1.6	1.5	1.4	1.3	1.2	1.1	1
	2.05	1.9	1.8	1.7	1.6	1.5	1.4	1.3	1.2	1.1	1
	2.1	2	1.9	1.8	1.7	1.6	1.5	1.4	1.3	1.2	1.1
	2.15	2	1.9	1.8	1.7	1.6	1.5	1.4	1.3	1.2	1.1
	2.2	2.1	2	1.9	1.8	1.7	1.5	1.4	1.3	1.2	1.1
	2.25	2.1	2	1.9	1.8	1.7	1.6	1.5	1.4	1.2	1.1
	2.3	2.2	2.1	2	1.8	1.7	1.6	1.5	1.4	1.3	1.2
	2.35	2.2	2.1	2	1.9	1.8	1.6	1.5	1.4	1.3	1.2
	2.4	2.3	2.2	2	1.9	1.8	1.7	1.6	1.4	1.3	1.2
	2.45	2.3	2.2	2.1	2	1.8	1.7	1.6	1.5	1.3	1.2
	2.5	2.4	2.3	2.1	2	1.9	1.8	1.6	1.5	1.4	1.3

TEST	Time	95%	90%	85%	80%	75%	70%	65%	60%	55%	50%
20M	2.55	2.4	2.3	2.2	2	1.9	1.8	1.7	1.5	1.4	1.3
	2.6	2.5	2.3	2.2	2.1	2	1.8	1.7	1.6	1.4	1.3
	2.65	2.5	2.4	2.3	2.1	2	1.9	1.7	1.6	1.5	1.3
	2.7	2.6	2.4	2.3	2.2	2	1.9	1.8	1.6	1.5	1.4
	2.75	2.6	2.5	2.3	2.2	2.1	1.9	1.8	1.7	1.5	1.4
	2.8	2.7	2.5	2.4	2.2	2.1	2	1.8	1.7	1.5	1.4
	2.85	2.7	2.6	2.4	2.3	2.1	2	1.9	1.7	1.6	1.4
	2.9	2.8	2.6	2.5	2.3	2.2	2	1.9	1.7	1.6	1.5
	2.95	2.8	2.7	2.5	2.4	2.2	2.1	1.9	1.8	1.6	1.5
	3	2.9	2.7	2.6	2.4	2.3	2.1	2	1.8	1.7	1.5
	3.05	2.9	2.7	2.6	2.4	2.3	2.1	2	1.8	1.7	1.5
	3.1	2.9	2.8	2.6	2.5	2.3	2.2	2	1.9	1.7	1.6
	3.15	3	2.8	2.7	2.5	2.4	2.2	2	1.9	1.7	1.6
	3.2	3	2.9	2.7	2.6	2.4	2.2	2.1	1.9	1.8	1.6
	3.25	3.1	2.9	2.8	2.6	2.4	2.3	2.1	2	1.8	1.6
	3.3	3.1	3	2.8	2.6	2.5	2.3	2.1	2	1.8	1.7
	3.35	3.2	3	2.8	2.7	2.5	2.3	2.2	2	1.8	1.7
	3.4	3.2	3.1	2.9	2.7	2.6	2.4	2.2	2	1.9	1.7
	3.45	3.3	3.1	2.9	2.8	2.6	2.4	2.2	2.1	1.9	1.7
	3.5	3.3	3.2	3	2.8	2.6	2.5	2.3	2.1	1.9	1.8
	3.55	3.4	3.2	3	2.8	2.7	2.5	2.3	2.1	2	1.8
	3.6	3.4	3.2	3.1	2.9	2.7	2.5	2.3	2.2	2	1.8
	3.65	3.5	3.3	3.1	2.9	2.7	2.6	2.4	2.2	2	1.8
	3.7	3.5	3.3	3.1	3	2.8	2.6	2.4	2.2	2	1.9
	3.75	3.6	3.4	3.2	3	2.8	2.6	2.4	2.3	2.1	1.9
	3.8	3.6	3.4	3.2	3	2.9	2.7	2.5	2.3	2.1	1.9
	3.85	3.7	3.5	3.3	3.1	2.9	2.7	2.5	2.3	2.1	1.9
	3.9	3.7	3.5	3.3	3.1	2.9	2.7	2.5	2.3	2.1	2
	3.95	3.8	3.6	3.4	3.2	3	2.8	2.6	2.4	2.2	2
	4	3.8	3.6	3.4	3.2	3	2.8	2.6	2.4	2.2	2
30M	4.05	3.8	3.6	3.4	3.2	3	2.8	2.6	2.4	2.2	2
	4.1	3.9	3.7	3.5	3.3	3.1	2.9	2.7	2.5	2.3	2.1
	4.15	3.9	3.7	3.5	3.3	3.1	2.9	2.7	2.5	2.3	2.1
	4.2	4	3.8	3.6	3.4	3.2	2.9	2.7	2.5	2.3	2.1
	4.25	4	3.8	3.6	3.4	3.2	3	2.8	2.6	2.3	2.1
	4.3	4.1	3.9	3.7	3.4	3.2	3	2.8	2.6	2.4	2.2
	4.35	4.1	3.9	3.7	3.5	3.3	3	2.8	2.6	2.4	2.2

TEST	Time	95%	90%	85%	80%	75%	70%	65%	60%	55%	50%
	4.4	4.2	4	3.7	3.5	3.3	3.1	2.9	2.6	2.4	2.2
	4.45	4.2	4	3.8	3.6	3.3	3.1	2.9	2.7	2.4	2.2
	4.5	4.3	4	3.8	3.6	3.4	3.1	2.9	2.7	2.5	2.3
	4.55	4.3	4.1	3.9	3.6	3.4	3.2	3	2.7	2.5	2.3
	4.6	4.4	4.1	3.9	3.7	3.4	3.2	3	2.8	2.5	2.3
	4.65	4.4	4.2	4	3.7	3.5	3.3	3	2.8	2.6	2.3
	4.7	4.5	4.2	4	3.8	3.5	3.3	3.1	2.8	2.6	2.4
	4.75	4.5	4.3	4	3.8	3.6	3.3	3.1	2.8	2.6	2.4
	4.8	4.6	4.3	4.1	3.8	3.6	3.4	3.1	2.9	2.6	2.4
	4.85	4.6	4.4	4.1	3.9	3.6	3.4	3.2	2.9	2.7	2.4
	4.9	4.7	4.4	4.2	3.9	3.7	3.4	3.2	2.9	2.7	2.5
	4.95	4.7	4.5	4.2	4	3.7	3.5	3.2	3	2.7	2.5
	5	4.7	4.5	4.2	4	3.7	3.5	3.2	3	2.8	2.5
	5.05	4.8	4.5	4.3	4	3.8	3.5	3.3	3	2.8	2.5
	5.1	4.8	4.6	4.3	4.1	3.8	3.6	3.3	3.1	2.8	2.6
	5.15	4.9	4.6	4.4	4.1	3.9	3.6	3.3	3.1	2.8	2.6
	5.2	4.9	4.7	4.4	4.2	3.9	3.6	3.4	3.1	2.9	2.6
	5.25	5	4.7	4.5	4.2	3.9	3.7	3.4	3.1	2.9	2.6
	5.3	5	4.8	4.5	4.2	4	3.7	3.4	3.2	2.9	2.7
	5.35	5.1	4.8	4.5	4.3	4	3.7	3.5	3.2	2.9	2.7
	5.4	5.1	4.9	4.6	4.3	4	3.8	3.5	3.2	3	2.7
	5.45	5.2	4.9	4.6	4.4	4.1	3.8	3.5	3.3	3	2.7
	5.5	5.2	4.9	4.7	4.4	4.1	3.8	3.6	3.3	3	2.8
	5.55	5.3	5	4.7	4.4	4.2	3.9	3.6	3.3	3.1	2.8
	5.6	5.3	5	4.8	4.5	4.2	3.9	3.6	3.4	3.1	2.8
	5.65	5.4	5.1	4.8	4.5	4.2	4	3.7	3.4	3.1	2.8
	5.7	5.4	5.1	4.8	4.6	4.3	4	3.7	3.4	3.1	2.9
	5.75	5.5	5.2	4.9	4.6	4.3	4	3.7	3.4	3.2	2.9
	5.8	5.5	5.2	4.9	4.6	4.3	4.1	3.8	3.5	3.2	2.9
	5.85	5.6	5.3	5	4.7	4.4	4.1	3.8	3.5	3.2	2.9
	5.9	5.6	5.3	5	4.7	4.4	4.1	3.8	3.5	3.2	3
	5.95	5.7	5.4	5.1	4.8	4.5	4.2	3.9	3.6	3.3	3
	6	5.7	5.4	5.1	4.8	4.5	4.2	3.9	3.6	3.3	3

GOOGLE SHEET CALCULATORS - SCAN QR CODE TO ACCES THESE.

Force Velocity Profile

Dynamic Strength Index

Effect Size Calculator

JUMP TRAINING PROGRESSIONS

The overview list below shows the serial order of the jumping methods which takes the training means for newbie youth athletes up all the way to the very elite athletes. I felt it was vitally important to include such a detailed appendix of these jump training modalities as they play a pivotal role in developing general speed.

Each of these 7 methods will be broken down into the theory of how and why to apply the method, appropriate timing within your programme and links to individual exercises for a visual demonstration on technical execution:

1. **Landing + Non-Countermovement Jumps**
   A. Drop Landings
   B. Non-Countermovement Jump + Land
   C. Countermovement Jump + Land

2. **Extensive Jumps**
   A. Pogo Series
   B. Extensive Series
   C. Advanced Extensive

3. **Intensive Jumps**
   A. Long Coupling
   B. Short Coupling
   C. Altitude Landings

4. **Introduction to weighted jumps**
   A. Weighted Non-Countermovement Jumps
   B. Weighted Eccentric Focus Jumps

5. **Extensive weighted Jumps**
   A. Medicine Ball Pogo Series
   B. Weighted Extensive Jumps
   C. Overspeed Jumps

6. **Intensive weighted Jumps**
   A. Long Coupling
   B. Short Coupling
   C. Drop Jumps

7. Depth Jumps

Landing & Non Countermovement Jumps	Extensive Jumps	Intensive Jumps	Introduction to Weighted Jumps	Extensive Weighted Jumps	Intensive Weighted Jumps	SUPRAMAX JUMPS
Drop Landings	Pogo Series	Long Coupling	Weighted NCMJ	Medicine Ball Pogo Series	Long Coupling	DEPTH JUMPS
Non-Countermovement Jumps	Extensive Series	Short Coupling	Weighted Eccentric Focus	Weighted Extensive	Short Coupling	
Countermovement Jumps	Advanced Extensive	Altitude Landings		Overspeed Jumps	Drop Jumps	

Within each of the methods listed above, there's a 3-step checklist to give indication and coaching guidance to practitioners when it's appropriate to progress different jumps and the right time to move onto the next method:

1. First, establish the correct technique
2. Second, apply higher force efforts using the correct technique
3. Third, higher level of work capacity is obtained due to improving the execution form and function of the athlete's organism

Jump methods and exercise progressions

Each of the following methods have a specific set of goals that aim to achieve specific adaptations and teach the body certain motor abilities. This should be clearly communicated to the athletes each session in how to perform the exercises and what's being developed. It's important that you should recognise the language you are using in terms of cues as this can affect the execution of the jumps.

1. Landing + Non countermovement Jumps

The first method phase is broken into 3 sections with focus on landing, jumping without a countermovement and jumping with a countermovement action. Always finish in a strong landing position to train the habits of being prepared to take off into another jump. This is a perfect starting place for your beginner or youth athlete. The method breaks down the 2 segments that occur when colliding with the ground in the ground contact phase of the jump. This closely resembles the same action that takes place during long coupling jumps (touchdown and rebound segment). The final section of the method links both segments together.

Drop Landings

When the foot initially collides with the ground to start the touchdown phase, this sees the highest peak in ground reaction forces. Performing drop landings will mimic the touchdown segment with the coordination, timing and sequencing of the legs going into flexion. Initially, you want to be in full control during the landing, quiet on ground contact to achieve the optimal joint angle and body alignment. The aim is to switch on and apply the brakes.

Once the technique is correct, you can apply higher forces by performing the movement faster by actively pulling the body downwards and catching at the optimal angle of joint flexion. This will begin teaching the muscles to contract whilst lengthening at a faster rate whilst developing the ability to slam on the brakes quicker (part of the contract relax timing). The ground contact will now be much louder as you start cueing to 'attack' the ground.

Single drop landing repetitions are performed with the emphasis of targeting of the hip and knee.

Progression No#	Exercise	Direction	Additional Notes / Options
1	Fall & Catch	Vertical	Dropping Centre of gravity and catching
2	Split Squat Fall + Catch	Vertical	Catch in a deep split squat position
3	Sprinters Lunge + Catch	Horizontal	Don't reach for the ground, keep leading foot closer to hips
4	Lateral Lunge Fall + Catch	Lateral	
5	Single Leg Fall + Catch	Vertical	Stability and correct posture
6	Single Leg 90 degree Turn Fall + Catch	Rotational	Stability and correct posture

Non-Countermovement Jump + Land

The second section objective is to train the rebound segment of the jumping movement during the ground contact phase. The emphasis is on leg extension with the adjustment of the timing sequence of the hip, knee and ankle of the push up action. Each rep will start with the legs in a flexed position with either a 3 second pause before take-off or start in from a seated position. All reps should finish in the correct landing positions in preparation to take off for another jump. The landing has been intensified with athletes coming down from a greater height than previously. To lower this intensity, you can elevate the height of the ground which will be jumping up onto a box. This can be an added regression to the variation of the following exercises below if you have boxes available at your facility.

Single jump repetitions are performed with the emphasis again targeting the hip and knee. However, you can instruct the athlete to hold that landing position for a minimum 3 seconds to demonstrate balance upon landing, stability and control.

Progression No#	Exercise	Direction	Additional Notes / Options
1	NCM Jump	Vertical	Can be performed with or without arms (hands on hips) – Jump on box if equipment's available.
2	NCM Broad Jump	Horizontal	
3	NCM Split Squat Jump	Vertical	
4	NCM Lateral Jump	Lateral	
5	NCM 90 / 180 degree Jump + Stick	Rotational	
6	NCM Bound + Stick	Horizontal	
7	NCM Skater Bound + Stick	Lateral	
8	NCM 90 degree Bound + Stick	Rotational	Inside edge + Outside edge of foot
9	NCM Hop + Stick	Vertical / Horizontal	
10	NCM Lateral Hop + Stick	Lateral	Inside edge + Outside edge of foot
11	NCM 90 degree Hop + Stick	Rotational	Inside edge + Outside edge of foot

Countermovement and Land

The third section will combine the first two sections together to create a smooth, fluid movement transitioning through leg flexion into leg extension action. The jump should be relaxed and effortless on the push up to train the contract relax timing. Once the athletes begin grooving the movement, the amortisation phase (the action period from a muscle lengthening to shortening) should start becoming shorter. This transition should look smooth and effortless. Again, the athlete should be able to demonstrate correct landing technique by being balanced and stable holding the position for the count of 3 seconds. Single repetition efforts for each of these jumps below targeting the sequential energy flow from hip, knee and ankle.

Progression No#	Exercise	Direction	Additional Notes / Options
1	Box Jump	Vertical	Can use a box or standard vertical jump if equipment isn't available
2	Broad Jump + Stick	Horizontal	
3	Split Squat Jump + Stick	Vertical	
4	Lateral Jump + Stick	Lateral	

Progression No#	Exercise	Direction	Additional Notes / Options
5	90 / 180degree Jump + Stick	Rotational	
6	Bound + Stick	Horizontal	
7	Skater Bound + Stick	Lateral	
8	90 Degree Bound + Stick	Rotational	Inside edge + Outside edge of foot
9	Hop + Stick	Vertical / Horizontal	
10	Lateral Hop + Stick	Lateral	Inside edge + Outside edge of foot
11	90degree Hop + Stick	Rotational	Inside edge + Outside edge of foot

2. Extensive

This method now includes a combination of both long and short coupling jumps that were described previously. The purpose of this method is to enhance and challenge the jumping motor skill through repeated repetitions:

- Submaximal Effort to focus on technique
- Challenge the contract relax pattern and timing through numerous progressive exercises
- Build coordination, rhythm, relaxation and lightness into all the movements with minimal energy cost
- Increase structural changes to create muscle and tendon stiffness

Once technique is established, higher force efforts can be cued through speeding up the ground contact on short coupling movements or increasing the height for long coupling movements but keeping the form. Depending on the athlete's current level of preparedness, start off with single exercises, 2-3 sets of 8-10 reps. With this method being submaximal in principle, the aim is then to link multiple exercises together of 10-20 reps in a circuit to build the athlete's alactic capacity.

Pogo Series

These exercises are all short coupling jumps to target the ankle joint. With these jumps being low intensity, they can be performed as a circuit for time or reps. It can be recommended to programme these in combination with the first method.

Progression No#	Exercise	Direction	Additional Notes
1	Jump Rope	Vertical	Use normal skipping rope if available – great warm up option
2	Pogo's on Spot	Vertical	

Progression No#	Exercise	Direction	Additional Notes
3	Forward and Back	Horizontal	
4	Side to Side	Lateral	
5	Criss Cross	Lateral	

Extensive Series

The progression jumps from the 3rd section of method 1. Key coaching tips is for all of this movements to be fluid, springy, bouncy and effortless with repetitions performed in a repeated manner.

Progression No#	Exercise	Direction	Coupling Time	Joints	Additional Notes
1	Squat Jump	Vertical	Long	Hips + Knee	
2	Lateral Jump	Lateral	Long	Hips + Knee	
3	Split Squat Jump	Vertical	Long	Hips + Knee	
4	Broad Jump	Horizontal	Long	Hips + Knee	
5	Bouncy Run	Vertical	Short	Ankle	
6	Skip for Height	Vertical	Short	Ankle	
7	Skip for Distance	Horizontal	Short	Ankle	
8	Horizontal Bound	Horizontal	Short	Ankle	
9	Skater Bound	Lateral	Short	Ankle	
10	Hop	Vertical	Short	Ankle	
11	Tuck Jump	Vertical	Short	Ankle	
12	Pike Jump	Vertical	Short	Ankle	
13	Rotational Jump	Rotational	Long	Hips + Knee	
14	Lateral Hop	Lateral	Short	Ankle	Inside and outside edge of foot
15	Rotational Bound	Rotational	Short	Ankle	Inside edge + Outside edge of foot
16	Rotational Hop	Rotational	Short	Ankle	Inside edge + Outside edge of foot
17	Hurdle Jump	Vertical / Horizontal	Long	Hips + Knee	Start low hurdle heights before making the hurdles higher or spacing them out
18	Double Alternating Bound	Horizontal	Short	Ankle	

Advanced Extensive

Subsequent steps taken in preparing the body for the increase in the intensity motor skill competency and tissue tolerance to greater demands. These groups of exercises also challenge the re-organisation of the body, varying heights of hurdles or the ground to manipulate the environment to make the athlete adjust their timing of the movements.

These jumps shall be performed in line to the previous extensive jumps.

Progression No#	Exercise	Direction	Coupling Time	Joints	Additional Notes
1	Box Rebound	Vertical	Short	Ankle	Start with a very low box and build slowly to a
2	Scissor Jump	Vertical	Long	Hips + Knee	30cm box height
3	Variable Hurdle Jumps	Vertical	Short	Ankle	
		Horizontal	Long	Hips + Knee	Alternate hurdle height or
4	Variable Hurdle Distances	Vertical	Long		change the ground elevations
		Horizontal	Long	Hips + Knee	Change up the distances between each hurdle to
5	Stadium Jumps	Vertical	Long		make athlete re-organise
6	Alternating Step Jumps	Vertical	Long	Hips + Knee	Only if stairs are available. Jump up individual steps. Jump up every other step

3. Intensive

This method generates a much higher stress on the central nervous system and skeletal tissue compared to extensive jumps due to the maximal intent expressed by the athlete. The goal of this method is to increase the body's power outputs and reactivity capability. Due to the longer ground contacts and lower stimulus in comparison, the intensive jumps will be performed in order of long coupling jumps first followed by short coupling. The outcome is for the athlete to create as much force as possible in the take-off movement or decrease the length of time spent on the ground. As the practitioner, every jump repetition should be measured and recorded to give feedback to the athlete to drive that maximal intent. In a group of several athletes, this can be a competition driver. However, though the execution of each jump is maximal, it's still imperative that the quality of the technique must be maintained.

Long Coupling

Aim for either the greatest height or distance. To obtain the appropriate adaptation, volume is much lower with increased rest time between sets for full recovery.

Progression No#	Exercise	Direction	Take Offs	Additional Notes
1	Squat Jump	Vertical	Single	Pause for 3 seconds before jumping
2	Countermovement Jump	Vertical	Single	Use arms or hands on hip
3	Broad Jump	Horizontal	Single	
4	Consecutive Broad Jump	Horizontal	Repeated	Progressing take offs from 3, 5, 8, 10 fold
5	Single Leg Countermovement Jump	Vertical	Single	

Short Coupling

The aim is for either minimal ground contact time or apply maximal effort. Again, volume will be kept lower with increased rest time between sets for full recovery.

Progression No#	Exercise	Direction	Take Offs	Additional Notes
1	Pogo's	Vertical	Multiple	Use ground contact or time
2	Horizontal Bound	Horizontal	Multiple	Use distance or time
3	Hop for Distance	Horizontal	Multiple	Use distance or time

Altitude Landings

When falling, accumulation of kinetic energy builds up internally. When colliding with the ground, large amounts of ground reaction forces are produced. The higher the fall, the greater the forces that are formed. We challenge the athlete's ability to withstand a higher amount of forces, still achieve the correct landing position by increasing the magnitude of muscle tension. Skeletal muscles have to work eccentrically and contract whilst lengthening to apply the brakes upon landing. This overloads the touchdown segment on ground reaction phase and drives a higher ability to stabilise the body quicker in preparation to apply a taking off movement.

However, it must be noted that when comparing altitude landings to drop jumps, the biomechanics aren't the same. Much larger forces are created when a take-off action is performed immediately after touching down on the ground rather than just sticking the fall. This method is therefore a regression from drop jumps to allow adequate landing positions to be learnt.

Single repetition with two leg landings from an elevated height. Progressively build up to a height of 100cm. Due to the large impact, keep the volume low and perform the landing safely.

Introduction to Weighted Jumps

At this stage of athletic development, the athlete is at an intermediate level and ready to be challenged to a higher degree. To stimulate the central nervous system to a greater extent, the next steps are to load both the extensive and intensive jumps. However, first there is a transition method to introduce the athlete to adding external load to the jumping movement. In a similar context to starting an athlete at the beginning of the first method, when adding resistance to the body, the aim is still to teach and execute with the same previous technique of the jump via the correct timing and sequencing of the hip, knee and ankle. With resistance now to overcome, the goal is also to increase the amount of force that can be produced in the rebound segment of the ground contact phase through the push up movement.

Now that external load is being placed on the system, it's time to consider which load is most appropriate. The following list are popular tools that can be used to provide extra resistance to the body:

- Barbell
- Medicine Ball
- Dumbbells
- Trap bar
- Kettlebells
- Weighted Vest
- Bands

It must be understood that different tools can have a different effect on the jumping performance. Holding either dumbbells, kettlebells, a trap bar, medicine balls or wearing a weighted vest adds the load much closer to the centre of mass allowing for a more natural jumping action to happen. Placing a barbell on the shoulders means that there's an increase in the height of the individual centre of mass, creating larger resistance moment arms. This could inadvertently change the natural jumping technique that has been trained unloaded. It is up to the practitioner's discrepancy and their own reasoning to choose which apparatus would be most appropriate for the following methods.

Weighted Non-Countermovement Jumps

Each jump repetition will be single take offs and performed by starting from a non-countermovement position either in a seated position or after a 3 second pause. Still finish the jump with a controlled and stable landing with the main target joints are the hip and the knee. It's recommended to begin by loading the jumps with dumbbells before barbells. However, other forms of adding resistance can be through holding medicine balls, wearing a weighted vest or bands.

Progression No#	Exercise	Direction	Additional Notes / Options
1	Squat Jump	Vertical	Weighted options listed above
2	Split Squat Jump	Vertical	Weighted options listed above (apart from Trapbar)
3	Lateral Jump	Lateral	Med Ball, DBs, KBs, Weighted Vest
4	Single Leg Hop	Vertical	Weighted options listed above

Weighted Eccentric Focus Jumps

The aim is to adjust and correct the contract relaxation pattern by loading the leg flexion regime when the muscle is lengthening with the combination of an effortless feeling during the unweighted regime of leg extension. Using either DBs, trap bar, medicine balls or holding bands attached to the floor will be best fit to allow the athlete to use it for the safest release. Perform with a smooth and fluid motion, correct technique is still very important.

Each repetition is again single take offs with the target joints being the hip and knee.

Progression	Exercise	Direction	Additional Notes / Options
1	Squat Jump	Vertical	Can jump onto a box if available
2	Split Squat Jump	Vertical	
3	Broad Jump	Horizontal	
4	Hop	Vertical	
5	Skater Bound	Lateral	Hold on to a Medicine ball – safer to release

Weighted Extensive Jumps

These jumps are performed in the same manner as the unweighted extensive jumps as explained above. Again, the aim for these jumps are to build physical capacity, rhythm, relaxation but now encouraging the athlete to produce a greater amount of force in this action. This training is emphasising greater CNS stimulation by adjusting the execution technique of the stretch shortening by increasing the external load on impact. The number of exercises performed in this phase is now reduced compared to the previous unweighted extensive method.

Weighted Medicine Ball Pogo Series

Holding the medicine ball in a different position will change the emphasis on which chain will be targeted. The medicine ball can manipulate the centre of mass to place emphasis on the anterior chain (holding out in front), posterior chain (holding from behind) or lateral chain (holding on your side). This can be used to train any weak links in any of the weighted extensive jumps.

For the weighted medicine ball pogo series, all jumps are short coupling with repeated repetitions. The feeling sensation should be lightness and being bouncy.

Progression No#	Exercise	Direction	Additional Notes
1	Pogo's on Spot	Vertical	Place the MB in different positions to challenge the athlete. Where the weight lies the athlete will be challenges opposing side or overloading a limb
2	Forward and Back	Horizontal	
3	Side to Side	Lateral	
4	Criss Cross	Lateral	

Weighted Extensive Jumps

Each jump is performed with repeated repetitions. The intent is to perform the movement submaximally with the external load not being too heavy that it will affect the execution of the movement.

Progression No#	Exercise	Direction	Coupling Time	Joints	Additional Notes
1	Kettlebell Squat Jump	Vertical	Long	Hip + Knee	Feet can be elevated on two boxes to allow to sink into deeper hip range
2	Trapbar Jump	Vertical	Long	Hip + Knee	Can be performed with DBs to begin with or a barbell
3	Pogo's	Vertical	Short	Ankle	Can add greater load such as Barbell's orDBs
4	Split Squat Jump	Vertical	Long	Hip + Knee	
5	Scissor Jump	Vertical	Long	Hip + Knee	
6	Alternating Step Jump	Vertical	Long	Hip + Knee	
7	Skater Bound	Lateral	Long	Hip + Knee	

Extensive Overspeed Jumps

Rather than applying extra load to the body, the overspeed method will do the opposite by unloading the body during the push up effort during the rebound phase. This aims to enhance the contract relax pattern to provide greater elastic recoil whilst causing greater stimulation of involuntary actions by falling from a greater height. The body will have to handle greater ground reaction forces upon colliding with the floor whilst being able to achieve a higher jump height that it won't normally be capable of doing without the use of the band.

For the set-up of these exercises, a band can either be attached from the ceiling or more commonly the top of a squat rack where the athlete will climb into the band, tucking it under the arm bits. Holding onto the band, actively pull yourself down and relax on the push up with the feeling of like you're floating and flying. This will teach the system to relax at a faster rate on the push up movement.

The jumps will be performed with repeated repetitions with the resistance of the band being progressed from a light to heavy band.

Progression No#	Exercise	Direction	Coupling Time	Joints	Additional Notes
1	Banded Pogo's	Vertical	Short	Ankle	
2	Banded Squat Jump	Vertical	Long	Hip + Knee	
3	Banded Scissor Jump	Vertical	Long	Hip + Knee	
4	Banded Hops	Vertical	Short	Ankle	

Weighted Intensive

This stage is now for advanced athletes with this method being performed in the exact same way as the previous bodyweight intensive method. The goal again is to either achieve maximal height, distance or reps in a preselected time. Resistance will be applied in the form of barbells, dumbbells, medicine balls and bands but not at the expense of the loss of technique. The objective is to create greater CNS stimulation to increase power outputs through these movements.

Long Coupling

Progression No#	Exercise	Direction	Take Offs	Additional Notes
1	Kettlebell Jump	Vertical	Single	Perform with either a pause or countermovement – maximal height
2	Squat Jump	Vertical	Single	Perform with either a pause or countermovement – maximal height
3	Trapbar Jump	Vertical	Single	Perform with either a pause or countermovement – maximal height
4	Split Squat	Vertical	Single	Perform with either a pause or countermovement – maximal height

Short Coupling

Exercise	Direction	Take Offs	Additional Notes
Pogo's	Vertical	Multiple	Perform to achieve quick ground contact times

Drop Jumps

Drop jumps are an extension from the extensive box rebounds and altitude landing exercise with the optimisation of sequential muscle activation developed. Start the athlete at a height of 12 inches (30cm) with a progressive increase of 2-inch box height overtime. Still being part of the intensive method, if possible, record ground contact time as this is key with this exercise. The end goal for this type of exercise is to be falling from a 24-inch (60cm) box.

The aim is to produce maximal height with minimal ground contact during the ground contact phase with execution involving low magnitude of leg flexion and no use of the arms. By falling from a height, the exercise will improve the capabilities to utilise greater elastic energy recoil. This reactive strength improves the maximal force output expressed during the rebound segment of the ground contact phase.

There are a few options at your disposal regarding the direction in which the athlete jumps after the collision with the ground (vertical, horizontal, lateral). If measuring ground contact with a vertical jump, it's highly suggested to use the formula to calculate the athlete's reactive strength index: jump height (mm) / ground contact time (seconds). The higher the number from the calculation, the better. This will give a good indication in how well each athlete is using their force abilities when interacting with the ground.

Drop jumps are a perfect training means for a smooth transition into the final method depth jumps

Exercise	Direction	Take Offs	Additional Notes
Drop Jumps	Vertical / Horizontal / Lateral	Single	30cm – 60cm: Fast off the floor and maximal height (hands on hips). Keep volume low – no more than 10 reps in one session.

Depth Jumps

We're in the end game now!

The trump card of true plyometrics! It's an aggressive and advanced training tool and the end vision of the shock method - the depth jump. This exercise places the highest amount of force that the organism has to absorb whilst possessing the ability to overcome and express force in a small amount of time. The shock method is a high training effect on the neuromuscular system. It's a very powerful training method to develop explosive strength but only when it's objectively necessary. It can be a very successful tool but equally can cause negative effects. If the athlete hasn't gone through the relevant previous steps of building up the body's overall capacity and skill, the organism won't be in preparation to fully utilise this specific training means. The shock method is a way to intensify the training stimulus like no other. This is not by external loading but by an accumulation of kinetic energy which is developed by falling from a height and the collision with the ground provokes the neuromuscular system to stimulate and create a large amount of muscular tension.

Yet, for the exercise to be classed as a depth jump, the athlete needs to fall from a 30- inch box (75cm). This box height has been found to be optimal for power output compared to higher box heights. This height will generate explosive strength adaptations as well as better reactivity with the ground with the quickest ground contact time for all the depth jump exercises. Yet, as you increase the box height, the ground contact will be too long which turns it into more of a max force effort (95-115 cm box). The highest force production is around 110cm with the body experiencing around 400 kg of falling weight. If maximal strength was the aim, this depth jump height is optimal to elicit that adaptation. Nevertheless, it's unnecessary to go any higher than a 45 inch box because the benefits of the exercise aren't as profound compared to lower box heights (Reactivity, power output, ground contact time and maximal force effort).

You'll only coach the jump height but allow for a natural landing position to occur. Maximal jump height should be intended after colliding with the ground with suggested target to reach above the head or jump towards.

Progressio n No#	Box Height	Take Offs	Additional Notes
1	75-95 cm	Single	Development of Explosive strength
2	95-115 cm	Single	Development of maximal strength

Programming considerations:

Where to place plyometrics in training sessions?

Low level plyometrics can be placed in the warm up if you're coaching team athletes or once an early method is achieved, this can be the warm up for higher intensity methods. An example of this can be using the extensive method to prepare the body and act as a potentiation for intensive jumps.

When placing higher intensity plyometrics in training or gym sessions, you want to be performing those jumps as fresh as possible. The only two training means that will come before plyometrics will be a warm up and sprinting.

When deciding on which type of jumps to use within your training week, each session can have a theme to pair up the sporting movement with the way you'll perform the jump. For example, with emphasis on training the acceleration movement, the force vector is horizontal dominant so you can pair this movement with horizontal dominant jumps (Max velocity – vertical and change of direction – lateral / rotational).

Methods can overlap. For example, originally you can programme 3 exposures of the extensive method in a week. Progressing forward you may take the decision to have 2 exposures of the extensive method and bring in 1 exposure of the intensive method. To progress volume, start with single sets and add reps before reducing the reps back down and adding multiple sets.

Overall, programming to take into considerations:

- Plyometric Method
- Direction
- Type of jump
- Volume
- Intensity
- Number of weekly exposures
- Density

Single or repeated repetitions

Plyometric and jump training must be a well thought out progressive training strategy which serves a developmental tool which enable more complex training to take place

Ballistic Exercise Progressions

Mel Siff (Supertraining, 2003) described a ballistic exercise as a movement initiated by a **strong muscle action**, namely an impulse from the agonist muscle group, which is followed by a **state of relaxation** where the **limb motion will continue** due to the build-up of momentum. For that strong muscle action to be stimulated, external resistance is placed upon the system for it to overcome.

The contractile muscle elements are very explosive in nature with great emphasis placed on the central nervous system to express as much force as possible within a small-time frame. Rate of force development (RFD) is a term that is well known and used frequently to describe this action.

The main outcomes from ballistic exercises are to displace either a weighted object or the athlete's centre of mass with the addition of load. The training effect will generate different adaptive responses depending on which exercise type is selected and how the exercise is executed. This will be discussed in greater detail later on.

A key consideration to know and recognise when selecting and coaching ballistics, is that the muscle contraction timings are very important. The antagonist needs to relax proceeding the agonist action in order to realise the greater force capabilities from the agonist muscle group. We don't want the antagonist muscles to fire too soon as this heightens the risk of an injury occurring as well as dampening effect on overall force output. This is what we are trying to develop through ballistic exercises and this is what separates these exercises from other modalities.

What is Ballistic training trying to develop?

Field sport movements, such as sprinting and changing direction, require large forces to be produced in a time constrained environment. Ballistic exercises stimulate the improvement of the neuromuscular system to increase the athlete's rate in which force can be expressed (RFD). The physiological adaptations will provide a positive transfer for these key sporting movements in order to increase athlete's competition performance.

Classifying a strength or ballistic exercise

Still, there can be a grey area and confusion over where to place exercises either within the strength or ballistic category. For example, some coaches may think to use the term 'ballistic exercise' with your standard gym exercises such as the squat or the bench when performing with a light weight and quick motion. By using Siff's definition of a ballistic exercise which was outlined in the second paragraph, these can't be considered as ballistic exercises as there are no moments of relaxation during the lift. The body is also in contact with the bar and must apply deceleration forces to stop the bar's momentum continuing along its path. It's been shown that up to the final 40% of the concentric phase that the barbell in a back squat or bench press at loads of 30% 1RM are actually being slowed down. This means simply that the braking actions are being taught to the CNS rather than propulsive forces.

Additionally, further research has suggested that by using accommodative resistance (such as bands or chains) will combat the braking moments in the concentric phase with the addition of load being constantly applied throughout. The muscle action has to continue in applying propulsive forces to overcome the resistance. This however is great to develop acceleration strength and should be considered as part of your strength training model but isn't listed as a ballistic exercise. The rationale for the lack of inclusion is the constant tension needing to be applied throughout the duration of the concentric phase of the lift.

Categorising Ballistic Modalities

There is a big cross over from the different types of strength training that applies to ballistic training. The definitions that describe each of these trained qualities remain the same (Verkhoshansky, 2004). The table below breaks down each of the four strength type lists, gives recommendations on the intensity loading as well as linking the ballistic modalities to each of the strength types.

With there being a spectrum between intensity loading, there must be recognition of the inverse relationship between force and velocity. When resistance is increased, this has a knock-on effect of lowering the speed of execution and total velocity of the exercise. When attempting to choose the most appropriate exercises and loading intensity, having the SAID principle at the forefront of your mind will guide you towards the most appropriate option.

Strength Type	Description	Lifting / Velocity	Ballistic Modalities
Accelerative Strength	Achieve a rapid maximum force effort in the final phase of muscular tension (this phase begins when the magnitude of force effort is achieved with the level of the external resistance).	65 – 85% 1RM; 0.75 – 0.50 m/s	Gym Based Exercises - Resisted Specific Movements
Strength- Speed	Power capability in sport with force dominating velocity	45 – 65% 1RM; 0.75 – 0.50 m/s	Gym Based Exercises - Resisted Specific Movements - - Weighted Jumps
Speed- Strength	High speed movements applied against small resistance	25 – 45% 1RM; 1.30 – 1.0 m/s	Weighted Jumps; Resisted Specific Movements
Starting Strength	Produce a rapid increases, of force effort at the beginning of muscular tension	10 – 25% 1RM; >1.3 m/s	- Weighted Jumps, Medball throws, resisted specific movements

Ballistic Exercises Based on Classification for Speed

Gym based Exercises

Aim: Displace an object
Classification: General Preparatory Exercise (GPE)
SAID Principles: Accelerative Strength / Strength-Speed

All the listed exercises can be performed in the gym with the aim to displace the barbell or similar. The only exception is the kneeling wall shoot but are general in nature. These movements require small amounts of movement competency to be able to execute effectively.

Name of Exercise	Resistance Method	Target Area	Notes
Push Press	Barbell	Full Body	Varying loading intensity
Power Shrug	Barbell	Full Body	Varying loading intensity
Sled Power Row	Sled, Plates	Full Body	Varying loading intensity
Kneeling Wall Shoot	Bands, Sled	Lower Body	Varying loading intensity
Kettlebell Swing	Kettlebell, Dumbbell	Lower Body	Varying loading intensity – banded or a partner pushing down on the kettlebell will increase eccentric RFD
Landmine Throw	Barbell	Upper Body	Can perform in a half kneeling or tall kneeling position. Can place emphasis just on the concentric phase with a dead start or through the full movement. Varying loading intensity
Bench Throw	Barbell, Smith Machine	Upper Body	Varying loading intensity

It must be mentioned that common weightlifting derivatives will also fall into this section even though they haven't been stated above. Weightlifting exercises are just one tool of many that can be utilised to achieve the desired adaptations. The extensive list provided above can be equal or potentially better in achieving those results. All these exercises are still pretty general in comparison to the competition movements and principles of dynamic correspondence.

Furthermore, a high requirement of skill is needed to perform weightlifting exercises effectively and safely. To teach the proper execution of these lifts, it can be very time consuming where training resources can be better applied towards specific competition skills such as sprinting or technical practice.

This isn't to completely discourage you from using these exercises in your practice, that is at your own discretion. There are just other favourable methods that can be used as an alternative. However, there are many resources that will discuss the technical approaches for weightlifting if you wish to further expand your knowledge.

Weighted jumps

Aim: Displace centre of mass
Classification: Special Preparatory Exercise (SPE)
SAID Principles: Strength-Speed / Speed-Strength / Starting Strength

When comparing the listed exercises below to loaded plyometric exercises, the ballistic exercises will be executed as single reps whereas plyometrics are continuous reps. Each exercise can be performed from a dead start with the emphasis being placed on the concentric RFD. Completing the full movement, to target eccentric RFD, the execution must have intent to pull themselves down before reversing the movement. This group of exercises achieves one of the sections from the principles of dynamic correspondence with the enhancement of the magnitude of force being produced in a shorter amount of time.

Exercise	Resistance Method	Notes
Kettlebell Jumps	Kettlebell	Varying loading intensity / technical execution
Barbell CMJ Jumps	Dumbbells, Barbell	
Split Squat Jump	Dumbbells, Barbell	
Trapbar Jumps	Trapbar	start with trapbar on the ground concentric RFD or hang position for Eccentric RFD
Lateral Step-Up Jump	Dumbbells, Barbell	Varying loading intensity / technical execution

Medicine Ball Throws

Aim: Displace object / centre of mass displacement / both **Classification:** Special Developmental Exercise (SDE)
SAID Principles: Starting Strength

This group of exercises have achieved a higher classification due to containing more sections from the dynamic correspondence principles. In particular the amplitude and direction of force application. Throwing medicine balls or any weighted object allows for specific loading of different force vectors (Vertical, Horizontal, Lateral) that are associated with sporting movements.

These movements can begin from a dead start position with emphasis on the concentric RFD. Execution of the exercise can progress with adding the eccentric phase of the movement. A third progression will conclude with the displacement of the athlete's centre of mass by following the medicine ball after release. Beginning in a dead start can teach youngsters or beginning athletes body position before adding progressions of the exercise before load.

Exercise	Target Qualities	Notes
Overhead Throws	Vertical RFD	1. Dead start
		2. Full movement of loading quads and glutes
		3. Full movement with vertical projection
Granny Toss	Horizontal RFD	1. Dead start
		2. Full movement of loading hinge movement of posterior chain
		3. Full movement with a horizontal projection
Side Toss	Frontal plane RFD	1. Dead start
		2. Full movement of loading outside leg
		3. Full movement with a lateral cross over projection
Overhead Slam	Eccentric RFD	1. Start with a medicine ball above your head, pull yourself downwards as you slam the medicine ball into the floor.
		2. Gain height by going onto tiptoes.
		3. Begin by standing on a low box.
Chest Throw	Upper Horizontal RFD	1. Ball starts on the chest
		2. Full movement - arms start outstretched

Resisted specific movement

Aim: Displace centre of mass
Classification: Special Developmental Exercise (SDE)
SAID Principles: Accelerative Strength / Strength-Speed / Speed-Strength / Starting Strength

This group of exercises tick many of the dynamic correspondence principles especially with increasing the accentuated region of force production through applying resistance of a sled or pulley rope. These exercises are very specific as they can load and replicate the sporting action movements that are commonly displayed in field-based sport. However, a high-level of movement competency before increasing load with execution velocity.

Name of Exercise	Resistance Method	Notes
Resisted Acceleration Push Out Step	Pulley, Sled, Heavy Band	From a static position, working on starting strength to increase force production on the first step only
Resisted Acceleration	Pulley, Sled, Medium – Heavy Band	Acceleration – Piecing together multiple acceleration steps
Resisted Prime Timers	Pulley, Sled, Medium – Heavy Band	Max Velocity – Hip extension force of the hamstring and glute
Resisted Open Step	Pulley, Sled, Medium – Heavy Band	Transitional movement – emphasis on outside push off
Resisted Cross Over Step	Pulley, Sled, Medium – Heavy Band	Transitional movement – emphasis on inside push off

Measuring & Tracking

Measuring and tracking key information can give a better representation of your athlete's relative power abilities. Using certain jump tests can be an easy, quick and non-evasive way in quantifying these metrics. The eccentric utilisation ratio (EUR) jump tests can give you a great insight in how your athlete recruits to produce force. The two jump tests used to determine EUR are a countermovement jump (CMJ) or a squat jump (SJ) with both tests normally performed with hands on hips (but not essential). Guidance on performing the two jump tests are as follows:

- CMJ: The athlete drops their hips down to around a half squat position and reverses the motion without pause to jump as high as they can.

- SJ: The athlete drops their hips down to around a half squat position again. However, this time, they pause in that position for 3 seconds before pushing straight up and jumping as high as they can. It's important that the athlete doesn't do a second dip to start the jump phase of this test, or this won't count.

Once the data has been collected, you'll take the two metrics and calculate to see the percentage differences. You can begin to build jump profiles to discover where your athlete is strong and where your athlete might be lacking in certain qualities. The points below list the desirable ratio as well as training recommendations:

Ratio	Dominance	Training Emphasis
CMJ 10% Higher than SJ	Ideal Balance	Evaluate the overall height scores – if relatively low, extensive plyometrics, increase relative strength + Ballistic starting strength
CMJ >10% Higher than SJ	Elastic Dominant	Relative strength + Ballistic Accelerative strength
CMJ <10% - Equal to SJ	Favouring muscle dominance	Concurrent training
SJ Higher than CMJ	Muscle Dominant	Plyometrics, Ballistic Speed-Strength

EXAMPLE PROGRAMS & SESSIONS

1. General Speed
2. Specific Speed
3. Special Speed
4. Tactical Speed

BIOMECHANICAL FACTORS OF SPEED IN SPRINTING

As touched on earlier in the book there are many biomechanical factors that contribute to efficient sprinting. Understanding these elements—such as muscle length-tension relationships, muscle moment arms, joint angles, and muscle activation patterns—is critical for athletes and coaches aiming to optimise sprinting technique. By dissecting these components, athletes can enhance stride length, generate efficient ground reaction forces, and minimise energy losses during each stride, ultimately improving performance. This section delves into these key biomechanical factors, offering insights on how athletes may differ and what coaches should observe to tailor training effectively.

1. Muscle Length-Tension Relationships

The length-tension relationship in muscles describes how muscle force production varies with changes in muscle length. Muscles generate the most force at an optimal length, where the overlap between actin and myosin filaments within the sarcomere is ideal.

Application in Sprinting

- **Optimal Muscle Length:** During sprinting, muscles such as the hamstrings and quadriceps must operate near their optimal length to maximise force production. The hamstrings, for instance, should be adequately stretched but not overstretched during the late swing phase to prepare for a powerful contraction during ground contact.
- **Stride Efficiency:** Athletes with optimal muscle length-tension relationships can produce greater force per stride, enhancing stride length and frequency.

Coaching Tips

- **Flexibility Training:** Ensure athletes maintain flexibility through dynamic stretches and mobility exercises to keep muscles within their optimal length range.
- **Strength Training:** Incorporate eccentric exercises to improve muscle length-tension properties, especially for the hamstrings and calves.

2. Muscle Moment Arms

The muscle moment arm is the perpendicular distance between the muscle's line of action and the axis of rotation at the joint. Larger moment arms generally allow muscles to produce greater torque.

Application in Sprinting

- **Joint Torque:** Larger moment arms at the hip and knee joints can enhance torque production, crucial for powerful strides.
- **Power:** Athletes with favourable moment arm lengths can generate more power during each stride, contributing to faster sprint times.

Coaching Tips

- **Specific Strength Training:** Utilising the specialised exercise as outlined in this book will increase the athletes ability to produce power when running.

- **Biomechanical Analysis:** Conduct assessments to understand individual variations in moment arms and adjust training to leverage these differences. This can be as simple as using slow motion video capture on a mobile phone.

3. Joint Angles

Joint angles influence the effectiveness of muscle force production and the efficiency of movement. Optimal joint angles vary depending on the phase of the sprint cycle. I have outlined some of the specific angles that are considered optimal in acceleration and maximum speed. Please do not over obsess with these specific angles. They are just a guide.

1. Hip Joint

Acceleration Phase:
- **Hip Flexion:** At the beginning of the push-off phase, the hip is flexed at approximately 60-70 degrees.
- **Hip Extension:** During the propulsion phase, the hip extends to about 10-20 degrees.

Maximal Speed Phase:
- **Hip Flexion:** At maximal speed, the hip flexes to around 80-90 degrees during the swing phase.
- **Hip Extension:** It extends to about 20-30 degrees during the ground contact phase.

2. Knee Joint

Acceleration Phase:
- **Knee Flexion:** During the initial contact phase, the knee is flexed at around 45-50 degrees.
- **Knee Extension:** It extends to nearly 180 degrees (full extension) during the push-off phase.

Maximal Speed Phase:
- **Knee Flexion:** During the swing phase, the knee flexes to about 90-100 degrees.
- **Knee Extension:** It reaches around 160-170 degrees during ground contact.

3. Ankle Joint

Acceleration Phase:
- **Ankle Dorsiflexion:** At the beginning of ground contact, the ankle is dorsiflexed at about 15-20 degrees.
- **Ankle Plantarflexion:** During push-off, it plantar flexes to approximately 20-25 degrees beyond neutral.

Maximal Speed Phase:
- **Ankle Dorsiflexion:** Around 10-15 degrees during initial ground contact.
- **Ankle Plantarflexion:** Reaches about 25-30 degrees during the push-off phase.

Coaching Tips
- **Technique Drills:** Incorporate drills that reinforce optimal joint angles as highlighted throughout the book.
- **Video Analysis:** Use video feedback to analyse and correct joint angles during different sprint phases. Athletes respond well to seeing themselves run

4. Muscle Activation Patterns

Muscle activation patterns refer to the timing and intensity of muscle contractions. Efficient activation patterns ensure that muscles contract at the right time and with the right force.

Application in Sprinting
- **Coordination:** Proper muscle activation sequences ensure efficient force transfer from the muscles to the ground, minimising energy losses.
- **Power Output:** Athletes with well-coordinated muscle activation patterns can produce higher power outputs during sprints.

Practical Examples and Coaching Considerations

Example 1: Stride Length vs. Stride Frequency
- **Athlete Differences:** Some athletes may naturally have longer strides but lower frequency, while others may have shorter, quicker strides.
- **Coaching Focus:** Analyse each athlete's natural stride mechanics. For those with longer strides, focus on improving stride frequency without compromising length. For those with shorter strides, work on lengthening strides while maintaining frequency.

Example 2: Ground Reaction Forces
- **Athlete Differences:** Athletes with different body compositions and muscle strengths will generate varying ground reaction forces.
- **Coaching Focus:** Tailor speed programs to enhance ground reaction force production.

Example 3: Energy Efficiency
- **Athlete Differences**: Energy losses during sprints can vary based on technique and biomechanical efficiency.
- **Coaching Focus:** Conduct regular biomechanical assessments to identify and correct inefficiencies in technique, focusing on minimising unnecessary movements and optimising force application.

BRODMANN AREAS OF THE BRAIN

Brodmann areas are regions of the cerebral cortex defined based on their cytoarchitecture, or the organisation of cells in the brain as seen under a microscope. The German anatomist Korbinian Brodmann first described these areas in the early 20th century. Brodmann used a staining technique to differentiate various cell types and their densities, which allowed him to map the cortex into 52 distinct areas, each hypothesised to be associated with different brain functions.

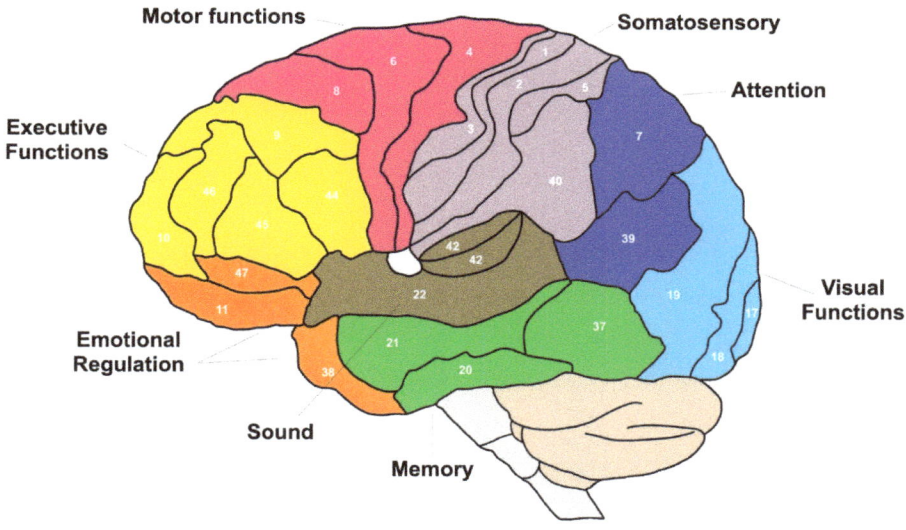

Below is an overview of all 52 Brodmann areas, including their general locations and associated functions:

Frontal Lobe Areas

1. Area 1, 2, 3: Primary somatosensory cortex - Processes sensory information from the body.
2. Area 4: Primary motor cortex - Responsible for voluntary movement.
3. Area 6: Premotor cortex and supplementary motor area - Involved in planning and coordinating movement.
4. Area 8: Frontal eye fields - Controls voluntary eye movements.
5. Area 9, 10, 11, 12: Prefrontal cortex - Involved in higher cognitive functions, decision-making, and personality.
6. Area 44: Broca's area (left hemisphere) - Important for speech production.
7. Area 45: Part of Broca's area - Language processing and speech production.

Parietal Lobe Areas

8. Area 5: Somatosensory association cortex - Processes sensory input related to touch.
9. Area 7: Posterior parietal cortex - Integrates sensory information and is involved in spatial awareness.
10. Area 39: Angular gyrus - Associated with language, number processing, and spatial cognition.
11. Area 40: Supramarginal gyrus - Involved in language perception and processing.

Temporal Lobe Areas

12. Area 20: Inferior temporal gyrus - Involved in high-level visual processing and object recognition.
13. Area 21: Middle temporal gyrus - Associated with auditory and language processing.
14. Area 22: Superior temporal gyrus - Wernicke's area (left hemisphere) - Language comprehension.
15. Area 37: Fusiform gyrus - Involved in facial recognition and visual processing.
16. Area 38: Temporopolar area - Involved in complex language and semantic memory.

Occipital Lobe Areas

17. Area 17: Primary visual cortex (V1) - Processes visual information from the retina.
18. Area 18: Secondary visual cortex (V2) - Further processes visual information.
19. Area 19: Associative visual cortex - Integrates visual information and is involved in higher-order visual processing.

Limbic Lobe Areas

20. Area 23, 24: Cingulate cortex - Associated with emotion formation and processing, learning, and memory.
21. Area 25: Subgenual area - Involved in mood regulation.
22. Area 26: Ectosplenial area - Part of the retrosplenial cortex, involved in memory and navigation.
23. Area 27: Piriform cortex - Related to olfactory processing.
24. Area 28: Entorhinal cortex - Important for memory and navigation.
25. Area 29, 30: Retrosplenial cortex - Involved in memory and spatial navigation.
26. Area 31: Posterior cingulate cortex - Associated with memory and visual processing.
27. Area 32: Dorsal anterior cingulate cortex - Involved in cognitive control and emotion.
28. Area 33: Part of the cingulate cortex - Plays a role in the limbic system and emotion.

Insular Cortex Areas

29. Area 13, 14, 15, 16: Insular cortex - Involved in diverse functions including perception, motor control, self-awareness, and emotional processing.

Additional Areas

30. Area 34, 35, 36: Parahippocampal gyrus - Involved in memory encoding and retrieval.
31. Area 41, 42: Primary auditory cortex - Processes auditory information.
32. Area 43: Primary gustatory cortex - Processes taste information.
33. Area 46: Dorsolateral prefrontal cortex - Involved in working memory and executive functions.
34. Area 47: Inferior frontal gyrus - Associated with language and cognition.
35. Area 48: Retrosubicular area - Involved in sensory and motor integration.
36. Area 49: Parainsular area - Less well-defined, but involved in processing multisensory information.
37. Area 52: Parainsular cortex - Involved in processing multisensory integration and emotional responses.

Understanding the Functionality

Each Brodmann area is defined by its distinct cellular structure and organisation, which correlates with specific brain functions. For instance:

- Motor areas (e.g., Area 4) are heavily involved in controlling voluntary muscle movements.
- Sensory areas (e.g., Areas 1, 2, 3) process input from various sensory modalities.
- Association areas (e.g., Areas 39, 40) integrate information from different sensory modalities to aid in complex cognitive functions such as language, spatial orientation, and problem-solving.

Importance in Neuroscience and Medicine

Brodmann areas have significant implications in neuroscience and clinical practice. Understanding the functions of these areas helps in diagnosing and treating neurological and psychiatric disorders. For example:

- Damage to Area 4 can result in motor deficits.
- Lesions in Area 22 (Wernicke's area) can lead to language comprehension problems.
- Abnormalities in the prefrontal cortex (Areas 9, 10, 11) are associated with mood disorders and cognitive impairments.

In summary, the Brodmann areas provide a foundational map for exploring the functional anatomy of the brain. They serve as a critical reference for researchers and clinicians in understanding how different regions contribute to behaviour, cognition, and sensory processing.